REAL ESTATE
A VALUE APPROACH

REAL ESTATE
A VALUE APPROACH

PETER G. GOULET
University of Northern Iowa

GLENCOE PUBLISHING CO., INC.
Encino, California
Collier Macmillan Publishers
London

For Meridith

A book and a child have one thing in common—
they can open your eyes to the future

Glencoe Publishing Co., Inc.
17337 Ventura Boulevard
Encino, California 91316
Collier Macmillan Canada, Ltd.

Library of Congress Catalog Card Number: 77-094768

1 2 3 4 5 6 7 8 9 10   83 82 81 80 79

ISBN 0-02-474530-8

PREFACE

Real estate occupies a unique and somewhat paradoxical place among the disciplines of business and economics because it is a uniquely integrative subject. It brings together material from at least six other major fields and makes it possible to study the interfaces among these disciplines from a useful perspective.

The paradox is that, in a great many schools, especially those without a major in the subject, real estate is something of an extremity. It is typically not well integrated into the rest of the business or economics curriculum, and is often taken as an unrelated elective by many students. This situation is unfortunate because it fails to exploit one of the major benefits of the course, its ability to highlight important interrelationships among decision making, the economic system, and exogenous influences in the social environment.

The diagram below shows how real estate ties together concepts from economics, finance, marketing, sociology, law, and geography.

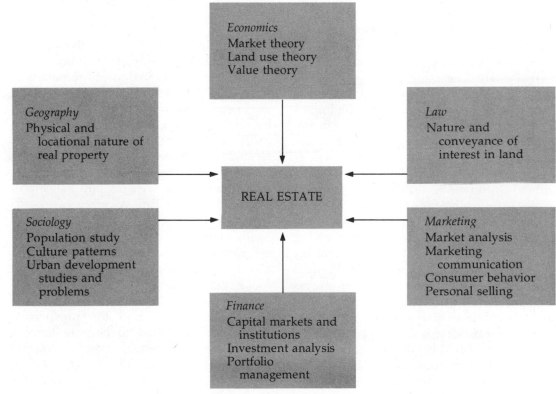

In writing this text, I had the following goals:

1. To introduce the student to the important terms and concepts of real estate
2. To lay a foundation for future study
3. To help provide background for a professional career while increasing the exposure of preprofessionals to some important topics missing from other approaches to the subject
4. To impress upon the reader the integrative nature of real estate

I have tried to accomplish these tasks within the framework of a typical business program; I wanted to develop an introductory text which would serve to educate both preprofessionals and interested business students in general.

I chose to accomplish these goals by altering the point of view of this text somewhat from that of its predecessors. A great many of the real estate texts currently available use a highly institutionalized approach to real estate. They emphasize the laws, instruments, and professional practices of the field at the expense of some of the important abstract issues. These texts also deemphasize decision making. The urban development approach also has deficiencies in that it fails to spend enough time on either institutions or decision making. There are texts with a balanced approach that corrects some of the above deficiencies, but these tend to be shallow in their coverage of most of the subject. While many of the current texts serve certain market segments quite well, I feel most tend to lack proper emphasis on decision making, value, and interdisciplinary relationships.

Decision making is the one central issue common to most business disciplines. The decision rules for most economic decisions are based on the notion of value. Thus, value is a central thread that joins most business fields. For that reason, the emphasis in this book is on the crucial notion of value. A significant portion of the text is devoted to explaining and estimating value for real estate. Much of the remainder of the book describes and analyzes factors affecting value and discusses some key decision-making processes.

Using this text, I hope instructors will be able to teach the subject in a way that will be consistent with knowledge from other business disciplines. At the same time, students will be able to learn enough to make some simple decisions about real estate investments, to understand the institutions of real estate, and to move towards a good professional career, if that is desired.

There is one thing this book cannot do, and does not intend to do: It cannot stand alone as a vehicle for a state license exam. Few—if any—introductory texts can do that.

Organization. This book is divided into three parts. The first eight chapters of Part 1 are a nuclear discussion of the nature of value in real estate. Value is first discussed in general terms; this discussion is followed by chapters on appraisal and investment analysis. The appraisal chapters are intended to describe common techniques; they are not designed to teach the reader to be an appraiser, a clearly impossible task for two chapters. The coverage of investment analysis is more detailed and serves to illustrate basic decision analysis. An intelligent and resourceful reader should be able to use these techniques, with care, to make some modest investments. The chapter on taxes in this section is somewhat general in nature, and the prospective investor is cautioned to become familiar with the rules in detail before proceeding to make investments.

The last chapter in the first part of the text is an optional discussion of portfolio theory and risk analysis. This chapter, unique among introductory real estate texts, demonstrates the close relationship between real estate concepts and finance. For the student of finance, this chapter and the investment chapter bring out the similarities and differences between securities and real estate investment.

Part 2 of the text is concerned with factors affecting real estate value. The first of these, chapter 10, uses a discussion of real estate markets to add a central structure to the text. This discussion is furthered by the use of a detailed model that ties all the various notions of value to the factors that affect value through the market mechanism. The remainder of Part 2 covers traditional topics such as law, financing, and physical and locational considerations. In addition to the market model, highlights in this part include a fairly advanced discussion of location theory and a detailed chapter on creative financing techniques with numerous real-world examples.

Part 3, the final three chapters, is concerned with decision making and real estate professional practices. Chapter 18 covers land development analysis. This chapter includes a decision model and coverage of economic base analysis. The chapter on real estate professional practices is broad and covers only the major processes, such as closings, that command most of the time of entry-level professionals. This discussion is intended to serve as a take-off point for prelicense study. Finally, the last chapter is a capstone presentation of the major issues and decisions involved in homeownership. The purpose of this chapter is to show students how some of the advanced value notions presented in earlier chapters apply to this common decision.

Learning Aids. The text includes a number of learning aids. The accompanying Instructor's Manual explains the nature and philosophy of these aids in more detail. Each part begins with an overview of its contents, and each chapter begins with a chapter outline. The study questions, problems, and key terms provided at the end of each chapter are designed to aid review of chapter material and to give the reader practice in dealing with the analytical issues. The annotated references at the end of the text are for the reader who is interested in pursuing certain specific topics further. A Glossary of the key terms is provided at the end of the text, along with an Appendix of the tables needed to solve the problems.

Acknowledgments. During the course of writing this text I have discovered two things that are difficult to comprehend without going through the process. The first of these is the length of time required for a book to move from its conception to fruition. The other thing an author learns to appreciate is the contribution of others to such a project.

I would like to start by thanking those people who made this book possible in the first place. It began as material for a series of seminars I prepared for presentation to members of the field sales staff of Sunmark Industries, a division of Sun Oil Company of Pennsylvania. These seminars were supported and paid for by the Training Division of Sunmark which has given me permission to use this material as the basis for a text. All the Sunmark people, especially Ed Hudgins and Frank Baumann, were extremely helpful to me in all aspects of my work there. I owe them a deep debt of gratitude.

To write a book while one is teaching a full load of courses requires a congenial and supportive atmosphere. The University of Northern Iowa and my colleagues there have provided that important atmosphere. I would especially like to thank my Chairman, Tom Reuschling, for his support and encouragement. I would also like to thank Guy Chiatello for contributing case material which added needed realism to many parts of the book.

I may have seemingly claimed the theme of the book, value, as if I invented it. I was strongly influenced in my approach to this subject by two of my major professors, Halbert Smith of the University of Florida at Gainesville and Ronald Racster of Ohio State University. Their guidance through both course work and the dissertation was invaluable in shaping my philosophy.

The development of this manuscript was significantly influenced by the input of its reviewers. William Brueggeman of Southern Methodist University and Rocky Tarantello of the University of Southern California both read the entire manuscript and made many incisive comments. I would also like to thank Franz Fischer, James A. Graaskamp, Alan A. Herd, Frank G. Mittelbach, W. D. Moore, and Ron Smith for their comments upon the outline and various portions of the manuscript.

Tanya Mink, my editor, and the rest of the Glencoe staff have worked hard and have been helpful, patient, and meticulous in editing and producing this book. I thank them sincerely.

Finally, I must thank my wife, Lynda, for her incredible contribution to this project. She not only did all the typing for the many drafts of the manuscript, but also helped to prepare the Instructor's Manual, checked all my math in the examples, prepared the charts and tables, and added much valuable editorial comment throughout. She has been a competent and patient partner.

Though I owe many debts of gratitude to all who contributed to this effort, I must accept the responsibility for any errors remaining. I hope the users of this text will find it both useful and enjoyable.

Peter G. Goulet
Cedar Falls, Iowa

REVIEWERS

William Brueggeman
Southern Methodist University
Franz Fischer
University of Southern California
James A. Graaskamp
University of Wisconsin
Alan A. Herd
University of California Extension
Frank G. Mittelbach
University of California at Los Angeles
W. D. Moore
Texas A & M University
Ron Smith
DeKalb Community College
Rocky Tarantello
University of Southern California

TABLE 3.3   INVESTMENT OPPORTUNITIES AT RISK LEVEL *x*

Investment 1	Return = 10.0%
Investment 2	Return = 9.5%
Investment 3	Return = 9.2%
Investment 4	Return = 10.5%
Investment 5	Return = 11.0%

Of the five investments shown in the table, the last one offers the highest return, 11%. Now consider a sixth investment which we would like to evaluate. What rate of return should be used to evaluate this sixth investment proposal? The answer is to use the *highest* rate of return which will be sacrificed by investing in the sixth investment instead of one of the other five proposals. Here the rate to be used would be 11%. This procedure has two assumptions in it:

1. Investing $1 in investment number six prohibits also investing that dollar in investment number five; and

2. The risks are the same for the alternative investments.

This approach for finding an appropriate rate of return is called the *market method* in traditional appraisal literature. The rate is called an *opportunity rate of return* or a market return in both finance and real estate literature. In our example, the investor can always buy a quantity of asset number five so the market rate of return for all other investments that might be considerd with the same risk is 11%. This will be one of our concepts of the appropriate rate of return for valuation throughout this text.[2]

Built-Up Rates—Summation Method

A second way of determining the rate of return is to view it as compensation for the time for which consumption is postponed, plus adjustments for risk. This is the **built-up rate of return** method. For example, we know that the basic rate of return for time for riskfree assets is about 3%. This is the rate usually associated with interest on U.S. Treasury Bills when no inflationary pressures are present. We then add extra compensation for various risks and also for expected inflation. This extra compensation is called a **risk premium.** We might find that Table 3.4 appropriately measures the various risks for our particular situation.

The **summation method** is another way of finding rates of return. However, it should be noted here that realistically it is virtually impos-

---

[2] We shall explore this concept in the context of modern capital market theory in chapter 9.

TABLE 3.4   BUILT-UP RATE OF RETURN SUMMATION METHOD

	Basic Riskfree Rate of Return	3.0%
+	Premium for Business Risk	2.0%
+	Premium for Financial Risk	0.5%
+	Premium for Lack of Liquidity	0.5%
+	Expected Loss in Purchasing Power	4.0%
	Total Rate of Return	10.0%

sible to construct a rate of return in this manner. Even though this method has little realistic, practical significance, it does serve as an appropriate hypothetical construct which may describe what a rate of return represents. The capital market theory described in chapter 9 enumerates a way to operationalize these constructs.

Band of Investment Technique

Our first two return techniques apply to the determination of the basic rate of return on investment (ROI) for funds supplied by *equity* or ownership interests. Not all funds are provided by equity, however. In fact, we have said that most real estate is financed with at least some debt. For this reason, we may use a combination rate based on a weighted average of the required returns for the various types of funds.

Assume that an investor is thinking of purchasing an investment property costing $20,000. Further, assume the investor has an opportunity rate of 12% on such investments and plans to borrow $12,000 at 8% to help finance the investment. What is the appropriate base rate of return for evaluating this project? We will ignore taxes for the present.

Debt   = $12,000 or 60% of total capital
Equity = $8000 or 40% of total capital

The rate of return on the investment is then calculated as:

Debt portion: 60% × 8% = 4.8%
Equity portion: 40% × 12% = 4.8%
ROI   = 9.6%

This overall rate of return becomes the appropriate return on investment for the capitalization process. This technique is commonly used by real estate practitioners for appraisal and is called the **band of investment technique.**

The rate of return on investment may then be seen as a two-step process. First, the opportunity rate of return for the investor would be determined. This rate for equity would then be combined with a debt rate and the proper proportions of debt and equity to find the *band of investment rate*.[3] The proportions, or weights, to be used in the band of investment technique are determined by the policy of the analyst or investor, who must look at the *average* expected proportions over the life of the investment because, as the debt is paid off, the proportion changes.

Summary of Capitalization Rates

A summary of the basic capitalization rates and their uses is listed here.

1. *Opportunity Rate of Return.*   This is the basic rate of return on investment (ROI) on equity funds supplied by the investor. It may be used directly or in combination with the debt rate to provide the proper ROI to be used in level annuity evaluations or present value calculations.

2. *Built-Up Rate of Return.*   This may be used as a substitute for the opportunity rate of return.

3. *Band of Investment Rate of Return.*   This is the rate of return on investment which is used when debt and equity are both used to finance the investment. This rate is used to value land or improvements when no adjustment for declining values needs to be made, as in the perpetual annuity calculation. This rate is also used for level annuity and present value calculations.

4. *Rate of Return for Straight-Line-Declining Income Streams.*   When the equation, first-year income divided by capitalization rate, is used to evaluate declining income streams, the capitalization rate which must be used is given by the formula:

$$ROI + (1/\text{useful life}) = \text{Cap rate}$$

Decision Rules

Net Present Value

An investor with limited assets has a number of important decisions to make. There are literally thousands of assets facing the investor as alternatives, competing for the limited wealth available. One decision that must be made is whether a given asset is a satisfactory use of the inves-

---

[3] Students of finance may recognize the band of investment rate as the weighted average cost of capital referred to in the literature of finance theory.

tor's funds. To make this decision, some kind of rule must be devised to enable the investor to choose among various competing alternative investments.

In order the devise a decision rule, we must first have an objective in mind. We cannot evaluate an economic decision without a frame of reference. As a result of much theoretical research, it is now commonly accepted that the appropriate objective for investors is that they seek to maximize their personal wealth. In general, a given investment will be satisfactory if, when properly valued, it does not reduce the net worth of its owner. In general terms, this means that the value of the expected benefits of an investment must not be less than the outlay required to acquire those benefits.

It was noted in chapter 2 that the value of any stream of cash benefits is affected by its quantity, quality, and the timing of the benefits. Thus, whatever decision rules we devise must conform to these constraints. As we have seen, the process of finding the present value does just that. It accounts for the ammount of each benefit in obvious fashion, for timing by considering each benefit separately when it occurs, and for risk through the discount rate. Referring to the summation method, the market method, or the capital asset pricing model in chapter 9 demonstrates that as risk increases, so does the rate of return used to discount the expected benefits. The application of a higher discount rate will result in a lower present value being imputed to the benefit stream, which is logically satisfactory. We would expect to pay less for something which has a greater risk attached to it.

One method we may use to make accept–reject decisions for investments is called the *net present value* (NPV) approach. Mechanically, it is very simple. Any investment whose benefits have a present value less than the cost of acquiring the benefits will be rejected. All other investments whose present values exceed their costs will be accepted. The difference between value and cost is called the **net present value.** Consider the following examples.

Example 3.4

An investor may purchase an investment which will yield five equal benefits of $2000 each. The investor's opportunity rate for investments of this risk is 10%. The investment costs $7000. Thus, the present value of the benefits is:

Benefit $\times PVAF_{5,10\%} = \$2000 \times 3.791 = \$7580$

The net present value = $7580 − $7000 = $580.
By using the decision rule, this investment would be acceptable.

Example 3.5

A second investment is available to our above-mentioned investor. This investment yields benefits of $2200 per year for five years and costs $9000. The risk is the same, so again the appropriate rate of return is 10%.

$$PVA = \text{Benefit} \times PVAF_{5,10\%}$$
$$= \$2200 \times 3.791 = \$8340$$
$$\text{Net Present Value} = \$8340 - \$9000 = -\$660$$

Here, the net present value is negative, so the investment must be rejected using the rule.

At the risk of making this issue more complicated, we shall now show why the net present value rule works. A couple of important points should be kept in mind. First, the key to understanding the analysis to follow is to remember that the 10% return applied to these two investments exists because the investor has other investments that are known to yield 10%. These alternatives have the same risk and provide known benefits sufficient to yield 10%. Second, the goal of the investor is to keep his or her wealth from being less than it should be, given the available alternatives. Now we can deal with the two examples.

Assume a hypothetical investor has $9000 available for investment and uses it to purchase the asset described in Example 3.5. Table 3.5 shows what might happen. When the investor gives up the $9000, his wealth temporarily declines to zero. However, he begins to receive benefits in return. If the investment were going to return exactly 10%, it would pay the return plus all of the principal back in exactly five years. Note what happens, however. The benefits are received, but the investor does not get all his principal returned. The investment in effect "keeps" $1064 of the investor's capital (worth $660 today). This amount is just equal to the negative net present value found in the previous calculation and represents a loss in wealth potential.

Column two in Table 3.5 shows what the investment should have paid for the investor's wealth to have remained as it should to yield 10%. Each payment should have been $2375 rather than $2200. The investor was "shorted" $175 each year for five years. The present value of this shortage is $660, as verified here:

$$PVA = \$175 \times PVAF_{5,10\%}$$
$$= \$175 \times 3.791 = \$660$$

Similarly, if we examine the investment from Example 3.4 we will find that in order to receive the scheduled benefits shown ($2000 per

TABLE 3.5   RETURN FROM THE INVESTMENT OF EXAMPLE 3.5

Investment As It Is		Investment As It Should Be	
$9000	Principal initially	$9000	
0.10		0.10	
$ 900	Interest 1	$ 900	
1300	From principal	1475	
$2200	Benefit 1	$2375	Benefit 1
$7700	Principal year 2	$7525	
0.10		0.10	
$ 770	Interest 2	$ 752	
1430	From principal	1623	
$2200	Benefit 2	$2375	Benefit 2
$6270	Principal year 3	$5902	
0.10		0.10	
$ 627	Interest 3	$ 590	
1573	From principal	1785	
$2200	Benefit 3	$2375	Benefit 3
$4697	Principal year 4	$4117	
0.10		0.10	
$ 470	Interest 4	$ 412	
1730	From principal	1963	
$2200	Benefit 4	$2375	Benefit 4
$2967	Principal year 5	$2154	
0.10		0.10	
$ 297	Interest 5	$ 215	
1903	From principal	2155	
$2200	Benefit 5	$2370[a]	Benefit 5
$1064	Unreturned principal	$ 0	Unreturned principal

PV of Unreturned principal =
$$\$1064 \times PVF_{5,10\%} =$$
$$\$1064 \times 0.621 = \$660$$

[a]Error due to rounding.

year) the investor must in effect be given some "extra" money by the investment. Table 3.6 illustrates this investment as it is and then as it should be. Notice that the only way the investor can receive the scheduled benefits of $2000 a year from the $7000 outlay is if the actual rate of return is 13.2%.

TABLE 3.6   RETURN FROM THE INVESTMENT OF EXAMPLE 3.4

Investment As It Is		Investment As It Should Be	
$7000	Principal initially	$7000	
0.10		0.132	
$ 700	Interest 1	$ 924	
1300	From principal	1076	
$2000	Benefit 1	$2000	Benefit 1
$5700	Principal year 2	$5924	
0.10		0.132	
$ 570	Interest 2	$ 782	
1430	From principal	1218	
$2000	Benefit 2	$2000	Benefit 2
$4270	Principal year 3	$4706	
0.10		0.132	
$ 427	Interest 3	$ 621	
1573	From principal	1379	
$2000	Benefit 3	$2000	Benefit 3
$2697	Principal year 4	$3327	
0.10		0.132	
$ 270	Interest 4	$ 439	
1730	From principal	1561	
$2000	Benefit 4	$2000	Benefit 4
$ 967	Principal year 5	$1766	
0.10		0.132	
$ 97	Interest 5	$ 233	
1903	From principal	1766	
$2000	Benefit 5	$1999[a]	Benefit 5
$ 936	Extra principal gained		

PV of "extra" principal =
    $936 \times 0.621 = 580$

[a] Error due to rounding.

Another way of looking at this is to say that the investment must give the investor $936 more than should have been earned in the fifth year. This extra benefit is worth $580 today and equals the net present value found earlier.

We may summarize our discussion of the net present value rule by saying that to make a proper accept–reject decision on an investment, we simply compare the present value of the investment's benefits to its cost. The difference between the two represents the change in wealth, at present value, that the investor will gain (or lose) from the investment. If an asset were purchased with a negative net present value, wealth would potentially be lost.

Internal Rate of Return

There is a second decision rule which may be used to make accept–reject decisions for investments. This rule is based on the information shown in Table 3.6. The rule, simply stated, is that if an investor requires a return of 10%, for instance, on investments of a given risk, any investment may be accepted which has a return greater than or equal to the required rate. The actual rate of return is the discount rate which, when applied to the investment, yields a net present value of $0. Thus, for the investment in Example 3.4, the actual return is 13.2%. The present value of the benefits of $2000 per year for five years at 13.2% is exactly $7000, which is also the cost of the investment. This actual rate is called the **internal rate of return.**

As a general rule, any investment which has a positive net present value also has an internal rate of return greater than the required rate. Similarly, any investment with a negative net present value has an internal rate of return below the required rate. Thus, both of these decision rules draw the same conclusions about the acceptibility of an investment. Both are consistent with the appropriate goal.

A question may arise for which rule is more acceptable. For simple accept–reject decisions, it does not matter which rule is employed. However, the internal rate of return (IRR) method has fallen out of favor in the last few years because it can cause trouble when comparing two competing investments to determine which is better. The two rules, IRR and NPV, may yield conflicting results. In such cases, it is better to use net present value and select the investment with the highest net present value. In chapter 8 we will use the NPV rule.

CHAPTER THREE SUMMARY

We have now completed two chapters concerned with the basic tools which will be used to evaluate values of real estate investment alternatives. Many of these concepts have been difficult and complex. We strongly advise that you work the problems for review at the end of the chapter, to become more comfortable with these tools.

Throughout both chapters 2 and 3, there may be a tendency to lose sight of their conceptual value. Among all the tools and calculations, there is an important point. The value of any income asset may be viewed as the present value of the future cash benefits to be expected from that asset. Note that only cash has real value—not profits, nor revenue, nor anything else, just cash.

KEY TERMS

Band of Investment
   Technique
Built-Up Rate of
   Return
Capitalization Rate
Economic Life
Internal Rate of
   Return

Net Operating
   Income
Net Present Value
Opportunity Rate
   of Return
Recapture of
   Capital

Return on
   Investment
Risk Premium
Straight-Line-
   Declining
   Income Stream
Summation
   Method

QUESTIONS FOR STUDY AND DISCUSSION

1. Differentiate between a *level annuity* and a *straight-line-declining income stream*. When is each likely to occur in the economic life of a property?

2. How is a stratight-line-declining income stream capitalized? How does this differ from the capitalization of a perpetuity?

3. Explain the concept of *principal recapture*. Under what situation is the concept not relevant?

4. How does the net present value method differ from the internal rate of return method as a decision rule? Under what circumstances would an investment be acceptable under each rule?

5. Attempt to determine your personal required rate of return on investment using different techniques and realistic expectations about economic conditions.

PROBLEMS FOR REVIEW

1. An asset has a useful life of twenty years. What is the appropriate rate to use for the recapture of capital?

2. An asset will provide a straight-line-declining stream of benefits starting with $50,000 in the first year. What will this asset's capitalized value be if you desire a 10% return on investment? The asset has a ten-year life.

3. What would the asset in problem 2 have as a value if it were a level annuity instead of a declining stream?

4. An apartment building is available which will provide a straight-line-declining stream of benefits for fifteen years beginning with $25,000 in year one. Your required return on investment is $13\frac{1}{3}\%$. What is the building's present value?

5. An investor finds she can invest in an apartment building which will provide a stream of benefits of $20,000 per year for ten years, at which time she may sell the building for $100,000 net cash. What is the most she should pay for the property if she wishes to earn a 12% return on her investment?

6. The investor in problem 5 has an option of using some debt in her purchase of the property. She will average 60% debt at 8.67% and 40% equity at 12% over the life of the asset. Find her weighted average rate of return and revalue the property.

7. An investor can buy a property with the following benefits: years 1 through 10—a level stream of $40,000 per year; years 11 through 20— a straight-line-declining stream beginning at $40,000. He can sell the property at the end of twenty years to yield $150,000 cash. What is the property's value using a 10% return on investment requirement?

4 INTRODUCTION TO VALUE ESTIMATES

IN CHAPTER 1 we saw that there are two ways to view real estate. One view is the value of the property as determined by the market. Market value is an historical fact which is never known for certain until the property changes hands. Investment value is a subjective value matched more closely to the investor's personal preferences for risk and return. In chapters 5 to 8 we will examine a number of techniques for estimating both types of value. Our discussions will be in some detail. They will rely heavily on the material in chapters 1 to 3, so it is essential that you have a good grasp of those principles at this point.

Appraisal

Appraisal is the process of *estimating* or *predicting* what the market value of a property will be at some particular point in time. Some practitioners argue that appraisal should properly be called an estimation process. Others argue that appraisal is really a prediction of the results of a future transaction. Estimation implies some degree of knowledge about the outcome. Prediction somehow carries the image of a gypsy reading tea leaves. There is probably no compelling reason to argue for one viewpoint over the other, however, since appraisal is to a great degree as much an art as it is a science. Any kind of estimation or prediction requires a great deal of insight and experience. Appraisal is no exception.

Market Value

In chapter 1 we briefly defined the concept of market value. Here we will discuss it in more detail. Smith quotes the definition used by the American Institute of Real Estate Appraisers. **Market value** is

> The highest price in terms of money which a property will bring in a competitive and open market under all conditions requisite to a fair sale, the buyer and seller, each acting prudently, knowledgeably and assuming the price is not affected by undue stimulus.[1]

> This definition goes on to set up a number of conditions which must prevail for a market transaction to be "fair." The buyers and sellers must be motivated and knowledgeable. The property should be exposed to the market for a sufficient amount of time to obtain active bidding for the property. However, there should be sufficient competitive properties to keep the price from becoming overinflated. Finally, there should be sufficient financing to enable a qualified buyer to purchase the property he has selected.

---

[1]Halbert C. Smith, *Real Estate Appraisal* (Columbus, Ohio: Grid, 1976), p. 5.

It is perhaps difficult to fully appreciate the subtleties of this definition and its conditions without some background in real estate markets.
We will, therefore, discuss the **market mechanism.**

From basic economics we learn that the *allocative mechanism* in our
economy is the *market.* A market is a place (or situation) where buyers—
those who demand goods—meet sellers who supply the goods. The
buyers and sellers negotiate a price at which they are willing to exchange
goods and money.

The market price occurs as a function of the quantity of goods supplied and the quantity demanded. If more goods are supplied than are
demanded, the price tends to become depressed, so that sellers may
entice buyers to take their goods. When demand exceeds supply, prices
tend to rise to help allocate the available supply to those most able to
pay. This market action may be illustrated by a graph such as the one
in Figure 4.1.

As you can see from the graph, when supply and demand are equal,
we have an equilibrium price, at P_e, and an equilibrium quantity, Q_e,
which will change hands. Real estate markets operate similarly. Price
is best determined when a fair number of similar, competing units are
offered for sale and a fair number of qualified buyers are available to
purchase them.

FIGURE 4.1   SUPPLY AND DEMAND FACTORS

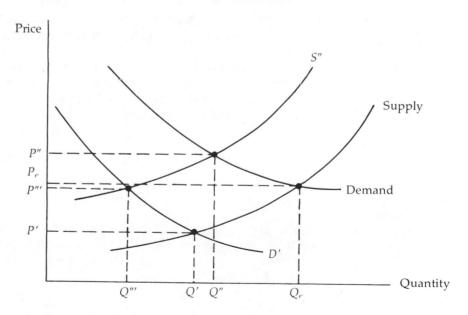

It should be pointed out that the market can be viewed in two time frameworks: the short run and the long run. The short run refers to near-term periods of time in which conditions are essentially temporary or in transition. The long run refers to periods of time during which short-run disequilibrium conditions may be ironed out. Theoretically, when a market is characterized by excessive supply or demand in the short run, we can expect to see the market gradually adjust itself until a long-run equilibrium is again established. We can show this by example below.

Example 4.1

One of the most common market disequilibrium situations occurs when a community suffers from economic distress. In many cities in the Northeast, the mid-twentieth century was a period of transition. The industrial bases which supported many communities became mature and stopped growing or closed down altogether. The resulting high unemployment and loss of income in the community generally resulted in an oversupply of all types of real properties. Many people began to move away from the community, resulting in a temporary oversupply of dwellings. Fewer people were available to purchase these units and less money was available to finance purchases.

The foregoing condition results in a shift in the demand curve in Figure 4.1 from D to D'. The result of this shift is that both the price and quantity of units transacted will fall to P' and Q'. In a depressed economy, this excess of supply over demand may temporarily depress prices below construction costs. However, in the long run, the market will react by reducing supply also. The figure shows the effect of supply's moving to S''. Fewer new units will be built and gradually a new equilibrium will be found. This long-run adjustment will be aided by the gradual loss of existing units which become uninhabitable. Once supply is restricted, the market may firm up somewhat, and prices will rise to P'' and once again represent investment value more fairly.

Example 4.2

Another type of disequilibrium occurs when demand gets out of line. Imagine a community of 20,000 population which has just been chosen by a major industrial firm to be the site of a new plant which will employ 2000 people. Temporarily the demand for housing and services will drive prices up dramatically. We may represent this in Figure 4.1 by starting at an equilibrium point designated P''' Q'''. Demand rises from demand curve D' to D as a result of the new industry. Prices rise to P'' as a result. This short-run disequilibrium may cause prices to rise by as much as 10% to 15% per year. This condition is great for sellers, but not so good for buyers of properties.

Developers in this community will see the problem and profit potential and begin to build new housing units and commercial properties. This will cause supply to move from S'' to S, resulting in a price drop from P'' to P_e. Quantity will increase from Q'' to Q_e. This gradual shift to long-run equilibrium will stop when supply and demand are once again balanced and growth returns to normal.

In the preceding two examples, we have seen how outside factors can alter the short-run balance of supply and demand for properties, causing a change in market values. In any such situation, the market will begin a process of long-run adjustment until market balance is again achieved.

Nature of Appraisal

In the job of estimating or predicting value, the appraiser is called upon to do a great deal of work. The process an appraiser must go through is:

1. The appraiser gets an assignment and defines the problem. This must be done so that the appraiser may select the correct technique or techniques to use. This problem definition also guides the data collection process.

2. The proper appraisal approach is then selected. The classic techniques will be described briefly in a section to follow.

3. After deciding how to proceed, the appraiser must gather the relevant information required to complete the analysis. This includes market data, local economic data, neighborhood data, income data, and anything else which might be required. For instance, many appraisal reports even include results of recent local elections. The party in power has a great deal to say about important factors such as zoning, taxes, and building codes, all of which may affect value.

4. Armed with the data and an approach, the appraiser then makes estimates of the market price of the property. There are two important

points here. First, the appraiser is approaching value by using perhaps two or three techniques. The resulting values from the various techniques are then *correlated* to form the *final* value estimate. Second, with each method and the final correlation, the appraiser is making an estimate of the *most probable value*. It is this last area which requires professional judgment.

Approaches to Appraisal

There are three classic approaches to appraising real property: the market comparison approach, the cost approach, and the income approach. These three will be described in detail in chapters 5 and 6. We will compare them briefly here.

Market Comparison Approach   The theory behind the **market comparison approach** is very simple. We know for a number of reasons that each parcel of real estate is technically unique. However, many properties are similar. In a typical housing subdivision, there may be a number of homes with similar structures, providing similar housing services, and having locations in the same neighborhood. These similar properties should all sell for similar prices. The procedure in the market approach is to find several properties, similar to the subject property, which have sold recently, and compare them to the subject property. A parcel of real property which is being appraised is called the **subject property.** The similar properties are called the **comparable properties,** or **comparables**. Because each of these comparables is a recent sale, the subject property's real value is probably very close to the comparables' sale prices. Thus, by making a few simple adjustments, the value of the subject property can be estimated. This approach is used most often to evaluate residences and raw land.

Cost Approach   The **cost approach** is based on a slightly different idea. The market value of a property should not, in theory, exceed the cost to reproduce it in its exact form. Let us say we wish to appraise a twenty-year-old factory building. First, we would find what it would cost to reproduce the characteristics of the property in today's terms. Since the building is not new, we then penalize our hypothetical reproduction for any depreciation inherent in the subject property. In this context, *depreciation* refers to a *real loss in value,* not just an accounting value for depreciation. The result of the penalized cost estimate is the appraised value of the subject property. This approach is used most often to evaluate older buildings. It is especially useful for properties with no income and few market comparables. Public buildings are an example.

Income Approach   Actually, there are three approaches to income appraisal. Each is based on the idea that a property should be valued as a function of the income it can produce. The property is worth the present value of its future benefits. Each of the three **income approaches** is a version of this idea. They differ only in their assumptions regarding the manner in which the property is compensated by its income. The three techniques are: the land residual, the building residual, and the property residual. These techniques are usually applied to income properties such as apartment buildings, office buildings, and commercial structures.

Importance of Appraisal

Appraisal is one of the most important functions in the field of real estate. Buyers and sellers in any market rely on information to help them determine the value of the goods or services they wish to exchange. Without this information the market would not function. The role of the appraiser is to provide value estimates for the market participants. Appraisal data facilitate transactions and help ensure a fair market.

Earlier we saw an example of a tight housing market in which prices were rising rapidly. In such a market, neither the buyer nor the seller may have a really good idea of a particular property's worth. The market participants may have a subjective opinion. However, if their opinions are not realistic, an unfair transaction may occur. It is the appraiser's job to make certain that fair, impartial, and accurate estimates are provided to those who need them, for a bad appraisal is worse than none at all. For this reason, these professionals require much training and must command a great deal of confidence through high-quality work. From a purely selfish standpoint, a good appraiser can give a shrewd investor a real edge in the market.

To summarize, appraisers serve an important function in the market for real property. They provide much of the vital information which facilitates the efficient operation of the market. Considering the high value of most real property, relative to other goods, and the high risks which may be involved, this is an important function indeed.

Appraisal Vs Investment Analysis

We can now complete our preliminary discussion of appraisal with a final comparison to investment analysis. Appraisal is the estimation of market values. These are values which will most probably ultimately occur in a transaction. The actual buyers and perhaps even the sellers may be unknown to the appraiser, so value must be estimated for the average buyer or seller. Appraisal does not generally account for personal tax situations, financing arrangements, or depreciation schedules of the form of organization under which the property will be owned.

Investment analysis, on the other hand, is personalized. Whether the benefits from an investment are substantial enough to compensate a specific owner for the risks involved will be a function of numerous variables, including the owner's tax rate, the method chosen for financing the property, the forms of depreciation allowed, and others.

A specific example may be beneficial here. Assume there are two investments available to investors Adams and Madison: a corporate bond selling for $1000 to yield 9% interest and a municipal bond selling for $1000 to yield 6%. Adams is in the 25% tax bracket and Madison is in the 50% bracket. As you may know, corporate bond interest is fully taxable, while municipal bond interest is tax-free for federal tax purposes. Table 4.1 shows how each investor will fare with these two investments.

For Adams, who is in a relatively moderate tax bracket, the corporate bond is a better investment than the municipal bond in spite of the tax-free nature of the municipal bond. On the other hand, because of Madison's high tax bracket he would clearly prefer the municipal bond. We have assumed the risks are similar for the two investment alternatives. The same idea applies to real estate. The investment value depends on the investors' personal characteristics. We will see exactly how to determine these values in chapter 8.

TABLE 4.1   COMPARISON OF INVESTMENTS

	Adams	**Madison**
Corporate Bond:		
Before-Tax Return	$90.00/year	$90.00/year
Tax	$22.50/year	$45.00/year
After-Tax Return	$67.50/year	$45.00/year
Rate of Return	$\frac{\$67.50}{\$1000} = 6.75\%$	$\frac{\$45}{\$1000} = 4.5\%$
Municipal Bond:		
Return After-Tax	$60.00/year	$60.00/year
Rate of Return	$\frac{\$60}{\$1000} = 6.00\%$	$\frac{\$60}{\$1000} = 6.00\%$

Value Principles of Appraisal

Highest and Best Use

There are three other concepts which should be explained before proceeding to the details of investment analysis and appraisal. The first of these is *highest and best use*. This concept is a very important one in the field of appraisal. A basic definition is given by Boyce. **Highest and best use** is:

> That reasonable and probable use that will support the highest present value, as defined, as of the effective date of the appraisal.
>
> Alternatively, that use, from among reasonably probable and legal alternative uses, found to be physically possible, appropriately supported and financially feasible, and which results in the highest land value.[2]

Highest and best use is applied to *land*. The main idea concerns the fact that a parcel of land may have a number of possible improvements put on it. Whichever improvement is "best" will determine what the land is worth in economic terms. In the previous section, we saw how different investments may differ in their effective value to a given investor. Similarly, a parcel of land may have a number of potential different uses, each with its own different effective value. In a downtown neighborhood in a big city, land will typically be very expensive. Thus, certain improvements, say, a one-story dentist's office, might not provide nearly as much income as another alternative use. A large office building built on the site would provide a great deal more income for the landowner. Alternatively, at the edge of town in a quiet, residential neighborhood, land is likely to be cheaper than in the downtown area. A less costly site could make the office building more profitable, but the landowner would probably not be able to obtain either the zoning or the traffic needed to permit such a development. Hence, this suburban site would favor the dentist's office or a small shop.

The highest and best use is a hypothetical concept. At any point in time, there is a highest and best use for any site. It may not coincide with the actual use of the property at that time. That is inconsequential for appraisal purposes. *Land is appraised as if it were being put to its highest and best use.*

To explain highest and best use more graphically, let us use an example. An investor wishes an appraisal on a small parcel of residential property. There are three feasible uses for this property: a one-story, four-unit apartment; a two-story, eight-unit apartment; and a twelve-

---

[2]Byrl N. Boyce, Editor, *Real Estate Appraisal Terminology* (Cambridge, Mass.: Ballinger Publishing Company, 1975), p. 107.

unit apartment. Which of these is best? The answer is found by dividing the income of the property into its constituent parts.

If a 10% return is required on the whole investment, we may also presume a 10% return is required on every part of the investment. The income to an investment can be divided to see if there is enough income to compensate all the parts adequately. Figure 4.2 shows how this might occur. In the figure, the total property's return is divided into two parts, each of which compensates the appropriate part of the investment: the building and the land. In real estate theory, the income accruing to the land is called **economic rent.** Using this idea, we can now analyze our three apartment alternatives.

Table 4.2 shows the costs and returns for each of these buildings. The table shows the actual income for each property and compares the actual income to the income required by the building at 10%. The difference between the required income and actual income is the income available to compensate the land.

As you can see from the table, the four-unit apartment building does not leave as much income for the land as the eight-unit use. The largest building does not give the land any positive income. The small building is not an intensive enough use. The large building is too intensive. The

FIGURE 4.2   DIVISION OF RETURN

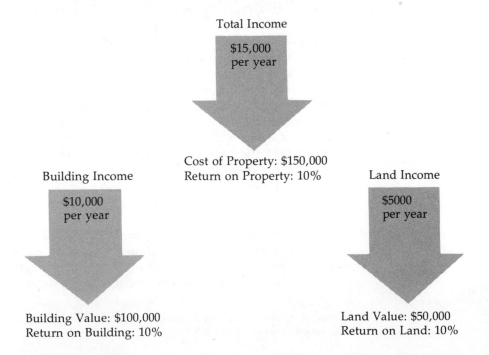

TABLE 4.2   HIGHEST AND BEST USE ANALYSIS

	Four Units	Eight Units	Twelve Units
Building Cost	$80,000	$160,000	$320,000
Required Return @ 10%	$ 8000/year	$ 16,000/year	$ 32,000/year
Total Property Income	$10,000	$ 20,000	$ 30,000
Less: Required Return	$ 8000	$ 16,000	$ 32,000
Available for Land	$ 2000	$ 4000	($ 2000)

middle-sized unit is just right, since with this alternative the income for the land is the highest. There may be other possible uses for this property in addition to the three mentioned. The appraiser would look at each feasible, hypothetical use until the one which provided the *most income for the land* was found. That would be the highest and best use.

It must be kept in mind that all these uses may be hypothetical. The property in question may have a five-year-old lumberyard on it at the time of the appraisal. The owner may be foregoing value on the land if it is not at highest and best use. Thus, the highest and best use, however hypothetical, is nevertheless relevant.

It may be noted that a return level must be specified (10% in our example). At a different level of return, there may be a different highest and best use. The reader may wish to verify that at a 5% return the highest and best use is the twelve-unit apartment with an income available to the land of $14,000. At a 15% return, however, all uses result in a negative income to the land. This would imply that the property put to its potential uses could not achieve that high a level of return. Since appraisal is an objective process, the return level chosen represents a "general" return for the risk level of the investment, not necessarily a specific investor's return level. However, if an investor requests an appraisal for his or her personal use, then that specific required return level would be used.

Principle of Substitution

The value of a property is affected by more than the principle of highest and best use as described above. No matter how unique a property is, there are substitutes for it. The reason a user occupies property is because it provides some service to that user. This service is what gives the property value to a potential owner or occupant. Any properties which provide similar services should have similar values.

The **principle of substitution** basically says that the upper limit on value of a given property A is the cost of acquiring an equally desirable property which provides the same service as A. This principle is limited by the need to replace A in a reasonable time.

Principle of Contribution

This principle guides the process of altering a property. Basically, it is the traditional equivalent in appraisal to the net present value rule we described in chapter 3. The **principle of contribution** says that a property should not be improved unless the capitalized value of the income added by the improvement exceeds the cost of making the improvement. This principle has some impact in cost and income appraisal, as we shall see in the chapters to follow. The reader may notice that the principle of highest and best use is similar to the principle of contribution, except that highest and best use specifies what improvements should be made to a parcel of land.

CHAPTER FOUR SUMMARY

This has been a brief introduction to the procedures and concepts of appraisal and investment analysis. We saw how and why the appraiser provides his service. We briefly outlined the major approaches to appraisal. The concepts of market value and investment value were compared and we saw how investment value considers many factors appraisal does not consider. Finally, we developed the concept of highest and best use of property which is integral to the process of appraisal—whatever leaves the most income available for the land.

KEY TERMS

Appraisal	Highest and Best	Market Value
Comparable	Use	Principle of
Properties	Income Approaches	Contribution
Cost Approach	Market Comparison	Principle of
Economic Rent	Approach	Substitution
	Market Mechanism	Subject Property

QUESTIONS FOR STUDY AND DISCUSSION

1. Distinguish between *real* and *accounting* depreciation values.

2. What is meant by *appraisal* in real estate? How does it differ from *investment analysis*?

3. If demand increases without a comparable increase in supply, the price of the resource would be expected to increase. What factors or conditions might lead to this situation in real property? What factors

might help remedy this situation? Would these remedial factors be short run or long run in nature?

4. This chapter mentioned that a high level of unemployment might result in an underpriced housing market. Can you think of other factors or conditions which might result in a depressed real estate market?

5. What are the three classic approaches to real estate appraisal? Describe each approach briefly.

6. What is meant by *highest and best use*? If a medical building is determined to be the highest and best use for a parcel of land today, will it necessarily be the highest and best use five years from now? Why or why not?

7. What techniques for appraisal might best be used for each of the following types of properties?

A. A personal residence, owner-occupied

B. 120 acres of farmland

C. A twenty-five-year-old factory, rented to tenants

D. A twelve-unit apartment complex

E. A pizza restaurant

F. A school building

G. A twenty-five-year-old service station on two acres of downtown land in a major city

8. Is highest and best use an objective or subjective concept?

PROBLEMS FOR REVIEW

1. Find the highest and best use from among the following feasible alternative uses. The applicable rate of return is 10%. The land is one acre near a shopping center.

A. A small cocktail lounge. Cost of building: $150,000. Net expected revenue per year: $17,500.

B. A twenty-four-hour convenience market. Cost of building: $100,000. Expected revenue per year: $14,000.

C. A fast-food restaurant. Cost of building: $250,000. Expected return per year: $28,000.

5

MARKET COMPARISON AND COST APPRAISING

IN THIS chapter we will examine two of the three classic appraisal techniques: the market comparison approach and the penalized replacement cost approach. These discussions are not intended to turn you into a qualified appraiser, but to give you an appreciation for the issues and concepts of appraisal technique.

Market Comparison Approach

As we stated earlier, the premise underlying the market approach to real estate appraising is that similar properties tend to sell for similar prices in the market. Kahn, Case, and Schimmel call this the **principle of substitution.**[1] When a property sells in the market and is a fair sale, its price tends to be a basis for the value of similar properties which will be sold in adjacent, succeeding time periods. At the heart of this method is a list of recent property transactions of various types. These serve as "benchmarks" or comparable properties to which the subject property under appraisal may be compared.

Process of Market Comparison

The structure of market comparison appraisal is simple. First, the subject property must be identified and described. This description must be very thorough with considerable detail. Because each parcel of real estate is unique, true comparisons with properties just like the subject will be impossible. By establishing a detailed description of the subject property, using a pre-established list of descriptive variables, critical points of comparison which affect value may be identified.

Second, the appraiser should find a list of comparable properties for the subject. These must be as similar to the subject as they can be in terms of their key characteristics (variables). Normally in a straightforward residential appraisal, three or four such comparable properties will be used. The appraiser can use as many as are needed to establish the value with a high degree of confidence.

Third, the appraisal involves the evaluation of the differences between the comparable properties and the subject. Taking each characteristic in turn, the appraiser estimates the *adjustment* that must be made to the price of each comparable property to account for dissimilarities between the comparable one and the subject. If the comparable one has a feature which is more valuable than a similar feature of the subject, the actual sales price of the comparable is adjusted downward for the

---

[1]Sanders A. Kahn, Frederick E. Case, and Alfred Schimmel, *Real Estate Appraising and Investment* (New York: Ronald Press, 1963), p. 87.

value of difference. Similarly, when the subject is more valuable, the price of the comparable is adjusted upward. This third step of making adjustments is a critical one and the appraiser needs to have a great deal of sound judgment.

When all adjustments have been made to the prices of the comparables, the adjustments are totaled and an *indicated value* determined for each comparable property. These indicated values are then correlated to derive the final estimate of value for the subject property. Notice that *all the adjustments are made to the value of the comparable properties*.

Data Requirements   The data requirement for a market comparison appraisal is based on the variables for which adjustments need to be made. You can probably think of most of these variables simply on intuitive grounds. Some of the major points of comparison include:

1. *Property Location*.   The appraiser needs the address and the characteristics of the neighborhood surrounding each property.

2. *Time of Sale*.   A time period must be established during which sales of any similar property will be considered to be comparable. In a housing market characterized by a relatively stable or small, constant change in housing prices, this time period may be of longer duration than the time period for a market in which housing prices increase rapidly or change unpredictably. An adjustment for the time of sale, even within this acceptable period, is still necessary to account for inflation or deflation which occurred between the time of sale of the comparable property and the present time.

3. *Size of Lot*.   In many properties, a large portion of the value will be contained in the lot, so its characteristics must be noted.

4. *Size of Building*.   For a personal residence, commercial or residential income property, this is usually a square-foot measure.

5. *Characteristics of Improvements*.   For personal residences, this category includes factors such as the number of rooms, the utilities supplied, the type of heating system, the presence of a basement, construction type and quality, age and condition of improvements, the architecture, and the presence of amenities such as fireplaces and landscaping.

6. *Financial Factors*.   Here we would like to know how the comparable sales were financed, if there are pending assessments against the property, and other financial factors which might affect the value.

7. *Miscellaneous Factors*.   Other factors for which adjustments might be made include the presence of personal property in the sale, income characteristics for income properties, and zoning and deed restrictions.

This list is partial, but representative, of the variables for which adjustments may be made. In general, any significant point of difference between the comparable and subject properties should be considered.

Data Gathering   These preceding data are generally gathered routinely by professional appraisers. The characteristics of any property can be used, providing it was purchased at arm's length in an open market transaction. There must have been no duress or pressure of any kind affecting either party to the transaction. These comparable sales data may be gathered from a number of sources. Often appraisers are also brokers and have data on transactions closed by their offices. Information may also be collected at the county courthouse where official records of real estate transactions are kept. Sometimes, however, this source may be incomplete. Other sources may include real estate professionals, the principals in sales transactions, or professional organizations such as local real estate boards. The most important point to remember here is that data should be of unquestioned quality and ethically obtained.

A Sample Appraisal

Table 5.1 shows how a grid or matrix may be constructed to facilitate estimating the value of a subject property. On the left side of the table is a list of factors for which adjustments may be made. Next, the description of the subject property is entered in the grid. Finally, the comparable properties' data are listed in the grid. At this point, the appropriate adjustments can be made to the comparable properties. The total adjustments and the adjusted values for each comparable appear at the bottom of the grid, along with the correlated, estimated value for the subject property.

Sample Property Description   The subject property may be described by the following characteristics:

1. Single-family residence located in a medium-sized Midwestern city;

2. Lot is 100 feet by 150 feet, zoned residential, has normal topography, and has full utilities provided;

3. Neighborhood is fully developed with single-family residences in the $20,000 to $40,000 range, the market is balanced in the neighborhood;

4. The house has 909 square feet with a living room, dining room, kitchen, three bedrooms, and a bath; is six years old; is a frame ranch-style house with a full basement; has hardwood floors with carpeting, forced air gas heat, drywall construction, and no appliances are to be included in the sale; has no garage, but a paved drive, parking slab, and

TABLE 5.1   MARKET COMPARISON DATA

Variable	Subject Description	Comparable #1 Sale Price: $33,000 Description	$	Comparable #2 Sale Price: $30,500 Description	$	Comparable #3 Sale Price: $34,500 Description	$
Location	average	average	0	average	0	good	−1000
Sale Date	present	8 months ago	+1500	3 months ago	+ 500	6 months ago	+1250
Site/View	100 × 150 lot	62 × 120 lot	+2000	66 × 118 lot	+2000	70 × 115 lot	0
Design	ranch	ranch	0	ranch	0	ranch	0
Age	6 years old	17 years old	0	7 years old	0	5 years old	0
Quality	good	good	0	good	0	good	0
Condition	good	good	0	good	0	good	0
Square Feet	909	908	0	912	0	940	− 750
Rooms	5, 3 bedrms.	5, 3 bedrms.	0	5, 3 bedrms.	0	5, 3 bedrms.	0
Basement	full, roughed in partitions	full, half-finished	−1000	full, half-finished	−1000	full	0
Utilities	average	average	0	average	0	average	0
Air Cond.	no	yes	−750	no	0	no	0
Garage	slab	1 car	−1000	nothing	+ 750	nothing	+ 750
Patios	patio slab	nothing	+ 250	nothing	+ 250	nothing	+ 250
Driveway	paved	rock	+ 500	rock	+ 500	rock	+ 500
Paved Street	no	yes	−1500	no	0	yes	−1500
Total Adjustments			0		+3000		− 500
Indicated Price	$33,500	$33,000		$33,500		$34,000	

patio slab; the improvements have an estimated remaining life of sixty-five years;

5. There are $2500 in liens against the property to pay for street and sewer improvements.

Using this description of the property and similar descriptions of the comparables, we can now proceed to estimate the subject's value as shown in Table 5.1.

Interpretation of Table   As you can see from the sample data in the table, the three comparables are very similar in description to the subject property. However, there are some substantial areas of difference. In all cases where the adjustment is a positive number, the subject property has a feature which the comparable property lacks. When the comparable property has a feature which is lacking in the subject property, the feature must be removed from it by subtracting an estimate of the value of that feature. For example, comparables #1 and #2 both have partially finished basements. The appraiser has determined that this feature adds $1000 to their values compared to the subject's unfinished basement. This is probably a rough estimate of the cost of finishing the basement of the subject in a similar fashion. The air conditioning in comparable #1 is worth about $750, the approximate cost required to add this feature to the subject property. Since all these features make the comparables more valuable, the values have been subtracted from the appropriate sale prices.

For features such as basements, garages, air conditioning, patio slabs, and the like, the adjustment is usually *an approximation of the cost of adding that feature to the property lacking it*.[2] In summary, if the subject has the feature, the value is added to the comparable. If the comparable has the feature, the value is subtracted to make the adjustment.

After subtotaling all the adjustments for each comparable, an adjusted price is derived. This adjusted price is called the *indicated value* of the comparable. In this case, when all the comparables have been made as similar to the subject as possible, the price range of the comparables varies from $33,000 to $34,000. This range is then used to estimate the value for the subject property. Here an average value was used for the appraisal of the subject, $33,500. Given the range and the basic description of the subject property the appraiser will use the value he or she feels is *most probable*. The range may even be used as the value. Notice in the example that the value chosen corresponds to the adjusted (indicated) value of comparable #2, which sold most recently. Because inflation is difficult to predict and this market is known to be under

---

[2]The appraiser can obtain aid in estimating these improvements from one of the numerous services supplying cost data for such purposes. These are generally the same firms referred to later in this chapter.

some inflationary pressure, the newest sale may be the most timely and most indicative of the subject's value.

In general, when estimating the value of anything, one can be more confident of the estimate if a number of approaches is used independently and each provides a similar indication of value. Here each comparable is, in essence, an independent estimator of value. Since the estimates result in a narrow range of $1000, the appraiser may have a reasonable amount of confidence in the final estimate. Some appraisers might also supplement this type of residential appraisal with the cost approach, which we will discuss shortly. The cost approach for this subject property is demonstrated in Table 5.2. The value estimate, $33,000, was slightly lower than the market comparison approach estimate. Nevertheless, it confirms the basic range of the value of the subject property.

Uses of Market Appraisals

The market comparison approach is used most often in the evaluation of residential property, especially single-family residences. It is also used to appraise land. Raw land, as well as improved land, may be valued using this technique. As we shall see in the next chapter, some approaches to income appraisal require an independent estimate of land value. The cost approach in this chapter also requires an estimate of the land value. The market comparison approach may be used for valuing land when these various other appraisal methods are used.

The market approach is not limited to single-family residential property and land, however. Whenever there is sufficient market data available from timely, arm's length transactions, the technique may be applied. For many income properties, an appraiser may apply an income capitalization method as well as the market comparison method to make the appraisal of the subject property. The use of more than one method allows the appraiser to confirm the estimate. Except in larger cities, the market comparison approach is difficult to apply to commercial properties because there is just not enough comparable data available to make a good analysis. However, commercial properties, such as service stations, which are found in large numbers even in smaller metropolitan areas, may be evaluated using this approach. When sufficient, timely data are scarce, the income approaches or cost approach must be used.

Limitations of the Market Comparison Approach

Even if enough comparables exist for the market approach to be feasible, there are some problems inherent in this method. First, for some types of property data may be difficult to gather. Data are often incomplete or cannot be validated properly. When any doubt exists for the validity of the data, a good professional will not use it.

Another problem arises in making adjustments. There are many types of adjustments for physical amenities which are reasonably easy to make. In our example, it was not difficult to validate the cost of a paved drive or air conditioning. However, difficulty arises in making adjustments for value differences based on quality of construction, appearances, condition of the improvements, and neighborhood differences. These adjustments are more subtle and require subjective judgment. There is a great deal of discretion in these qualitative judgments, which may result in an estimated value which is more "convenient" than real.

Our sample did not contain many really qualitative judgments, but there was one of note. Refer to the item in Table 5.1 entitled "site/view." The lots for comparables #1 and #2 are much smaller than the subject's lot. Large adjustments were made to the comparables for this deficiency. Comparable #3 also has a small lot. However, no adjustment was made. The explanation for this is that a superior view apparently offset the lot's smaller size. This was indeed convenient. If a pure size adjustment of $2000 had been made, comparable #3 would have been valued at $36,000, well above the values of the other two comparable properties. The range of values for the comparables would be increased and the confidence in the appraisal value for the subject property would be decreased. Situations with such subjective judgments tend to cast some doubt on the objectivity of the market comparison appraisal process.

This discussion is not meant to be an indictment of market comparison appraising. However, when you might be using such an appraisal, for instance, as a potential seller of your own residence, you can at least be warned of the fact that there are many areas of qualitative judgment in this method. You can use this information to help you draw your own conclusion concerning a property's worth.

One final area of difficulty in this type of appraising involves the underlying premise of the technique. Market comparison is based on the data from the activity in real estate markets which are presumed to be reasonably efficient indicators of value. Price is an indicator of value at the moment of the transaction and a major part of the environment of that transaction is the market itself. However, as we saw in chapter 4, markets sometimes get out of balance, causing prices to be inadequate reflectors of economic worth.

A property has an **intrinsic value** also, based on the benefits it provides its owner. In a normal market the value of the benefits—cash or psychic—accruing to the owner of a property should be reflected in the market price. In an abnormal market this will not always be the case. The market value may not be a substitute for intrinsic value. Buying a property that is overpriced by the market structure may be justified by the market itself but not by either of the other two measures of value we have (cost and income approaches to value). If you buy a property when the market price exceeds intrinsic value then you are practicing the "greater fool theory" that caused the downfall of many investors in the stock market crash of 1929. You must be wary of market appraisals *not supported* by similar results in the income or cost approaches.

Cost Approach

The second of the three major appraisal techniques is called the cost approach. The procedure is relatively simple, although it may require a great deal of work. The basis for the approach is the idea that a property should never be valued at a price above what it would cost to replace it. We, therefore, estimate this cost of replacement as a first step. All properties depreciate as they are used, so we must penalize the hypothetical replacement building for the accrued depreciation of the subject property. The resulting difference (cost less depreciation) is the estimated value of the improvement. We then must add an appropriate land value to obtain the appraised value for the property.

Estimating Replacement Cost

The first step in the cost appraisal procedure is to devise an estimate of the cost of replacing the subject property with a hypothetical substitute which would perform the same functions. Often building codes and construction methods will have changed between the time the subject was built and the time of the appraisal. The hypothetical replacement structure will be developed on the *basis of current standards*. Consequently, any functional or physical improvements will be removed to compensate for deficiencies in the subject property.

The cost to reproduce a structure includes more than just building costs. There are **direct costs** such as the materials and labor in the building. There are **indirect costs,** including architects' fees, financing costs, permits, and any other such costs required before the building would be habitable. The sum of both the direct and indirect costs is the total cost to reproduce.

There are several methods for estimating the replacement cost of a property. The method (or methods) used will depend on the information available, the complexity of the problem, and the speed required for the appraisal. Ring defines four methods for estimating the direct costs:[3]

1. Builder's detail inventory method,
2. Quantity survey method,

---

[3]Alfred A. Ring, *The Valuation of Real Estate*, 2nd Ed. (Englewood Cliffs, N.J.: Prentice-Hall, 1970), pp. 166–173.

3. Unit-in-place construction method, and

4. Comparative market method.

These will be explained next.

Building Specifications   The basis for the cost approach to appraisal is a set of specifications which describes the subject improvements. The building **specifications** enumerate the type of materials and construction to be used in each part of the improvement. The specifications for the basement might call for walls eight inches thick made of reinforced concrete with a six-inch concrete floor, and so forth.

For convenience in appraisal, the specifications are often divided into functional units. These units coincide with parts of the structure as they would be built by a subcontractor. A sample list for a single-family residence is shown in Table 5.2. Each one of the units in the list is composed of a number of materials as well as a certain quantity of labor. The labor and materials constitute the value of the functional unit.

TABLE 5.2   SUBCONTRACTORS' SPECIFICATION LIST
SINGLE-FAMILY RESIDENCE

Item	Finished Cost
Site Clearing	$400
Excavation	500
Foundation	xxx
Exterior Walls	xxx
Subflooring	xxx
Framing and Carpentry	xxx
Roofing	xxx
Windows and Doors	xxx
Dry Wall	xxx
Flooring and Covering	xxx
Cabinet Work	xxx
Plumbing	xxx
Electrical	xxx
Heating and Cooling	xxx
Fixtures,	xxx
etc.	$\vdots$
Financial, Closing, and Permits	xxx
Total Cost	$37,000

Builder's Detail Method   The most comprehensive and accurate method of estimating the cost of reproduction for a subject improvement is the **builder's detail method.** The appraiser using this approach first divides the building into units such as those shown in Table 5.2. Then, using the specifications for the subject property, the appraiser develops a full list of the amount of labor and materials required for each unit. To derive the cost of each unit, these materials and the appropriate amount of labor are multiplied by their costs. Finally, the units are summed to provide the direct cost of the whole structure. Indirect costs are then added.

The cost as derived by this approach is based on *current building codes and specifications for a building providing the same service as the subject property.* The appraiser will design the specifications to be as close to the description of the subject property as current law allows.

Because so much detail is required for the builder's approach, the appraiser must have a good working knowledge of building techniques, codes, and construction plans and specifications. The amount of detail in the unit breakdowns makes this process time-consuming and expensive. It is used when the appraiser wishes to achieve great accuracy without tight time or cost restrictions.

Quantity Survey Method   Similar results to those of the builder's method may be achieved through the **quantity survey method.** This method is also based on the specifications for the units in the building, such as the foundation and the roof. However, the appraiser short-cuts the work involved by estimating the total direct cost for the units *without regard to internal detail.* It is possible to do this because commercial data sources provide basic costs for units of varying construction. If, for example, a roof of 2000 square feet of average construction were to be valued, a total cost figure for the constituent labor and materials would be obtained from the data source.

The fact that the appraiser need not be concerned with the internal detail of the various units makes the quantity survey much easier to use than the builder's method. The appraiser must still have a good understanding of construction techniques, however, so that sufficiently detailed specifications can be developed. It is the specifications which dictate the particular cost figures to be selected from the commercial data sources.

Unit-in-Place Method   In the **unit-in-place method,** the building under appraisal is again specified and divided into parts. However, in this case, the appraiser does not look at functional units. Rather, he or she considers *the total quantity of the various materials in the entire building.* For instance, the appraiser would determine the total quantity of lumber in the structure by adding the lumber requirements for the roof, the walls, the framing, the floor, and so forth. The two previous methods treated this material as it was found in a functional unit. In the unit-in-place method, a building is treated as consisting of so many board feet of lumber, so many cubic yards of concrete, so many squares of shingles, so much wire, etc. When the specifications are put in these terms, it is relatively easy to find the total cost of the materials. A labor estimate is then added to derive the direct cost of the reproduction.

Comparative Market Method   The easiest and fastest approach to estimating the reproduction of a structure is the **comparative market method.** This approach applies a *market-derived multiplier* to the general size specifications of the property to be appraised. For this method to be used, the appraiser must have a set of hypothetical structures of various specifications which have had total material and labor costs estimated. These total costs are divided by the total number of square feet in the structure to derive a standard constant multiplier, which may then be applied to any structure of similar specifications. Again, commercial data sources are available which provide total cost estimates for different specifications. The data available for this method are tailored for differences in labor and material costs for every major community in the United States, so local price differences are accounted for.

Assume we must estimate the cost of a simple warehouse structure of concrete block construction. The appraiser finds the appropriate value for this type of structure, say, $15.31 per square foot, and simply multiplies this cost by the square footage of the structure to be appraised. If a few pieces of miscellaneous equipment or amenities are not included in the standard structure, these items must be valued separately and added on to the cost of the basic structure.

The comparative market method is not the most accurate of the cost approaches, but it is inexpensive and easy to apply. It is especially popular for use in single-family residences for which less costly appraisals are desired. We will use this approach in the example which follows shortly.

For the appraiser to make any of these cost estimates, a knowledge of construction techniques and costs is required. Sources for accurate information must be located and developed. Today commercial services do provide much information which can be used for the comparative market, unit-in-place, and quantity survey methods. We have distinguished between all these methods, but, in practice, the forms used by appraisers may actually be mixed combinations of the described approaches.

Estimating Depreciation

Thus far we have seen how the appraiser might estimate the cost of a hypothetical reproduction of the subject property. Now we must look at the adjustment for depreciation which must be made. All older, used structures suffer from some sort of loss in value. This is *accrued depreciation*. The appraiser must estimate this loss in value and adjust the reproduction cost downward by the appropriate amount.

The purpose of the accrued depreciation adjustment is to account for the differences between the subject property and the hypothetical reproduction of it. Suppose an appraiser is trying to estimate the value of a unique fifty-year-old factory building. The market comparison appraisal approach is not applicable, so the cost approach may be used. The cost of the building fifty years ago is not relevant. Instead, the cost of a similar structure built today must be substituted as a basis for the value of the old structure. If this new structure performs the same functions as the subject property, the appraiser knows that prospective buyers of the subject property could build the new substitute for their needs. Thus, the reproduction cost is an *upper bound* on the value of the service provided by the subject property.

The appraiser also knows that if the subject property provides any functional utility at all, then it must have some value. The *difference* between the subject property's value and the new hypothetical structure's value is the *real accrued depreciation inherent in the subject property*. The appraiser must estimate this accrued depreciation and subtract it from the reproduction cost to obtain the value of the subject property.

Prospective buyers of the subject property know that they will be getting a less valuable property than if the structure were reproduced new. However, buyers would be willing to sacrifice some value as long as they need pay only for the actual service they would obtain from the subject property. The cost approach attempts to value the *actual service that a buyer will receive by purchasing the subject property.*

Depreciation can arise for one of three reasons. A building may simply wear out physically. **Physical deterioration** involves minor problems such as cracked plaster and peeling paint and major items such as inadequate wiring and structural weakness. A second type of depreciation is **functional obsolescence.** As a structure is used for a length of time and for various purposes, it may begin to become functionally obsolete. This means the structure no longer provides adequate service to the user compared to newer structures with technological advances. A warehouse building with low ceilings will not compete well with newer, high-ceiling warehouses. The owner would be losing some value by retaining the older structure. The third form of accrued depreciation is **economic obsolescence.** This arises in relation to the site of the property. Because of changing neighborhoods, loss of traffic circulation, increased nuisances, and so forth, a building may lose value because it is on a particular site. The methods for estimating the accrued depreciation of the subject property are described here and illustrated in the example to follow.

Physical Deterioration   Physical deterioration (or obsolescence) is the measure of the wear and tear on a building. As a structure grows old, the walls weaken, the floor will not support as much weight, and so forth. This means the building has a diminished capacity to provide the owner with the service required. There are two types of physical deterioration: curable and incurable. **Curable deterioration** refers to problems which can be fixed at a cost which is reasonable in relation to the value of the structure. **Incurable deterioration** refers to a loss in value which either cannot be fixed without razing the building or which has a very high cost in relation to the value of the whole building.

For example, let us hypothesize a fifty-year-old factory building with three floors. The top floor is in such bad condition that it will only support fifty pounds of weight per square foot. This renders it virtually useless. The floor can be strengthened at a cost of $250,000. If the whole building is only worth $200,000 as is, then the weak floors would be considered an incurable problem. Fixing them would increase the service of the building by only 50%, but the cost of the building would be increased by over 100%.

The appropriate adjustment for curable physical deterioration is the cost required to fix the problem. The cost of minor repairs, and even major curable repairs, is estimated and subtracted from the reproduction cost of the structure. Incurable problems are more difficult to adjust for. There are two methods which may be used to account for incurable physical obsolescence.

Let us assume that an industrial building has a 10,000-square-foot wing which is no longer structurally sound. It cannot be fixed at a reasonable cost, but it may be used in its diminished capacity. One way of adjusting for this problem is to penalize the cost of reproducing this part of the building for the percentage of the original structure's useful life which has expired. This is, in effect, straight-line depreciation. If the structure had an original life of fifty years and thirty years has expired, then 60% (30/50) of the structure's life would be over. Thus, the appraiser would subtract an amount equal to 60% of the cost of reproducing the defective area from the cost of the whole structure. If the wing would cost $80,000 to reproduce, then 60% of $80,000, or $48,000, would be subtracted for this incurable physical obsolescence.

A second approach to incurable obsolescence of any type, not just physical, is the **liability to replace** method described by Ring.[4] Again suppose our hypothetical building had an original life of fifty years when new. Further suppose thirty years has expired, leaving twenty years of useful life remaining. The penalty in this approach is based on

---

[4]Ring, *Valuation of Real Estate,* p. 190.

the present value of the benefits lost up to the time of appraisal. Let us say the general (or market) rate of return on factory building is 10%. The present value annuity factor (*PVAF*) for level benefits accruing to a structure for fifty years at 10% is 9.915. The *PVAF* for twenty years, the remaining life, at 10% is 8.514. The difference between these two factors is the relative value lost by the incurable obsolescence.[5]

$PVAF_{50,10\%}$	9.915
$PVAF_{20,10\%}$	8.514
Present Value Lost	1.401

The liability to replace adjustment factor is viewed as a percentage of the present value of benefits lost to the present value of the benefits available at the onset of the building's economic life. In this case, the adjustment factor is approximately 14%, 1.401/9.915.

Using the calculation shown, we may determine that incurable physical deterioration is about 14% of the reproduction value of the building. Estimates of the useful life and the rate of return to be used are critical and make this method difficult to apply properly. Notice that the straight-line penalty is applied to the reproduction cost of the incurable problem, while the percentage factor from the liability to replace method is applied to the reproduction cost of the entire structure.

Functional Obsolescence   Curable functional obsolescence is measured by the cost of upgrading the functional quality of the structure. As with physical problems, curable functional deterioration involves difficulties which can be feasibly and economically repaired. Incurable functional problems may be treated in various ways. One method is to reflect the estimated cost of "getting around" the functional problem, if that is possible. Another method is to penalize the structure's replacement cost for the expected loss in value in the sale of the property because the structure will perform only limited functions. The low-ceiling warehouse might be penalized by 15% of its value because of its less competitive position relative to warehouses with high ceilings. Again, the penalty involves much judgment and is difficult to apply for that reason.

Economic Obsolescence   Economic obsolescence is by its nature incurable. The general approach to treating this problem is to *compare the replacement structure on an ideal site with the same* (replacement) *structure on the subject site.* The difference in economic rent which the owner would collect on the ideal site is compared to that from the subject site.

---

[5]This calculation is described in detail in the appendix to chapter 2.

This difference is capitalized as an annuity or a declining stream to generate the value adjustment. A form of the liability to replace method may also be used. For this method the useful *economic* life of the hypothetical structure on the ideal site is compared to its estimated life on the subject site. These estimates can be treated in present value terms as illustrated in the physical deterioration section.

Sample Appraisal

To illustrate the cost approach to appraisal we will return to the example from the market comparison approach to appraisal involving the single-family ranch home shown in Table 5.1. The cost approach for this dwelling is shown in Table 5.3. The basic data are presented next.

1. Subject has 909 square feet with average construction. The replacement cost of this type of construction in the relevant market area is about $32 per square foot, using the comparative market method to estimate cost. In addition to the basic house, there is a garage floor, paved driveway, shed floor, a patio, and landscaping.

2. Physical deterioration: The subject property needs painting, some repairs to the walls in two rooms, and the carpeting needs replacement in two rooms.

3. Functional obsolescence: The property has two functional problems. First, there is no shower in the bathroom. Second, the bedrooms are too small for the average family in the relevant market at the present time.

4. Economic obsolescence: Though the neighborhood in which this house is located is neither old nor unbalanced, it is not connected by a good arterial street. In addition, a small factory has been built two blocks from the subject property, which is on the edge of the neighborhood. It is estimated that the hypothetical replacement structure would have an economic life of seventy years on an ideal site compared to an economic life of forty years on the subject site. The market rate of return is about 10%.

5. The land of the subject property would be worth $6000 if vacant.

From Table 5.3 we can see that the indicated value of the subject property is $33,000 or $500 less than that derived by the market comparison approach. The penalties for curable repairs are fairly straightforward. The penalty for the small rooms is based on an estimated loss in sales price that will be suffered at the time of the sale. The economic depreciation is based on a seventy-year useful life on an ideal site compared to a forty-year life on the subject site using the liability to replace method. This is a function of the traffic problems and the recent nuisance.

The alert reader may have noticed that some of the adjustments to

TABLE 5.3   PENALIZED COST TO REPLACE SINGLE-FAMILY HOUSE

Estimated Cost:		
909 Square Feet @ $32/sq. ft.		$29,100
Plus: Garage Floor		600
Paved Driveway		1,000
Shed Floor		100
Patio and Landscaping		1,000
Total Cost to Reproduce		$31,800
Physical Deterioration:		
Curable: Painting	$400	
Wall Repairs	400	
Carpeting	800	(1,600)
Functional Obsolescence:		
Curable: Install Shower	$ 500	
Incurable: Small Rooms	2,000	(2,500)
Economic Obsolescence:		
Ideal Structure on Ideal Site: $PVAF_{70,10\%}$		
Ideal Structure, Subject Site: $PVAF_{40,10\%}$		
9.99 − 9.78 = 0.21		
% Depreciation = 0.21/9.99 = 2.1%		
Penalty (2.1% × $31,800)		(700)
Value of Improvements		$27,000
Plus Land Value		$ 6,000
Indicated Value of Subject		$33,000

the comparable properties from Table 5.1 differed from the cost estimates shown for the subject property in Table 5.3. These two types of appraisals are measuring different things. The market approach deals with *adjustments to the market value* of comparable properties compared to the subject. Th cost approach is concerned with the cost to create a property today which would most nearly replace the subject.

Uses of Cost Approach

The cost approach is used primarily to appraise older structures and buildings which are somewhat unique. Factories, commercial buildings, and public buildings are good examples of properties which might be valued using this approach. The cost approach is also used to confirm market and/or income appraisals, as we demonstrated with our market appraisal of the single-family residence.

The purposes which are well suited to cost appraisals are numerous. One primary purpose for appraising older structures is for fire insurance. Cost is also used as a basis for many condemnation appraisals, as these often involve older structures.

Limitations of Cost Appraising

The main limitations of the approach are based on the complexity of the estimates that must be made. The process of estimating replacement cost requires a great deal of judgment and experience. It also requires much data and time. The adjustments are also difficult to make accurately. Curable obsolescence is relatively easy to estimate because it is related to the cost estimation process. However, the adjustments for incurable obsolescence may be somewhat arbitrary. Useful lives are difficult to estimate, which makes comparisons based on this factor difficult. The effects of nuisances and functional problems on sales and rental values may also cause difficulties in estimation.

CHAPTER FIVE SUMMARY

In this chapter we have examined two of the three major approaches to the appraisal of real property. The market comparison approach was based on the similarities in prices of like properties. In this approach the appraiser uses properties comparable to the subject property and adjusts the prices of these comparables. The adjusted prices provide a range of value for the subject.

The cost approach is based on the premise that the value of a property may be determined as the penalized cost to reproduce it as closely as possible. We saw four different methods for finding the cost of reproducing the subject property. The adjustments to this cost are based on accrued depreciation inherent in the subject property. There are three types of depreciation involved: physical, functional, and economic depreciation. Physical deterioration is based on the physical wear and tear inherent in the property. Functional obsolescence refers to the inability of the property to perform its intended function as efficiently as it should. Economic depreciation accounts for the effects of location.

We have seen how these methods of appraisal may be used and what their limitations are. This chapter presented a general overview of the basic methods and uses of these types of appraisals, rather than a cookbook methodology for using the approaches. The references at the end of the text provide sources for you readers who desire greater detail in these two appraisal approaches.

KEY TERMS

Builder's Detail Method

Comparative Market Method

Functional Obsolescence

Incurable Deterioration

Physical Deterioration

Principle of Substitution

Curable	Indirect Costs	Quantity Survey
Deterioration	Intrinsic Value	Method
Direct Costs	Liability to Replace	Specifications
Economic		Unit-in-Place
Obsolescence		Method

QUESTIONS FOR STUDY AND DISCUSSION

1. Explain the premise underlying the *market approach* to appraisal. Compare this to the premise underlying the cost approach.

2. How would you adjust a comparable property for the presence of amenities not present in the subject property? How would you adjust for the subject's amenities not present in a comparable property?

3. How is the value of the subject property determined under the market approach to appraisal? How confident might an appraiser be of the value obtained for the property? Under what circumstances might the appraiser be more confident of the value estimate?

4. Describe and compare the four methods of estimating reproduction cost. Under what circumstances might one method be more appropriate than other methods?

5. Describe and compare the three kinds of depreciation adjustments used in the cost approach. How is curable depreciation distinguished from incurable depreciation?

6. What are some of the limitations of the market comparison and cost approaches to appraisal?

PROBLEMS FOR REVIEW

1. Using the data given here, find the indicated value for the vacant lot shown as the subject property. Inflation is approximately 10% per year in the subject area. Treat each amenity as an independent factor. For simplicity, base all percentage adjustments on the sale prices of the comparables.

Item	Subject	Comparable #1	Comparable #2	Comparable #3
Price	?	$8,000	$15,000	$9,000
Size	65 × 150	65 × 120	130 × 120	65 × 150
Time of Sale	present	9 mo. ago	3 mo. ago	6 mo. ago
Terrain	good	good	5% worse	5% worse
Location	average	5% better	average	10% worse
Subsoil Conditions	good	5% worse	good	good

2. A small store is available for purchase. It is a twenty-year-old building on ¼ acre near a shopping area in a small town. The store has 7000 square feet which could be reproduced at a cost of $15 per square foot. The property needs painting worth $2000 and minor repairs costing $3000. The lighting in the store is inadequate for most uses and could be replaced for $4000. Incurable functional depreciation will restrict the sale price by approximately 10%. The subject property is on the wrong side of the street for most uses, so it is felt that the site would reduce the economic life of the replacement structure to thirty years from fifty years on an ideal site. A good market rate of interest is 12% for this type of property. The land is worth $10,000 vacant. Find the indicated value for this property using the cost approach.

6

INCOME APPRAISAL

THE THIRD of the classic appraisal techniques is the income approach to appraisal. The underlying premise of this approach is that the value of real property is equal to the capitalized value of its future cash benefits. In this chapter we will explore a number of approaches to appraising the value of the future benefits of an income property. We will also use this chapter to summarize our discussion of appraisal in general.

Structure and Data Requirements

In order to discuss income appraisal, we will have to draw heavily on the material presented in chapters 2, 3, and 4. It is suggested that you briefly review the concepts of capitalization, present value, and highest and best use, if necessary, before proceeding.

Income Characteristics of Property

During the economic life of an income-producing property, a number of changes may take place. The way the property will be appraised depends on the stage in its life and the expectation of its future income characteristics. We can see this best by looking at a diagram of the benefits accruing to a parcel of newly improved income property. Figure 6.1 shows the income stream that would most probably accrue to a newly constructed residential or commercial building during its economic life.

As you can see from the figure, the income may rise gradually for a few years as the building attains prime occupancy and is still new enough to have relatively low maintenance and repair expenses. Stage one in the property's life is the period in which this rise in income takes place. Stage one ends when net income has declined to its original level.

The second stage in the life of the property is characterized by a steady decline in income. During this period, occupants will be willing to pay less rent while expenses will be rising as the building becomes relatively less efficient and more expensive to operate.

During stage three, the income decline will stop because the building will be at the end of its economic life. At this point, the improvements may well be razed or abandoned. We do see some income in stage three, however.[1] That income is a basic income level accruing to the property for its value as land. If the improvements should continue to be occu-

---

[1]In Figure 3.2 from chapter 3 we showed income dropping throughout the life of a property until it reached zero. This diagram is a simplistic representation and essentially disregards the characteristic nature of the income decline.

FIGURE 6.1   INCOME STREAM FOR A NEW PROPERTY

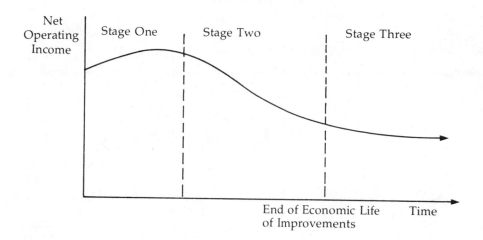

pied in stage three, the income derived will be to compensate the property essentially as land.

The stages we have just described are important, for they help establish the assumptions which must be made for income appraisal and
investment analysis. The three most straightforward capitalization
methods we have seen are the straight-line-declining method, the present value of a level annuity, and the present value of a perpetuity. None
of these methods by itself really fits the overall income curve shown in
Figure 6.1. In the classic appraisal techniques to be described here, the
assumption is nonetheless made that one basic technique, which is best-
suited to the actual income expectation, should be used. To see how the
basic models may be fitted to the property income curve from Figure
6.1, refer to Figures 6.2 and 6.3.

Figure 6.2 shows the property income approximated *in stages* by the
standard capitalization models. Figure 6.3 illustrates the relationship of
the various model approximations (the income curve is omitted).

Underlying the income and value in all three stages is the perpetual
income accruing to the land. In stage three the land income is seen as
the total income. In stage one the income accruing to the improvements
is best-approximated as a level annuity of finite duration. In stage two
the income accruing to the improvements is best-approximated as a
straight-line-declining income. We can now apply these presumptions
to the problem of estimating the value of these income streams.

To make an appraisal for the economic life of a property beginning
in stage one, the appraiser should probably treat the income of the improvement in two parts to match the income stream approximated by
Figure 6.3 (refer to the solid lines in stages one and two of that figure).

FIGURE 6.2   STANDARD INCOME MODELS APPLIED TO PROPERTY IN-
COME IN THREE STAGES

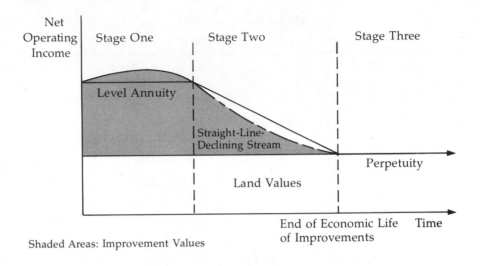

Shaded Areas: Improvement Values

FIGURE 6.3   APPROXIMATION OF PROPERTY INCOME STREAM BASED
ON MODELS

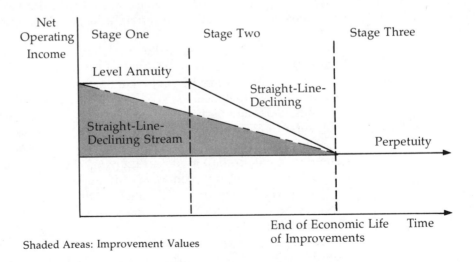

Shaded Areas: Improvement Values

We will actually do this later in Example 6.6. However, this approach
is nontraditional. Typically, the appraiser would estimate the value for
the entire economic life of the property using only the declining stream
(refer to the dashed line in Figure 6.3). This declining stream will yield
a conservative value for the property compared to the value derived
from estimates by stages. Sometimes, because of inflation in rents, the

decline in income of a property is so slight that a level annuity capitalization can be used to approximate the income stream for a new property. This can be done only when the error is expected to be slight compared to a more precise two-stage valuation. The error is most likely to be small when stage one lasts for perhaps fifteen to twenty years. The incremental present value of the benefits received after that time is very low.

An appraisal for a property whose improvements are currently in stage two can be approximated very well as a straight-line-declining stream. Generally, properties in stage two are older properties and the probability is high that the straight-line-declining stream will best approximate the income, as opposed to the level annuity. Similarly, an appraisal for a property in stage three can easily be treated as a perpetuity.

Approximating the income for the entire economic life of a property (stage one and stage two) by a single line may also be accomplished by using one of the more advanced techniques such as the Babcock premises, number 2 or 3.[2] The basic idea of the Babcock premise is illustrated by the dotted curve in Figure 6.4.

For the entire economic life of the improvements the dashed curve in the figure can be seen to be a better fit to the income stream than the use of a single straight-line-declining stream (shown as the lower solid line). It can also be seen to fit the income stream about as well as the estimates by stages (the upper solid lines). However, this method re-

FIGURE 6.4   BABCOCK PREMISE FOR THE INCOME STREAM

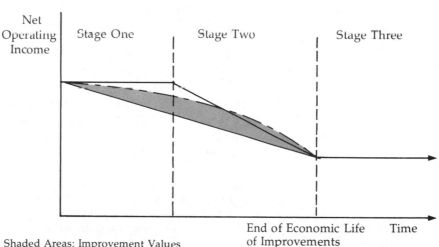

Shaded Areas: Improvement Values

_____

[2]For a description of these techniques see: Alfred A. Ring, *The Valuation of Real Estate,* 2d Ed. (Englewood Cliffs, N.J., Prentice-Hall, 1970), p. 264.

quires special tables for its use. From a mechanical standpoint, this type technique would be applied in the same fashion as the present value annuity factor used in the examples which follow in the technique sections. We will not explore these advanced techniques any further here. The straight-line-declining stream approach will instead provide an easy, conservative approximation of property values for the economic life of the improvements.

One other valuation technique deserves some attention at this point. On some occasions the appraiser may be interested in appraising only the equity interest in a property on which there is a sizable mortgage. The result of such an appraisal is the price which this equity should be expected to bring in the open market. To perform such appraisals, many appraisers use tables devised by Ellwood (see Appendix 2, references, at the end of the text). These tables are especially constructed to provide present value factors for equity values using the band of investment approach. The tables allow for the mortgage rate, duration, and proportion of total value automatically. The tables also account for the change in the mortgage proportion over time as the debt is paid off.

Because only the equity in the property is being valued with the Ellwood approach, the present value factor is applied to the stabilized cash flow after mortgage payments have been met, rather than to the net operating income as is the case with the other techniques we shall examine shortly. The more traditional residual techniques described next do not account for mortgage payments because the equity value is assumed to be equal to the total property value. As more and more properties trade in the market with large mortgage balances, equity valuation using the Ellwood approach will become increasingly appropriate.

In this section we have shown how the income stream for an average income property might look. We have seen how this may be approximated by both traditional income valuation models and the more sophisticated models such as the Babcock premises and the Ellwood technique. We have also proposed that an even closer approximation might be achieved by partitioning the income stream based on the stages in the life of the property. This technique will be described more fully in an example later on. However, the bulk of the description of technique will be based on the traditional models because of their widespread use and simplicity. What must be kept in mind here is that in any appraisal the techniques used must provide a good estimate of the real expected benefits over the remaining life of the property, whatever shape the benefit stream takes on.

Income Measurement

Before discussing the specific techniques that will be used in income appraisal, we must examine the nature of net operating income, which is the major input to all the income appraisal methods.

Revenue   The major source for operating income is the revenue generated by the rental of the property or the revenue derived by the owner from the operation of the property. Many forms of income real estate are, in essence, small businesses. If they are owner-operated commercial properties, then the revenue comes from sales. If the owner is the landlord, then the revenue source is rent.

For residential or commercial property, the revenue is estimated in two parts. First, the *gross rent* is calculated. This is the rent that would be derived from having all available space rented all year. The gross rent for an owner-operated commercial building is an estimate of expected sales. In addition to rental income, any miscellaneous income to be derived from the property is also added to **gross income.** The second part of the revenue estimate involves the subtraction of an *allowance for vacancy and collection losses*. The difference between these two is called **effective gross income.** A sample calculation of effective gross income is shown in Table 6.1.

Expenses   The expenses which will be subtracted from effective gross income are divided into two groups. First, a property may have **operating expenses.** These include expenses such as maintenance, repairs, utilities, and a management fee. The management fee cannot be overlooked. Even though a property may be managed on a part-time basis on the owner's free time, there must be some compensation for this effort. This compensation may be real or implied, but it must be included.

The other major category of expense items is called **fixed expenses.**

TABLE 6.1   CALCULATION OF EFFECTIVE GROSS INCOME FOR A TWELVE-UNIT APARTMENT BUILDING

Panther Arms Apartments

Gross Income	
11 units @ $260/month:	
11 × 12 months × $260	$34,320
1 unit @ $230/month:	
1 × 12 months × $230	2,760
8 garages @ $15/month:	
8 × 12 months × $15	1,440
Washers and dryers @ $40/month:	
12 months × $40	480
Total Gross Income	$39,000
Less: Vacancy and Collection Losses	
5% of gross income:	
0.05 × $39,000	1,950
Effective Gross Income	$37,050

These are expenses which are purely a function of the property's identity as real estate. These charges are not directly related to the operation of the property. In this category we include such items as property taxes, insurance, and the reserve for replacements. This last item is very important and will now be discussed in more detail.

A real property improvement is made up of many components. These components wear out at different rates and must be replaced. These replacements require additional cash outflows which take place on a periodic basis throughout the life of the improvement. To take these eventual replacements into account, the cash stream is penalized each year. The amount of this penalty is determined by the amount of money which must be set aside each year to yield sufficient cash to replace the worn-out parts at the appropriate time. This, you may recall, is the sinking fund concept. If a part is to be replaced in ten years, then specific yearly deposits at bank rates for each of the ten years will provide sufficient cash for the replacement at the end of the period. The **reserve for replacements** for the Panther Arms Apartments is shown in Table 6.2.

It is evident from the table that there are five components in the apartment building which are wasting parts that must be replaced periodically. These items account for $32,500 of the total building value. The reserve allocation is slightly over $3000 per year.

Table 6.3 illustrates all the expenses for the Panther Arms Apartments: $13,300. The operating expenses are $4070 and the fixed expenses are $9230. Note that a management fee had to be imputed to the project. This fee was derived as a percentage of effective gross income.

Net Operating Income   Net operating income (NOI), which is the heart of income appraisals, is derived from the revenue and expense considerations described previously. The NOI is equal to the effective gross income less operating and fixed expenses, including the reserve

TABLE 6.2   RESERVE FOR REPLACEMENTS FOR PANTHER ARMS APARTMENTS

Item	Life	Value	SFF @ 5%	Reserve Amount
Roof	7 yrs.	$ 5,000	0.123	$ 615
Appliances	10 yrs.	$ 7,500	0.080	$ 600
Air Conditioners	10 yrs.	$10,000	0.080	$ 800
Parking Lot	10 yrs.	$ 5,000	0.080	$ 400
Carpeting	7 yrs.	$ 5,000	0.123	$ 615
				$3,030

TABLE 6.3   EXPENSES FOR PANTHER ARMS APARTMENTS

Operating Expenses:

Utilities (house meters) @ $40/month	$ 480
Water @ $25/month	300
Maintenance @ $100/month	1,200
Garbage Collection @ $20/month	240
Management Fee @ 5% of Effective Gross	
Income from Table 6.1	1,850
Total Operating Expenses	$ 4,070

Fixed Expenses:

Real Estate Taxes	$5,400	
Insurance	800	
Reserve for Replacements	3,030	
Total Fixed Expenses		9,230
Total Expenses		$13,300

for replacements. The final statement for the Panther Arms Apartment building is shown in Table 6.4. The resulting NOI of $23,750 will be used to explain the various income appraisal techniques which follow.

For purposes of income appraising, the NOI estimates which are used must be *stabilized*. An appraiser must estimate normal expected income for a property, rather than use, say, last year's income statement. Sometimes a poorly managed property will have less income than it should or will have an erratic income stream. The value of a property at any point in time is a function of its future expected benefits from that point on. The appraiser must base value on a reasonable estimate of income, given sound management and an appropriate expectation of economic conditions. This is the **stabilized income** concept.

The Residual Concept

The techniques used to value income property are based on the residual concept. In this form of analysis, we presume that the income from a property must compensate the two parts of the property—the land and the building. The basic presumption we will make in both the building and the land residual techniques is that the appraiser knows the value of one of the two parts, but not the other. This presumption allows the appraiser to determine what portion of the total income must be allocated to the known part of the value. The remaining portion of the in-

TABLE 6.4   OPERATING STATEMENT FOR
PANTHER ARMS APARTMENTS

Revenue (Table 6.1):		
Gross Possible Revenue		$39,000
Less: Vacancy and Collection Losses		1,950
Effective Gross Income		$37,050
Expenses (Table 6.3):		
Operating Expenses		
Utilities	$ 480	
Water	300	
Maintenance	1,200	
Garbage	240	
Management	1,850	(4,070)
Fixed Expenses		
Taxes	$5,400	
Insurance	800	
Reserve For Replacements	3,030	(9,230)
Net Operating Income (NOI)		$23,750

come is then *available as* **residual income** for the unknown value. Figure 6.5 graphically illustrates the residual techniques.

From Figure 6.5 we see that in the **land residual technique** the value of the building is presumed to be known and the income residual is used to determine the value of the land. In the **building residual technique,** the value of the land is known and the residual is available to determine the building value. However, the **property residual technique** presumes that neither part of the value is known and all income is a residual.

Once the residual has been determined it is capitalized to derive the value of the unknown portion of the property.

The concept of the residual was previously employed in the description of highest and best use in chapter 4. In Table 4.2 we saw that the property which had the most income available to the land, the eight-unit apartment, provided $4000 in residual income. For appraisal purposes, this $4000 would then be capitalized to find the value of the land. We will now proceed to describe the three income appraisal techniques.

Land Residual Technique

Description of Technique

The first of the residual techniques we will discuss is the land residual technique. The appraiser uses this method for properties whose build-

FIGURE 6.5   INCOME RESIDUAL TECHNIQUES

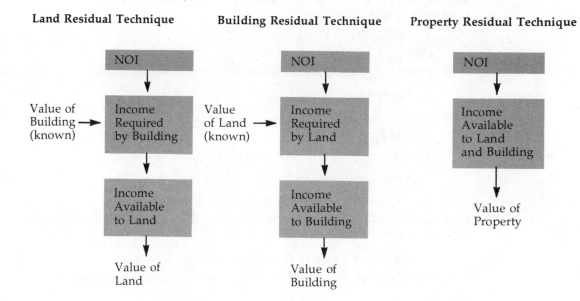

ing value is known. The building value may be known because it is brand new or because it is hypothetical, as in the case of highest and best use analysis. To apply the land residual technique we use the following five steps.

1. The first step involves the determination of the **building capitalization rate** which must be applied to the improvement to derive its required return.

a. If the building is presumed to be earning a straight-line-declining income stream, the appropriate capitalization rate is the sum of the required rate of return on investment plus an allowance for the recapture of capital.

b. If the building is presumed to be earning an income which is a level annuity, then the capitalization rate would consist of the return on investment only, as recapture is automatic in the level annuity model.

The required return on investment in all appraisal calculations is a market-determined rate of return because the value being estimated is a market value. The appraiser derives these rates from the actual returns for properties in the market similar to the subject property.[3]

---

[3]See chapter 9 for a further discussion of the theory of market-determined rates of return.

2. After the capitalization rate has been determined, the **building income** can be derived. This is the income required by the building to provide the appropriate return.

   a. **Straight-Line-Declining Stream:**

   Building Income = Building Value times Building Capitalization Rate

   b. **Level Annuity Stream:**[4]

   Building Income = Building Value divided by $PVAF_{\text{remaining life, ROI}}$[5]

3. The next step is to determine the residual.

   Land Income Residual = NOI − Building Income

4. The land value is calculated by capitalizing the land income as a perpetual annuity. The appropriate factor is the required market rate of return on investment.

   Land Value = Land Income divided by ROI.

5. The value of the property is the sum of the building and land values.

   Total Value = Building Value + Land Value

Examples of Land Residual Valuation

We will now apply the preceding steps to derive a value estimate for the Panther Arms Apartments. The NOI derived earlier was $23,750. Assume the building is new and cost $180,000 to create. The life of the structure is expected to be fifty years. The market rate of return on investment for properties of this type is 10%. The calculations are summarized step-by-step next.

Example 6.1

Assume the building income is a straight-line-declining stream.

1. Building Capitalization Rate:

Market return on investment (ROI)	10%
Recapture rate (100%/50 years)	2%
	12%

---

[4]In the annuity approach, the building value is treated as the present value of the building income, which is unknown. To solve for this income, we must divide the present value by the present value annuity factor. The algebra is the same as we used in chapter 2 during the discussion of the calculation of mortgage payments.

[5]ROI = Return on investment.

2. Building Income:

Building Value times Building Capitalization Rate =
$180,000 × 0.12 = $21,600

3. Land Income (Residual):

NOI less Building Income =
$23,750 − $21,600 = $2150

4. Land Value:

Land Income divided by ROI =
$2150/0.10 = $21,500

5. Property Value:

Land Value + Building Value =
$21,500 + $180,000 = $201,500

Example 6.2

Assume the building income is a level annuity.

1. Building Income:

Building Value divided by $PVAF_{50,10\%}$ =
$180,000/9.915 = $18,155

2. Land Income:

NOI less Building Income =
$23,750 − $18,155 = $5595

3. Land Value:

Land Income divided by ROI =
$5595/0.10 = $55,950

4. Property Value:

Land Value + Building Value =
$55,950 + $180,000 = $235,950

The value in the second example is higher than the value under the assumption of a declining income stream because of the extra income assumed to be earned during the life of the level annuity.

Summary

The land residual technique is based on the knowledge of the building value. Usually, this is true for new, nearly new, or hypothetical structures. We can use either a straight-line-declining or level annuity assumption to make the estimate of value. This provides a range of value within which the real property value probably falls.

Building Residual Technique

Description of Technique

The building residual technique is very similar to the land residual technique. The only real difference is the order in which the steps are performed. We will now assume the land value is known independently. The land is given its required return first and the building earns the residual. This approach is generally used on older properties where the current improvement is *not* for the highest and best use. The land is valued using the market comparison approach or using the land residual technique with a hypothetical improvement that is the highest and best use. Once the land value has been assumed, we may then proceed with the building residual technique, using the following four steps.

1. The first step in the building residual technique is the determination of land income. **Land income** is found by multiplying the land value by the required rate of return for land. Remember, this stream is perpetual. This calculation is unaffected by the nature of the building income.

Land Income = Land Value times Market ROI

2. Building income is then determined by subtracting land income from NOI.

Building Income (residual) = NOI less Land Income

3. Now that the residual has been derived, the value of the building can be calculated. This calculation depends upon the assumption made for the nature of the building's income stream. If the income is thought to resemble a straight-line-declining stream, the value is found using the building capitalization rate which was employed in the land residual technique.

a. Straight-Line-Declining Stream:

Capitalization Rate = ROI + Recapture Rate
Building Value = Building Income divided by
    Building Capitalization Rate

b. Level Annuity:

Building Value = Building Income times *PVAF*

The present value annuity factor here is for the life of the building at the market required return, ROI.

4. The total property value is the sum of the building value and the assumed land value.

Examples of Building Residual Valuation

To demonstrate how the building residual technique is applied, the Panther Arms Apartments will again be used. Now it will be assumed that the land can be valued using the market technique and has an indicated value of $20,000. The value calculations are shown below. The rates of return and capitalization rates are the same ones as used in the land residual technique examples.

Example 6.3

1. Land Income:

   Land Value × ROI = $20,000 × 0.10 = $2000

2. Building Income:

   NOI − Land Income = $23,750 − $2000 = $21,750

3. Building Values:

   a. Straight-Line-Declining Stream:

   Building Income divided by Capitalization Rate =
   $21,750/0.12 = $181,250

   b. Level Annuity Stream:

   Building Income times $PVAF_{50,10\%}$ =
   $21,750 × 9.915 = $215,650

4. Property Values:

   a. Straight-Line-Declining Stream:

   Land Value + Building Value =
   $20,000 + $181,250 = $201,250

   b. Level Annuity Stream:

   Land Value + Building Value =
   $20,000 + $215,650 = $235,650

Summary

The building residual technique is used mostly for older properties. As with the land residual, we have a range of value. Note that the range is similar to that found by the land residual technique.

Property Residual Technique

Description of Technique

The last of the three types of income appraisal techniques is the property residual technique. Sometimes the appraiser may not know the value of either the land or the building independently. In such a case, it cannot be determined to which part the residual belongs. Thus, the appraiser assumes the whole property gets the residual. The procedure in this technique is much easier than the procedures for the other two techniques. The NOI for the property is simply capitalized based on the appropriate assumption and a residual value is added for the estimated residual value of the land at the end of the economic life of the improvement. The steps in the property residual technique are summarized here.

1. The residual income is the NOI for the property.

   a. If we assume that the residual is a straight-line-declining stream we must apply the building capitalization rate to value the income stream.

   Capitalization Rate = ROI + Rate of Recapture
   Property Value = NOI divided by Capitalization Rate

   b. If we assume that the income stream is a level annuity, then we must use the appropriate present value annuity factor. This factor is based on ROI and the life of the improvement.

   Property Value = NOI times $PVAF_{\text{remaining life, ROI}}$

2. The last step is to add a residual value for the land. This must be done because either of the methods used in step one make the tacit assumption that the entire value of the property has been recaptured. The land has not really depreciated, however, and cannot be recaptured. Thus, the appraiser must add back the present value of the land residual which will exist at the end of the life of the improvements. A regular present value factor is used here for the ROI and the life of the improvements.

   Residual Value = Land Residual $\times PVF_{\text{life, ROI}}$

Examples of Property Residual Valuation

To illustrate the property residual, the same basic data from the Panther Arms Apartments will be used. We will assume the land will be worth $20,000 at the end of the life of the improvements. The first of the next two examples will assume NOI is a straight-line-declining stream and the second example will assume it is a level annuity stream.

Example 6.4

Straight-Line-Declining Stream

1. Building Capitalization Rate = 12%

   Property Value = $23,750/0.12 = $197,915

2. Residual Value = $20,000 × $PVF_{50,10\%}$

   $20,000 × 0.008 = $160

3. Total Value = Property Value + Residual Value

   $197,915 + $160 = $198,075

Example 6.5

Level Annuity Stream

1. Property Value = NOI × $PVAF_{50,10\%}$

   $23,750 × 9.915 = $235,480

2. Land Residual Value = $20,000 × 0.008 = $160

3. Total Value = Property Value + Residual Value

   $235,480 + $160 = $235,640

Summary and Modified Example

Again, there is a large difference between the values under the two income assumptions. This is a function of the size of the income stream and the mathematics of recapture. Note that the values derived by the property residual technique are very similar to those derived in the other two techniques. Because the range of value is so wide based on the two assumptions about income, the same example will be recalculated using the stages we illustrated in Figure 6.2 earlier. We will assume NOI is a level annuity for ten years and a straight-line-declining stream for the next forty years until the improvements have worn out. At that point, the land residual will earn $2000 per year perpetually.

Example 6.6

Property Residual Technique Calculated by Income Stages

1. Value of Level Annuity Stage:

$$\text{Present Value}_1 = \$23{,}750 \times PVAF_{10,10\%}$$
$$= \$23{,}750 \times 6.145 = \$145{,}950$$

2. Value of Declining Stream Stage:

Building Capitalization Rate = ROI + Rate of
Recapture = 10% + (100%/40 years) = 12.5%
Value of Declining Stream = NOI divided by
Capitalization Rate = $23,750/0.125 = $190,000

This value must be brought back to the present, as it is a value which will be received ten years hence. Therefore,

$$\text{Present Value}_2 = \$190{,}000 \times PVF_{10,10\%}$$
$$= \$190{,}000 \times 0.386 = \$73{,}340$$

3. Value of Land Residual Stage:

Value of perpetuity of $2000 per year:
$2000/0.10 = $20,000

This land residual value must be brought back to the present.

$$\text{Present Value}_3 = \$20{,}000 \times PVF_{50,10\%}$$
$$= \$20{,}000 \times 0.008 = \$160$$

4. Total Value = Sum of the three present values

$145,950 + $73,340 + $160 = $219,450

A graphic representation of this three-stage valuation appears as Figure 6.6. As you can see, with a more realistic assumption about the shape and duration of the constituent parts of the income stream, the value of the modified property residual falls in the middle of the range derived in examples 6.4 and 6.5. This is to be expected since the level annuity assumption is the most liberal premise of value and the straight-line-declining stream is the most conservative. The modified three-stage approach lies in between. The interested reader may try the three-stage approach for both the land and the building residual approaches to the Panther Arms Apartments valuation as an exercise.

FIGURE 6.6   THREE-STAGE APPROACH TO PROPERTY RESIDUAL

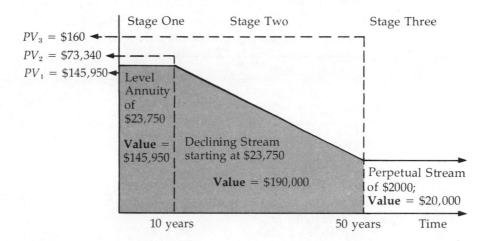

Summary of Income Appraisal Techniques

In this chapter we have examined three major techniques for determining the value of income real estate based on a capitalization of its benefits. The land residual technique assumed that the appraiser could determine the value of the property improvements independently, as would be the case with new buildings. Based on this assumption, the appraiser can compute the portion of NOI required to compensate the improvements, leaving a residual income for the land. Capitalization of the land income residual sets a maximum value for the land and the property as a whole.

We then reversed the assumptions of the land residual technique and assumed the value of the land might be independently determined. This method may be used when the improvements are old. The land is compensated first and the improvements earn the residual in the building residual technique. Finally, we looked at the property residual technique where it was assumed that neither the value of the land nor the value of the building could be independently determined. This technique is the most general and produced the widest range of value under our group of income assumptions. The last example presented was based on the staged income assumption using the property residual technique. This example resulted in a more realistic value for the property. The derived value fell in the middle of the range of value determined by the level annuity and declining stream assumptions. The results of the various values derived for the Panther Arms Apartments property are shown in Table 6.5.

TABLE 6.5   SUMMARY OF INCOME APPRAISALS

Technique Used	Example no.	Values		
		Building	Land	Total
Land Residual: Declining Stream	6.1	$180,000	$21,500	$201,500
Land Residual: Annuity	6.2	$180,000	$55,950	$235,950
Building Residual: Declining Stream	6.3	$181,250	$20,000	$201,250
Building Residual: Annuity	6.3	$215,650	$20,000	$235,650
Property Residual: Declining Stream	6.4			$198,075
Property Residual: Annuity	6.5			$235,640
Property Residual: Stages	6.6			$219,450

Ranges

Land Value: $20,000 to $55,950
Building Value: $180,000 to $215,650
Property Value: $198,075 to $235,950

Indicated Value: around $220,000

As you can see from the table, the range of value is roughly from $200,000 to $235,000, with an intermediate value established at $220,000. This latter figure is probably a fair estimate of value. Just for informational purposes, you might be interested to know that the total cost to create for this property, including land, was actually $200,000 and the property sold for $225,000 to the original buyer.

Chapter Six Summary

In chapters 5 and 6, we have examined the complex topic of real estate appraisal from many angles. The bulk of the discussion centered on the description of the numerous techniques employed by professional real estate appraisers. The easiest way to appreciate the concepts of appraisal is to look at the techniques and their underlying assumptions. However, with all this technical material, it is important not to lose sight of the implications for our main concern in this book—real estate value.

Appraisal is complex and requires much judgment and experience to perform. Probably income appraisal is the most objective and has the most practical value for the potential investor. For that reason, more detail was presented in that area. The purpose of these two chapters was not to try to train the reader as an appraiser. A glance at the material presented by Ring, for instance (see the references in Appendix 2), will show the reader that these two chapters are too brief to serve as a training tool. The purpose of these chapters was to try to give the reader a sense of the elusiveness and subjectivity of real estate value. It has been stated on numerous occasions that market values are objective. Historically, this is so. However, it can easily be seen that *estimates of market values* are very subjective and fragile.

Each of the appraisal techniques presented in these two chapters represents an approach, an independent estimate of value. Though not all of the techniques can be applied to every property, often more than one will work. Appraisers must select two or three techniques which should be applicable theoretically and use them to increase their confidence in their estimate. After all the appropriate estimates have been derived, the appraiser will correlate (not just average) the indicated values to obtain the *most probable estimate of value*. This estimate, along with the appropriate supporting information, is presented to the client.

The Appraisal Report

When an appraiser presents a good professional report to a client, the report usually follows a prescribed format. The format will depend on the purpose of the appraisal. A simple single-family residential appraisal may be presented very briefly without much supporting material to a potential seller. However, for the seller of a piece of reasonably valuable commercial property, a good appraisal document can easily be fifty to seventy-five pages long.

A report of this latter type will include much of the detailed information upon which the appraiser based the opinion. The report will also detail the various methods used and show the derivation of the various value estimates. The appraiser will present a statement of the appraisal assignment, the conditions prevailing at the time of the appraisal, descriptions of all properties discussed, and even his or her personal qualifications as an appraiser. A good quality appraisal report is an interesting document for the real estate student. For the interested reader, Ring provides a list of the contents as well as samples of appraisal reports.[6]

---

[6]Ring, *Valuation of Real Estate.* See pp. 376–482 and chapter 23.

Concluding Comments

Even though you cannot become a qualified appraiser just by reading these two chapters, you should be better able to judge any appraisals you might use in your activities in real estate. The material on income appraisal can be used as a basis for the investment analysis to follow in chapter 8. The detail in that chapter will provide the student with some good, basic knowledge of a practical nature. The techniques in chapters 6 and 8 should be enough to keep the beginning investor from making any foolish decisions on many types of reasonably simple investments in real estate.

KEY TERMS

Building Capitalization Rate	Gross Income	Property Residual Technique
Building Income	Land Income	Reserve for Replacements
Building Residual Technique	Land Residual Technique	Residual Income
Effective Gross Income	Net Operating Income	Stabilized Income
Fixed Expenses	Operating Expenses	

QUESTIONS FOR STUDY AND DISCUSSION

1. Describe the three residual techniques for income appraisal. Compare each of the three methods. How do their assumptions differ?

2. What items are considered when NOI is calculated?

3. Explain the concept of a *reserve* for a wasting part. How is the reserve for replacements calculated?

4. What are the three stages in the life of an income stream accruing to a newly improved income property? Describe each stage briefly. How would an income appraisal based on stages differ from income appraisals based on level annuity and declining streams?

5. Using the information from both chapters on appraisal, determine which methods an appraiser could apply to each of the following properties.

   a. A new single-family residence

   b. A used residence, tenant-occupied

   c. A small town's water tower

   d. A new downtown office building

   e. A twenty-year-old neighborhood shopping center

   f. A vacant lot

   g. A county court house

   h. A downtown parking garage (not highest and best use)

PROBLEMS FOR REVIEW

The following data apply to the problems which follow.

An investor finds that he can buy an abandoned fast-food restaurant building and the land under it. The investor knows a tenant who would be willing to occupy the restaurant if it were improved. The building is nearly new and may be valued at $100,000, including the improvements. The land has a value determined by market analysis of $70,000. The property will be rented to the restaurant operator for $2750 per month. The owner would agree to maintain the property and pay all taxes and insurance. The tenant will pay all utilities. The building will have a life of thirty-three years and the market rate of return for such investments is 12%.

1. The property has the following wasting parts. Calculate the reserve which should be allowed for each item. Use a 6% bank rate for these calculations.

Item	Life	Value
Roof	8 years	$5000
Air Conditioning	10 years	$4000
Parking Lot	10 years	$6000

2. The investor has presented the following estimate of income and expenses to the appraiser. Put it in the proper form and calculate NOI.

Rent: $2750 per month, effective

Insurance: $3135 per year

Taxes: $1800 semiannually

Maintenance and repairs: $100 per month

Snow removal: $500 per year

Management: 5% of effective gross income

Depreciation: $3000 per year

3. Find the value of the property using the land residual technique. Assume both a straight-line-declining income and a level annuity income for the improvements to get a range of value.

4. Find the value of the property using the building residual technique. Assume both a straight-line-declining income and a level annuity income.

5. Find the value of the building using the property residual approach. Again assume both types of income streams are possible for the improvements. Assume the land has a residual value of $50,000.

6. Summarize your findings from the three residual techniques. Do you feel the asking price, including improvements, of $170,000 is reasonable? Would it be more or less reasonable if the market rate of return were 10%?

7. As an exercise, return to examples 6.1 and 6.2 in the chapter. Assume the building income will be an annuity for ten years and a straight-line-declining stream for forty years. Find the indicated value.

8. Make the income assumptions listed in problem 7. Recalculate the property value using the information from example 6.3.

7 TAX CONSIDERATIONS

REAL ESTATE is largely a tax-oriented investment. The market prices and rents on real property are to some extent a function of the federal income tax laws. In this chapter we will discuss the areas in which taxes of all types affect cash flows and values in real estate. The discussion will be simplified as much as possible. It will be keyed to the regulations in effect after the Tax Reform Act of 1976 (H.R. 10612).

General Tax Structure

Everyone knows the old saying about the certainty of taxes. It is safe to say that most taxpayers are also painfully aware of the variety of taxes to which they may be subjected. The power to levy taxes is given by the U.S. Constitution, Article I, and the Sixteenth Amendment. The power to tax is one of the major restrictions on the freedom to profit from one's assets. The owner of real property is faced with three sets of taxes: local, state, and federal.

State and Local Taxes

The primary method of raising money in most municipal governments in the United States is the **ad valorem tax** on real property. This is a tax dating back to the Middle Ages which is based on the concept of taxing an individual's ability to pay. The wealthier (in terms of property) one is, the more tax one pays. The tax is on the value of property, hence ad valorem, in proportion to the value.

The amount of the tax on a given piece of property is found by multiplying a millage rate times an assessed value for the property. The **assessed value** is what the property is worth for tax purposes only. The **millage rate** is a rate of tax which will spread the budget of the municipality over the assessed value available. The methods of calculating the millage and the assessed value differ in various communities. Often these procedures are guided by state law. In California, for instance, the general procedure is to assess a property at roughly its market value. There is often a time lag here, however, causing assessments to be somewhat less than the current market values. This type assessment generally has a relatively low millage rate. In other states, such as Ohio, property is assessed at a percentage of market value. Assessments of this kind, say, 25% of market value, are likely to have higher millage rates than assessments at market value.

Because **property taxes** are levied on the property directly and are deductible for calculating federal income taxes, we will treat them as a fixed expense in our investment analyses.

There are other types of taxes which may affect the real property owner at the local level. Some major municipalities, New York City, for instance, levy income taxes like those of the federal government. These taxes are also deductible for federal income tax purposes and may be treated as operating expenses in investment analysis. Municipalities also levy excise taxes on certain types of real estate, such as the motel-room tax used in some cities. The property tax is still the most common.

The primary state taxes are the sales tax, which does not affect real estate directly, and the income tax, which directly affects real property. The state income tax will be treated in much the same way as the local income tax previously mentioned.

Federal Taxes

The prime source of revenue for the U.S. Government is the graduated **income tax.** This will affect property owners directly no matter what kind of organizational structure they use. Owners will pay tax on the income they derive from their property, whether they are incorporated or not. An owner who is incorporated may pay both business and personal income taxes on the profit from property. The rest of this chapter will be concerned with the structure of these federal taxes. It should be noted that real estate is treated with some favor by the tax laws. This favoritism has been diminished to some extent by the last two major tax reforms, in 1969–70 and 1976. These reforms were induced by political pressures to remove the "loopholes" felt to be enjoyed by rich property owners.

Personal Tax Structures   To put the tax situation in perspective, we will now briefly outline the structure of the personal income tax form. There are four major components to the income tax calculations. First, you must calculate your **gross income.** This includes salary, wages, and business and investment income. If you own real estate as a corporation and pay yourself a reasonable fee to manage the property, this fee will appear as personal income. If you organize your property as a partnership or proprietorship, the business income after expenses will appear as part of personal gross income. There are other ways your gross income could be affected. An incorporated property might distribute dividends, which are considered to be personal income. Finally, you might lend money to your incorporated real estate and you will pay tax on the interest you earn from the loan. The income section of the tax form then closes with a series of *adjustments* which are a special class of expense deductions. This yields **adjusted gross income.**

Once you have derived the adjusted gross income, you then consider two classes of items which will be subtracted from adjusted gross income to yield **taxable** income. **Exemptions** are subtracted, supposedly to account for minimal cost living expenses—a theoretical justification. The second group of items, **deductions** for specific expenses, are itemized here.

1. Medical expenses

2. Interest expenses—interest paid on debts, especially mortgage debt for a residence, is deductible here.

3. Taxes—these are deductions for taxes paid to governmental units such as state and local property, income, and excise taxes.

4. Charitable contributions

5. Miscellaneous deductions

It should be stressed that these deductions are primarily for personal expenses. Operating expenses for a piece of income property would be accounted for on a separate business income form with only the net profit transferred to personal tax (for unincorporated property only).

If the taxpayer does not have sufficient deductions (over $3200 on a joint return), he may elect to use the zero-bracket tax tables. These new tables have replaced the old **standard deduction** by allowing the taxpayer $3200 in income which is not taxed.

Once you have subtracted the appropriate deductions and exemptions from the adjusted gross income, yielding taxable income, the next step is to calculate the tax liability. This liability is based on the tax rate schedule shown in Table 7.4 at the end of this chapter.

One important item has been omitted from explicit consideration up to this point—capital gains. This important investment income source will be discussed shortly in a separate section.

Business Tax Structures   The treatment of taxes for a business, in our case, income real estate, depends on the form of organization chosen by the owner.[1] If the property is *incorporated*, the gross income of the property is reduced by operating and real estate expenses to determine taxable income. Taxes are then paid and the net profit after taxes is available for dividends. If less than 100% of the net profits is paid out in dividends, the remaining earnings are retained in the business as earned surplus (equity). One of the deductible expenses for corporate taxes is a reasonable management fee (salary) for the owner. This salary and any dividends distributed are taxable as personal income.

If the owner chooses a *noncorporate* form such as the proprietorship or partnership for the property, income from the property is considered

---

[1]See Beaton and Robertson, *Real Estate Investment*, 2d Ed. (Englewood Cliffs, N.J.: Prentice-Hall, 1977), for a discussion of forms of ownership.

to be part of personal income. There are several tax advantages to the nonincorporated form. If there is a loss for tax purposes in a noncorporate form, the loss is used to offset personal income which may have been earned from other sources. The loss may arise if the deductible expenses exceed gross income. This loss results in a savings in the personal taxes the owner would have paid if there had *not* been a loss. This personal tax savings becomes part of the cash flow of the investment project. We shall explore the mathematics of this in more detail in chapter 8. In the corporate form, a loss will allow the owner to avoid corporate taxes on the income from the property, but will not result in tax savings on a personal basis.

Another advantage to the unincorporated forms is the avoidance of **double taxation.** A corporation pays taxes on its income and the owner then pays taxes again on the dividends he received. By combining personal and business income in the unincorporated forms, this situation is avoided.

There are some advantages to the corporate form, however. The owner's personal assets are not subject to the debts of the corporation. In a partnership, for contrast, if an owner defaults on a debt, personal assets can be liquidated to pay the business debt. In general, though, the unincorporated forms of ownership are very popular in real estate because of the tax advantages. The ability to carry losses against personal income gives rise to the **tax shelter** characteristics of real estate.

Organization of the Discussion   Federal income tax considerations affect real estate investors in three important areas. First, when the property is acquired, one consideration must be the establishment of a depreciable base for the property. Second, during the life of the investment, the investor is concerned with the operating expenses, especially depreciation. Finally, tax implications are important when property is disposed of at the end of the desired holding period. In addition to the foregoing topics, we will also look at some personal considerations in the discussion to follow.

It is important to establish a philosophical note here. The federal tax code is immense and complex. Even those portions affecting real estate specifically are too lengthy for one chapter in a text such as this one. For that reason, the primary purpose of this chapter will be to explain the main areas of concern in tax-oriented decisions in real estate. Wherever possible, extensive coverage of the details of the tax code will be omitted. When it is advantageous, the reader will be referred to those sections of the tax code which will be of most immediate concern. Tax laws change almost every year. The sophisticated investor must keep abreast of these changes to gain the full protection of the code. Here we merely wish to outline the key areas of concern.

Tax Considerations at Acquisition

Concept of Depreciation Base

Most fixed assets, with the notable exception of land, are presumed to wear out during their lives. We defined *economic life* earlier as the length of time over which a fixed asset provides a positive benefit to its owner. Because an asset loses its productivity during its life, the tax laws permit the owner to subtract from income some amount of money which is supposed to reflect the loss in value of the asset in a given accounting period. We will discuss the rules for taking depreciation in the next section of this chapter.

When an asset is acquired, some rule must be followed to determine the depreciable base for the property. Only this base may be depreciated. Basically, the **depreciable base** is the total price of the depreciable part of the property, including the costs required to put the property to the use for which it was intended. However, the details vary depending on the method of acquisition. In addition to the original cost, major improvements to the property are also added on to the base. Besides controlling the amount to be depreciated, the base also serves as a major input to the capital gains calculations we will describe later.

Determination of Depreciable Base

Depreciable property may be acquired in three ways: purchase, gift, or exchange. Each of these methods of acquisition has an affect on the determination of the base of the property.

1. The basis at acquisition for purchased property is the total cost of acquisition, less any estimated salvage value.

2. The basis for property acquired by gift or through a will (as an heir) is the value at the time of the receipt of the property.

3. The basis for property received in an exchange is more complicated to determine. Generally, the basis for such property is the adjusted basis of the property, plus adjustments for additional consideration received by the recipient, less any consideration given up in the exchange.

We may summarize these rules a bit by saying that the depreciable basis for any property will be the same as the basis for determining the gain from a sale of the property. Sometimes depreciable improvements and land are purchased together for one lump sum. In these cases, the basis is the proportion of *value* accounted for by the depreciable part of the property. Finally, for depreciation to be taken, the basis must be established without question. If the taxpayer cannot prove the amount of the basis, no depreciation can be taken.

Tax Rules Relating to Operations

In general, expenses incurred in the operation of real property are deductible in the period in which they are incurred, which includes depreciation. There are some exceptions, however. Interest is one deductible expense. However, there are limits on the deductibility of interest incurred during the construction of new property. Now this interest must be capitalized and deducted gradually. The general rule is that interest can only be deducted when it is a liability to the taxpayer. Interest which is not actually owed cannot be deducted.

For real estate the major deductions are for operating expenses, interest, and depreciation. Because of its special features, depreciation will be discussed next.

Nature of Depreciation

One of the most important periodic expenses which is deducted from the periodic (ordinary) income of a business is depreciation. It is important because it does not involve the periodic outlay of cash. One of the major principles in accounting is that in each accounting period income should be matched with the expenses incurred to earn it. As a fixed asset is used to generate income year after year, it wears out. Eventually, the asset will have to be replaced. For this reason, the owner of real property, which is a fixed asset, is permitted to make periodic adjustments for this assumed depreciation. This process has some important tax implications.

It is worthy of note that not all owners of depreciable real property may take depreciation. A dealer or a broker who buys property for resale may not take depreciation. The property must be held primarily to earn periodic income.

The basic calculation of depreciation is reasonably simple to make. A *useful life* is determined for the asset, guided by certain rules of the IRS. Useful life is not the same concept as economic life, as it is merely a construct for determining depreciation schedules. Both real and personal property involved in a parcel of income real estate may be depreciated. Real property, as previously stated, is land and everything permanently attached to it. Personal property is property owned by the investor that is not real property. *Land is not depreciated*. The value of the asset is reduced by any expected *salvage value* when the depreciable portion of the asset is determined. This depreciable portion is divided into periodic charges using depreciation methods to be described in this section.

Depreciation Methods

There are three major methods for calculating the depreciation for an asset. These are straight-line, declining balance, and sum-of-the-years' digits. The latter two methods are called accelerated depreciation methods.

Straight-Line Depreciation   An apartment building is purchased new for $225,000. Of this amount, $25,000 is land. We will assume the building will have a useful life of fifty years and no salvage value. The **straight-line depreciation** is calculated as follows. Divide the depreciable value of the asset by its useful life. Depreciation will be the same in each year and equal the value found by this division calculation. Another way of viewing this type of depreciation is to find the percentage of the asset's value which is presumed to be lost each year. This percentage is found by dividing 100% by the useful life of the asset. Note the similarity to the recapture of capital rate calculated in chapter 3. For our example, we can calculate the depreciation both ways to illustrate the process.

Total Purchase Price	$225,000
Less: Land	25,000
Depreciable Value	$200,000

Method One

$$\frac{\$200,000}{50 \text{ years}} = \$4000 \text{ per year}$$

Method Two

$$\frac{100\%}{50 \text{ years}} = 2\% \text{ depreciation per year}$$

$$\$200,000 \times 2\% = \$4000 \text{ per year}$$

Accelerated Depreciation Methods   For a number of reasons the taxpayer is allowed to use **accelerated depreciation** on certain assets. Accelerated depreciation does not generally change the total amount to be depreciated nor the length of time. It merely changes the timing of the deductions. Higher deductions are allowed in the early years with lower deductions later on in the life of the asset. The total tax one pays is the same as with straight-line. However, in present value terms, the *cost* of the taxes is lowered. This is a definite advantage for the investor.

Declining Balance Methods   The **declining balance** methods are different from straight-line depreciation in three ways:

1. The rate of depreciation is accelerated rather than constant.

2. Depreciation is based on the *undepreciated balance* each year rather than the original depreciable value.

3. Salvage value may be ignored with the declining balance methods, resulting in a potential change in the total value depreciated.

There are actually two ways to approach declining balance depreciation. One way is to ignore salvage value and apply the declining rate to each year's undepreciated balance. The other method, preferred by some, uses the same type of depreciable base as straight-line. The declining rate is applied to this base and the declining balance thereafter. At some point during the life of the asset, the annual depreciation taken will fall below the corresponding straight-line depreciation. At this crossover point, the remaining undepreciated balance may be divided by the remaining number of years in the asset's useful life and a straight-line depreciation deduction may be taken. This can be seen in the calculations in Table 7.1.

The most liberal declining balance method is the *double* or *200% declining balance* rate. To calculate it we use the following steps:

1. Find the straight-line percentage lost each year in the asset's life. For our apartment house this was 2% per year.

2. Double this rate. This would yield 4% as the new rate.

3. This new rate is used as the percentage of the remaining balance to be depreciated each year.

For our apartment house the first two years' depreciation changes are shown here.

> Year One
> Balance × Rate = $200,000 × 0.04
> First Year's Periodic Charge = $8000
>
> Year Two
> Balance = $200,000 − $8000 = $192,000
> Balance × Rate = $192,000 × 0.04
> Second Year's Charge = $7680

There are two alternative forms of this declining balance method: 150% of straight-line (3% of the balance in our example) and 125% of straight-line. These are permissible under certain circumstances enumerated by the IRS.

Sum-of-the-Years' Digits   In present value terms the most liberal accelerated method over the life of the asset is the **sum-of-the-years' digits**

method. Here the rate of depreciation is again based on the asset's initial value, as it is in straight-line depreciation. Salvage value is also used, as with straight-line. The annual charge is determined as follows.

1. Add up all the digits for the years in the useful life of the asset. With a five-year life the sum would be: $1 + 2 + 3 + 4 + 5 = 15$.

2. Taking the largest digit first, calculate the percentage charge for each year by dividing the year digit by the sum of the digits. The first year's percentage charge for a five-year life would be $5/15 = 33\%$. The second year's charge would be $4/15 = 27\%$.

3. To find the dollar depreciation charge, multiply the year's percentage charge by the asset's initial value.

A formula can be used to find the sum for extended periods, like fifty years. If the number of years of useful life is N, the sum-of-the-years' digits would be given by:

$$\frac{N(N + 1)}{2}$$

For fifty years, the sum would be 1275, or 50(51)/2. For our apartment building, the first year's percentage charge would be 3.9%, 50/1275.

To illustrate the differences among the three methods of depreciation, Table 7.1 has been constructed. Here we have taken a $100,000 depreciable asset and given it a ten-year life with no salvage value. With the double-declining balance method, toward the end we switch over to straight-line depreciation. This is permissible and in the best interest of

TABLE 7.1   COMPARISON OF DEPRECIATION METHODS

Year	Straight-Line		Double Declining		Sum-of-the-Years' Digits	
	Annual	Accumulated	Annual	Accumulated	Annual	Accumulated
1	$10,000	$ 10,000	$20,000	$ 20,000	$18,182	$ 18,182
2	10,000	20,000	16,000	36,000	16,364	34,546
3	10,000	30,000	12,800	48,800	14,545	49,091
4	10,000	40,000	10,240	59,040	12,727	61,818
5	10,000	50,000	8,192	67,232	10,909	72,727
6	10,000	60,000	6,554 [a]	73,786	9,091	81,818
7	10,000	70,000	6,554	80,340	7,273	89,091
8	10,000	80,000	6,554	86,894	5,455	94,546
9	10,000	90,000	6,554	93,448	3,636	98,182
10	10,000	100,000	6,552	100,000	1,818	100,000

[a]Switched over to straight-line method.

the investor. The reader may wish to check these calculations as an exercise.

Notice in the table that after the second year the accumulated benefits of depreciation will be the greatest with the sum-of-the-years' digits method. This will usually be the case, except for extremely short-lived assets.

Component Depreciation

Under certain circumstances, it is permissible to divide an asset into parts which are readily separable and have different lives. Let us return to our $200,000 apartment building. We can actually view that building as the sum of a number of different parts. These parts are itemized in Table 7.2, along with their useful lives. As each part wears out it will be replaced and redepreciated. The approach results in superior cash flows and tax advantages compared to the depreciation of the entire property as a unit. The table shows the first-year depreciation for each component and for the total property taken as a unit. Different depreciation methods are used. Notice the advantage using component depreciation.

Depreciation Cash Effects

The importance of depreciation to the investor can be shown very simply. Depreciation is a deductible expense which does *not* require the

TABLE 7.2   COMPONENT DEPRECIATION

Components	Cost($)	Life	Straight-Line Depreciation First Year	Double-Declining Balance Depreciation First Year	Sum-of-the-Years' Digits First Year
Shell	120,000	50	$2,400	$ 4,800	$ 4,706
Roof	15,000	15	1,000	2,000	1,875
Utilities	20,000	20	1,000	2,000	1,905
Elevator	15,000	15	1,000	2,000	1,875
Air Conditioning	30,000	10	3,000	6,000	5,455
Total	200,000	50	$8,400	$16,800	$15,816
Entire Property					
Building	$200,000	50	$4,000	$ 8,000	$ 7,843

Adapted from Halbert C. Smith, Carl J. Tschappat, and Ronald L. Racster, *Real Estate and Urban Development*, rev. ed. (Homewood, Ill.: Richard D. Irwin, 1977), p. 234.

periodic outlay of cash as do taxes, utilities, maintenance expenses, and other costs. Thus, the depreciation expense lowers the tax payments without reducing cash. Table 7.3 shows the tax and cash flow effects of depreciation.

Some relationships may be seen from observation of this table.

1. When there is no depreciation, cash flow and income after taxes are identical.

2. When there is depreciation, cash flow and net income differ by the amount of depreciation, giving rise to the false notion that depreciation is a source of funds. *It is not.* However, because it is not a cash outflow, all other things being equal, cash will exceed income by this amount.

3. Because depreciation is an expense, income and taxes will be lowered with depreciation.

Net income equals pretax income minus taxes. If pretax income is decreased, then taxes are decreased by the amount of the expense times the tax rate. Income after taxes is decreased by the amount of the expense times (1 − tax rate). Depreciation expense is $20,000 in our example and the tax rate is 40%. Thus, taxes should fall by $20,000 × 40%, or $8000, as can be seen in Table 7.3. Income should fall by $20,000 × (1 − 0.40), or $12,000, as it does. While depreciation does not provide cash, it *protects cash*. Cash flow is increased in our example by $8000 when depreciation is present. This is the amount of taxes saved by this noncash expense.

Rules for Depreciation

Depreciable property can be classified according to several categories. Depending upon these classifications, only certain forms of depreciation

TABLE 7.3   CASH EFFECT OF DEPRECIATION

	Without Depreciation Income	Cash Flow	With Depreciation Income	Cash Flow
Rents	$50,000	$50,000	$50,000	$50,000
Operating Costs	30,000	30,000	30,000	30,000
Operating Profits	$20,000	$20,000	$20,000	$20,000
Depreciation	0	0	20,000	0
Taxable Income	$20,000	$20,000	$ 0	$20,000
Tax (40%)	8,000	8,000	0	0
Net Income	$12,000	$12,000	$ 0	$20,000

may be used. The depreciation rules concern whether the property is new or used, personal or real property, or residential or nonresidential. Rather than compound this text with excessive detail, we will generalize these rules a bit.

In general, new residential property (first-user owned) may be depreciated with any method. Used residential property cannot be depreciated with the fast write-off methods. Generally, straight-line is used, but, in some cases, when the life remaining is twenty years or more, 125% of straight-line declining balance may be used. New commercial property is treated with straight-line or limited acceleration. Used commercial property must use straight-line. Component depreciation may be used on new and used property if the value of the components can be allocated properly. Finally, low-income housing gets the most privileged position in the use of depreciation if the property is properly qualified (Sec. 167K of IRS code).

Tax Effects of Disposals

Perhaps the most complex tax calculations arise at the time property is sold or disposed of by exchange. The tax effects of disposals basically center on the computation of capital gains and losses and the recapture of depreciation. There are tax preferences for capital gains (as of 1978), so the ability to allocate sale gains to this category can greatly influence the cash flow from the sale.

Nature of Capital Gains

We examined the basic structure of taxes in the first section of this chapter. Now we will look at a major area of preference which is allowed to taxpayers making investments. **Ordinary income** refers to **periodic income**, including investment income. However, when a fixed or capital asset is sold a profit may be earned on that asset. This profit is called a **capital gain.**

A capital gain occurs when an asset is sold at a price in excess of **book value** (also called the **adjusted basis**) of the asset. Book value is determined by taking the original price of that asset and deducting the accumulated depreciation to the date of sale. Improvements to the property are added to the basis as they are made. A **capital loss** occurs when an asset is sold for a price less than its adjusted basis.

The amount of time an asset has been owned affects the tax paid on the capital gain. An asset purchased after January 1, 1978, must be owned for one year to receive preferential tax treatment as a **long-term capital gain.** If an asset is owned less than one year, then the entire gain is a **short-term capital gain** and is treated as ordinary income. A sample capital gain is shown in Example 7.1.

Example 7.1

A twelve-unit apartment building was purchased five years ago for $250,000. To date, $10,000 in improvements have been made to the property and total depreciation has been $50,000. The building was just sold for $240,000. What is the amount of long-term capital gain?

Original Price	$250,000
Add: Improvements	10,000
Gross Value	$260,000
Less: Accumulated Depreciation	50,000
Adjusted Basis	$210,000
Sale Price	$240,000
Less: Adjusted Basis	210,000
Long-term Capital Gain	$ 30,000

Tax Treatment of Gains

The determination of the appropriate tax for capital transactions is complicated and occupies a great deal of space in the code. The rules which follow will be somewhat abbreviated and generally aimed at the rules most often affecting real estate transactions. The basic procedure is as follows.

1. Determine net short-term gain or loss. Short-term losses are subtracted from gains to obtain the net position.
2. Determine long-term gain or loss. Long-term losses are subtracted from long-term gains.
3. Total position from capital transactions comes from combining (1) and (2) above.

If the overall position is a loss in (3), then some or all of this loss will be deductible. Those rules will follow in the next section. If the result in (3) is a gain, some tax will be incurred. The calculations vary depending on the type of gain realized. Generally, the procedure is as follows. One-half of any net long-term gain is deducted from the total gains and the result is added to adjusted gross income in the return. Notice the following two examples.

Example 7.2

Salary		$20,000
Capital Gain or Loss		
Net Long-term Gain	$3,000	
Net Short-term Gain	2,000	
Net Gain Before Deduction	$5,000	
Less: ½ of Long-term Gain	$1,500	
Net Gain in Income		$ 3,500
Adjusted Gross Income		$23,500

Example 7.3

Salary		$20,000
Capital Gain or Loss		
Net Long-term Loss	($1,000)	
Net Short-term Gain	3,000	
Net Gain Before Deduction	$2,000	
Less: ½ of Long-term Gain	0	
Net Gain in Income		$ 2,000
Adjusted Gross Income		$22,000

There are obviously numerous combinations of losses and gains possible here. The best advice is to follow the instructions on Form 1040 Schedule D closely.

If the taxpayer desires, an alternative computation may be used to calculate the tax due on capital transactions. The approach is enumerated here.

1. Tax on income is calculated exclusive of capital gains or losses.

2. To this tax is added 25% of any long-term gain of $50,000 or less (joint return).

3. If the net long-term gain exceeds $50,000 the tax is:

  a. Regular tax on ordinary income

  b. Plus $12,500 (25% of $50,000)

  c. Plus the difference between tax on income with ½ of gain included and the tax on the sum of taxable income excluding gain plus $25,000.

If the net long-term gain is less than $50,000, this computation is easy to follow. If the gain exceeds $50,000, however, it is somewhat more complicated. Example 7.4 shows both methods of computing the tax on a long-term gain of $60,000.

Example 7.4

Regular Computation

Salary		$ 75,000
Capital Gain or Loss		
Net Capital Gain (long-term)	$60,000	
Less: Deduction (½ of long-term)	30,000	
Net Gain included in Income		30,000
Adjusted Gross Income		$105,000
Less: Deduction and Exemptions		5,000
Taxable Income		$100,000
Tax (see Table 7.4)		$ 43,260

Alternative Computation

Regular tax on ordinary income of $70,000		
($75,000 less 5000)		$ 29,960
Tax on first $50,000 long-term gain		12,500
Tax on excess gain		
Tax on income with ½ of gain		
included	$43,260	
Less tax on sum of taxable		
income excluding gain		
plus $25,000 ($95,000)	40,260	
		3,000
Total Tax		$ 45,460

Here the lowest tax comes through the regular computation.

We said at the beginning of the chapter that there would be a minimum number of rules for this chapter. However, the preceding rules are included because they were new in 1977 and something of a departure from previous calculations. Further, tax planning for real estate investors is critical and this area of tax preference is very important. One other point deserves to be mentioned here. The tax calculations above may be affected by the surtax on preferential income. That area will be discussed later in the chapter.

Treatment of Capital Losses

Capital losses arise when assets are sold for prices below their book values. The losses in each category, short-term and long-term, are offset by capital gains as previously mentioned. Long-term losses are written off against long-term gains; short-term losses are written against short-term gains. If there are *net losses* in these two categories, they may be written against ordinary income by strict rules.

1. *Net short-term losses* up to $3000 can be written off against income beginning in 1978. This is a recent liberalization.

2. *Net long-term losses* may be used to offset income using one-half of the net loss up to $3000.

3. The total losses which can be written off against ordinary income in any one year are $3000. These losses may be *carried forward* indefinitely by individuals, however, to offset future gains and income by a specific formula. The reader is referred to the references in Appendix 2 for details on some of these rules.

No losses may be written off from the sale of a personal residence, though gains are taxable. Corporations are restricted from taking net losses against ordinary income. Losses must be written off against gains only. They may be carried forward and backward a few years, but if gains are not made sometime, losses cannot be written off. Corporate gains are taxed at a maximum rate of only 30%, which may be more advantageous than the rate for individuals.

Section 1231 Property

The foregoing description of the tax status of capital transactions applies in general to *any* capital asset. However, certain depreciable property, such as real estate, receives some different treatment. In general, these special items fall under the category of **Section 1231 property** and include:

1. Depreciable personal property used in trade or business and held over one year. This would include furniture and equipment, not considered real property.

2. Real property used for trade or business (commercial or industrial buildings) and held over one year.

3. Property held for production of income (such as rental real estate) and held over one year.

4. Leaseholds used in trade or business and held over one year.[2]

These categories include virtually all of the property which would be involved in a typical real estate investment. The segregation of these items from other capital assets such as securities is important because

---

[2]We will discuss leaseholds in chapter 13.

they receive *preferential treatment.* The rules for calculating the taxes on the disposal of this property are based on the general rules presented earlier. However, the important differences for Section 1231 property involve the determination of the *size* of the gain or loss to be taxed and include:

1. The methods for determining whether or not the gain receives preference, and
2. The fact that some or all of the depreciation taken during the life of the asset must be "recaptured" and taxed as ordinary income.

The segregation of Section 1231 losses and gains between short- and long-term begins in the general fashion. However, *all* gains and losses are netted together. If *gains exceed losses,* all gains and losses are treated as *long-term.* If *losses exceed gains,* all losses are treated as *short-term.* This gives the taxpayer the maximum preferential treatment for losses and gains. These gains and losses are exclusive of recaptured depreciation. Recapture will be discussed as it applies to the two subcategories of Section 1231 property called **Section 1245 property** (personal) and **Section 1250 property** (real).

Section 1245 Property   Section 1245 property includes all personal property such as equipment, furniture, and other items not part of the real property structures. If the sale price of such property is in excess of the adjusted basis at the time of sale, it is taxed as *ordinary income to the extent of depreciation taken.* If the gain exceeds the accumulated depreciation, the excess is a Section 1231 gain.

Example 7.5

A batch of office furniture is sold along with a building in a separate transaction. The gain on the sale of this furniture is calculated as:

Original cost of Section 1245 property	$50,000
Less: Accumulated Depreciation	20,000
Adjusted Basis	$30,000
Sale Price	$60,000
Less: Adjusted Basis	30,000
Total Gain	$30,000
Depreciation Taken:	
Section 1245 Gain (taxed as	
ordinary income)	$20,000
Section 1231 Gain	$10,000

Section 1250 Property Real property is subject to **depreciation recapture** only to the extent *depreciation taken over its life exceeds what would have been taken under straight-line*. The steps for calculating this recapture are extremely complicated because there have been two tax reforms since 1968 and both of them changed these rules. Thus, property is segregated and treated in pieces with different rules applying to depreciation after 1975, before 1976 but after 1969, and before 1970.

In general, for new property acquired after 1975, the rule is that all excess depreciation must be recaptured and treated as ordinary income on all property except low-income housing. For the latter category the recaptured amount is reduced by 1% for each month the property is held over 100 months. Thus, after 200 months there is no recapture and all gains are treated as Section 1231 gains. An example of recapture for new property, purchased after 1975, is included as Example 7.6. For the other rules refer to *Federal Tax Course—1978* listed in the references in Appendix 2.

Example 7.6

A rental apartment is purchased in 1977 for $100,000 and sold after two years for $120,000. The gain is treated as follows. Note the original life was computed to be forty years for depreciation purposes.

Depreciation:	
2 years double-declining balance, 40-year basis	$9,750
2 years straight-line, 40-year basis	$5,000
Amount to be recaptured	$4,750
Gain:	
Sale Proceeds	$120,000
Adjusted Basis ($100,000 − $9,750)	90,250
Total Gain	$ 29,750
Division of Gain:	
Total Gain	$29,750
Less: Recapture (Section 1250)	4,750
Long-Term Section 1231 Gain	$25,000

Thus $25,000 is treated as a long-term Section 1231 gain and $4,750 is treated as ordinary income.

Concluding Comments

Capital gains treatment as we have described it may be taken only by bona fide investors. Real estate brokers cannot take gains on a property they have purchased for resale. It should also be noted that there are many detailed categories of capital gains relating to specific types of properties. The reader is referred to the tax service listed in the references.

Gains may be postponed by a number of legitimate means. For instance, if a property is sold on an installment basis with no more than 30% of the total price collected in the year of the sale, the gain may be prorated over the life of the installment contract. Exchanges also permit gains to be postponed. Again, the investor should consult a tax authority for the specific qualifications.

The capital gain provisions of our tax laws provide some preferences. It should be stressed that these gains are not an everyday occurrence for a real estate investor. They are more episodic than periodic in nature.

Miscellaneous Concepts

Surtax on Preferences

In addition to the normal tax considerations we have seen so far, there is another rule which may affect real estate investors. Certain items affecting income are called tax preferences. Chief among these are capital gains and accelerated depreciation, as previously mentioned. When a large amount of preference income is present, as in the case of the capital gains for the investor in Example 7.4, a 15% surtax may be applied.

To calculate the **surtax on preferences,** we find the total of all preference items, subtract an exemption, and multiply the resulting figure by 15%. The total preference item is found by taking one-half of the long-term capital gains and adding the excess by which accelerated depreciation exceeds straight-line for the period (similar to the depreciation recapture, except the property need not have been sold). The exemption is $10,000 or one-half of the regular tax liability, whichever is *greater*. Now we will see an example of these calculations.

Example 7.7

Mrs. Adams has ordinary income of $100,000 after a deduction of $40,000 for accelerated depreciation. The depreciation on her property would have been $20,000 by straight-line. In addition, there was a long-term capital gain of $50,000. The basic tax liability the regular way would have been $45,180, assuming the deductions and exemptions shown here.

Ordinary Income		$100,000
Long-term Capital Gain	$50,000	
Less: Deduction		
(½ of long-term gain)	25,000	
Net Gain in Income		25,000
Adjusted Gross Income		$125,000
Less: Deductions and Exemptions		21,800
Taxable Income		$103,200
Tax		$ 45,180
Preference Income		
Accelerated Depreciation	$40,000	
Less: Straight-Line	20,000	
Depreciation Preference	$20,000	
Add: ½ of capital gain	25,000	
Total Preferences		$45,000
Less: Exemption (½ of tax liability)		22,590
Subject to Surtax		$24,410
Surtax at 15%		$ 3,360

Total Tax = $45,180 + $3,360 = $48,540

There are other preference items in addition to the ones we have discussed. However, capital gains and accelerated depreciation are the more important ones which affect real estate investors. Finally, it may be stated for clarification purposes that surtax on preferences is a periodic tax, whereas the recapture provision applies only when an asset is sold for a gain and accelerated depreciation has been used.

Tax Considerations in Rate Calculations

In chapter 3 we discussed the calculation of weighted average rates of return for use in the capitalization of earnings. These calculations were made on a pretax basis in that chapter. However, we know that interest is a deductible expense. This makes debt a cheap source of funds. It also lowers the effective rate of return required by the investor.

In this chapter it has been seen that the effective after-tax cost of an expense is the before-tax cost times the quantity (1 − investor's tax rate). Thus, an 8% interest rate on debt financing may be calculated on an after-tax basis by using the relationship for the effective after-tax cost of the interest expense. Assuming a 30% tax rate, the effective cost becomes:

$$8\% \times (1 - 0.3) = 8\% \times 0.7 = 5.6\%$$

Note that *equity is not adjusted for taxes*. Return on equity is automatically an after-tax figure. The cost of debt, only, requires an after-tax adjustment when the weighted average cost of capital is to be determined.

We may now calculate our weighted average return on investment from chapter 3. An investor can borrow at 8%; has a 30% tax rate; and requires a 12% return on equity. Debt will compose 60% of his total average capital requirement. The overall rate of return may be seen as:

After-tax Debt: 60% × 5.6% = 3.4%
Equity: 40% × 12.0% = 4.8%
Overall Rate   8.2%

The overall rate of return on investment of 8.2% is indeed lower than that found in chapter 3 using the before-tax debt rate (9.6% was the overall rate of return determined in chapter 3). In general, sophisticated investors will probably use the after-tax rate in their investment calculations. A before-tax rate is more likely to be used in appraisal work since each individual investor's tax rate will differ.

Exchanges

A final area which we will only briefly discuss is the property exchange. Capital gains taxes on long-term capital gains may be at preferred rates, but they may still be sizable. Imagine an investor owned a piece of raw land purchased for $200,000 ten years ago. Now the investor desires income from her investments. She finds she can sell the land for $1,000,000, exactly the equity required to invest in a shopping center. There is a problem, however. If she sells the land she will pay taxes on a gain of $800,000. This will reduce the cash she nets from the sale to around $750,000. She will be short of the amount needed to buy the shopping center. Further, the shopping center owner may have a similar problem with large capital gains taxes.

The solution to these problems may lie in the ability to consummate a **tax-free exchange.** By trading properties, or groups of properties, owners may be able to *postpone* capital gains taxes on their transactions. These taxes will eventually be paid when the properties are finally sold. However, these future payments may be made at a more convenient time in the investor's life.

The rules for exchange are complex and interesting, though really beyond the scope of this book. There may actually be some tax on the exchange depending upon whether certain consideration changes hands.[3] The challenge of consummating tax-free exchanges on large parcels of property has given rise to a whole group of specialists who excel in this area. There are even some clubs whose members try to outdo each other in putting together such transactions. A really complex

---

[3]*Consideration* is a legal word meaning value given up.

exchange is an exciting look into the true art of negotiation, bargaining, and appraising the real worth of property.

CHAPTER SEVEN SUMMARY

This chapter has been somewhat detailed in dealing with the very important area of taxes. We have seen the basic structures of business and personal taxes which are likely to affect a real estate investor. As we saw in Figure 1.1, taxes are one of the many factors affecting the value of *investment real estate*. We do not consider taxes to be a consideration in market value estimation, however. We have seen that the net cash flow of income real estate is definitely affected by such items as depreciation, interest, operating expenses and other deductions, and the taxes themselves. A change in the tax rate will change the income. We have also seen that without taxes depreciation would not provide its tax-shelter effect. Real estate value is heavily influenced by the presence of taxes. The Tax Reform Act of 1976 has had a great deal of impact on the value of real property. Many of the former shelters have been weakened or removed. Most professionals now seem to be saying that the best way to invest in real estate is to take taxes into account, but *make certain the investment is a good one no matter what its tax benefits are.*

It should be noted that some details concerning the treatment of capital gains and depreciation have been omitted for the sake of clarity and brevity. They are not unimportant details. Their absence was merely to avoid undue confusion. Even the details included have been simplified a bit. The point here is that taxes are a very important consideration in any income real estate investment. The services of a capable professional, such as a tax attorney, will be beneficial in such transactions. It is wise to consult one before the investment is made, not after the deal has been consummated. For your own information, some references have been included in Appendix 2 at the end of the text which will provide extra insight into this area if you so desire.

KEY TERMS

Accelerated Depreciation	Depreciable Base	Section 1231 Property
Adjusted Basis	Depreciation Recapture	Section 1245 Property
Adjusted Gross Income	Double Taxation	Section 1250 Property
Ad Valorem Tax	Exemptions	Short-Term Capital Gain
Assessed Value	Gross Income	Standard Deduction
Book Value	Income Tax	Straight-Line
Capital Gain	Long-Term Capital Gain	
Capital Loss	Millage Rate	
Component	Ordinary Income	

Depreciation	Periodic Income	Depreciation
Declining Balance	Property Taxes	Sum-of-the-Years'
Depreciation		Digits
Deductions		Surtax on
		Preferences
		Taxable Income
		Tax-Free Exchange
		Tax Shelter

QUESTIONS FOR STUDY AND DISCUSSION

1. What are the important taxes affecting a real estate investor?

2. Differentiate between the income tax ramifications of incorporated and unincorporated real estate investments.

3. What are the most important differences between the various depreciation schedules?

4. Explain the concept of a *capital gain*. How is it treated differently from ordinary income?

5. What are the advantages of accelerated depreciation? Is it always better to choose accelerated depreciation methods if one has a choice for a given piece of property?

6. Under what conditions might real estate investors wish to trade properties rather than sell them?

7. What are the basic components which affect an individual's tax liability?

PROBLEMS FOR REVIEW

1. An investor purchased a property for $100,000. Since owning it he has made $20,000 in improvements. Total accumulated depreciation is $30,000. The property is sold after five years for $100,000. What is the capital gain (loss)?

2. A new property is purchased for $300,000. This property includes land worth $50,000 and an expected salvage value (excluding land) of $50,000. Its useful life is twenty-five years. Find the first year's depreciation using straight-line, double-declining balance, and sum-of-the-years' digits methods.

3. What will be the accumulated depreciation using each method for the property in problem 2 after ten years?

4. The property in problem 2 is sold after ten years for $200,000. If the investor used straight-line depreciation, what would his capital gain (loss) be?

5. Assume the property in problem 2 was sold for $200,000. If the investor had used double-declining balance depreciation, what would the capital gain (loss) be? Ignore depreciation recapture.

6. How would the gain in problem 5 be divided between ordinary income and capital gains if depreciation recapture were considered? How would the loss be divided if there were a loss rather than a gain?

7. Repeat problems 2 through 6 for a different property purchased for $500,000 ten years ago. The land component was $50,000 for the property. It was sold for $325,000 after ten years. When purchased originally the property had a life of thirty years and no salvage value for the building.

TABLE 7.4   TAX SCHEDULE:—1977[a]

Married Filing Joint Returns and Qualifying Widows and Widowers

Use this schedule if you checked **Box 2 or Box 5** on Form 1040—

If the amount on Schedule TC, Part I, line 3, is: Enter on Schedule TC, Part I, line 4:

Not over $3,200 . . . .   —0—

Over—	But not over—		amount over—
$3,200	$4,200	14%	$3,200
$4,200	$5,200	$140+15%	$4,200
$5,200	$6,200	$290+16%	$5,200
$6,200	$7,200	$450+17%	$6,200
$7,200	$11,200	$620+19%	$7,200
$11,200	$15,200	$1,380+22%	$11,200
$15,200	$19,200	$2,260+25%	$15,200
$19,200	$23,200	$3,260+28%	$19,200
$23,200	$27,200	$4,380+32%	$23,200
$27,200	$31,200	$5,660+36%	$27,200
$31,200	$35,200	$7,100+39%	$31,200
$35,200	$39,200	$8,660+42%	$35,200
$39,200	$43,200	$10,340+45%	$39,200
$43,200	$47,200	$12,140+48%	$43,200
$47,200	$55,200	$14,060+50%	$47,200
$55,200	$67,200	$18,060+53%	$55,200
$67,200	$79,200	$24,420+55%	$67,200
$79,200	$91,200	$31,020+58%	$79,200
$91,200	$103,200	$37,980+60%	$91,200
$103,200	$123,200	$45,180+62%	$103,200
$123,200	$143,200	$57,580+64%	$123,200
$143,200	$163,200	$70,380+66%	$143,200
$163,200	$183,200	$83,580+68%	$163,200
$183,200	$203,200	$97,180+69%	$183,200
$203,200	. . . .	$110,980+70%	$203,200

[a] Source: Internal Revenue Service.

8
REAL ESTATE INVESTMENT

IN CHAPTER 1 the value of real estate was defined three ways: as market value, investment value, and cost. At this point we have discussed market value and cost and will now turn to the details of investment value. The reader will notice many similarities between investment value and market value as estimated by the income approach, but, in addition, there are many differences. The investment value of a property is a subjective value which is affected by depreciation, taxes, and financing arrangements. These are all factors which are often ignored in market value estimates.

In this chapter we will be presenting sufficient information for you to use the methods described for personal investment analysis. A basic worksheet format will be presented which can be used for any basic investment project. All major aspects of investment analysis will be discussed. Real estate is perhaps one of the best investments an individual can make, but it is easy for the average individual to make conceptual errors in investment analysis. One of the main purposes of this chapter is to help you avoid these errors.

Investment Characteristics

Investment Attributes

An *investment* may be defined as a commitment of resources, or, more specifically, funds, in order to obtain future benefits. The value of any investment, whether it is securities, commodities, or real estate, depends on the relative strength of the investment on a number of common attributes.

1. *Return.*   The **return** from an investment is often a combination of two returns. First, most investments offer some form of periodic flow such as interest, dividends, or businesstype income. Second, most investments provide a residual value from their sale at the end of their economic life or holding period. Any capital gain realized by this value provides some (or all) of the asset's return.

2. *Safety.*   **Safety** refers to the probability that the investment will produce the total return which the investor expected it to produce.[1] Essentially, this attribute relates to the stability or predictability of the return.

3. *Liquidity.*   An asset is said to have high **liquidity** when it can be sold quickly for cash while retaining a high percentage of its economic value.

4. *Manageability.*   **Manageability** is the ability of an investment to

---

[1]*Safety* is most often discussed in terms of its complementary concept, *risk.* We, too, shall do this in the discussion to follow.

be managed by its owners or their agents to help ensure that the investment will produce its expected return.

5. *Taxability*.   **Taxability**, the last attribute, refers to the degree to which an investment is subject to taxation. Generally, this refers to federal income taxation, but there are other taxes as well, which we have discussed in chapter 7.

The choice among various investment alternatives is generally made by measuring the extent to which these various attributes are in evidence for each available alternative. Some of the attributes such as return, taxability, and, to some extent, safety can be measured fairly objectively. Manageability and liquidity can only be compared on a subjective basis.

When various investment alternatives are analyzed, the question of safety is often treated in an indirect way. Rather than measuring the safety of an investment, we generally look at risk instead. *Risk* may be defined as the probability that an investment will *not* provide its expected return. Risk may be viewed as the absence of safety. There are many types of risks, not all of which apply to all categories of investments.

1. *Market risk*.   The risk that an adverse change in the market value of an investment will cause the investor to suffer a loss in value is the **market risk**. This applies mostly to securities. Market risks may be avoided in some instances if the investment can be held through the down market trend. This may result in an opportunity loss, however, if the investor passes up a good alternative investment while waiting for the market to recover.

2. *Business risk*.   **Business risk** refers to the potential for loss, especially to business investors, which arises when economic fluctuations cause a loss in operating income to the business. This type of loss is totally independent of the type of financing employed.

3. *Financial risk*.   The additional risk in a business investment in a company financed by interest-bearing debt is the **financial risk**. Fluctuations in operating income affect debt-financed companies more than those with no debt-financing (unlevered firms).

4. *Purchasing power risk*.   In an economy subject to inflation, investments may lose value because of a loss in the purchasing power of the dollar. This is **purchasing power risk**. Fixed value, fixed income securities are especially susceptible to this type of risk.

5. *Political risks*.   The category of **political risk** includes a multitude of potential problems which arise from the actions of governmental units. These can include changes in laws, regulations, zoning, and even takeovers of assets by foreign governments.

Real Estate Attributes

At the risk of overgeneralizing we will now examine how real estate fares in relation to the attributes listed above.

1. *Return*.   Real estate earnings are among the highest of the common investments available to the individual investor. The type of return is a function of the type of real estate purchased, however. Raw land typically provides its return in the form of capital gains. Residential and commercial income property provide much more return in the form of periodic cash flows, although a great deal of the return may be derived from the residual value of the property.

2. *Risks*.   Real estate is potentially subject to a great many risks. However, it does protect the investor from one of the most insidious risks—purchasing power risk. Real income property is probably the only real hedge against inflation for the individual investor.[2] When investors make good real estate investments they can be relatively certain the purchasing power of their investment returns will be maintained. Real estate is affected by market risks. The residual value of real property may be adversely affected by market conditions. Real estate may also suffer a loss in expected value from unforeseen expenses or losses in revenue which cause net operating income to be lower than expected. Because real estate is normally highly leveraged, it is susceptible to financial risks. We shall examine this in more detail later in this chapter. Finally, real estate is affected a good deal by political factors. Zoning, changes in building codes, tax law changes, and other political concerns may all adversely affect the value of a real estate investment.

3. *Liquidity*.   Real estate is one of the *least* liquid of all investments. This can be a problem. If an investor makes a poor investment, it may be very difficult to sell the property. Either the investor will have to sell at a large loss or suffer the opportunity loss of having funds tied up in an asset with a low return.

4. *Manageability*.   Real estate is one of the *most* manageable of all investments. Many adjustments can be made when the income from a real estate investment does not perform adequately. If a stock market investment does not perform as planned, the investor's only real choice is to sell it. However, even major high-quality projects sometimes cannot be managed well enough to save them. In 1978 the huge Omni complex in Atlanta failed because its income was insufficient even to cover its debt service. Market rents were too low to permit the owners to charge enough for the space available for rent.

---

[2]There are people who would argue this point, saying that stocks are also a good hedge against inflation. However, there is increasing evidence that this is no longer true. See Warren E. Buffet, "How Inflation Swindles the Equity Investor," *Fortune*, May 1977, pp. 250–267.

5. *Taxability*.   The income from real property is taxable, but it does provide a tax shelter when depreciation is large enough. In addition, since so much of the return comes from capital gains at preferred tax rates, real estate investors often pay lower taxes on this type of investment than they would pay if they held securities.

Investment Process

Assumptions and Approach

The process of analyzing the value of a real estate investment will be discussed in detail here. However, at this point, we will look at the general process as it applies to any investment alternative. It should be realized at the outset that the analytical framework of investment is based on a foundation of several critical assumptions.

1. Investments must be judged in context. Investments should be analyzed in relation to alternative uses for the funds. Without this assumption we have no standard of risk and return by which to judge the worth of an investment.

2. Investors are risk-averters. This is a complex and difficult assumption, in the author's view. We assume that investors will try to avoid risks if given the choice. However, the taking of risks is essential to the process of capital formation in the economy. The seeming paradox is resolved by taking the position that investors will not take undue risks. They wish to be compensated fairly for the risks they do incur.

3. Hand-in-hand with the second assumption is the presumption that investors have a diminishing marginal utility for money. This means that each additional unit of money received provides the investor with slightly less additional satisfaction than the previous similarly sized unit. Because of the lower satisfaction for this extra return, investors tend to avoid trying to make extremely large returns. The reason for this is found in assumption four.

4. Excessive returns from investments are obtained by taking excessive risks. There is a trade-off between risk and return. Because high risks must be incurred to obtain high returns and the excessive returns have decreasing marginal satisfaction, investors tend to avoid seeking excessive returns.[3]

---

[3]It may be obvious that what may seem excessive to one investor may be unsatisfactory to another. Similarly, not all investors are risk-averters or rational investors. These assumptions apply to investors as a group; individually, exceptions can be found. For a further discussion of these assumptions see chapter 9.

5. Investors are economically rational. This assumption implies that investors have the foregoing assumed characteristics and use a rational judgment process to evaluate alternative investments.

6. Finally, we assume investors are operating in an efficient, economic market where they have access to perfect information and open market prices. The full impact of these assumptions will be evident as we proceed.

Investment decisions involve a number of trade-offs. As we have seen, the primary trade-off involves risk and return. Another trade-off involves return and liquidity. To obtain more return an investor typically must take a higher risk and also sacrifice liquidity. There are also trade-offs among the other attributes, but they are more difficult to generalize. Evaluating the trade-offs for alternative investments is a subjective process which requires that each investor compare measures of the various attributes for each alternative to his or her own personal goals and preferences.

The investment process begins with a determination of the investible wealth available for commitment. Next, investors must define their preferences for risk, return, and the other investment attributes, so they can evaluate the trade-offs. Next, investors should find those categories of investments which meet their general criteria. The investors are now ready to evaluate specific alternative investments. Finally, the satisfactory investments are combined to obtain the best overall group of investments.

In order to make the individual evaluations, one of two possible criteria may be used. One approach is to find the value of the benefits from the investment, given the rate of return required by the investor. This value may be called the *maximum justified price* of the investment which will still permit the investor to earn the required return. This value is then compared to the cost of the investment. If the value exceeds the cost, then the investment may be considered viable. It should be noted further that the required rate of return has already been adjusted for risk, so both risk and return are accounted for. This is simply the net present value rule discussed earlier.

A second approach to this analysis is to find the specific rate of return of an investment when the value of the benefits equals its cost. This method is not preferred for a number of technical reasons. Both this method and the first method were described in chapter 3 in the decision rules section.

Investment Yield

For any investment, including real estate, there are two basic ways to look at the return on investment: the short run and the long run. As we shall see later, the long-run measure is generally more important and acceptable for decision-making. However, one-period (short-term) measures are appropriate for historical analysis. The period is usually considered to be one year, although shorter periods such as a month can be adjusted to yield annual figures. The concept of risk can be explained conveniently using one-period measures of yield.

The yield, or return, can be shown by the following formula:

$$\frac{PR + (P_1 - P_0)}{P_0} = HPY$$

where

PR is the periodic return for one period,
P_0 is the original price of the investment,
P_1 is the price after one period, and
HPY is the **holding period yield.**

Assume you purchase an investment for $10,000 and you receive $500 in the first year as a cash return from the investment. Further, you can now sell the investment for $10,500 after the year is over. Your HPY may be calculated as:

$$HPY = \frac{\$500 + (\$10,500 - \$10,000)}{\$10,000} = 10\%$$

This simple relationship generally shows how well you have done in a single period. As long as you restrict this approach to single periods, the method will be compatible with the time-adjusted yields (long-run) mentioned earlier.

Risk Measurement

The concept of risk measurement in investing is more difficult to describe, and, for this reason, it will be treated separately in chapter 9. At this point, it can be said that, in general, the risk of an investment is measured by its variability. The more variable the returns from an investment, the riskier it is.

Concluding Comments

The presentation in this chapter thus far has served to introduce the fundamentals of investment in general. We have looked at the process of investing as well as basic concepts of risk and historical return. This material was intended to give you some perspective for investment analysis which should be helpful for you, as an investor, to make choices among alternatives.

It is also worth noting here that the concepts of risk and expected value presented are useful to the appraiser. When the appraiser makes a judgment of the most likely value for a property, he or she is making a subjective judgment of the expected value of the property. The appraiser is also making a relative judgment for the potential variability in the estimate. Even if the risk is not measured directly, it should at least be taken into account subjectively. The greater the risk is, then the greater is the return the investor will seek.

Real Estate Investment Analysis

In this section we will discuss the specific processes that should be used to analyze the acceptability of prospective real estate investments.

There are two major categories of cash benefits from a real estate investment, the periodic cash flow and the net cash value of the property when it is sold. The main factors affecting the periodic cash flow are the size of the net operating earnings, the amount of depreciation, the cost of financing arrangements, and the investor's tax liability. The net cash from the sale of the property is affected by the sale price, the presence of a capital gain or loss, the investor's tax bracket, and the presence of any unpaid balance from the financing arrangements.

Periodic Cash Benefits

The estimation of the periodic flow requires several steps. These are described here and summarized in Figure 8.1.

1. The first step is to determine the inputs to the investor's taxable income from the property. This is equal to the taxable portion of NOI less expenses for interest and depreciation. The taxable portion of NOI is the net operating income plus the reserve for replacements. These reserves are cash charges affecting value, but they are not tax deductible. We call the sum of NOI plus reserves the **taxable operating income, TOI.** The interest charge to be deducted will be explained shortly. Depreciation is calculated as it was described in chapter 7.

2. After obtaining the taxable income, we can then calculate the tax liability. The proper way to find the tax liability is to compare the income of the investor under the assumption that the investor does not make the investment with his or her tax liability when the investment income is included. The difference is the tax arising from the investment. Note if the investment shows a loss for tax purposes, the investor's tax liability will decrease. This results in a tax savings which is added to the cash flow from the investment. This gives rise to the tax-shelter characteristic associated with real estate.

FIGURE 8.1   SUMMARY OF NET CASH FLOW CALCULATIONS

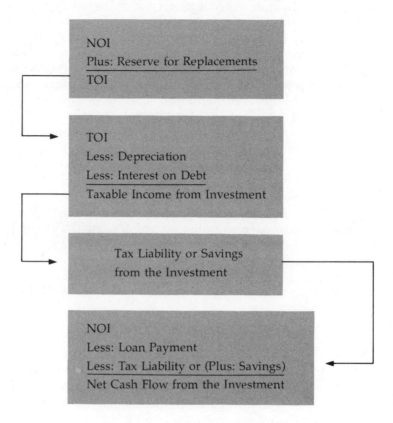

3. The next step is to compute the net cash flow from the investment. The net cash flow is equal to NOI, not TOI, less the periodic loan payment and the tax liability found in step 2. A tax savings would be added to NOI. The net result of these calculations is the **periodic net cash flow.** This process is repeated for each period in the life of the investment.

Debt Service and Interest   In the preceding periodic income calculations, there are two important elements which are somewhat new to our discussions thus far. The calculation of the tax liability included a deduction for interest on debts. A loan payment, also called **debt service,** is composed of two parts—the interest on the unpaid balance and a repayment of a portion of the principal. *Only the interest portion is tax deductible.* The interest amount decreases from period to period as more of the principal is repaid. There is no easy way to find the amount of interest in each period unless you use a table. Some selected tables of this type have been included in Appendix 1 at the end of this book. They are called Interest Amortization Tables. An excerpt from one of these tables is presented in Table 8.1. The portion illustrated is for a ten-year loan at 9%. The tables have been constructed for annual loan payments only. The difference in interest percentages and outstanding balances between annual and monthly payment schemes is slight. Thus, for ease of calculation only annual payment schemes are used.

At the left-hand side of the table the numbers represent the number of annual payments which have been made. They also indicate the number of years the loan has been outstanding. Across from each of these figures in the main body of the table a pair of numbers is presented. The first number of the pair is the percent of that year's loan payment which is interest. The second number is the percent of the original loan which is unpaid at the end of that period.

In order to find the interest deduction for each period, the annual loan payment must first be calculated. You may recall that the calculation of the loan payment is made using the AMF table in the appendix and equation [2.15] from chapter 2.

$$\text{Loan Payment} = \text{Loan Amount} \times AMF_{n,i}$$

The payment for a $30,000 loan for ten years at 9% is determined as:

$$\text{Loan Payment} = \$30,000 \times AMF_{10,9\%}$$
$$= \$30,000 \times 0.156 = \$4680 \text{ per year}$$

The loan balance outstanding during the first year is $30,000, so at 9% interest the total interest amount in the first year is $2700 ($30,000 $\times$ 0.09). This is 57.7% of the first annual loan payment ($2700/$4680).

TABLE 8.1   INTEREST AMORTIZATION TABLE:
9% INTEREST; 10 YEARS

Years	% of Annual Payment Which Is Interest	% of Loan Unpaid at End of Year
1	57.7	93.4
2	53.9	86.2
3	50.3	78.4
4	45.2	69.8
5	40.3	60.5
⋮	⋮	⋮

This percentage appears as the first number in the Interest Amortization Table shown in Table 8.1. Because $2700 of the first payment is interest, the remaining $1980 represents the principal repayment ($4680 − $2700). This means that at the end of the first year $28,020 is unpaid ($30,000 − $1980). This is 93.4% of the original loan amount ($28,020/$30,000). This percentage figure is also found in the table. In the second year $28,020 is the outstanding balance and the interest charge is calculated using that amount. The entire table may be generated in this manner. The reader may wish to complete the calculations for this example.

Tax Liability Calculations   To avoid any confusion, we will now examine the calculation of the tax liability for an unincorporated real estate investment. Assume an investor has a taxable income of $36,000 before considering a real estate investment. His tax liability on that income is $8,996 based on Table 7.4. Now this prospective investor wishes to calculate his tax liability based on the addition of a taxable income of $16,000 from a real estate investment. His total taxable income would now become $52,000 ($36,000 + $16,000). The tax liability for $52,000 based on Table 7.4 is $16,460. The tax liability incurred by the investment is shown here.

Tax with Investment	$16,460
Less: Tax without Investment	8,996
Tax Liability of Investment	$ 7,464

Assume now the same investor is analyzing an investment with a loss for tax purposes. The loss is $8000 before taxes. Now the investor has a taxable income of $28,000 including the investment ($36,000 − $8000). The tax on this would be $5948. The investment then offers a tax savings of $3048.

Tax with Investment	$5948
Tax without Investment	8996
Tax Savings from Investment	$3048

For our next examples we will short-cut these calculations by using the appropriate tax bracket (percentage charged on additional income) for a hypothetical investor. This technique works satisfactorily for smaller sized investments. For instance, the investor in our first example would have been charged around 46% for income added on to his $36,000. Forty-six percent of the $16,000 investment income results in an estimated tax liability of $7360 compared to the actual $7464 liability. It is nevertheless a good, fast approximation.

Sample Calculation of Periodic Benefits   To illustrate the techniques described up to this point, we will look at an example, the Panther Arms Apartments described in chapter 6. Table 8.2 presents a condensed statement of income for this investment. Other key data are presented here.

1. NOI = $23,750 per year
TOI = $26,780 per year

2. Life of Building Shell = forty years
Life of Wasting Parts = ten years[4]

3. Building Cost (new) = $180,000
Wasting Parts Cost (part of building) = $32,500
Land Cost = $20,000

4. Property is to be bought and held for five years and then sold for $195,000. Today's purchase price is $200,000.

5. Property will be financed with a loan of $150,000 payable over twenty years @ 9% interest.

6. The investor making the purchase expects the property income to be taxed at 50%. The investor feels a 12% return will be acceptable for this property.

The calculation of the periodic cash flow involves a number of preliminary calculations. These will be done for the first year in detail here. The periodic income for the five years is summarized in Table 8.3. Tables 8.4 and 8.5 show the details of depreciation and interest amortization schedules, respectively.

TABLE 8.2   PANTHER ARMS APARTMENTS CONDENSED STATEMENT OF INCOME

Gross Income		$39,000
Less: Vacancy and Collection Loss		1,950
Effective Gross Income		$37,050
Less: Operating Expense	$4,070	
Less: Fixed Expenses	$9,230	13,300
NOI		$23,750
Add: Reserve for Replacements		3,030
TOI (Taxable Operating Income)		$26,780

[4]For ease of calculation a ten-year life is being used uniformly in depreciation calculations for the group of wasting parts. This tends to reduce the depreciation expense, increase the tax liability, and decrease net cash flows. As an exercise the reader may recalculate these figures using the lives of the wasting parts given in Table 6.2.

TABLE 8.3   PANTHER ARMS—FIVE-YEAR CASH FLOW

	Year One	Year Two	Year Three	Year Four	Year Five
Tax Liability					
Taxable Operating Income	$26,780[a]	$26,780	$26,780	$26,780	$26,780
Less: Interest	13,500	13,230	12,935	12,615	12,265
Less: Shell Depreciation	7,375	7,005	6,655	6,325	6,005
Less: Parts Depreciation	3,250	3,250	3,250	3,250	3,250
Taxable Income	$ 2,655	$ 3,295	$ 3,940	$ 4,590	$ 5,260
Tax at 50%	$ 1,325	$ 1,650	$ 1,970	$ 2,295	$ 2,630
Cash Flow					
Net Operating Income	$23,750	$23,750	$23,750	$23,750	$23,750
Less: Debt Service	16,500	16,500	16,500	16,500	16,500
Pretax Cash	$ 7,250	$ 7,250	$ 7,250	$ 7,250	$ 7,250
Less: Taxes	1,325	1,650	1,970	2,295	2,630
Net Cash	$ 5,925	$ 5,600	$ 5,280	$ 4,955	$ 4,620

[a]Figures are rounded to the nearest $5

TABLE 8.4   PANTHER ARMS DEPRECIATION SCHEDULE

Building Shell Using Double-Declining Balance

Year	Initial Balance	Depreciation Rate	Depreciation Charge	Ending Balance
1	$147,500[a]	5%	$7,375	$140,125
2	$140,125	5%	$7,005	$133,120
3	$133,120	5%	$6,655	$126,465
4	$126,465	5%	$6,325	$120,140
5	$120,140	5%	$6,005	$114,135
			$33,365	

Wasting Parts Using Straight-Line

$3,250 each year
Total Depreciation for five years = $16,250
Undepreciated Balance at end of five years =
$32,500 − $16,250 = $16,250

TABLE 8.4   PANTHER ARMS DEPRECIATION SCHEDULE (CONTINUED)

Total Undepreciated Balance

Building Shell	$114,135
Wasting Parts	$ 16,250
Total	$130,385

Total Actual Depreciation

Building Shell	$ 33,365
Wasting Parts	$ 16,250
Total	$ 49,615

[a]Figures rounded to nearest $5

Depreciation of Building Shell, first year;
Using a forty-year life and double-declining balance:

Straight-line rate = 100%/40 = 2.5%/year
Double-declining rate = 2 × 2.5% = 5%/year
Building shell value = $180,000 − Wasting parts
    = $180,000 − $32,500 = $147,500
First year depreciation charge =
    Building shell value × 5% =
    $147,500 × 0.05 = $7,375
Balance at the end of the first year =
    $147,500 − $7,375 = $140,125

Depreciation of wasting parts, first year;
Using a ten-year life and straight-line:

Straight-line rate = 100%/10 = 10%
First year depreciation charge =
    Wasting parts value × 10% =
    $32,500 × 10% = $3250

TABLE 8.5   PANTHER ARMS INTEREST AMORTIZATION

Year	(1) Beginning Balance	(2) 9% Interest	(3) Principal Repayment	(4) Total Payment	(5) Unpaid Balance At End of Year
1	$150,000[a]	$13,500	$3,000	$16,500	$147,000
2	$147,000	$13,230	$3,270	$16,500	$143,730
3	$143,730	$12,935	$3,565	$16,500	$140,165
4	$140,165	$12,615	$3,885	$16,500	$136,280
5	$136,280	$12,265	$4,235	$16,500	$132,045

[a]Figures rounded to nearest $5
Column (1) × 9% = Column (2)
Column (4) − Column (2) = Column (3)
Column (1) − Column (3) = Column (5)
Column (5) becomes Column (1) in the following year

Debt Service, first year:

$$\text{Annual payment} = \$150,000 \times AMF_{20,9\%}$$
$$= \$150,000 \times 0.110$$
$$= \$16,500 \text{ per year}$$

$$\text{First year's interest} = \$150,000 \times 9\%$$
$$= \$13,500$$

$$\text{Principal reduction at end of first year} =$$
$$\$16,500 - \$13,500 = \$3,000$$

$$\text{Outstanding balance at end of first year} =$$
$$\$150,000 - \$3,000 = \$147,000$$

Comments   The cash flow from the five-year investment can be seen to average about $5300 per year for the five-year holding period of the investment. We have used this short holding period for two reasons. First, this is a common practice in real estate. Second, it made the calculations easier to show. One trouble with this periodic cash flow analysis is that it is cumbersome. With accelerated depreciation and decreasing interest payments, each year's cash will be different. This is a nuisance, but not difficult to handle for short holding periods. There are some short-cut methods for examining this uneven cash flow. However, with the number of good business calculators available today, it is recommended that these short-cut methods not be used.

Some ease of calculation can be provided by using the formats in the tables such as 8.3–8.5 to make the internal and summary cash calculations. Blank copies of these table formats have been provided in the appendix to this chapter. They can be reproduced and used for personal analysis.

We may now proceed to a treatment of the residual cash which accrues from the sale of the property at the end of its life or holding period.

Residual Cash Benefits

The **residual cash benefits** from the sale of an operating property often provide the owner with a large cash flow at the end of a short holding period. As with the periodic benefits, the first step in the calculation process is to measure the tax liability. We will recall some of the details of the calculations from chapter 7. The steps are summarized in Figure 8.2.

The steps shown in the figure allow the investor to calculate the total tax liability that will apply to the sale of the property. At this point the cash flow can be determined.

Cash Flow   The calculations required to derive the final cash flow are summarized as:

> Sale Price
> Less: Tax Liability or (Plus: Savings)
> Less: Mortgage Balance
> _____
> Net Cash from Property
> Plus: Unused Reserve for Replacements
> _____
> Net Cash Residual

Notice that the taxes and the mortgage balance are subtracted from the sale price to derive the cash flow from the property. The analyst must then add back the unused balance of the reserve for replacement account. If the property is to be held for a short period, the balance can be estimated as the future value of an annuity (opposite of the sinking fund calculation used to determine the reserve for replacement amount). Recall equation [2.11]:

$$FA_n = S \times AF_{n,i}$$

Sample Calculation of Residual Cash Flow   We can now use the analysis just described to find the cash accruing from the sale of the Panther

FIGURE 8.2   TAX CALCULATION

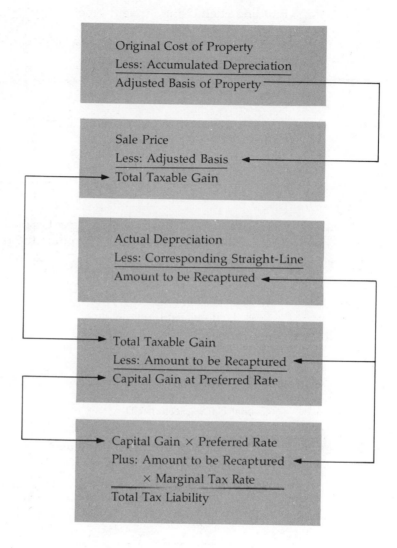

Original Cost of Property
Less: Accumulated Depreciation
Adjusted Basis of Property

Sale Price
Less: Adjusted Basis
Total Taxable Gain

Actual Depreciation
Less: Corresponding Straight-Line
Amount to be Recaptured

Total Taxable Gain
Less: Amount to be Recaptured
Capital Gain at Preferred Rate

Capital Gain × Preferred Rate
Plus: Amount to be Recaptured
      × Marginal Tax Rate
Total Tax Liability

Arms in five years. First, we will find the amount to be recaptured. This will help to determine the capital gains tax. From Table 8.4 we see the total depreciation taken during the five years amounts to $49,615. Using straight-line depreciation, this amount would have been $34,685 as determined here.

Building Shell Using Straight-Line:

$147,500/40 years = $3,687 per year
$3687 × 5 years = $18,435

Wasting Parts Using Straight-Line:

$16,250 for five years (from Table 8.4)

Total = $18,435 + $16,250 = $34,685

The amount to be recaptured and taxed as ordinary income is $14,930 ($49,615 − $34,685). We can now compute the tax calculation. Refer to Figure 8.2 for these steps.

Original Cost of Property	$200,000
Less: Accumulated Depreciation	49,615
Adjusted Basis	$150,385
Sale Price	$195,000
Less: Adjusted Basis	150,385
Total Taxable Gain	$ 44,615
Less: Amount to be Recaptured	14,930
Capital Gain—Section 1231	$ 29,685

Tax (Regular Way)		
Ordinary Income Amount Recaptured		$14,930
Section 1231 Gain	$29,685	
Less: Deduction	14,843	
Amount Added to Income		14,842
Taxable Income		$29,772
Tax at 50%		$14,886

Before proceeding to the final cash calculation, the unused reserve balance will be determined. The reserve deduction is $3030 per year. This was assumed to be accumulated at 5% per year. The calculation of the accumulated reserve is:

$$FA_5 = \$3030 \times AF_{5,5\%}$$
$$= \$3030 \times 5.526 = \$16,745$$

We may now complete the residual cash flow determination.

Sale Price	$195,000
Less: Mortgage Balance (Table 8.5)	132,045
Less: Tax Liability (rounded)	14,885
Residual from Property	$ 48,070
Plus: Unused Reserve	16,745
Total Cash Residual	$ 64,815

Comments   This last calculation completes the derivation of the cash flows from the five-year investment in the Panther Arms Apartments. The last step in the analysis is to determine whether the value of these cash flows exceeds their cost. The cash flows derived in this section and the previous section are summarized in Table 8.6 of the following section.

Present Value of Benefits

The value calculations for a real estate investment are something of an anticlimax compared to the cash flow determinations themselves. Table 8.6 shows the cash flows and the appropriate present value factors at 12%. The total value of the benefits is $56,035. Because the downpayment is only $50,000 ($200,000 purchase price less the $150,000 loan), the investment shows a value in excess of its cost, at 12%, and should be made. The net present value of $6000 provides some cushion should the analyst's projections be in error. The use of a ten-year straight-line depreciation on the wasting parts provides some additional cushion to the investment analysis.

TABLE 8.6   PANTHER ARMS PRESENT VALUE CALCULATION

Year	Cash Flow		$PVF_{12\%}$	Present Value
0	($50,000)[a]	Downpayment	1.000	($50,000)
1	$ 5,925		0.893	$ 5,290
2	$ 5,600		0.797	$ 4,465
3	$ 5,280		0.712	$ 3,760
4	$ 4,955		0.636	$ 3,150
5	$ 4,620		0.567	$ 2,620
5	$64,815	Residual	0.567	$36,750
			Net Present Value	$ 6,035

[a]Figures rounded to nearest $5

Concluding Comments

This completes our basic discussion of investment analysis. In this discussion we have seen all the details of simple investment analysis. Even the most complex problems can be dealt with using the same methods. Only the flows may be more complex. To reiterate the process of investment analysis, another case problem will be presented in the appendix to this chapter.

The Role of Leverage

The investment calculations we have just seen take into account the presence of debt in the financial structure of the investment. Most real estate investments—virtually all large structures—are somehow supported by debt. The use of debt has two important characteristics. First, the use of debt, often called **leverage**, serves to magnify the owner's earnings when used properly. Second, leverage increases the risks of investing. The reasons for these two characteristics will be examined next.

Earnings Magnification

When an investor puts up all the money for an investment, he or she is entitled to all of the earnings. Let's presume an investor puts up $20,000 to purchase an investment earning $3000 per year. In this case, the owner earns 15% on his investment during the yearly period.

$$\text{Yield} = \frac{\$3000}{\$20,000} = 15\%$$

Now presume another investor buys a similar investment using $10,000 of her own money while borrowing the other $10,000 from a creditor. This investor promises to pay her creditor 10%, or $1000, in interest per year for the use of the money. The second investor now earns $2000 from her investment ($3000 less $1000 to the creditor). Her return on her investment is 20%:

$$\text{Yield} = \frac{\$2000}{\$10,000} = 20\%$$

The reason the second investor does better, in spite of a lower dollar benefit, is that her creditor put up half the capital while taking only one-third of the return. The creditor is willing to do this because he has a contractual claim which carries a lower risk than the owner's claim on the earnings. This is shown graphically in Figure 8.3.

Additionally, because of the leverage employed in the second case

FIGURE 8.3   EFFECTS OF LEVERAGE

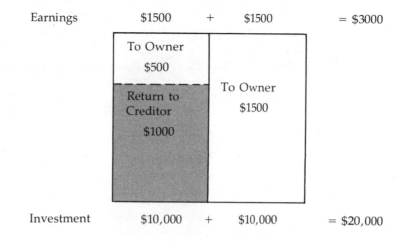

the owner could suffer a decrease in the total return from the investment to $2500 and still have the same return on her own equity as the all-equity investor had. The owner would be compensated $1500 ($1250 + $250 after paying the creditor). This is 15% of the $10,000 equity.

The Risk of Leverage

Along with its obvious ability to increase investor's returns, leverage carries with it a major risk. The same magnification of returns which occurs when returns are high also increases losses when returns are less than they should be. Let us return to our two hypothetical investors. Presume returns, instead of being $3000, now fall by 50% to $1500. The first investor in this case earns 7.5% on his $20,000 equity:

$$\text{Yield} = \frac{\$1500}{\$20,000} = 7.5\%$$

This represents a 50% decrease from his original 15% return on investment. The percentage decrease in investment earnings is the same as the percentage decrease in investment return.

The second investor is not in such a good position, however. She must always pay her creditor $1000. Thus, when total return drops to $1500, this investor has only $500 left for herself. This means her return on investment falls to only 5%:

$$\text{Yield} = \frac{\$500}{\$10,000} = 5\%$$

This decrease from 20% return to 5% return represents a 75% decrease in return when investment earnings only decrease by 50%. The more leverage employed, then the higher is this risk.

Thus, we have seen that leverage may have a benefit for the investor who uses it, but it also carries some risk. Many major buildings and projects in our large urban areas are financed with complex layers of debt. In the past this has caused the demise of the ownership interests in many of those projects. Indeed, in the middle 1970s, many of the nation's large real estate investment trusts (REIT's) found themselves in a good deal of trouble because of the high risks associated with leverage and the difficult economic times.

CHAPTER EIGHT SUMMARY

In this chapter we have discussed the analysis of real estate investments. Our analyses have taken into account a number of factors such as financing, depreciation, and income taxes which were not included in income appraisal. The chapter began with a detailed discussion of the process of investing and the factors, especially risk, which must be dealt with in any analysis of an investment. We concluded with a discussion of the role of leverage.

In the middle of the chapter the analytical framework of investment analysis was discussed. Though we only used one major example, the process can be easily extrapolated to any situation by simply adjusting the formulas to include the relevant information. The analytical process is summarized here.

1. Calculate periodic cash flows

   A. First calculate taxable income

   B. Calculate the tax liability

   C. Derive periodic net cash benefits

2. Calculate residual cash flow

   A. First find the adjusted basis of the property

   B. Derive the capital gain (loss)

   C. Compute all applicable taxes

   D. Derive the net cash flow

3. Find the present value of the periodic and residual cash benefits using a discount rate appropriate for the risk assumed. Compare this value to the equity required for the investment to find net present value.

It should be noted here that while risk has been accounted for in the discount rate, the investor is also expected to consider each cash benefit as an expected value with a possible variation (standard deviation). It may be difficult to deal with these variations directly. However, the investor can use sensitivity analysis to check the risk inherent in the project. **Sensitivity analysis** refers to the process of varying certain critical assumptions about the investment returns to see if they have an effect on the ultimate decision. For instance, for the Panther Arms project, we could have asked what would happen if the final sale price were only $150,000 instead of $195,000. We could have asked what would the decision have been if expenses were to rise by 10% during the last three years of the holding period. Sensitivity analysis of the residual value would be called for if the market for real property would be expected to change during the holding period. Sensitivity analysis could also be used on the income expectation for the investment. Subjective risk assessments can be objectively treated in this manner.

To aid the reader in understanding and applying investment analysis, there are a number of exercises included at the end of the chapter. There is another fully solved investment problem in the appendix following the end-of-chapter exercises. The techniques used in this chapter will be applied later in our analysis of creative financing (chapter 17) and home ownership (chapter 20).

KEY TERMS

Business Risk
Debt Service
Financial Risk
Holding Period
    Yield
Leverage
Liquidity

Manageability
Market Risk
Periodic Net Cash
    Flow
Political Risk
Purchasing Power
    Risk
Residual Cash
    Benefits

Return
Safety
Sensitivity
    Analysis
Taxability
Taxable Operating
    Income

QUESTIONS FOR STUDY AND DISCUSSION

1. What are the main attributes of any investment? Discuss each briefly.

2. How does real estate investment fare in terms of these attributes when compared to other investments?

3. How can we estimate the risk inherent in an investment? How can several investments be compared in terms of their riskiness?

4. How can we treat investment risks in analysis? What is the role of sensitivity analysis?

5. Outline the major steps in investment analysis of real estate.

6. What is meant by *leverage*? Why is it important? Discuss the pros and cons of using leverage in real estate investing.

7. Describe the differences between investment analysis and appraisal analysis.

PROBLEMS FOR REVIEW

1. An investor is going to finance an investment in a duplex with a $50,000 twenty-year loan at 9% interest. What are his annual payments? Devise an amortization schedule for the first ten years of this loan and find the unpaid balance at the end of the tenth year. Check your results with the Interest Amortization Table found in Appendix 1 at the end of the text.

2. An investor may purchase a duplex which rents for $450 per side per month. Total operating expenses are expected to be $800 per year and fixed expenses, including the reserve for replacements, are $3000 per year. The reserve for replacements is $600. The property is new and costs $80,000. The investor borrowed $50,000 for twenty years at 9%. The useful life of the building is forty years. Land was $10,000 of the original cost. Depreciation is double-declining balance on the whole building, including components. The investor's tax bracket is 50%. Find the cash flow for each of the first two years.

3. Suppose the investor in problem 2 sold the property at the end of five years for $75,000. Calculate the residual cash proceeds. Assume all the reserve for replacements is unused and has been invested at 5%.

4. Calculate the remaining three periodic cash flows for the property in problem 2 (the rest of the first five years). Evaluate the total cash flows at 10%. Should the investor make this investment? What kinds of sensitivity analysis might be performed before the investor makes a final decision on the investment?

5. Using the data presented for the Panther Arms Apartments, find the net present value of the project if all equity were used to purchase the property. Should the investment be undertaken in this circumstance?

6. Using the data presented in the chapter for the Panther Arms Apartments, perform the sensitivity analysis suggested in the summary.

a. Use $150,000 as the sale price in the fifth year.

b. Increase all operating and fixed expenses by 10% in the third, fourth, and fifth years of the holding period.

c. Decrease revenue by 10% in the first and second years of the holding period.

d. Combine the situations listed in parts B and C. Do any of these four situations change the investor's investment decision?

APPENDIX
TO CHAPTER 8

THE SUPER SUPPER RESTAURANT: A CASE STUDY; WORKSHEETS FOR INVESTMENT ANALYSIS

The Super Supper Restaurant: A Case Study   Mr. Gregory is analyzing a prospective investment in a fast-food restaurant. The project involves a theme-type restaurant which will be developed as a leasehold on an existing site. In a medium-sized city, there is a parcel of land located near the downtown center which would work well for Mr. Gregory's purposes. It is near several other well-known fast-food restaurants. The parcel has an existing restaurant building on it. The building is abandoned and the owner of the land is anxious to have it occupied by an operating business. The existing building is not owned by the landowner. The building is suitable for Mr. Gregory with some modifications. The building is being offered for $70,000 as is and will require $30,000 in modifications and new equipment. Additionally, Mr. Gregory will have to put up $10,000 for working capital. The land lease can be assumed by Mr. Gregory for $600 per month, the current rate. The lease has eleven years to run and is not renewable.

Mr. Gregory has performed an analysis of his expected cash flows, which is shown in Table 8.7. Sales have been estimated to be constant for the first five years, then rising for the last six years. The cash flow estimates are based on an existing project so the returns are fairly certain. The building owner must pay all taxes and insurance, which is one reason the lease is inexpensive. Also notice there are no reserves for replacements because the property will be abandoned in eleven years and repaired only as necessary.

The building investment will be financed with a $75,000 loan for ten years at 9% interest.[1] A loan amortization is shown in Table 8.8. Table 8.9 shows the annual depreciation for the leasehold improvements. Because the lease will expire in eleven years, the investor can depreciate the improvements over the remaining lease term. Straight-line depreciation will be used. A $1000 salvage value has been assumed for the restaurant equipment for depreciation purposes.

---

[1]Normally this loan would be for a longer time but, generally, a lender will not lend money for a building on leased land longer than the period of the lease.

TABLE 8.7   SUPER SUPPER RESTAURANT—CASH FLOWS FOR ELEVEN YEARS

	1	2	3	4	5	6	7	8	9	10	11
Sales	250,000	250,000	250,000	250,000	250,000	300,000	300,000	300,000	300,000	300,000	300,000
Less: Cost of Sales	94,300	94,300	94,300	94,300	94,300	113,200	113,200	113,200	113,200	113,200	113,200
Less: Variable Operating Costs	72,500	72,500	72,500	72,500	72,500	87,000	87,000	87,000	87,000	87,000	87,000
Less: Fixed Operating Costs[a]	28,000	28,000	28,000	28,000	28,000	28,000	28,000	28,000	28,000	28,000	28,000
Operating Income	55,200	55,200	55,200	55,200	55,200	71,800	71,800	71,800	71,800	71,800	71,800
Less: Fixed Expenses:											
Property Tax	3,600	3,600	3,600	3,600	3,600	4,500	4,500	4,500	4,500	4,500	4,500
Insurance	3,200	3,200	3,200	3,200	3,200	4,000	4,000	4,000	4,000	4,000	4,000
Land Rent	7,200	7,200	7,200	7,200	7,200	7,200	7,200	7,200	7,200	7,200	7,200
NOI = TOI[b]	41,200	41,200	41,200	41,200	41,200	56,100	56,100	56,100	56,100	56,100	56,100
Less: Depreciation (Table 8.9)	9,000	9,000	9,000	9,000	9,000	9,000	9,000	9,000	9,000	9,000	9,000
Less: Interest (Table 8.8)	6,750	6,305	5,820	5,295	4,720	4,090	3,410	2,665	1,850	965	0
Income Before Tax	25,450	25,895	26,380	26,905	27,480	43,010	43,690	44,435	45,250	46,135	47,100
Tax at 30%	7,635	7,770	7,915	8,070	8,245	12,905	13,105	13,330	13,575	13,840	14,130
NOI	41,200	41,200	41,200	41,200	41,200	56,100	56,100	56,100	56,100	56,100	56,100
Less: Income taxes	7,635	7,770	7,915	8,070	8,245	12,905	13,105	13,330	13,575	13,840	14,130
Less: Debt Service (Table 8.8)	11,685	11,685	11,685	11,685	11,685	11,685	11,685	11,685	11,685	11,685	0
Net Cash Flow	21,880	21,745	21,600	21,445	21,270	31,510	31,310	31,085	30,840	30,575	41,970

[a]Includes a management fee
[b]NOI = TOI because there are no reserves for replacement

TABLE 8.8   SUPER SUPPER RESTAURANT—LOAN AMORTIZATION

Annual Payment = $75,000 × $AMF_{10,9\%}$
= $75,000 × 0.1558 = **$11,685 per year**

Year	Beginning Balance	Interest at 9%	Principal Reduction	Payment	Ending Balance
1	$75,000[a]	$6,750	$4,935	$11,685	$70,065
2	$70,065	$6,305	$5,380	$11,685	$64,685
3	$64,685	$5,820	$5,865	$11,685	$58,820
4	$58,820	$5,295	$6,390	$11,685	$52,430
5	$52,430	$4,720	$6,965	$11,685	$45,465
6	$45,465	$4,090	$7,595	$11,685	$37,870
7	$37,870	$3,410	$8,275	$11,685	$29,595
8	$29,595	$2,665	$9,020	$11,685	$20,575
9	$20,575	$1,850	$9,835	$11,685	$10,740
10	$10,740	$ 965[b]	$10,740[b]	$11,685[b]	$ 0
		$41,870[b]	$75,000[b]	$116,850[b]	

[a]Figures rounded to nearest $5
[b]These numbers do not add up exactly due to rounding errors in the interest calculations

TABLE 8.9   SUPER SUPPER RESTAURANT—DEPRECIATION

Building Value of $70,000 with an 11-year life;
Using Straight-Line Depreciation:
$70,000/11 = $6,364 per year

Additional Improvements with 11-year lives;
Using Straight-Line Depreciation:

Value	$30,000
Less: Salvage Value for depreciation purposes	$ 1,000
Depreciable Value	$29,000

$29,000/11 = $2,636 per year

Total Depreciation per year:
$6,364 + $2,636 = $9,000

The cash flows themselves are capitalized at a 20% rate of return to allow for the risk inherent in the project and the owner's required return. It has been assumed that the equipment can be sold for $5000 at the end of the project's life and that the working capital will be returned.

The residual calculation is shown in Table 8.10. The cash flow summary at present value appears in Table 8.11.

As you can see, this project is extremely lucrative. The investor is actually going to be earning about a 65% return on his investment! This is the internal rate of return of the project.

This example was chosen for inclusion at this point for a number of reasons. First, it is a real example and serves to show just how spectacular returns on even small real estate investments can be. As a matter of fact, the investor in this example actually decided not to pursue this investment because another property was found which provided even

TABLE 8.10   SUPER SUPPER RESTAURANT—RESIDUAL CASH FLOW

Cash in Residual at end of 11th year:		
Return of Working Capital		$10,000
Salvage of Equipment	$5,000	5,000
Less: Book Value	1,000	
Gain—Section 1245	$4,000	
Tax on Section 1245 Gain		
(treated as ordinary income)		
30% × $4,000		(1,200)
		$13,800

TABLE 8.11   SUPER SUPPER RESTAURANT—PRESENT VALUE OF FLOWS

Year	Cash Flows		PVF @ 20%	Present Value
0	($35,000)	Equity[a]	1.000	($35,000)
1	$21,880		0.833	$18,225
2	$21,745		0.694	$15,090
3	$21,600		0.579	$12,505
4	$21,445		0.482	$10,335
5	$21,270		0.402	$ 8,550
6	$31,510		0.335	$10,555
7	$31,310		0.279	$ 8,735
8	$31,085		0.233	$ 6,930
9	$30,840		0.194	$ 5,980
10	$30,575		0.162	$ 4,955
11	$41,970		0.135	$ 5,665
11	$13,800	Residual	0.135	$ 1,865
			Net Present Value =	$74,390

[a]Includes $25,000 downpayment + $10,000 working capital

higher returns. In this example, there is no significant residual value for the property. It is basically supporting itself from periodic cash flow alone. For certain investors, this type of property could provide a sizable income flow and a comfortable living as well as the additional cash to expand investment holdings. The expenses have a management fee deducted from them, so the return is all on investment. Also, it is interesting to note that there is no tax shelter in this investment. With a 65% return, who needs a tax shelter! The important point here is that even though taxes are being paid on this cash flow, the return is spectacular. This is a good, sound investment in its own right which does not have to rely on the tax laws to make it so, and may be very important in the future as more and more "loopholes" are closed.

This project serves as a good contrast to the apartment project we analyzed in the body of the chapter. One final caveat is worth noting before we finish. Not all real estate investments are this good. Many are offered which only return 5% to 6%. In real estate the investor has many choices. To make these choices intelligently requires rational analysis such as we have illustrated in this chapter. Sound judgment of risks and variations from expected revenue and expense estimates is also a major requirement of analysis. Finally, creativity and a good deal of "footwork" is required to find good investment opportunities.

Worksheets for Investment Analysis   As an aid for analyzing investment projects, several worksheet formats have been included in this appendix. Copies of these may be made and used either for the reader's personal investment analyses or to complete the exercises included in this and later chapters.

The worksheets included here are:

1. Income Worksheet for the determination of NOI and TOI;

2. Periodic Cash Flow Worksheet for the determination of periodic tax liability and periodic cash flow;

3. Residual Cash Flow Worksheet for the determination of the residual tax calculation and residual cash flow; and

4. Net Present Value Worksheet for the determination of the net present value of the investment project.

INCOME WORKSHEET

Gross Income	$_____
Less: Vacancy and Collection Loss	(_____)
Effective Gross Income	$_____

INCOME WORKSHEET (CONTINUED)

Less Operating Expenses:

Management Fee $_____

_____   _____

_____   _____

_____   _____

_____   _____

_____   _____

_____   _____

_____   _____

        Total $_____   (_____)

Less: Fixed Expenses:

    Real Estate Taxes $_____

    Insurance   _____

    Reserve for Replacement   _____

        Total $_____   (_____)

Net Operating Income (NOI) $_____

Add: Reserve for Replacement   _____

Taxable Operating Income (TOI) $_____

PERIODIC CASH FLOW WORKSHEET

	Year 1	Year 2	Year 3	Year 4	Year 5
Net Operating Income (NOI)	$_____	$_____	$_____	$_____	$_____
Less: Annual Debt Payment	(_____)	(_____)	(_____)	(_____)	(_____)
Pretax Cash Flow	$_____	$_____	$_____	$_____	$_____
Less: Tax or Plus: Savings*	_____	_____	_____	_____	_____
Net Periodic Cash Flow	$_____	$_____	$_____	$_____	$_____

*Calculation of Tax (Savings) follows

	Year 1	Year 2	Year 3	Year 4	Year 5
Taxable Operating Income (TOI)	$_____	$_____	$_____	$_____	$_____
Less: Interest on Debt	(_____)	(_____)	(_____)	(_____)	(_____)

PERIODIC CASH FLOW WORKSHEET (CONTINUED)

	Year 1	Year 2	Year 3	Year 4	Year 5
Less: Annual Depreciation	(_____)	(_____)	(_____)	(_____)	(_____)
Taxable Income or (Shelter)	$_____	$_____	$_____	$_____	$_____
× Marginal Tax Rate (%)	× ___%	× ___%	× ___%	× ___%	× ___%
Tax Liability or (Savings)	$_____	$_____	$_____	$_____	$_____

RESIDUAL CASH FLOW WORKSHEET

Sale Price	$_____
Less: Tax or Plus: Savings*	_____
Less: Mortgage Balance	(_____)
Net Cash from Property	$_____
Plus: Unused Reserve for Replacements	_____
Net Cash Residual	$_____

*Calculation of tax follows:

Original Cost of Property	$_____
Less: Accumulated Depreciation	(_____)
Adjusted Basis of Property	$_____

Sale Price	$_____
Less: Adjusted Basis of Property	(_____)
Taxable Gain	$_____
Less: Amount to be Recaptured	(_____)
Capital Gain (Section 1231)	$_____

Capital Gain	$_____	$_____	Recapture Amount
× Preferred Rate	× ___%	× ___%	× Marginal Rate
Tax or (Savings)	$_____ +	$_____	= $_____

NET PRESENT VALUE WORKSHEET

Year	Cash Flow	$PVF_{n,i}$	Present Value
	Downpayment and Working Capital		
0	($_____)	1.0000	($_____)
	Periodic Cash Flows		
1	$_____	.____	$_____
2	$_____	.____	$_____
3	$_____	.____	$_____
4	$_____	.____	$_____
5	$_____	.____	$_____
6	$_____	.____	$_____
7	$_____	.____	$_____
8	$_____	.____	$_____
9	$_____	.____	$_____
10	$_____	.____	$_____
11	$_____	.____	$_____
12	$_____	.____	$_____
13	$_____	.____	$_____
14	$_____	.____	$_____
15	$_____	.____	$_____
	Residual Cash Flow		
____	$_____	.____	$_____

Net Present Value = $_____

9

CAPITAL ASSET PRICING AND RISK ANALYSIS

ON MANY occasions in the past few chapters we have alluded to the nature of risk and its relationship to value. In chapters 3 and 4 a number of references were made to the nature of the relationship between risk and return. In chapter 8 we looked at the types of risks affecting investments without really operationalizing the concept. The purpose of this chapter will be to present a thorough discussion of a number of important ideas relating to risk, the risk–return relationship, and some of the current thinking concerning the practical treatment of risk in value analysis. The discussion will involve four areas of modern financial theory:

1. The nature of risk;
2. Market-based risk–return relationships;
3. Capital asset pricing; and
4. Portfolio considerations in investment decisions.

The discussion on which we are about to embark may be difficult for some of you not already versed in some of these ideas. For that reason, the presentation will be at a very basic level. This chapter cannot be taken as a substitute for a thorough knowledge of these topics. Rather, it is an introductory summary which is presented to provide some background in risk analysis and also to help tie together financial and real estate investment decision-making.

The Nature of Risk

Risk as Variability

The concept of risk is difficult to describe. For this discussion we need to involve the ideas of probability and expected value. Historically, the return from an investment is a unique, discrete amount. However, when estimating yields in the future we do not know exactly what benefits will be received. Generally, the most likely result is used as the estimate. This "most likely" estimate can be obtained more precisely by using expected values.

For every *state of nature* (condition of the world, the economy, etc.) there is a corresponding benefit (*outcome*) from an investment. To use a simple example, assume the economy can be in one of three states next year: boom, normality, or recession. The probability of each of these events and the resulting outcome from a hypothetical investment under each state of nature are shown in Table 9.1.

The determination of the expected outcome in this situation is made by multiplying each outcome (return) by its corresponding probability

TABLE 9.1 HYPOTHETICAL INVESTMENT UNDER THREE STATES OF NATURE

State of Nature	Probability	Investment Return
Boom	0.30	$2000
Normality	0.40	$1000
Recession	0.30	$ 0
	1.00	

of occurrence. The sum of all these products is called the **expected value,** EV. Thus,

$$EV = O_1 (P_1) + O_2 (P_2) + O_3 (P_3)$$

where

O is the outcome and
P is the corresponding probability

More generally,

$$EV = \sum_{i=1}^{n} O_i (P_i)$$

We can see this result conveniently in Table 9.2.

The expected return estimated in the example is $1000. Notice, however, that the outcome actually could have been $2000, $1000, or $0. This is a rather wide range of outcomes. Further, one might not be very

TABLE 9.2 EXPECTED VALUE OF THE HYPOTHETICAL INVESTMENT

State of Nature	Probability	Outcome	$O_i (P_i)$
Boom	0.30	$2000	$ 600
Normality	0.40	$1000	$ 400
Recession	0.30	$ 0	$ 0
	1.00		$1000 = EV

happy with the $0 result if it actually occurred. Thus, we now introduce the concept of risk. Risk is defined as the *variability* in the potential outcome of an investment. It also can be called *dispersion*. Look at a second investment alternative shown in Table 9.3. Compare it to the first investment and make an intuitive judgment: which one do you prefer?

Both investments have the same expected return, yet the first investment is riskier. You might receive a higher return with the first investment, but it is equally likely you would receive less than with the second investment.

To measure the degree of risk we may use the concept of **standard deviation. Variance,** the square of the standard deviation, may alternatively be used as a measure of risk. This measures the amount of variability. The standard deviation, S, is found by:

1. Comparing each outcome to the expected value;
2. Squaring this difference;
3. Multiplying the difference by the probability;
4. Summing the products of (3) above; and
5. Taking the square root of (4) above.

Table 9.4 shows these calculations for the two investments shown in Tables 9.1 and 9.3.

Table 9.4 demonstrates that our intuitive impression of the riskiness of the two investments was correct. Investment alternative two is much less risky than the first investment.

Total Risk

The approach we have taken to risk thus far deals with the **total risk** of the investment. All of the risks described in chapter 8, taken together, cause the variability that may be measured by the standard deviation (or variance). This is not the only way to look at risk, however. As we shall see, total risk may be subdivided mathematically to explain investment behavior more effectively.

TABLE 9.3   EXPECTED VALUE OF A SECOND HYPOTHETICAL INVESTMENT

State of Nature	Probability	Outcome	$O_i\,(P_i)$
Boom	0.30	$1500	$ 450
Normality	0.40	$1000	$ 400
Recession	0.30	$ 500	$ 150
	1.00		$1000 $= EV$

TABLE 9.4   STANDARD DEVIATION CALCULATIONS

Investment One

Outcome	EV	O − EV	(O − EV)²	Probability	(O−EV)²(P)
$2000	$1000	+$1000	$1,000,000	0.30	$300,000
$1000	$1000	$ 0	$ 0	0.40	$ 0
$ 0	$1000	−$1000	$1,000,000	0.30	$300,000
				1.00	$600,000

$$S = \sqrt{\$600,000} = \$775$$

Investment Two

Outcome	EV	O − EV	(O − EV)²	Probability	(O−EV)²(P)
$1500	$1000	+$500	$250,000	0.30	$ 75,000
$1000	$1000	$ 0	$ 0	0.40	$ 0
$ 500	$1000	−$500	$250,000	0.30	$ 75,000
				1.00	$150,000

$$S = \sqrt{\$150,000} = \$387$$

Capital Asset Pricing

We have seen previously that the values of most investment assets are determined by the market. We have also seen that the value of a risky asset is affected by the degree of risk associated with it. In this section we will examine the relationship between the return of an individual risky asset and the return on the market for that asset. We will show how this relationship can lead to a method for determining the discount rate which may be used to find the appropriate value for the asset. Before proceeding to that discussion, however, it is necessary to digress briefly in order to explain the nature of a linear relationship.

Linear Relationships

Often it is useful in analytical situations to understand the relationship between two variables when one is believed to affect the other. For instance, it may be reasonably hypothesized that, as activity in the economy as a whole fluctuates, there will be resulting fluctuations in various segments of the economy. In such a case, the appropriate measure of economic activity—whether it be Gross National Product (GNP), the Index of Industrial Production, or whatever—is called an **independent variable**. This means that it is thought to be a causal agent in some type of relationship involving another variable. The measure of the other activity thought to be influenced by the independent variable would be designated as the **dependent variable**.

One way to show these relationships is by using a two-dimensional graph. Figure 9.1 shows such a relationship. The horizontal (or x) axis of the graph measures values of the independent variable. The vertical (or y) axis measures values of the dependent variable. Table 9.5 shows the actual values of the three variables, which will be used in the two following examples.

The plotted points in Figure 9.1 illustrate the *actual* values of the two variables, GNP and Housing Starts, for the years 1967 through 1976.

The equation which may be derived to describe a linear relationship between two variables (such as the ones in Figure 9.1) is called a **linear regression equation**.

In Figure 9.1 the equation

$$y' = 1.67 - 0.000045\,x$$

is the equation of the straight line in the graph. The line is determined by a mathematical technique called "least squares." This process determines which linear equation will estimate the relationship between the two variables with the least degree of error. By using this **regression equation**, a value for x may be substituted into the equation to generate an *estimated* value for the dependent variable. This estimated value is y'.

(In general, any linear relationship of two variables may be expressed as $y = a + bx$. The a is the value for y when x is zero (called the *y-intercept*). The b shows the rate of change in the y variable for a one-unit change in the x variable (called the *slope*). However, in a regression

TABLE 9.5   ACTUAL VALUES FOR THREE VARIABLES

Year	GNP (billions)	Housing Starts (millions)	Contract Construction (billions)
1967	$ 796	1.292	not available
1968	$ 868	1.508	not available
1969	$ 935	1.467	not available
1970	$ 982	1.434	$ 94.9
1971	$1063	2.052	$110.0
1972	$1171	2.357	$124.1
1973	$1307	2.045	$137.9
1974	$1413	1.338	$138.5
1975	$1528	1.160	$132.0
1976	$1706	1.538	$144.8

Compiled from *Statistical Abstract of the U.S.*, 1978.

equation, y' is generally used rather than y in order to differentiate the estimated value from the actual value. Alternatively, the regression equation could be expressed as $y = a + bx + e$, where e indicates the error involved (the difference between y' and y).)

According to the equation, relating housing starts and GNP, a GNP of $1700 billion should result in about 1.6 million housing starts. To the extent that each plotted point is not on the line, the value estimated for the y variable by the equation is in error. The particular straight line shown in Figure 9.1 is the best fitting line for the points shown, but as you can see there is a great deal of error.

Any two variables can be related through regression but these relationships do not necessarily have meaning. We can see how closely the two variables are related by calculating a statistic called R^2. This statistic tells how much, what percent, of the *total variation* in the dependent variable is explained by the independent variable. To the extent that the

FIGURE 9.1   GNP AND HOUSING STARTS

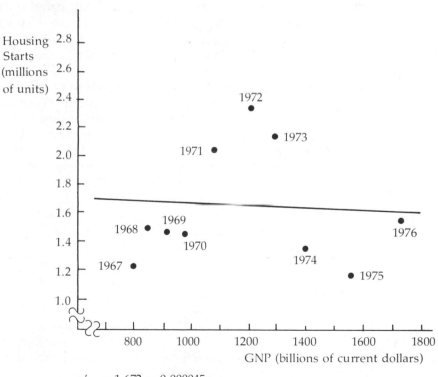

$$y' = 1.672 - 0.000045x$$
$$R^2 = 0.001$$
$$R = 0.034$$

regression equation can estimate a value for the dependent variable, some portion of the dependent variable's total variation can be "predicted" by the equation. In Figure 9.1 only 0.1% of the variation in housing starts is explained by GNP—which is not very much.

In addition to R^2, we can use the statistic **R** (the square root of R^2) to explain how well the two variables are related. When R equals 1, the two variables are said to be perfectly related (correlated). **Correlation** means they move together perfectly. If the value of the independent variable increases, then the value of the dependent variable will also increase, and the exact increase can be predicted using the linear relationship. If R equals -1, the two variables are also perfectly correlated, but they move in opposite directions. If the independent variable's value increases, the dependent variable's value will decrease to the exact amount predicted by the equation. If R equals 0, there is no relationship between the variables. In this case, knowing the value of the independent variable will in no way help you estimate the value for the dependent variable. That is nearly the case in Figure 9.1.

It should be stated that the existence of correlation between two variables does not necessarily indicate a causal relationship between these variables. Frequently, two variables are correlated because they are each, individually, correlated with some other variable or variables. If causation is lacking, the relationship *may not* be a valuable predictive tool regardless of the degree of correlation. Furthermore, a low correlation does not imply the variables are not related, merely that they are not linearly related. A nonlinear relationship could exist.

In Figure 9.2, we see a relationship contrasting to the one shown in Figure 9.1. This graph shows the relationship between GNP and contract construction. Notice how the regression line is much closer to all the plotted points. R^2 for this functional relationship is 0.773. Thus, this regression equation explains 77% of the total variation in the dependent variable. The correlation coefficient, R, is much closer to one than in the first example. In this case, an analyst might have a fair degree of confidence that this regression equation will be able to help predict the rate of contract construction, given the level of GNP.

The Beta Model

Because the value of most risky assets is a function of the market, so, too, is the return on a risky asset investment a function of market activity. In fact, financial theory now specifies, to the satisfaction of most, that the return on any risky investment is a linear function of the return on the market as a whole. The specific function is equation [9.1]

$$R_i' = a + bR_m \qquad\qquad [9.1]$$

FIGURE 9.2   GNP AND CONTRACT CONSTRUCTION

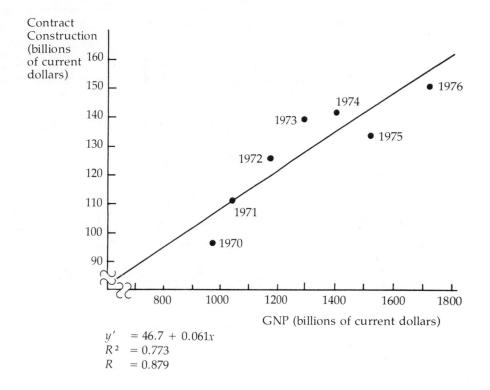

$$y' = 46.7 + 0.061x$$
$$R^2 = 0.773$$
$$R = 0.879$$

where

R_i' = total return for asset i

R_m = total average return for the investment market

a = return on asset i when $R_m = 0$

b = slope of regression line, called *beta*

The line described by equation [9.1] is called the **characteristic line** for an investment. For any given return of the market, R_m, a return of R_i, can be estimated for an asset i. The foregoing returns are calculated in the same manner as the holding period yields described in chapter 8. Table 9.6 shows the returns which were used to derive the characteristic line illustrated in Figure 9.3. In the table the returns shown are quarterly returns.

The relationship between this asset and the market is fairly close. The value of R^2 is 0.81 which says that 81% of the total variation in the in-

TABLE 9.6   RETURNS FOR A STOCK AND
THE MARKET

Period	Market Return	Stock Return
1	0.02	0.02
2	0.03	0.02
3	0.03	0.03
4	0.04	0.04
5	0.04	0.05
6	0.05	0.05

$$R_i' = -0.006 + 1.182 \, R_m$$

$$R^2 = 0.809$$

$$R = 0.900$$

FIGURE 9.3   CHARACTERISTIC LINE FOR A STOCK

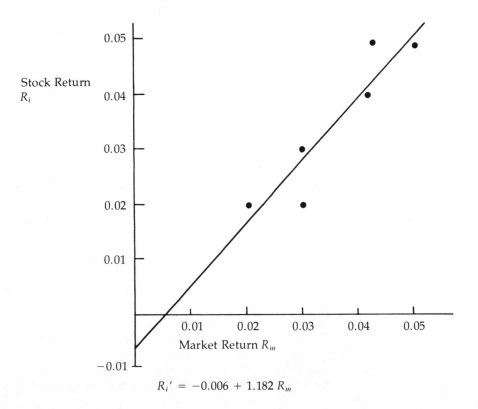

$$R_i' = -0.006 + 1.182 \, R_m$$

vestment's return is explainable by the action of the market. This part of the total variation in the return of the asset has been called **systematic risk**. The 19% of the variation that is not explained by the market is called **nonsystematic risk.** As we shall see later, some or all of nonsystematic risk may be removed by combining investments with different functional relationships to each other. This process is called **diversification.**

The beta in the regression equation shown in Figure 9.3 shows the manner in which this investment's return moves relative to the market movements. The equation tells us that if the market return is 4%, then the return on the investment should be 4.1%. If the market return rises to 5%, the investment's return would be estimated to rise to 5.3%. You can see that when the market return goes up 1% the investment return goes up 1.18%. This relationship between investment and market is expressed by the beta in the equation.

The basic idea which is important in the foregoing discussion is that risk may be partitioned into two segments—risk which comes from the market and risk which relates to nonmarket forces. The latter portion of the risk of an asset is subject to the power of diversification, leaving the investor in a position to simply "cope" with the action of the market. Armed with this knowledge, the investor's strategy becomes one of diversifying and buying assets with "good" betas. When the market is rising, a group of diversified assets with a combined beta of more than one will give the investor a better return than is achieved by the market as a whole. When the market's return is falling, the beta should be less than one so that the assets' returns will fall to a lesser extent than the market's return.

Implications for Real Estate   The technique described for relating the returns of individual assets to the market seems straightforward enough. In fact, the practical implications as the theory now stands are dramatic. However, one should not rush out and try to locate apartment buildings with betas of 1.5, for example, because they will be difficult to find. A number of practical problems exist which make this theory difficult to apply.

The main development of the beta model has been done using common stocks for which there is an active national market. This makes the determination of R_m relatively easy. Similarly, R_i can be determined with some alacrity. Even so, we find problems. Many researchers have found that beta is not stable over time. Beta also depends on the type of data used, whether they be quarterly, weekly, or monthly, for instance, and the number of periods used in the calculations.

A second problem arises specifically with real estate. What should the relevant market return be? Should it be a local market return or an average return from across the country? Further complicating the issue is the fact that income real estate is essentially a private phenomenon and data are extremely hard to develop.

One final problem causes trouble with the beta model. As we saw in Figure 9.1, not all regressions, despite the existence of an equation (and, hence, a beta), have any real meaning. When R is near zero the equation will not have a great deal of predictive validity. The existence of a numerical value for beta does not guarantee its usefulness for a given asset.

Overall, the beta model is compelling in its simplicity and implications for investment strategy, but there are problems. Many investment services now supply beta estimates for common stocks. However, in truth we are just not far enough along in the development of this model to say that the technique is ready for successful, general use—and for real estate, the problems are much greater than for common stock.

The astute reader may be tempted to ask a question at this point. If beta does not work very well as an operational technique for real estate, why has it been presented? The answer to this question lies in three areas. First, the beta model presents the state of the art theoretically in the development of a generalized model of investment behavior. Real estate investors are no different from stock or bond investors in terms of their overall desire to make money. So we must presume this theory should be developed to help understand real estate, too. Second, by looking at this theory in relation to real estate, we can help tie the field more closely to the field of finance, which is, in many ways, the parent discipline to real estate. Third, the idea that risk may be partitioned is important. We do know that the ideas of diversification implied by the beta model and the portfolio theory to be discussed later in this chapter do have real merit. Thus, there is some inherent value in our model.

Capital Asset Pricing Model

We may now proceed from the beta model to a more general understanding of the relationship between risk and return in the capital markets. We will start from the premise that *only systematic risk has any real meaning to the investor* because nonsystematic risk may be handled through diversification. It is then possible to let beta serve as a substitute measure of systematic risk.[1] If this is done we may say that the return on a risky asset can be measured in terms of two considerations. First, as we stated earlier, underlying the return on every investment is compensation for time. This is generally measured as the return on short-term government securities which are presumed to have no risk. Second, there is a premium attached for the extra risk taken with a risky investment. This premium is measured as the difference between over-

---

[1]Mathematically, systematic risk equals beta squared times the variance of the market returns.

all market return, R_m, and the risk-free return called R_o.[2] Using the linear model again we can express return on an individual asset as:

$$R_i' = R_o + b\,(R_m - R_o) \tag{9.2}$$

Equation [9.2] says that the return on an individual security should be the risk-free return plus beta times the compensation for extra risk. The implications of this idea are very important. In effect, equation [9.2] allows one to create a custom-made rate of return for the valuation of any risky asset. This permits the direct calculation of the appropriate rates of return for use in income appraisal and investment analysis. This model substitutes directly for the summation method described in chapter 3. Rather than trying to estimate the market premiums individually as described in the summation approach, we may use equation [9.2] instead. R_o in the equation is a constant for any given period, as is the quantity $(R_m - R_o)$. These constants can be estimated from historical data, so that all that remains to be found is beta. Of course, the use of this equation, often called the **capital asset pricing model** or CAPM, is limited by the problems with beta described earlier. However, at this point we are closer to operationalizing the summation method than ever before.

The mathematical procedures for calculating beta and estimating R_i using the CAPM are relatively simple. Although we cannot go through all the underlying mathematics here, we can show the calculations by example. The procedures are not difficult, but the calculations are numerous. For that reason, the use of a programmable calculator which can determine covariance and correlation is extremely helpful.

Example 9.1

Table 9.7 presents historical data which may be used to estimate R_i using equation [9.2]. These data are for a hypothetical real estate market. The method, however, would be the same if real data were used. We will assume an investor is interested in buying an apartment building with twelve units in a large metropolitan area. The investor will estimate the beta for this investment based on historical data from similar properties. The general method of calculation is outlined here.

1. Estimate the risk-free return, R_o, for each of the periods in which market returns and similar property returns are available. Then determine the expected value of these returns.

---

[2]This premium is determined in the market, is stable at any one point in time, and can be derived theoretically. This risk premium can be seen to be the slope in the security market line which follows in a later section.

2. Calculate the expected value of the market returns for the periods being considered. Also calculate the variance of the market returns.

3. Calculate the covariance of the returns from the market and the returns from similar properties. **Covariance** is found by:

(a) *For each period multiply* the following two quantities:

$(R_m$ − expected value of $R_m)$
$(R_i$ − expected value of $R_i)$

(b) Sum these products for all the periods involved.

(c) Divide by the number of periods.

4. Calculate beta. Beta is the covariance from (3) above divided by the variance of the market returns, from (2) above.

5. The estimated value, R_i' can be calculated using the CAPM equation. R_o in the equation is the expected value of R_o found in (1); R_m will be the expected value of R_m found in (2); and beta will be the value determined in (4).

The preceding calculations described are shown in Tables 9.7 and 9.8. From Table 9.7 we see that the expected risk-free return is 6.3% and the expected market return is 9.5%. This means the expected premium, R_m − R_o, is 3.2%. Beta is calculated in Table 9.8 and equals 1.12.

Using the variables from the tables and the CAPM equation, we find that R_i' equals 9.9%, or approximately 10%.

$$R_i' = 0.063 + 1.12\,(0.095 - 0.063)$$
$$= 0.063 + 0.036 = 0.099$$

Using this relationship, we have found that this investor should be compensated at about 10% for the prospective investment, given the risk that he or she will be assuming and the average market return level.

In spite of what may appear to be a dazzling and complex array of numbers in the two following tables, a closer look reveals that it is remarkably easy to derive a required rate of return for investment evaluation using the capital asset pricing model. This is true provided the data are available. For real estate the data problem is the real drawback to the use of this technique. Even so, it is probably safe to say that as this model (and others similar to it conceptually) becomes more widespread, astute real estate investors will begin accumulating the data required for their use. These investors may well develop an edge in the market by scrutinizing their investments more carefully on the basis of the appropriate risk-adjusted yields.

TABLE 9.7   DATA FOR CAPM EXAMPLE

Year	Risk-free Return R_o	Real Estate Market Return R_m	$(R_m - E(R_m))^2$	Apartment Building Returns R_i
1968	0.05	0.07	$(-0.025)^2$	0.05
1969	0.07	0.09	$(-0.005)^2$	0.08
1970	0.07	0.12	$(0.025)^2$	0.11
1971	0.05	0.13	$(0.035)^2$	0.16
1972	0.05	0.10	$(0.005)^2$	0.10
1973	0.07	0.06	$(-0.035)^2$	0.08
1974	0.08	0.07	$(-0.025)^2$	0.08
1975	0.07	0.09	$(-0.005)^2$	0.10
1976	0.06	0.10	$(0.005)^2$	0.10
1977	0.06	0.12	$(0.025)^2$	0.13
Totals	0.63	0.95	0.00505	0.99

Expected Value of $R_o = 0.63/10 = 6.3\% = E(R_o)$

Expected Value of $R_m = 0.95/10 = 9.5\% = E(R_m)$

Variance[a] of $R_m = 0.00505/10 = 0.000505$

Expected value of $R_i = 0.99/10 = 9.9\% = E(R_i)$

Variance[a] of $R_i = 0.000829$ (calculation is similar to that of finding the market variance)

---

[a]The earlier method of calculating variance was (Return $- EV)^2$ (probability) for each state of nature, summed. When there are periods rather than states of nature, we may simply divide $(R - EV)^2$, summed for all periods, by the number of periods.

Investment Market Considerations

Security Market Line

Given the basic models of the foregoing individual investment behavior, one additional step may be taken. We will now describe the behavior of markets for these individual assets. This is illustrated in Figure 9.4 as the **security market line.** It can be stated that this line describes the return for every level of risk in the market. Further, when the market is in equilibrium every asset's real return should lie on this line.

The security market line is derived by considering risk and return to be the relevant variables. Risk is considered to be systematic risk only and beta is used as a proxy for this measure. The asset with no risk, the risk-free asset, should have a return equal to R_o. The market itself has a beta of 1, by definition, and a return of R_m. When these two points

TABLE 9.8   CALCULATION OF BETA AND R^2

Year	$R_i - E(R_i)^a$	$R_m - E(R_m)^a$	$(R_i - E(R_i))(R_m - E(R_m))$
1968	−0.049	−0.025	0.001225
1969	−0.019	−0.005	0.000095
1970	0.011	0.025	0.000275
1971	0.061	0.035	0.002135
1972	0.001	0.005	0.000005
1973	−0.019	−0.035	0.000665
1974	−0.019	−0.025	0.000475
1975	0.001	−0.005	−0.000005
1976	0.001	0.005	0.000005
1977	0.031	0.025	0.000775
			0.005650

Covariance = 0.00565/10 = 0.000565

Beta = Covariance/market variance^a = 0.000565/0.000505 = 1.12

R^2 may be calculated using the following relationship:

beta^2 (market variance)/(asset variance)^a =
1.12(1.12)(0.000505)/(0.000829) = 0.764

---

^{a}Values of R_i, $E(R_i)$, R_m, $E(R_m)$, variance of market, and asset variance are from Table 9.7.

FIGURE 9.4   SECURITY MARKET LINE

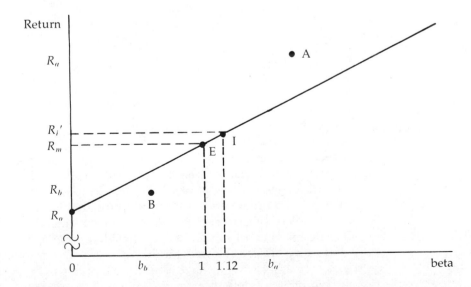

are plotted as in Figure 9.4, the resulting linear relationship will have a slope of $(R_m - R_o)$. One should be able to describe the relationship of any asset's return to its risk by the linear relationship depicted in the figure when the market is in equilibrium.

From the data presented in Table 9.7, we calculated the beta for a hypothetical apartment building. Its beta was 1.12 and its expected return from equation [9.2] was 9.9%. If the market is in equilibrium, this asset's risk–return relationship should lie on the security market line. That relationship is illustrated in Figure 9.4 as Point I. Two other points, A and B, are also illustrated. Both of these points are lying off the line. These points represent assets which are in disequilibrium. Point A which lies above the security market line represents an asset which is earning a higher return than it is expected to. This means that it is not selling for a high enough price in the market and will eventually have to rise in price until its return falls to the equilibrium level. Point B, on the other hand, represents an asset which is earning less than it should for the risk involved. That means B is overpriced and should be expected to fall in price until its return is in equilibrium. It should be stated that our example asset in reality may or may not lie on the security market line, depending upon its actual rate of return. Point I represents the fact that the *estimated* return must lie on the line based on its beta. Whether the asset's *actual* return is greater than or less than 9.9% will determine if the asset is in equilibrium or if it is underpriced or overpriced. From Table 9.7 the expected return of similar assets is 9.9% based on the historical data presented. If the asset under consideration is priced similar to the comparable properties (as it should be), then we would find that indeed the actual risk– return relationship of that asset falls on the security market line.

Implications for Real Estate

The ideas described in Figure 9.4 have important implications for the real estate investor or appraiser. Because of the incredible inflationary pressures in the 1970s, many properties sold for prices far in excess of their value. As we can see from this market model, these prices will have to come down eventually. There is a temptation in a "hot" market to subscribe to the "greater fool theory." Many investors buy overpriced property because they feel there is always a "greater fool" around to take it off their hands. Perhaps in the short run, for some investors, this will actually be the case. However, the rational investor, the professional appraiser, and the mortgage loan officer must be careful not to fall into this trap. If the income of a property, capitalized at the appropriate value, does not justify the price, then this fact should not be hidden. It is tempting to fall back on continued appreciation as a protection against insufficient value, but we cannot succumb to this temptation.

Portfolio Considerations

We pointed out earlier in this chapter that by selecting appropriate groups of risky assets for purchase an investor could lower the overall risks of the investments. Further, we mentioned that by diversifying, nonsystematic risk could be ignored. This lowering of risk is an important concept which is often misunderstood. The investment decision process described in chapter 8 implied that all one needed to do to make responsible decisions was to find assets with positive net present values. There is more to it than that. What investors desire, overall, from risking their funds, is the *highest* possible return for the risks assumed for all the assets as a group. Another way of saying this is that investors wish to *minimize the risk assumed for a given overall return.*

Portfolio Return

Overall return in a portfolio, a group of investment assets, is a function of two things: the return of the individual assets purchased and the proportion each is of the total investment. The expected return on the portfolio is simply the weighted average of the expected returns of the individual assets.

Assume an investor can buy two assets, A and B, with returns of 10% and 8%, respectively. If half of the investor's total dollars are invested in each of these assets, then the portfolio return will be 9%.

$$\text{Portfolio Return} = R_A \text{ weight}_A + R_B \text{ weight}_B$$
$$= (0.10)(0.5) + (0.08)(0.5)$$
$$= 0.09 \text{ or } 9\%$$

By changing the proportions, the total return can be altered to range from 8% (buying all of B) to 10% (buying all of A).

Portfolio Risk

The risk of a portfolio is not as easy to determine. Table 9.9 shows the returns and variances for three different assets using the analysis from the first part of this chapter.

Assume assets A and B are purchased in equal proportions. Table 9.10 shows the portfolio return and the portfolio risk. Now assume assets A and C are bought in equal proportions. Table 9.11 shows the risk and return for this portfolio. Both assets B and C are identical in terms of individual risk and return, so something else must account for the different results of the two portfolios. This extra factor is the *correlation* of the returns between the assets in the portfolios. Assets A and B are positively correlated. This means that both move in the same direction as economic conditions change. However, assets A and C are negatively correlated. They move in opposite directions when economic conditions

TABLE 9.9 SAMPLE INVESTMENT ASSETS

	State of Nature	(1) Investment Return	(2) Probability	(1) × (2)	(Return−EV)²(Probability)
Asset A	Boom	0.05	0.3	0.015	$(-0.05)^2 (0.3) = 0.00075$
	Normal	0.10	0.4	0.040	$(0.00)^2 (0.4) = 0.00000$
	Recession	0.15	0.3	0.045	$(0.05)^2 (0.3) = \underline{0.00075}$
				$EV =$ .10	Variance = 0.0015
Asset B	Boom	0.06	0.3	0.018	$(-0.02)^2 (0.3) = 0.00012$
	Normal	0.08	0.4	0.032	$(0.00)^2 (0.4) = 0.00000$
	Recession	0.10	0.3	0.030	$(0.02)^2 (0.3) = \underline{0.00012}$
				$EV =$ 0.08	Variance = 0.00024
Asset C	Boom	0.10	0.3	0.030	$(0.02)^2 (0.3) = 0.00012$
	Normal	0.08	0.4	0.032	$(0.00)^2 (0.4) = 0.00000$
	Recession	0.06	0.3	0.018	$(-0.02)^2 (0.3) = \underline{0.00012}$
				$EV =$ 0.08	Variance = 0.00024

Summary	A	B	C
Expected Value	10%	8%	8%
Standard Deviation	3.87%	1.55%	1.55%

TABLE 9.10 PORTFOLIO I—50% ASSET A AND 50% ASSET B

State of Nature	(1) Portfolio Return	(2) Probability	(1) × (2)	(Return −EV)²(Probability)
Boom	0.5(0.05) + 0.5(0.06)	0.3	0.0165	$(-0.035)^2 (0.3) = 0.0003675$
Normal	0.5(0.10) + 0.5(0.08)	0.4	0.0360	$(0.000)^2 (0.4) = 0.0000000$
Recession	0.5(0.15) + 0.5(0.10)	0.3	0.0375	$(0.035)^2 (0.3) = \underline{0.0003675}$
			$EV =$ 0.09	Variance = 0.000735
		Standard Deviation = 2.71%		

TABLE 9.11   PORTFOLIO II—50% ASSET A AND 50% ASSET C

State of Nature	(1) Portfolio Return	(2) Probability	(2) × (3)	(Return $-EV)^2$(Probability)
Boom	0.5(0.05) + 0.5(0.10)	0.3	0.0225	$(-0.015)^2(0.3) = 0.0000675$
Normal	0.5(0.10) + 0.5(0.08)	0.4	0.0360	$(0.000)^2(0.4) = 0.0000000$
Recession	0.5(0.15) + 0.5(0.06)	0.3	0.0315	$(0.015)^2(0.3) = \underline{0.0000675}$
			$EV =$ 0.09	Variance = 0.000135

Standard Deviation = 1.16%

change. This negative correlation dampens the fluctuations and reduces total risk for the portfolio. In fact, the portfolio risk for the A and C combination is less than the risk of either asset alone. This is called *diversification*. Assume an investor currently has all of his investment dollars in asset C and wishes to increase his overall return. With appropriate diversification through the purchase of asset A, the investor could *raise his return and lower his risk,* even though the asset to be purchased is riskier than the asset already owned!

We have just seen that under the proper circumstances the right mix of assets can increase an investor's return and lower overall risk. The amount of change in risk is a function of the individual asset risks, the degree of correlation, and the proportion of each purchased. One final refinement can be performed on this example. The best overall portfolio combination is not necessarily the one we have shown. By varying the proportions of the total portfolio invested in each asset, risk can be *minimized*, given a desired level of return. The best overall combination is called the **efficient portfolio.**

Diversification must be dealt with carefully. It is not enough just to buy many different assets. One must look at assets which are negatively correlated. If the investor has started with asset B and added asset A to his portfolio, the return would have risen from 8% to 9%, but the total risk would also have risen from 1.6% to 2.7%.

One other point needs to be made concerning portfolios. The capital asset pricing model and the security market line both rely on the assumption that nonsystematic risk is ignored. In this section we have only addressed total risk of a portfolio. Determining total risk for a large portfolio is a complicated process. However, calculating systematic risk for a portfolio is simpler, provided the betas of the assets with the market are known. Studies involving common stocks indicate that as the number of assets in a portfolio is increased, the proportion of systematic risk rises. For a large portfolio, say over twenty-five stocks, most of the total risk is systematic risk. We also know mathematically that merely increasing portfolio size does not guarantee an increase in the proportion of systematic risk. However, larger portfolios tend to become more representative of the market in general. If this is true, the systematic risk proportion would rise. Unfortunately, research in this area has been limited to securities and securities markets. Whether the generalization concerning systematic risk and portfolio size is valid for other markets is open to question, although theoretically, at least, it should be.

Implications for Real Estate

The preceding portfolio analysis can be applied to any kind of investment assets. The implication is that real estate investors must consider diversifying their overall portfolios with either securities or some other types of assets in order to gain the best overall risk–return combination. Investors must be aware that the process of investment selection involves more than net present value or internal rate of return calculations.

The fact that portfolio considerations must be accounted for is clear. However, the example in this discussion was extremely simple. In a real world situation a great deal more work will be needed. At this time there are no good, practical solutions for the average investor to implement with, say, the use of a calculator to help make such investment decisions. The best approach seems to be to balance one's portfolio with assets which tend to have different relationships to economic conditions. For the energetic reader, the references at the end of the text (Appendix 2) reveal sources for the general structure of the mathematics involved in the more realistic decision situations. Hopefully, with the advent of the microcomputer, it will become easier to apply some of these analyses.

CHAPTER NINE SUMMARY

This has been a difficult chapter. In it we covered a number of complex and important theoretical issues relating to the processes of appraisal and investment analysis. First, we identified the concepts of expected value and the nature of risk. This was followed by an introduction to the nature of linear regression. Based on these two major constructs, we described the essence of capital asset pricing. We saw how the returns of an investment asset may be related to the market in order to develop a required rate of return for valuation. We also discussed the limitations of this model for practical use.

We then turned our attention to the nature of the market for investment assets and the implication of disequilibrium conditions in that market. We saw how astute investors might exploit underpriced assets to make "extra" returns for the risks they would assume. Finally, we developed the idea of the portfolio and saw how the proper grouping of assets may be used to alter the risk and return patterns of individual assets.

Even though this chapter was long and complex, it barely scratched the surface of the details of these important models. Although these models bring us closer to operationalizing many of the concepts we described earlier in this text, many refinements must be made before they can be adapted to the needs of the average investor or appraiser.

KEY TERMS

Capital Asset
    Pricing Model
Characteristic Line
Correlation
Covariance
Dependent variable
Diversification
Efficient Portfolio

Expected Value
Independent
    variable
Linear Regression
    Equation
Nonsystematic
    Risk
R
R^2

Security Market
    Line
Standard Deviation
Systematic Risk
Total Risk
Variance

QUESTIONS FOR STUDY AND DISCUSSION

1. Differentiate between the estimated return of an asset and the actual return. How may the estimated return be calculated?

2. What is the equation for a straight line? What is meaning of the y-intercept, called a? What is the meaning of the slope, called b or beta?

3. What is the *capital asset pricing model*? How can we use it to help evaluate a real estate investment?

4. Relate the concept of the *security market line* to the tasks of the appraiser and the investment analyst.

5. What is meant by *diversification*? What effect may diversification have on the desirability of a given individual investment? What risk may we control with diversification?

6. Identify the pros and cons of the CAPM technique for use in investment analysis. What are the major strengths and weaknesses of the technique?

PROBLEMS FOR REVIEW

1. A real estate investment is expected to earn the following returns each year for the next ten years, depending upon the condition of the

economy (states of nature A through E). Find the expected value of these annual cash flows.

State of Nature	Cash Flow	Probability
A	$36,000	0.10
B	$30,000	0.20
C	$27,000	0.30
D	$24,000	0.25
E	$20,000	0.15

2. Find the standard deviation for the distribution of returns found in problem 1.

3. The expected risk-free rate of return in the market is 6%. The return on the real estate market is expected to be 11%. A shopping center development is expected to have a beta of 1.4. What rate of discount should be used to analyze this investment opportunity?

4. An investor in the same general market as in problem 3 is analyzing two investments. The investor can afford only one. Which, if either, should be purchased? Why?

Investment A: beta = 1.4; actual IRR = 13%
Investment B: beta = .8; actual IRR = 11%

5. An investor may buy the two assets shown below. Assuming that 40% of the total amount invested is used to purchase investment 1 and 60% is used to purchase investment 2. Find:

a. The expected return on this two-asset portfolio;

b. The standard deviation of the two-asset portfolio.

State of Nature	Probability	Return for Investment 1	Return for Investment 2
State A	0.25	0.08	0.16
State B	0.40	0.10	0.12
State C	0.35	0.14	0.04

PART 2

CHAPTER TEN—REAL ESTATE MARKETS

The first chapter in this part presents a comprehensive model of the real estate market. The discussion builds a basic model explaining the consumer choice process and continues to show what factors determine the level of supply and demand in the market. The chapter concludes with a discussion of market dynamics.

CHAPTER ELEVEN—PHYSICAL AND LOCATIONAL FACTORS

This is the first chapter to provide an in-depth discussion of the major factors affecting the value of real estate. The first part of the chapter develops some simplified models which are used to explain why particular land uses occupy particular urban land areas. The last part of the chapter describes many of the physical factors affecting value.

CHAPTER TWELVE—LEGAL FACTORS I

In this first of three chapters on legal factors affecting value, the discussion centers on a description of the various forms of ownership interest in real property. The chapter also discusses the ways in which title to property may be conveyed and the various forms of evidence of title.

CHAPTER THIRTEEN—LEGAL FACTORS II

In this chapter the discussion continues to cover the degrees of interest one may hold in land. The main part of the chapter is concerned with lease interests. However, interests such as easements and reversions are also discussed.

CHAPTER FOURTEEN—LEGAL FACTORS III

The last of the legal factors chapters is concerned with

FACTORS AFFECTING VALUE

the various limitations which may be placed on the use of property. The private limitations include deed restrictions and liens. The public limitations discussed include zoning, eminent domain, police power, taxing power and building code restrictions.

CHAPTER FIFTEEN—REAL ESTATE FINANCE I

This is the first of three chapters concerned with the financing of real estate. The discussion in this chapter centers on the major instruments of finance. The most important of these tools is the mortgage. The

characteristics, varieties, and default remedies for mortgages are all discussed. The chapter concludes with descriptions of several other major financing instruments, both long term and short term.

CHAPTER SIXTEEN—REAL ESTATE FINANCE II

This chapter is concerned with the structure of the market for real estate finance and the major sources of these funds. The chapter begins with a discussion of the role of individual savers and financial intermediaries in

the market. The various institutional sources of funds are then described. The chapter concludes with a discussion of government participation in both the primary and secondary markets.

CHAPTER SEVENTEEN—REAL ESTATE FINANCE III

The final chapter in part 2 discusses the effect of financing on real estate value. In this presentation, numerous examples of the creative use of financing tools are used to illustrate how they can increase the investment value of a property and stimulate development.

10 REAL ESTATE MARKETS

A DIAGNOSTIC model was presented in Figure 1.1 to show the major relationships affecting the various values associated with real property. This figure is reproduced as Figure 10.1. We will now proceed from our original view to derive some of the key structures of real estate markets.

Figure 10.1 shows the major factors relating to the various measures of value we have discussed. This representation is a very simple view, however, with none of the internal interactions represented. In the sections to follow we will expand this figure to develop a much more detailed view of the market and what affects it. The new model will be developed step-by-step and then assembled later in this chapter.

Real Estate Market Structure

To begin our discussion of real estate markets, we will examine the decisions that must be made by market participants. We will then look at some theories describing how these decisions are made. Finally, we will examine the various factors affecting these decisions.

Market Decisions

To make our discussion easier, we will begin by talking about the housing market. The mechanisms for understanding housing markets and other markets are very similar, so we can extend them later. The deci-

FIGURE 10.1   REAL ESTATE VALUE MODEL

Factors Affecting Value   **Types of Value**

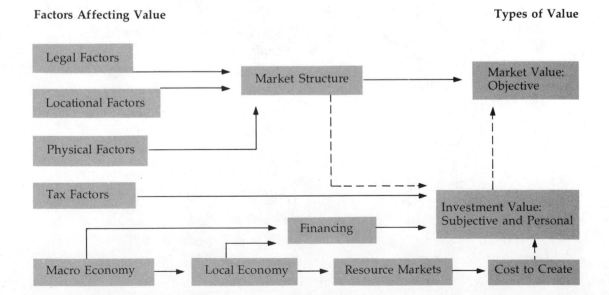

sions that must be made in the market involve two groups of participants: those supplying property and those demanding it.

Demand   The demand side of the market is characterized by potential buyers who have a number of choices to make. First, they must decide how much they wish to spend for the property. Buyers have a certain fixed quantity of monetary resources which they may spend on all the goods which provide satisfaction for them. Some of their monetary resources are likely to be applied to housing. Each consumer must decide which combinations of goods will be most satisfying.

When the consumer has chosen the *quantity* of housing he or she wishes to buy, the next choice must be how to divide the money over various combinations of features that may be obtained. Similar decisions are made by the demanders of industrial property. A businessperson contemplating a new factory building must make trade-offs between various features so that the total expenditure may be kept within economic limits. These decisions are *quality* decisions.

Supply   Those who supply units to the various real estate markets must also make decisions and trade-offs. The supplier must decide how much property to supply. Because improved real estate is a manufactured product, the exact specifications of what will be supplied must be determined. The supplier must be able to use information about market demand to supply the right property in the right quantity.

The supplier must also make quality decisions. A new home builder must decide what features will satisfy potential customers. Again, the builder needs to utilize information about the market and its participants.

Market Allocation

In chapter 4 we saw that the basic allocative mechanism in real estate is the market. The market transactions that occur depend on the price established between buyers and sellers. In order to sell property, sellers must feel they are receiving compensation for the investment value they perceive for their properties. This subjective value serves as a *floor* for the price accepted by a seller. Buyers similarly have their views of the investment value of the properties they demand. This value serves as a *ceiling* on the amount a buyer will pay.

The price which will allow transactions to take place depends on the structure of the market. In a good, efficient market, there must be a sufficient number of potential buyers for each offered property to ensure that there will be enough offers to give sellers their investment value. There must also be enough competitive properties offered to ensure that sellers aren't monopolists, thereby allowing them to extract more value than they are entitled to.

Thus the price in the market is a function of overall supply and demand. We saw how this might be portrayed using the graph shown as Figure 4.1. This figure illustrated how any real estate market might clear itself.

Figure 10.2 shows how the overall market structure might appear in terms of our original value model. As you can see, the market value is a function of the levels of supply and demand which determine the overall market structure. We can also see the role of information in market activity. The market value serves as information to both sellers and buyers, enabling them to readily determine the decisions they must make.

Individual Choice Decisions

We have shown in chapter 4 and reiterated here how the overall market operates. Now we will look at the mechanism for individuals making choices in this market setting.

The Budget   An individual making choices among competing goods for consumption has some finite amount of money he or she can spend. In Figure 10.3(a) this is shown as the **budget line.** On the x-axis of the graph we will put the units of housing service consumed. Housing service rather than houses per se are reflected by this scheme. **Housing service** refers to the benefits received from a particular house. To raise the amount of housing service, a consumer generally buys a larger house, not two houses. On the y-axis we will put the unit consumption of alternate good B. Good B represents everything besides housing which the consumer demands. The unit consumption represented at the intersection of the budget line with each axis (points B_0 and H_0) is found

FIGURE 10.2   THE MARKET FOR REAL ESTATE

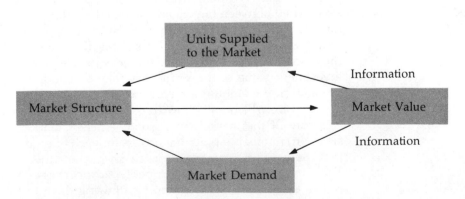

→ means "has an effect on."

FIGURE 10.3   INDIVIDUAL CHOICE DECISIONS

(a)   Units of Good B

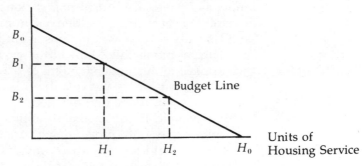

(b)   Units of Good B

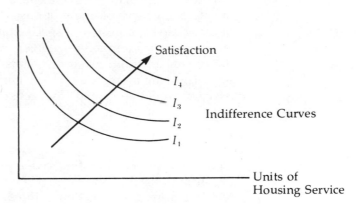

(c)   Units of Good B

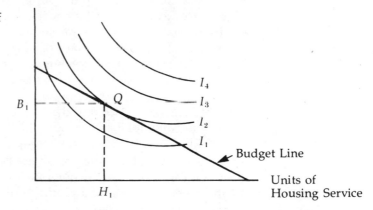

by dividing the total budget by the price of the item (good B or housing service). These prices are assumed to be constant. Anywhere on the line we see the combinations of goods which may be consumed. The budget line represents what is possible for the consumer.

Satisfaction   In order to make the trade-off decision between combinations of goods, the consumer has to decide what combination will be most satisfying, also called *utility*. Satisfaction is characterized as the overall benefit value to be derived from consuming something. Economists make several assumptions about people when they discuss utility, such as rationality. Many of these assumptions are similar to those we applied to our understanding of markets in chapter 4. We also assume that consumers derive a **diminishing marginal utility** from consuming a good. If one unit of a good is consumed, the consumer might derive ten units of satisfaction from that consumption. The second unit consumed may only provide eight units of satisfaction, and so forth. Each additional unit consumed provides relatively less satisfaction.

Figure 10.3(b) shows how satisfaction is depicted graphically by economists. Each curve on the graph is called an **indifference curve.**[1] Each of these curves represents a specific total level of satisfaction. Any combination of consumption on a given curve provides *equal* satisfaction to the consumer. If the consumer wants more satisfaction, then he or she must consume more in total. In Figure 10.3(b) the highest level of satisfaction would be gained from consuming a combination of goods on indifference curve I_4.

Choice Decisions   The final consumption choice can be depicted by a graph such as that shown in Figure 10.3(c). The indifference curves (called a map) are a function of the individual's tastes and preferences. We impose these desires on the budget curve which represents the level of resources available to the consumer. The appropriate quantities for the individual to consume are shown by the point indicated by Q in Figure 10.3(c). This is the point of tangency between the highest indifference curve (here I_2) and the budget line. Any other indifference curve would provide either more or less satisfaction than the consumer can afford. In the case illustrated in the figure, the consumer would buy H_1 units of housing service and B_1 units of everything else (good B). This would provide a total satisfaction of I_2.

It should be noted that even though the figure only shows four indifference curves, there are an infinite number, corresponding to every level of satisfaction the consumer may have. Furthermore, the shape of the indifference curves for a specific individual can be determined mathematically. Figure 10.3 illustrates the general shape of indifference curves for consumers as a whole.

---

[1]The shape of these curves is a function of the assumptions which were applied. This shape is mathematically derived from these assumptions. For further discussions of consumer choice decisions, please refer to any standard economics text, such as the book by Samuelson in the references.

Summary The consumer choice decision is determined by the relationship between one's desired level of satisfaction and the funds available to be spent. The choice is influenced by the *consumer's income*; the *prices* and the *number of* the various *goods competing* for his or her dollars; and that consumer's *overall tastes and preferences*. This model can be used to explain any choice decision between various competing goods when limited funds are available. This discussion has been very simple and many details have been omitted. However, we do have sufficient information to continue our examination of the real estate market.

A Model of the Overall Market

In order to develop a model of the real estate market as a whole, we need to deal with three major groups of variables.[2] First, we must look at the factors which affect the level of demand in the market. Second, we must examine the factors which affect the amount of property supplied to the market. Finally, we will look at the interaction between these two sets of factors.

Factors Affecting Market Demand

The factors which control the overall level of demand in the market follow directly from the preceding discussion of individual choice. These major factors were:

1. The pattern of consumer preferences;
2. The level of liquid assets; and
3. The level of income.

The factors affecting individual choice-making also affect the market as a whole, since all the individual choice-makers, taken together, form the market as a whole. Thus, we can say that any environmental input which alters one of the foregoing three major factors, such as a change in household income, will cause a change in demand in the market. This may be short-run (temporary) change or a long-run, more permanent change.

Short-Run Variables There are several specific factors which affect demand in the short run:

1. A change in the level of property prices or rents;
2. A change in prices of competing budget items; and
3. A change in consumer expectations.

---

[2]This model is based on structures summarized by Goulet (see references).

From the discussion summarized by Figure 10.3, it is obvious that if the prices of property or competing goods change, the budget line for most consumers would have to change. It is difficult to alter one's income in the short run, so if prices rise, total demand must fall. This drop in demand may be dampened if sufficient liquid assets (savings) are available for emergency purchases. Similarly, the availability of cheap credit may allow the consumer to adjust to rising prices more easily in the short run. Obviously, falling prices are less difficult to cope with.

A change in consumer expectations may also affect demand. If price rises are perceived to be temporary the consumer may postpone purchases that are felt to be priced too high. If the consumer has a foreseeable major need looming in the near future, a saving may occur. Of course, there are times when this is not entirely possible. However, in a general price rise, major purchases typically are postponed first. If the price rise becomes sustained, then other adjustments may be made in long-run behavior. The point is that the way consumers react to short-run environmental changes is at least partially a function of their expectations about the permanency of the change.

Changes in rents have the same effect on consumers of rental properties as do changes in prices of property available for sale. However, changes in rents have a different effect on investors. A rise in rents may mean a rise in NOI. A rise in NOI causes the investment value of the rental property to rise and the demand for existing properties by investors may rise correspondingly. Thus, where prices represent costs, a rise in price will cause demand to fall. However, where prices represent a rise in revenue, demand may rise in the short run.

Long-Run Variables   There are a number of underlying factors which will cause overall demand to change more permanently. These include:

1. Net new family formations;
2. Net in (out) migration;
3. Changing family preferences;
4. Asset holdings; and
5. Growth in real income.

We can see the relationship of these variables fairly easily. If the total number of people or families in a local market changes significantly, demand must be affected. Similarly, if there is a significant change in overall income and savings levels, the budget line will move up and to the right (see Figure 10.3). This means more of everything may be demanded and, in general, higher levels of satisfaction achieved. Finally, as overall preferences and needs change, entire classes of properties may lose or gain value from changes in demand.

Summary and Model   Market demand may thus be summarized as being a function of the following overall variables:

I. Consumer preferences (needs);

II. Individual monetary resources;

III. Economic characteristics of new and existing properties;

IV. The price of the product, including financial costs such as interest rates; and

V. The total number of demanders in the market.

These variables and the environmental relationships which affect them are illustrated in the rather complex Figure 10.4. This figure expands the information seen in Figure 10.2 to account for some of the interactions we have described in this section. We will now examine this model a bit further.

As shown in Figure 10.2, the upper right-hand quadrant of the model depicts market structure. Using the information presented in chapter 8, we can easily imagine what factors will affect the investment values of new and existing properties (see the lower right-hand quadrant in the figure). Changes in rents, expenses, initial price (downpayment), expected terminal value, taxes, and interest costs will all cause variations in the cash flow stream and thus affect value and ultimately demand for properties by investors. The various arrows leading into the Economic Characteristics box depict the factors just mentioned, including the costs required to create new properties.

Working from these inputs to the Economic Characteristics box towards the lower left and upper left quadrants in the figure, we may obtain a view of the factors which affect these investment-oriented inputs. Taxes are a function of both local and national economic conditions and policies. The cost and availability of mortgage financing, a vital cost in real estate, is determined in its own market. Both these inputs to investment value are primarily affected by local conditions of supply and demand. However, as we shall see later in the text, national economic policy and government intervention also have an impact. The major resource markets for labor, land, and materials, which also affect investment values, are also affected by local economic conditions.

Since real estate markets are basically local in nature, we have systematically worked back to the section of Figure 10.4 to the Local Situation box. At this local level, the two major concerns are the overall nature of the population and the strength of the underlying economy. In chapter 18 we will see how these factors are analyzed by the developer of real estate. Figure 10.4 illustrates that these two major local factors are interrelated. The local economy affects the monetary resources of the people who, in turn, are responsible for the functioning of the

FIGURE 10.4   MARKET WITH DEMAND FACTORS

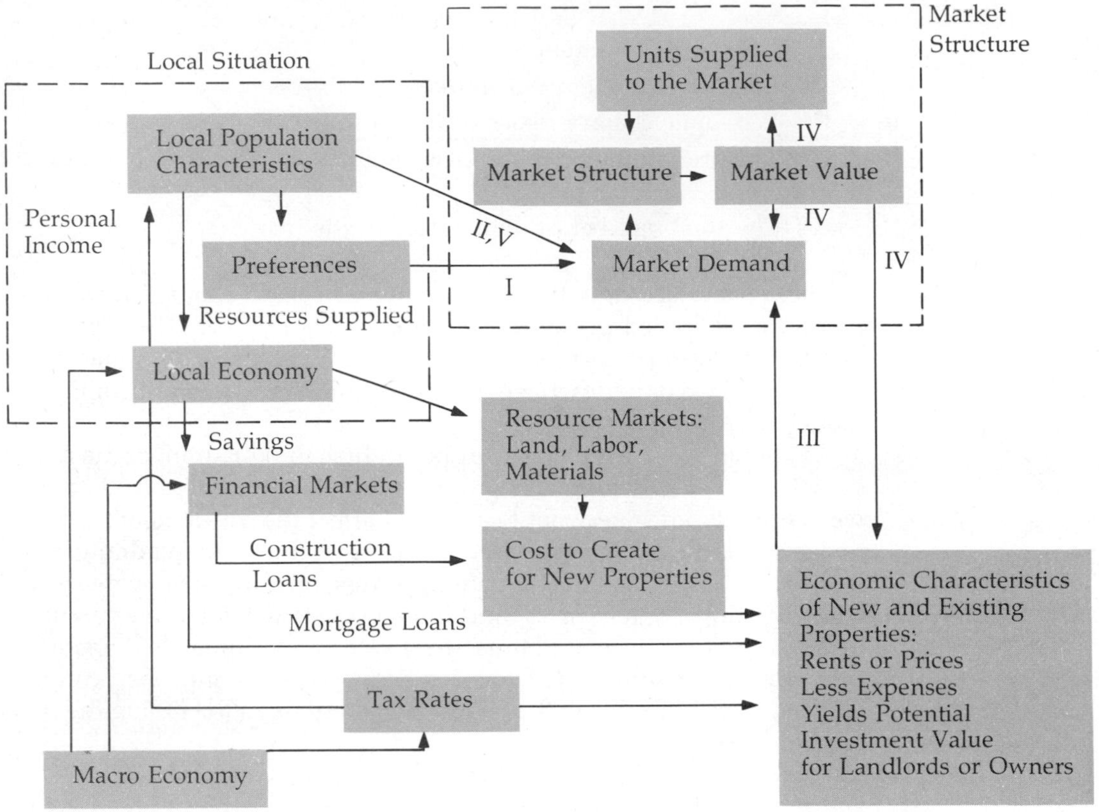

→ means "has an effect on."
Roman numerals relate to the summary variables from the discussion.

local economy. We may complete the circle by pointing to the effect on market demand by local population characteristics and preferences.

Figure 10.4 is complex, but when it is viewed in the context of the long- and short-run variables affecting demand, the figure does fall into sections fairly easily. The Roman numerals in the figure help relate the illustration to the summary demand variables listed on p. 209. This figure shows in more detail the tremendous number of interrelated areas in our economic system. If any one of these many factors underlying demand is altered, even in the short run, there will probably be an effect throughout the vast, interconnected network we have seen. Adjustments are not always fast, but they are usually inevitable. Good real estate professionals must understand this structure and its environment to make the right decisions for themselves or to advise their clients.

Factors Affecting Market Supply

The supply of real property in the market is affected by many of the same variables which affect demand. The change is one of perspective. The important factors include, to name a few, the costs associated with producing or selling units of property, overall price levels, downpayment requirements, rates of competing construction, and others. Supply is really a function of the relationship between the perceived demand for properties of a given type and the cost to create these properties. If short-run demand is perceived to be so low that a potential supplier of a newly improved property cannot create the property for a price below the expected selling price, then the new unit will not be supplied. Similarly, the owners of existing properties will not relinquish the benefits derived from their properties unless they perceive demand to be high enough to guarantee them a satisfactory price. Of course, there are exceptions.

In the long run the main adjustment to the supply side of the market is in the form of new construction. A sharp developer will supply new properties only when demand is perceived to be strong enough to absorb all the new, similar units that are expected to be offered at the same time. This means the developer must estimate both demand and competitive supply. Even a favorable result in this analysis is not enough, however. The property to be supplied must have an investment value which is high enough to command a price higher than its cost to create, as was mentioned previously. Therefore, the property's characteristics must be evaluated in advance, along with both short- and long-run demand and supply, in order to select the proper characteristics which will provide sufficient economic benefits to the supplier. This long-run adjustment mechanism is explained more fully in the section on filtering in this chapter.

Figure 10.5 illustrates how the supply side of the market depends on value and economic characteristics. The supply side appears in the upper right corner of Figure 10.5. The needs of the local population affect demand, rents, and the economic value of properties, as we saw in Figure 10.4. Rising investment values stimulate new construction and the discretionary supply of existing units to the market. In essence, supply is stimulated by the presence of sufficient basic value.

Demand–Supply Interaction

The interaction of supply and demand in the marketplace gives the market its structure and helps set the prices at which properties will change hands. The activity on both sides of the market provides information which is used by potential participants in the market. Therefore, appraisal plays an important role as an information processing mechanism. The long- and short-run dynamics of the market depend on its structure as well as the expectations about changes in this structure.

FIGURE 10.5   COMPLETE MARKET AND VALUE MODEL

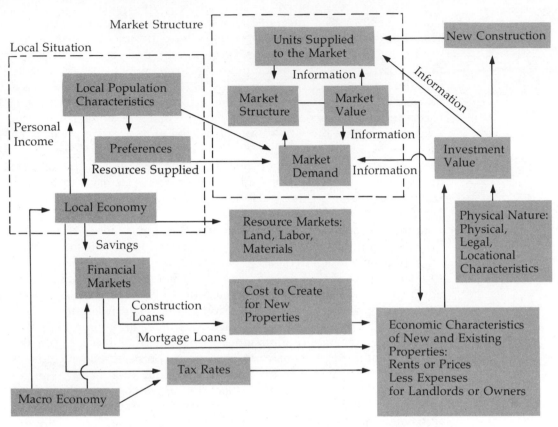

→ means "has an effect on."

Summary of Market Structure

In the preceding sections we have developed a model for the overall structure of the market for real estate. In many ways, this is a very simplified model, in spite of its complex appearance. To conclude this discussion and lead the way for the coming sections, we can list a few conclusions.

1. The overall allocative mechanism is the market. The market is cleared when buyers and sellers come together and prices are agreed upon.

2. Individual housing or other real estate choice decisions are a function of prices, incomes, prices of competing goods, and personal pref-

erences. These items become the major factors influencing demand when taken in the aggregate.

3. Supply in the market is largely a function of value perception. The economic and physical characteristics of a property influence the construction of new units, a major input to the supply side of the market.

4. Many economic factors interacting among themselves influence both the supply and demand for property.

We have thus far seen a fairly static view of the structure of the overall market for real property. We have kept this model as general as possible, though much of our discussion related to the housing market. You can probably use this basic model structure to provide yourself, intuitively at least, with a similar model for other types of real property.

We will now move from our static view of the market to a discussion of the long-run adjustment mechanism.

Market Dynamics—Submarket Analysis

Submarkets

The market model in Figure 10.5 relates to the entire local market for real estate. However, studies of market dynamics have shown that the market is most probably divided into many individual submarkets, each operating more or less on its own.[3] A **submarket** is an area which contains property units, say housing, which are roughly substitutes for each other. All the dwellings in a given submarket are likely to provide roughly equivalent utility to the consumer. Submarkets are generally defined first by location and then by the physical characteristics of the units in the area.

A logical question may arise at this point. So, what about submarkets, what good is all this detail? Think about this a moment. If you wish to buy a home appliance, what do you do? You shop around various stores until you find the one you want. You then buy it and take it home. Housing does not work that way. It must be consumed at a static location. You move to it; you do not take it to where you are. It is this static location which gives rise to many of the peculiarities of real estate markets.

Let us define a community with four major submarkets. Figure 10.6 shows a diagram of this hypothetical community. Each submarket is characterized by housing units with similar value levels and occupied

---

[3]For a thorough discussion of submarkets, see Grigsby in the references.

FIGURE 10.6   HOUSING SUBMARKETS

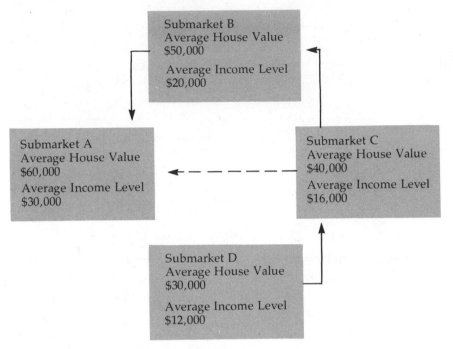

Arrows indicate linkages.

by individuals with similar income characteristics. Each submarket is also "linked" to at least one other submarket, as shown by the arrows. You will understand the nature of these **linkages** shortly.

Filtering

Using Figure 10.6 as a guide, imagine what would happen if say fifty families in submarket B find that their incomes have increased to around $30,000. This would represent a change in one of the long-run variables affecting demand. Also imagine that their dwellings had deteriorated slightly and were worth somewhat less than the average house in submarket B. These fifty people would now be prime demanders for units in submarket A to which B is linked, provided units were available in A. A sharp developer would see these increasing income levels and would proceed to build fifty new units in A. The lucky families could move to these new units, leaving fifty vacancies in submarket B.

There are undoubtedly some people in submarket C who also have been lucky enough to get an increased income during the same time. They see the vacancies developing in B, units which are more in their new price range, and they decide to move. The units in B are more attractive because, even though they have deteriorated somewhat, they are still superior to units in C. They are also more affordable because of their deterioration.

When the submarket C families have moved, they will also have left vacancies and some submarket D families may also decide to move. It can be noted that there may also be moves *within* submarkets in much the same fashion because not all the units are exactly alike. If many families from submarket C moved directly to A (dotted line in the figure), as well as to submarket B, then C would be linked to both submarkets. Since there are many submarkets in most communities, each submarket is likely to be linked to more than one other submarket.

The upshot of all this activity is that those families who find themselves with the appropriate resources and preferences can increase their housing consumption. This change in consumption can be seen in Figure 10.3 as moving to a higher indifference curve. The movement of families between submarkets is stimulated by new construction, a change in overall incomes, or a change in housing values. Ultimately new construction becomes necessary to facilitate the process.

Used units **filter** down the economic ladder so that their remaining value can be utilized effectively. The units at the lower end become ideal for new families who cannot afford newly constructed housing. As units get too old and dilapidated, they filter out of the system completely, having been replaced by new construction.

This system of market dynamics should ideally provide an effective allocation of the housing resources. Unfortunately, it does not work perfectly. The price of new construction is currently too high, causing used units to command increased demand and, thus, higher prices. If this trend in construction costs continues, by the early 1980s, so few people will be able to afford a brand new home that the market mechanism we have just described may be all but disabled. New families will be closed out of reasonable low-end homes because no one will be moving out. This will have important policy implications for our society in the not-too-distant future. If the housing market mechanism does not operate properly on its own, the government will inevitably step in, making the market model we illustrated in Figure 10.5 even more complex.

The Housing Cycle

For many years real estate scholars and practitioners have talked about the presence of an overall **housing cycle** in the national economy. This cycle had an important role to play because it was supposed to run counter to the overall economic cycle. This meant that housing and real estate construction, in general, would *lead* the economy out of a recession. The housing cycle was considered to be the self-correcting mechanism which would help dampen the business cycle. In this brief section, we will look at the way the housing cycle is supposed to operate and examine its current status. In actual fact, there is not one cycle affecting real estate, but several. Some are local in nature and some are more general.

The Macro Housing Cycle

To understand the conventional explanation of the housing cycle, one must understand the structure of a macro business cycle. As the economy expands and prosperity is on the rise, our theory of consumer choice dictates that budgets increase and anticipation and demand rise. Business confidence causes an increase in capital spending plans by business concerns. Consumer confidence causes consumers to buy on credit in anticipation of continued prosperity. All this expansion puts heavy demand on money markets, resource markets, and industrial capacity. This stress causes interest rates, resource costs, and goods prices to rise—and eventually causes an erosion of confidence, inflation, an end to the "boom." The system then "cools off" and eventually recycles.

The rising of interest costs, wage rates, and resource costs all cause the potential builder to think twice before making a large commitment which is difficult to reverse, once begun. Thus, housing starts to decline as the business cycle begins to peak, workers are laid off, and the housing cycle begins its downturn. Demand for housing drops because of high prices and the high costs of credit. After this contraction in activity in the housing market begins, other dependent industries such as manufacturers of home appliances, air conditioners, carpets, and so forth also begin to suffer losses in demand, in turn, causing these industries to lay off workers.

It used to be felt that when a recession was well underway money would become cheaper to obtain since the demand for it would have tapered off, laid-off workers would take any jobs they could get, and so forth. At this point, builders would rush in and begin building less-expensive units to offer for sale, using some of the unemployed labor force. This would help create the money incomes needed to facilitate the filtering mechanism. In this way, the building industry would lead the economy out of the recession—the housing cycle would be the first to begin its upturn.

There was only one problem: recessions do not operate in this fashion anymore. In the recession of the mid-seventies, the housing market followed the rest of the economy out of the recession. It was the last major sector of the economy to wake up. The reason for this seemed to lie in a phenomenon economists call **stagflation.** Normally, in a recession, goods become cheaper. The general price level retreats. However, it now appears that under certain circumstances we may suffer the inflation of a boom in the depths of a recession, which means that mortgage money remains scarce and expensive. Discretionary housing purchases are not made. Further, it appears that wages do not drop radically, even temporarily, to make cheaper labor accessible to builders. Thus, until the rest of the economy gets on its feet and inflation slows, housing cannot recover. It remains to be seen whether this pattern will continue in the future.

Local Cycles

Often, regardless of the national situation, particular local submarkets may suffer boom–bust cycles. Sometimes these are very local, are regional, or even statewide. The basic source of these cycles lies in the overzealous developers. In the Florida condominium boom in the early 1970s, every builder felt he would be able to capture a full share of the market for condominiums. The developers all measured potential demand a bit optimistically without real regard to the overall supply. Someone else was going to build the surplus units. At one time in that period, there were well over 100,000 extra units. A similar phenomenon occurred involving motel units in the Lake Buena Vista, Florida, area surrounding the Walt Disney World complex.

For whatever reason, it appears that when a particular type of development begins in a given local area it may "catch on." Probably, this is a result of a number of builders acting as followers, each under the assumption that someone else has done the necessary analysis. Early profits and rising demand only serve to complicate the situation, attracting more developers. Eventually, demand tapers off, prices begin to decline, leaving the last layer of "greater fools" holding the bag. There is some evidence that the massive California building boom of the mid-1970s will have begun to burst by 1980. Owners of used homes, especially those purchased just before the downturn of the local cycle, will probably be locked into their properties for years.

It should be noted that local cycles are not always violent. When developers do their homework and the city fathers keep a sharp eye on land-use patterns and other economic signs, the cycles need not be as previously described. Growth can be orderly and still be profitable.

Summary

Because of the nature of the market structures described in this chapter and because of many participants in the housing market all eager to profit from new construction, there is a great deal of cyclical behavior in real estate markets. A sharp developer can carefully exploit a knowledge of these cycles by being a leader rather than a follower. Cyclical behavior is part of the short-run market mechanism and needs to be understood by any real estate professional.

CHAPTER TEN SUMMARY

This book is concerned with value analysis. It is built around the notions of value and the value relationships described in chapter 1 and again in more detail here. We will conclude this chapter with a discussion of the ways our market model in Figure 10.5 relates to the rest of the text.

Up to this point, we have been concerned with the economic value of real estate from an operational point of view. We have looked at the process a potential buyer or seller would go through to correlate information about real estate benefits and costs to obtain an estimate of value. Potential investors, for example, would make estimates of revenues and expenses, including local taxes and financing costs, to determine the value of an investment they are contemplating. They might look at local economic conditions, population trends, and the nature of the current stock of units to make their estimates, thereby following the path we took in Figure 10.4.

We have already looked at one major input to this value analysis, taxes. We have also defined the other inputs without discussing them in detail. In the next chapters we will look at the various physical, locational, and legal factors which influence the investment value and indirectly the market value of a property.

The discussions of physical, locational, and legal factors will be followed by an examination of the nature of financing for real estate. We will see how it works and how it affects the economic nature of the property.

Part 3 of this text will center on some special topics. We will look at land development in chapter 18 and see how a developer goes about estimating the various elements of the market model shown in Figure 10.5 to help make critical development decisions. In chapter 19 we will see markets from a "process" standpoint rather than from a theoretical view as we did in this chapter. We will be talking in chapter 19 about brokerage and other services performed by market professionals. Finally, we will take one last look at the value analysis process in housing by examining the pros and cons of home ownership.

KEY TERMS

Budget Line	Housing Cycle	Linkages
Diminishing	Housing Service	Stagflation
Marginal Utility	Indifference	Submarket
Filtering (Filter)	Curves	

1. Explain the basic factors which influence the price of housing service in the market.

2. Explain the factors influencing the individual choice process for deciding the consumption of various competing goods and services. How do we explain this choice process in economic theory?

3. A number of factors directly affect the demand for housing and real estate in general. Enumerate these factors and briefly explain how each influences demand.

4. Explain the factors affecting the supply of real estate.

5. What is meant by a *housing submarket*? How does *filtering* work to allocate housing within the market structure?

6. Describe the *housing cycle* and its relationship to business conditions in the economy as a whole. In what ways has it not operated as it theoretically should? What explanation is there for this fact?

7. As an exercise, graph the national GNP, national housing starts, and your local housing starts by months for the past few years. What differences are apparent? What does your graph indicate about the macro and local housing cycles?

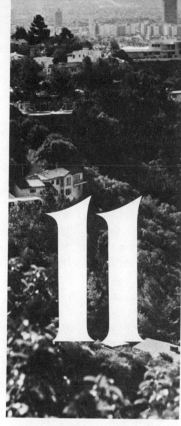

11
PHYSICAL
AND LOCATIONAL
CHARACTERISTICS

AS WE saw in the model in chapter 10, a portion of the value of real estate results from its physical nature. As we have said before, real estate is largely an urban, manufactured product—in value terms. All real estate, regardless of its location, occupies a unique space. In addition to its location, real property is identified and distinguished by its physical characteristics such as topology and soil and subsoil conditions.

Besides the aforementioned characteristics, real estate has other physical characteristics. The supply of real estate is fixed. Because real estate markets are primarily local, fixed supply takes on even more meaning. Land cannot be shipped from where it is to where it is needed. The supply of oil is also fixed, but if one country runs short, it can buy the oil it needs from someone who has it, at least until the supply runs out.

This last point is important. Even though the supply of real estate is fixed, land is basically indestructible. Land used for extractive purposes such as coal and iron mining does lose some of its value, but not permanently. Old strip mines can be filled in or graded and used for other purposes. Urban land is generally not used for these type destructive reasons, however. The fact that land is basically indestructible does not preclude the fact that the value of land can be changed by altering its physical characteristics. Relatively low-valued land can sometimes be improved by engineering activities which upgrade its physical characteristics. Likewise, land which has a relatively high value in one use can lose its value with improper management of its physical characteristics.

In this chapter we will explore the physical and locational aspects of real estate to see what factors should be understood to help determine the value of the land. We will see what the important factors are and how to analyze the physical and locational characteristics of a specific site. Before proceeding to the analysis, we will look at the methods used for describing the location of a piece of property.

Land Location and Description

The physical nature of real property is not limited to the surface of the land. As we mentioned in chapter 1, the owner of land in fee simple owns his property from the center of the earth out into the sky more or less indefinitely. (*Fee simple* is the highest degree of interest one may have in land.) As we shall see in the legal discussions later, fee simple rights are not absolute. The use of air space as well as the use of the land itself may be restricted by government action.

If one places a piece of property on the earth's surface, the property can be defined by extending straight lines from the edge of the property down to the center of the earth, forming a wedge much like you would remove from a watermelon. These lines extend the wedge into the sky. This is shown in Figure 11.1.

Location of property must be determined with precision. A share of stock or a bar of gold may be held in one's hand and is easy to identify. When a person buys a piece of land, however, it is essential that the property be precisely identified. There are three methods which are used to do this: metes and bounds, rectangular survey, and the platting method. These will be illustrated and described next.

Metes and Bounds

The earliest method used for identifying real property was the **metes and bounds** technique. This method involves the use of landmarks to describe property. A piece of farmland might be described as the property running along the east side of Apple Creek from the big oak on the north to county road 13 on the south over to county road 26 on the east in Henderson County.

There are many problems with this method. What if the big oak is destroyed by lightning or the creek changes its flow? If the landmarks are moved or destroyed the land description is lost. Further, it is difficult to define landmarks which are not ambiguous. Further difficulties arise

FIGURE 11.1   FEE SIMPLE OWNERSHIP

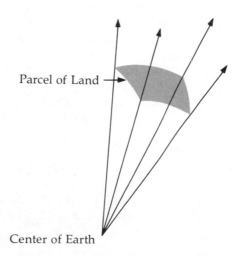

with small residential properties such as those found in subdivisions. To counteract these difficulties, we now utilize the rectangular survey and platting methods throughout much of the United States.

Rectangular Survey

The **rectangular survey** is based on the arbitrary division of large areas of land into smaller six-mile-square areas called **townships.** These townships are described in relation to two types of imaginary lines which divide the larger area. First, a north–south line called the **Principal Meridian** is described in a large area. On either side of this line, other parallel meridians are described. These are spaced every six miles. Similarly, an east–west line, perpendicular to the meridians, called a **baseline,** is described. Again a number of other lines are laid down parallel to this baseline at six-mile intervals. Together these lines all divide large areas into six-mile-square townships, each of which can be related to the principal meridian and the baseline. This pattern is illustrated in Figure 11.2. T refers to Township; R refers to Range.

The rectangular survey is used to describe a particular township by designating the distance and direction from the reference lines. Distances from the principal meridian are designated as **range** east or west. Distances from the baseline are designated township north or south. Thus, township A in the figure would be designated as Range 3E, Township 2N. Township B in Figure 11.2 is Range 2W, Township 2S. Thus, we are provided with a precise description of each township area.

We now subdivide each township into thirty-six one-mile-square areas called **sections.** These are described numerically as shown in Figure 11.3. The northeast section is numbered one and the others numbered in serpentine fashion as shown. We have chosen Township A from Figure 11.2 for our illustration.

Figure 11.4(a) shows Section 18 from Township A. Each section is described by subsequent divisions into halves and quarters. In the description the smallest quarter (or half) is described first. An "x" has been placed in Section 18. We may describe this piece of land as follows: north ½ of northwest ¼ of northwest ¼ of Section 18 of Township A. The property can be totally described as N ½, NW ¼, NW ¼, Section 18, Range 3E, Township 2N. This description shows very precisely where this small property is in terms of the very large original area. In terms of area, a section is 640 acres or one square mile. How big is our subject property?[1]

Similarly, Figure 11.4(b) describes a property located in Section 20. It should be noted here that even though there is a certain precision in

---

[1]Answer: ¼ × ¼ × ½ × 640 acres = 20 acres.

FIGURE 11.2   RECTANGULAR SURVEY METHOD

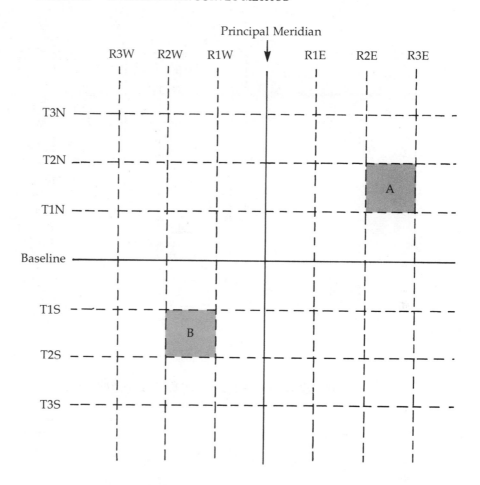

the survey method, it is not used in all areas of the United States. In the places where the survey is used, the method is based on U.S. Government surveys.

Platting Method

Let us now presume that the twenty acres we described in Figure 11.4(a) is a residential subdivision in the suburbs. We wish to continue our description to locate the lot marked "20" in the map shown in Figure 11.5. This could be extremely difficult using the rectangular survey. Instead, the subdivider who develops this twenty-acre property files a

FIGURE 11.3   TOWNSHIP A

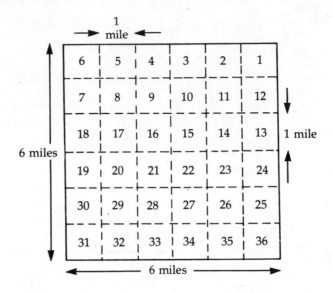

FIGURE 11.4(a)   SECTION 18, RANGE 3E, TOWNSHIP 2N

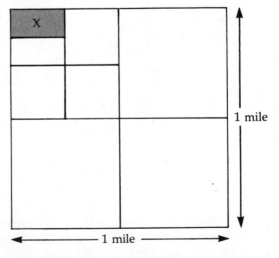

N½, NW¼, NW¼, Section 18

(a)

FIGURE 11.4(b)   SECTION 20, RANGE 3E, TOWNSHIP 2N

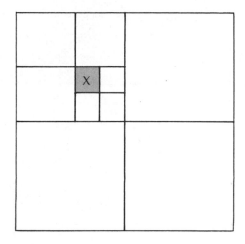

NW¼, SE¼, NW¼, Section 20

(b)

precise map of these lots and places an approved map of the subdivision in the courthouse for the county in which the property is located. This is the **platting** method. Mr. Smith was responsible for the property shown in Figure 11.5, so he filed the **plat plan** shown in that figure. A purchaser buying the property numbered 20 would have a sufficient description if his land was described as Lot 20, Smith's Subdivision, such-and-such County. The subdivision itself might be formally described as we did earlier using the rectangular survey.

We have seen how even a small, irregularly shaped plot of land can be described precisely. Now we will describe the dynamics of location and its effect on value.

Location and Value

One of the oldest cliches in real estate says there are three important influences on the value of any property: location, location, and location. In this section, we will explore the influence of location on value and discuss some of the theoretical models which are used to explain land use patterns.

FIGURE 11.5   SMITH'S SUBDIVISION

N ½, NW ¼, NW ¼, Section 18, Range 3 E, Township 2 N

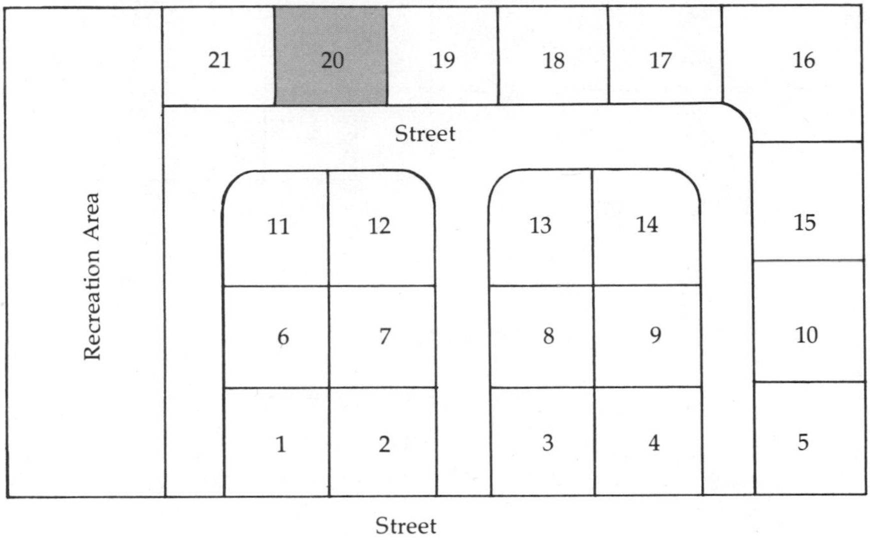

Street

The Nature of Urban Areas

To begin to understand the relationship between location and value requires a mixture of common sense and elementary economics. The economic system in the United States is basically a free market system. As we have seen, goods and services, including those provided by real property, are allocated in markets. Our system operates because individual owners of property rights are allowed to profit from the exploitation of these rights. However, society does demand that by and large these profits be earned under competitive conditions so they do not become excessive. If we assume that all producers of private goods and services intend to have maximization of profits from their enterprises, we may proceed to develop some reasons behind the nature of land use patterns and land values.

The processes of production may use varying amounts of the three classical economic inputs: land, labor, and capital. The most intensive use of the land resource is for agriculture, while industry produces its output by using larger quantities of labor and capital relative to output. Another intensive use of land is for housing, ranking right behind agriculture. The amount of land a particular user needs will have a great influence on the price that user is willing to pay and, as we will see shortly, it will also influence the patterns of land use.

Bid-Rent Theory   In our specialized economy, the key to the operation of resource allocation is the existence of markets. All producers of goods and services must eventually deliver their output to the appropriate markets. The farther away a producer is from the market, the greater the transportation expense, and the higher the cost of the product. Thus, all other things being equal, profits would be higher if producers could locate close to their markets. Similarly, a worker is a seller in the market. Workers, too, can profit by being closer to the market for their services. Thus, all other things being equal, workers would rather live close to their place of employment than far away. The logical presumption from all this is that for a given producer or seller, land close to the market will have a higher value than land farther away. How does all this translate into land use and value patterns?

If all land everywhere were the same price, some producers of a particular good would make more profits than competing producers of the same good by locating nearer to the market than their competitors. It is assumed that all similar producers know which land is "best" for them. Hence, the demand for those choice parcels is highest and the prices (or **economic rents**[2]) accruing to those parcels are also the highest. In fact, theoretically, the rents accruing to land will be distributed in such a manner that, in equilibrium, no producer of a particular good will have any advantage over another producer regardless of location— at least as far as costs are affected by market distance. This means, in general, that rents will fall as the distance to the market increases.

Not all industries are greatly concerned about the costs associated with distance to the market, however. For that reason, even though land rents always decline with distance from the market, the *rate* of decline varies among different industries. In general, the rate of decline in land rents is greatest when transportation of either raw materials or finished goods is very important or when land inputs to production are relatively unimportant. If transportation cost is large in relation to output value, then producers will try to reduce this cost by substituting a less expensive cost, land. If producers do not need much land to produce their output, then they can afford to bid a relatively large amount for a choice location because total costs will not be greatly affected by the additional rent charge.

We can see this diagrammatically in Figure 11.6. The curves R_a and R_b show the relationship between the rents offered for a unit of land and the distance to the market for producers in two different industries. The curve R_a, for industry A, drops very sharply as distance increases. This is the curve for an industry with a high transportation input or a low land input. Certain sellers of consumer goods or office space might

---

[2]As you may recall from chapter 4, *economic rent* is defined as the income accruing to the owner of the land over and above the basic required return.

FIGURE 11.6   BID-RENT CURVES

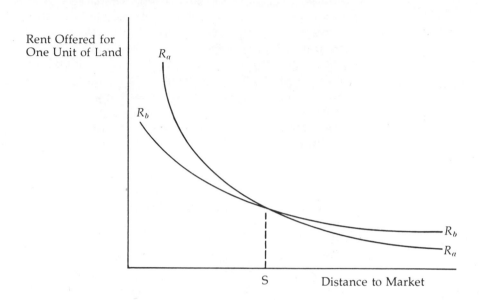

have a curve like this. Curve R_b, for industry B, falls much more slowly. This might be the curve for a farmer or a high-valued industrial goods producer.

In general, a given parcel of land will be obtained by that user who is willing to provide the highest economic rent to the landowner. Thus, from Figure 11.6 land of distance S, or less, from the market will be used by industry A; land of S distance or more from the market will be used by producers in industry B. The results of the relationships portrayed in this example can be used to explain much of the general nature of land use patterns of our urban areas. Cities, in general, are characterized by more or less concentric ringlike groups of use types. The central core of the city, called the **central business district** (CBD), is occupied by users with the steepest bid-rent curves such as office space and retail stores. Surrounding the CBD are various residential rings and some types of industrial uses.

The basic model we have presented thus far is very simplified and explains only a few general tendencies. We do find clusters of uses and a tendency for declining rents with market distances. However, the spatial organization of urban areas is more complex than that described for a number of reasons. We will now expand our model somewhat to account for additional details.

Spatial Organization of Cities   The preceding discussion tacitly assumes that the CBD and the market around which sellers wish to locate are more or less coincidental. A look at most cities shows that indeed the highest market concentration in terms of output per square foot of land is in or very near the CBD. This is only natural because as the city was formed the CBD was the first market area. As the city evolves and grows outward from the center, we find the densities of both the population and market activity fall.

The relationship between the population per unit of land, for instance, a square mile, and the distance to the city center forms a ratio called the **population density gradient.** Studies have repeatedly shown that as distance increases the density gradient falls. Further, over time this relationship has flattened out, leaving less difference between the gradient at the CBD and the city's edge than was formerly the case when the city was young. This means that the concentrations of population and market activity in large cities are gradually becoming less concentrated in the CBD. As a city evolves, grows, and occupies more area, it can more easily support shopping centers and other decentralized market areas. Smaller, younger cities are more dependent on the CBD and fit our earlier view better.

As cities evolve and population becomes more generally distributed, rents, too, follow the same pattern. We can similarly develop a **rent gradient** measure to show how unit rents relate to distances from the CBD. The pattern of rent gradients over time has generally followed the changes in population concentration we would expect from the bid-rent approach.

The reasons for changes in population and rent gradient relationships over time are difficult to pin down. However, at least one important factor influencing the changes is the drop in transportation costs. Even with the energy crisis, transport costs have fallen if one considers all the costs such as travel time, road quality, frustration, and fuel costs. As transportation costs fall and become less important, rents outside the CBD may rise and become closer to those at the center, thus flattening the overall curve. Another factor may be the wider distribution of employment. As the city becomes large and jobs are more generally distributed, it becomes easier for a family to locate far from the CBD and still be close to employment. The mechanism for residential location will be explained next. There is some disagreement whether the movement of population or jobs leads the decentralization process, but the falling density gradients are pervasive.

Residential Location   Urban areas are populated by numerous classes of land uses. The most important of these is the residential use. For this reason, housing has received a good deal of attention in the literature on the theory of location. Basically, as we saw in the previous chapter, housing can be viewed as a good providing a bundle of services leading to a particular level of satisfaction. In general, housing is no different from any other good consumed by an individual.

Housing is composed of a number of inputs: land, building materials, labor, and so forth. Housing has both land and nonland inputs. Land prices vary throughout a local area, but most nonland goods can be purchased at similar prices anywhere in the local area. Thus, land becomes the major reason why housing prices vary. Further, since land in cities may be considered roughly homogeneous physically (we will modify this later in the chapter), location becomes the primary differentiation in housing service costs.

The main ingredient in the location of housing is transportation cost. Because land is fixed in location, residential dwellers must travel to those markets to which they supply services (the job) and from which they derive services (stores, schools, church, etc.). Thus, the location of housing for a given family can be thought of as striking a balance between housing service costs and transportation costs. The trip required to obtain service from a given market establishment is called a **linkage.** Linkages are a function of distance, frequency of the trip, frustration, and other factors. The longer or more costly the linkages from a given residential location are, then the lower the rent a given family will pay for that location. This notion is actually quite compatible with our earlier general notions of location for businesses.

Each family has different service requirements or market connections. Thus, each family is willing to bid a different amount for a given housing location. Again, that family who can pay the most will obtain a given location. Each family can be thought of as having different bid-rent curves, just as different industries were shown to have in Figure 11.6. Again, this concept ensures that each parcel, in equilibrium, should earn the maximum economic rent.

In order to keep this discussion from getting out of hand, we will make a few generalizations at this point. If the preceding analysis is carried through to its logical conclusion, we find some patterns begin to emerge. First of all, we know from empirical study that higher income families tend to locate fairly far from the CBD. The reasons for this tendency can be deduced from economic theory. However, there is also a simple explanation for this pattern. Higher income families tend to occupy newer dwellings (remember filtering) which tend to be located away from the CBD because of land availability.

The sites occupied by residential users are larger as one progresses away from the CBD. The reasons for this are somewhat complex. Basically, housing service comes from the whole package of benefits supplied by housing. Deriving the appropriate satisfaction from the level of housing service purchased depends on how much each of the pieces of the package costs relative to the others. At a given location housing service may be increased by simply buying more service, implying a larger house. However, as we go farther away from the CBD land rents fall, but structure costs do not. Thus we may find housing service may be increased more by adding more land than through increases in dwelling size. It is true that dwelling sizes do tend to increase away from the CBD, but lots tend to increase relatively more rapidly. In effect, the homeowner uses the savings in land rent to increase total service by increasing the size of the lot. The savings in land rent also offset higher transportation costs. Close to the CBD where land is more expensive, housing service tends to be supplied by more structure, rather than more lot size. Thus we find high-rise apartments near the CBD, newer detached homes on fairly large lots far from the CBD, and moderately sized detached dwellings on small lots or garden-type apartments in between the two extremes.

Nonresidential Uses   Besides residential uses, urban areas also have major areas of land allocated to industry, retail trade, service establishments, public buildings, streets, and other uses. The bid-rent concepts we have examined above can also be used to explain the general locations of these types of establishments. If you wish to pursue more detail on the location of these uses, there are several excellent sources listed in the references.

A General Model of Location—Equilibrium

To summarize and organize what has been said up to this point we will present a simple, general equilibrium model of how land is allocated in urban areas.[3] Land may be viewed as deriving value from four broad classes of characteristics:

1. Site physical characteristics;
2. Site climate;
3. Neighborhood characteristics; and
4. Accessibility to service establishments (linkages).

A potential user for any site will evaluate the site on the basis of each of these variables to establish a value for the site. This is the investment value we have described previously. However, it should be added that probably this value is best explained in terms of utility or satisfaction rather than money.

For each site, there will be many potential users bidding for the property. In general, each bidder will be willing to pay a rent up to the amount of value perceived. If more than this were paid, some wealth would be sacrificed. The ultimate purchaser will be the highest bidder, who coincidently will have assigned the highest value to the site. In a

---

[3]This discussion is based on a presentation by David Segal in *Urban Economics* (Homewood, Ill.: Richard D. Irwin, 1977); see Chapter 5.

free competitive market, this will assign the highest and best use to every site.

As a given bidder is outbid on his or her first choice, that bidder falls back to the second choice, and so forth. Eventually all land will be under highest and best use and each user will be on the best site he or she can afford.

This model relates directly from the bid-rent approach we described. It is easy to see how the various appraisal and investment concepts we described in part 1 fit into this general model, in theory at least.

Important Trends and Factors in Urban Land Usage

A look at the map of any large city will show that in spite of the basic theory presented above, not all cities look alike. Some are larger than others. Some have more suburban areas than others. The list of differences is legion. Why do these differences exist?

Effect of Transportation Routes   If location is a function of market linkages, then any adjustment in the cost or length of the linkages for a given parcel will alter its value. Improved transportation routes in cities have definitely changed the value of properties located near these routes. The interstate highway system has had a great impact on many cities. The changes in transportation routes have changed the effective cost of getting to a particular market, so land which was far from the CBD now commands a higher rent because of improved access to markets. As more and more producers locate along these newer transportation routes, more jobs become located away from the CBD. This means that a family in the suburbs might suddenly find it is possible to lower the overall cost of a given location by changing jobs. Because of this fact, wage rate differentials in some cities have arisen between the CBD and the suburbs to erase these potential gains from switching employment locations.

Effect of Zoning   As we shall see in chapter 14, zoning is a prime limitation on the free market process for determining land use. Zoning may restrict a given parcel in a given location from being used in the manner in which its rent would be maximized by limiting the classes of users who may bid for the property.

The argument in favor of zoning is based on the maintenance of overall value or welfare. When an inappropriate land use is located in a given neighborhood, the surrounding sites may lose value. This loss in attractiveness causes rents on these parcels to fall. By prohibiting a given use on a particular site, say, a tannery in a residential neighborhood, some rent may be lost on the restricted site. However, if zoning is properly applied, the rent loss through the restriction should be smaller than that lost on the neighboring sites if there were no restriction. It is impossible to say if zoning always works to maximize neighborhood value, but it seems that zoning is a power communities generally desire to retain.

Factors Affecting City Growth   The reasons for differences in the size of metropolitan areas are not easy to determine. A number of writers have proposed various theories relating to the size, spatial dimensions, and other similar characteristics of cities. These theories are based on extremely complex mathematics and are not really compatible with the level of this discussion.

One theory, which we shall explore in detail in chapter 18, is the export base idea. This theory says that city growth is a function of growth in the demand for products which are sold outside the city's boundaries. If the demand for these exported goods rises, workers will be attracted to the job opportunities and growth will occur. Another argument for growth says simply that growth will occur when the labor supply grows. Which occurs first, an increase in labor or an increase in demand? We shall say that when export employment increases, whether from the demand for the output or from increased labor supply, the city will grow and so will the demand for property development.

Summary of Location Analysis

Theories which are used to explain the economics of urban areas are among the most fascinating in the social sciences, perhaps because urban development is explained by inputs from many seemingly unrelated disciplines. Major inputs to these theories come from sociologists, geographers, economists, political scientists, and others. Many questions still remain unanswered, however. Why are slums, urban blight, de facto segregation, cultural centers, and financial centers all found in cities?

In this section, we have presented a basic idea of how land rent is determined and why different land areas are used for different purposes. In general, land values are determined by those who can best afford to bid for it. Rent decreases as the distance from the market increases for a given class of user. Since value is the capitalized value of rent under highest and best use, the location of a parcel of land is a direct influence on its value. Finally, because so much of the total market for goods and services is concentrated in a few areas in a city (the CBD and perhaps some suburban shopping centers), the values of land outlying these areas are generally lower than values for land close by.

Physical Factors Affecting Value

There are a number of important physical characteristics which affect the productive capacity and, therefore, the value of land or improved property. Some of these will be discussed briefly next. These factors will be divided into those affecting the site itself and those affecting the site with improvements.

Factors Affecting the Site

Size and Shape of Site   The most obvious physical characteristics of a parcel which affect its value are its overall size and shape. There must be enough space in a particular site to improve it properly with the desired improvement. This must include space for the building as well as parking and perhaps some landscaping which would improve the appearance of the overall package. It is not sufficient just to have a lot which is large enough in terms of square feet. The lot must also have the proper shape.

There are some specific features of site size and shape which must be taken into account when evaluating a particular site. The **frontage** or width of a site will affect its value—it is the most valuable part, especially when the lot is not located on a corner. However, a given lot must have sufficient depth relative to its width or it may actually lose value relative to surrounding parcels. In general, we may say that if a lot is deeper than normal (compared to neighboring sites), relative to width, the front-foot value increases, but the overall value per square foot decreases relative to normal values. If a lot is shallower than normal, relative to width, front-foot values will be lower, but square-foot values will be higher.

Besides frontage and depth relationships, the location of a site on a corner may influence its value. For many users a corner location will be a positive influence, as it gives the site more accessibility, prominence, light, and air. However, in some areas corner lots command higher taxes and decreased privacy, making them less desirable. This may be especially true in the case of residential lots. In general, it is difficult to set forth any rules of thumb for this influence.

One final factor we may examine is the concept of **plottage.** It is possible to increase the value of a small site by combining it with other adjacent parcels. It is not unusual for the value of the combined site to exceed the sum of the values of the individual parcels! This happens because the larger, combined site permits a wide variety of more intensive uses which, in turn, allow a larger rent to be paid for the property as a whole. Plottage is an important factor in the private redevelopment of declining urban areas.

Topography   **Topography** refers to the overall "lay" of the land. Is the site hilly or flat? If the topography of a site is not right for the intended use, it must be altered. If the buyer must do too much work to alter the topography, then he can afford to bid much less for the site. Even so, a site with particularly unusual topography may be in heavy demand because of its unique character. In such a case, unusual topography may increase the value of a particular site.

Soil and Subsoil Conditions   Different uses require different soil and subsoil conditions as bases for adequate economical construction. When the Hancock Building in Chicago was being constructed, the builders miscalculated the subsoil conditions, causing them to put in an inadequate foundation. As the building began to be constructed, the first two stories started to sink and had to be rebuilt on new, deeper pilings. This type of mistake is expensive. For some uses, soil or subsoil conditions are not important. However, for improvements like skyscrapers and nuclear power plants, the economics of readying the site may be a key variable in the site-selection decision.

Factors Affecting the Improvements

Relationship of Improvement to Site   Frank Lloyd Wright showed us with his house and site combinations how important it is for a site and its improvements to work together and give the appropriate appearance. The improved site must have all its constituent parts in concert with each other in order to maximize value. A trip to many large cities today shows some interesting changes in the philosophy of site improvements for particular types of uses. In cities such as Minneapolis, Philadelphia, and Washington, D.C., new office buildings are often built in the suburbs on large, rolling sites with easy access to highways. They include attractive architecture, landscaping, and a parklike setting. Often, several buildings will be near each other for convenience. The overall appearance of these new developments is much more pleasing than many of their older counterparts and they provide attractive, valuable working environments.

Building Functional Characteristics   The value of any building improvement will depend to a great extent on the economical use of its space. We must know how much space we need to allocate to hallways, utilities, and service areas as these spaces cannot be rented to a tenant except indirectly. In most buildings, a proper balance needs to be struck between aesthetics and practicality. Factory-type buildings must contain a useful floor plan which allows their areas to be flexible and economically useful. High ceilings allow goods to be stacked, permitting more value to be assigned to a certain amount of floor area. We must keep in mind that an improvement must work well for its intended purpose to maximize value.

In this category, we are also concerned with the overall soundness of the structure. Are lighting and utilities adequate? Today energy usage is important. A well-planned, energy-saving structure will be more and more valuable in the coming years. We must also see what mechanical equipment is available and know its condition, whether it is to be purchased new or used or leased. The quality of the construction in the structure is also extremely important.

Other Factors   The value of a structure and its site will also be affected by the adequacy of off-site improvements such as utilities, road connections, railroad spurs, and street lighting.

One of the more important physical features affecting value is the flexibility of the improvement. A structure which has a variety of potential uses and which can be altered with minimum expense is inherently more valuable than a structure which is built for one special purpose. If it is for a special purpose only, then the market for a structure will obviously be restricted only to those users who need that type of structure. Since city characteristics do change over time, users for a particular site are also likely to change. Therefore, an improved property should be as flexible as possible to take advantage of city dynamics.

The preceding lists are hardly exhaustive, nor are they fully detailed. However, you can see that the physical analysis of a site involves a number of important variables, especially if it is improved. A potential investor must know what is needed in a site in order to receive the maximum productivity per dollar of cost.

CHAPTER ELEVEN SUMMARY   In chapter 10 we presented a detailed model of the factors affecting the market and investment values of real estate. In this chapter we have begun to explore two of the major categories of causal variables: location and physical characteristics. The value of a piece of property is a direct function of its productivity. We have looked at this in dollar terms in part 1 of this text. Now we are beginning to look behind the dollars to see what affects the productive capacity of the property.

The location of a property affects its ability to do work. Since all properties require services, a given site is linked to every establishment which provides those services. The cost of these linkages will definitely affect the cost of the benefits provided by the subject site. We have seen in this chapter how these transportation costs provide us with a theoretical nature of why particular land uses occupy particular locations. We have also examined a number of the more important physical characteristics which affect the value of a site. We have looked at factors which affect the site itself, as well as those which relate to the improvements.

We will now move on to a discussion of the legal foundations of value, which will be in contrast to the one we have just finished because the relationships to value will be much more subtle.

KEY TERMS

Baseline	Metes and Bounds	Range
Central Business	Plat Plan	Rectangular Survey
District	Platting	Rent Gradient
Economic Rent	Plottage	Sections
Frontage	Population Density	Topography
Linkage	Gradient	Townships
	Principal Meridian	

QUESTIONS FOR STUDY AND DISCUSSION

1. Describe the three major methods of legal description for real property.

2. What is a *linkage*? How do linkages affect value? Explain why the concept of a linkage discussed in this chapter is compatible with the idea of linked submarkets from the previous chapter.

3. Why do certain land uses fit well on a particular land location while others do not? (Explain in terms of linkages.)

4. How does bid-rent theory explain patterns of land use?

5. What are some of the common characteristics which seem to typify the locational structure of most urban areas?

6. What are some of the more important physical characteristics affecting the value of property?

7. Bid-rent theory is a static (equilibrium) concept. Describe the general changes which have occurred in cities over time and relate these changes to bid-rent theory.

8. What kind of population density gradient would you expect to find for a city such as Los Angeles? Boston? Why?

9. Why are slums so pervasive in our major cities? Why can we not eliminate them easily through the private enterprise system? Try to explain these questions using the economic theories described in this chapter.

12 LEGAL FACTORS AFFECTING VALUE I– OWNERSHIP INTERESTS

IN CHAPTER 10 our model of real estate value showed that the physical nature and, indirectly, the economic value of property is influenced by its physical, locational, and legal factors. In this chapter and the two which follow, we will look at the legal factors which affect real property values.

Property law, especially real property law, is extremely complex. It has many of its roots in English common law. Many of the concepts we will discuss here date back to the Middle Ages. As you read through this chapter with these historical roots in mind, it is easier to understand the rationale for many of the ideas that will be presented.

Because of the complexity of the legal interests involved in the ownership of real property, or *realty,* as it is called, you will be able to appreciate the necessity for the use of professional legal advice in the analysis process. This brief discussion cannot hope to instruct you in all the legalities of realty. However, what we can do here is note the general areas of concern and how the legal characteristics of a property may affect its value. Further, you can use this presentation to help introduce you to some of the more common terms and concepts about which you should be aware. It cannot be too strongly emphasized, however, that there is no substitute for good legal counsel in a real estate transaction.

Property Rights

In the introduction we described property ownership as a "bundle of rights" to the possession or use of the property. The number of rights a person owns in property determines the *degree of interest* that person has in the property. We will discuss the various degrees of interest one may hold in real property shortly. Some of the rights which constitute the elements of ownership in real property include:

1. Possession,
2. Use,
3. Right to withdraw minerals, and
4. Right to divide and sell the rights.

These rights apply not only to the land and what is under it, but also the air above the land. The ability to divide the property and its rights and sell them in whatever form the owner desires adds a great deal to the flexibility of real estate as an investment medium.

Normally the world of property is divided into two parts: real property and personal property. **Realty** is described as the land (and the air above it) and all appurtenances (structures) attached directly and permanently to the land. Any property which does not fall into this category is called personal property. Furniture, lamps, rugs, curtains, and the like are all examples of personal property, at least intuitively. However, there are some times when real property and personal property may become confused.

Sometimes personal property may be attached directly to a building which is, in turn, attached to the land. Items of personal property in these circumstances become real property and are designated **fixtures.** If a rug is simply laid on a floor it may be rolled up and moved when the property tenants move. In that case, the rug is personal property. However, wall-to-wall carpet nailed to the floor becomes real property. Similarly, a free-standing bookcase would probably be considered personal property, whereas a built-in bookcase would no doubt be considered part of the real estate.

The concern over the definition of these items may seem like a purely academic question, but it is not. When a piece of property is transferred, the rights to the ownership of a location are transferred. Legal description does not list each item being transferred. The buildings and other items are transferred automatically. If there are items of personal property involved some determination must be made as to the ownership of these items. If the sale contract specifies certain items that will or will not transfer with the property and all parties sign the contract, then the problem is taken care of. In the absence of specific provisions, however, conflicts may arise during property transfers. There are some legal tests which are applied to sort out these conflicts.

A fixture will transfer with a parcel of real property if it meets one of the following conditions.

1. If the removal of the item will injure the property. If built-in shelves were removed and would leave holes or unsightly damage, then they would be considered part of the property.

2. An item of personal property will be considered part of the real estate if it is required for the real estate to perform its intended function properly.

3. A judge may also look at the intent of the parties to the transaction. If the parties both seemed to intend the fixture to transfer with the property, then it will be treated as realty.

4. Finally, if all else fails, the new owner will be given priority.

Some items, such as trade and agricultural fixtures, are, in general, treated separately and do not come under these doctrines. Generally, these items are always considered to be personal property.

As you can guess, the value of a property will be obviously affected by its definition. The presence of fixtures and their retention may make the property more valuable. There is a lesson in this. Because of the effect of fixtures on value and the possible difficulties involved in defining them, it is a good idea to settle any doubts in writing before the transaction is consummated. Such agreements will save all parties confusion and prevent a loss in value for the owner.

Ownership Interests in Real Property

There are a great many degrees of interest one may hold in a piece of real property. To help you sort these out, we will divide them into some useful categories. The various degrees of interest are summarized in Table 12.1.

One of the major divisions of property interest is between *freehold* and *less-than-freehold* (sometimes erroneously called *leasehold*) estates.[1] A **freehold estate** is held by its owner either for its life or with the right to pass on the estate through inheritance. **Less-than-freehold** estates are not passed on through inheritance, except by agreement between parties. There are also two major divisions in the category of less-than-freehold estates: those which permit possession of the property and those which do not. We will now describe some of the major types of estates in more detail. In this chapter, we will deal only with freehold estates. The others will be covered in the next chapter.

Freehold Estates

The most important form of freehold estate is fee simple, the highest form of estate an owner may have in real property. Owners in fee simple have all the rights to possession, use, and transfer in a piece of property unless they deed some of these rights to someone else. The only real constraints on the freedom of owners in fee simple to use and dispose of their property as they wish come from government, with its police and taxing powers. A fee simple interest lasts indefinitely unless the property owner dies without having designated any heirs, at which time the property reverts to the state. Owners of a fee simple may voluntarily restrict the use of their property through deed restrictions or the granting of easements. These restrictions may last the life of the fee. (A *fee* refers to an inheritance in land.)

A rare form of fee simple is called **fee tail.** This type of estate has its roots in the medieval custom of passing property to one's oldest male heir. It is a qualified fee which is restricted from use in most states in the United States.

Qualified Fees   There are a large group of estates called **qualified fees.** These estates convert a fee simple interest into a restricted fee which prescribes or proscribes certain land uses for the remaining life of the fee.

---

[1]Webster defines the term *estate* as "the degree, nature, extent, and quality of interest or ownership one has in land or other property. Estate also refers to the property itself."

TABLE 12.1   SUMMARY OF DEGREE OF INTEREST
IN LAND

I. Freehold Estate
   A. Estates of Inheritance
      1. Fee Simple
      2. Fee Tail
      3. Qualified Fees
         a. Determinable
         b. Condition Subsequent
         c. Condition Precedent
   B. Life Estates
      1. Conventional Life Estates
      2. Legal Life Estates
         a. Dower
         b. Curtesy
         c. Homestead

II. Less-Than-Freehold Estates
   A. Leaseholds
      1. Tenancy for Years
      2. Periodic Tenancy
      3. Tenancy at Will
      4. Tenancy at Sufferance
   B. Incorporeal Rights
      1. Reversions and Remainders
      2. Potential for Reversions and Remainders
      3. Easement
      4. License
      5. Profit
      6. Lien
         a. Mortgage Lien
         b. Mechanics Lien
         c. Tax Lien

III. Number of Owners (applicable to I and II above)
   A. Tenancy in Severalty
   B. Tenancy in Common
   C. Joint Tenancy and Tenancy in Entirety
   D. Miscellaneous Groups

1. *Determinable Fee.*   The **determinable fee** interest requires that the property be used for some specific purpose, such as a church. If the property is put to some other use, the property will revert to the original owner who qualified the fee or to his heirs. The process of qualifying the fee creates a potential reversionary interest for the heirs of the grantor who qualified the fee.

2. *Fee Simple Subject to Condition Subsequent.*   Perhaps the owners of a property in fee simple wish to prevent their property from ever being used for a particular purpose. When the owners sell the property, they may put a restriction in the deed which states that the property can *never* be used for some purpose—a bar, for instance. If this qualification is subsequently violated, the property again would revert to the original grantors or their heirs.

3. *Fee Simple Subject to Condition Precedent.*   In this form of qualified fee, the grantor may put a clause in the deed which says that title will not pass to the grantee (purchaser or heir) unless a certain act is performed. Occasionally, a father with an unmarried daughter may deed his property to his daughter at death with the title to pass only if the daughter gets married, for instance.

There are some practical considerations with these qualified fees. Some number of generations after the death of a grantor who has qualified his or her fee, the original grant may be violated without anyone's knowing. These violations may make it difficult to subsequently sell the property, but the owners will not likely lose their interest simply because no one complains about the violation.

Life Estates   There is a group of freehold interests which cannot be inherited. These are called *life estates*. A life estate is held either for the life of the grantor or the life of some other designated person. A **conventional life estate** may arise in the following manner. A property owner has a piece of farmland which he is not using, so he deeds it as a life estate to his tenant farmer. When the grantor dies (or his wife, if he so chooses) the property reverts to a named beneficiary such as the grantor's son. This beneficiary is called a **remainderman.** Anyone can be named as remainderman in such a situation. This type of grant, in a similar fashion to the qualified fee, creates a potential interest for the remainderman. This potential interest becomes freehold when the original grantor dies and the property reverts to the remainderman or the remainderman's heirs.

There are also a number of so-called **legal life estates.** A wife has a legal interest in the real property of her husband which vests at his death. This is called the **dower right** and cannot be extinguished except by permission of the wife. If a man owns a piece of land which he subsequently transfers without his wife's signature, the new owner may find later, when the grantor dies, that his wife can claim an interest in this land. Obviously, the buyer of a piece of property may lose some of the value of his property if he does not demand the wife of the grantor to give up her dower rights. It should be noted here that if the wife of a grantor does not sign the contract for sale in a property transaction, she cannot be forced to sign the deed when the transaction is closed.

The dower right is not the same as community property. With community property both husband and wife have a real interest in the property of the other. The dower right vests only at death. A husband has a similar right in the property of his wife. This is called **curtesy right.**

Another legal life estate protects the family of a grantor from losing their interest in the property of a dead husband and father. This is called the **homestead right.** It offers the widow and children of a dead spouse protection from creditors and others by allowing a certain percentage of the value of any property as a homestead.

All these legal rights are designed to protect the families of landowners from losing all the interest in property to which they might be entitled. However, the exercise of these rights may be harmful to a grantee who has bought a parcel in good faith. For this reason, some state laws and courts have modified the common law rights of dower, curtesy, and homestead to minimize the injury to all parties in transactions where these rights are involved. One should not minimize the effect of, for instance, the dower right. Nothing could be more disastrous than for a property owner to have to give up a valuable property because of the exercise of a dower right which could have been avoided.

Number of Owners

Many of the preceding degrees of interest may be held by more than one owner simultaneously. The structure of the multiple ownership is important in determining the nature of the interest involved. When only one owner holds a given estate this is called **tenancy in severalty.** There are various types of multiple ownership which will be described next.

Tenancy in Common   With **tenancy in common** there are a number of owners, each of which has full rights to use and dispose of his or her interest, whatever it is, as that owner sees fit. This is analogous to the ownership of stock in a corporation. Each stockholder may buy as many shares as he or she can afford and can dispose of them without affecting the rights of the other owners. Each owner has the same basic rights as designated by law and the corporate charter.

Joint Tenancy   Joint tenants are in much more restrictive positions than tenants in common. First, joint tenants must each have the same proportional interests. For instance, two joint tenants must each own 50% of the property. When there are more than two joint tenants and one dies, that person's interest automatically reverts to the other tenants equally. A **joint tenancy** can exist only if all tenants share the same degree of interest, time of interest, degree of possession, and title. A joint tenancy involving only a husband and wife is called **tenancy in entirety.** A joint tenant cannot sell his or her interest without destroying the tenancy. There are many reasons for choosing joint tenancy instead of tenancy in common, and vice versa. An individual contemplating multiple ownership must explore the specific ramifications for each form before making a commitment.

Other Forms   In addition to the preceding, there are numerous other forms of interest which can be used in appropriate situations. Corporations may own property. In such a case, the corporation is treated as a person. Several corporations could be tenants in common in a property, involving thousands of people indirectly. Condominiums are a form of ownership which saw rapid growth in the 1970s. Being a condominium owner involves the joint ownership of parts of the property and the personal ownership of other parts. There are many other arrangements such as cooperatives, partnerships, trusts, and community property.

Summary

In this section, we have discussed a myriad of degrees of interest which may be held in real property. Because the value of property is a function of the benefits which may be derived, the degree of interest will have a great deal of bearing on property value. The more rights an owner has, and the more the owner controls those rights, the higher is the potential value. Before buying an interest in a piece of property, the potential investor should be careful to obtain the degree and type of interest which maximizes the value of the rights to be obtained.

Acquiring Title to Real Property

Having seen the variety of freehold estates one can have in a piece of real property, we will now discuss the legal aspects surrounding the acquisition of title.

Evidence of Title

The title to an interest in real property must be established without doubt in order for the owners to preserve the full value of their fee. There are a number of ways for this to be done.

Let us suppose a man buys a property. In most jurisdictions in the United States, he receives a **deed** which conveys the appropriate rights he will have in the property to him. However, there is more to it than that. For two reasons, the simple exchange of money for a deed is insufficient to establish title. First, the buyer does not really know if the seller owned what was sold. There are unscrupulous people who would try to sell land they do not own. Therefore, a system is needed to help buyers be assured that they are obtaining the degree of interest they desire in the property they are purchasing. This brings us to the second, related difficulty. The new owner must be able to establish for others that he does own the property so the seller will not try to resell the property to a third party later.

Abstract of Title   To provide a unified solution to both of the above-mentioned problems, we use the recording system. When our owner acquired property, he obtained a deed which is the instrument of conveyance of the title. The deed itself is some evidence of an interest. To establish the title properly, the new owner should go to the appropriate authority, generally the county clerk at the courthouse for the county in which the property is located, and *record* the deed. This recording process establishes the new owner in the chain of previous owners of the property. A recorded deed is a matter of public record, so the owner may be found by anyone who might be interested in buying the property, especially if the seller does not turn out to be the real owner.

Along with the deed, other things are recorded which affect the title to a property. Liens against the property, as well as other encumbrances, are also recorded. This assures that all the relevant facts defining the interest of a given owner in a particular fee are a matter of record. Prospective buyers may then go look at this record to assure themselves that they are buying what they want from the rightful owner.

To facilitate the search for the relevant information and also to provide additional evidence of title, we have the *abstract*. A **title abstract** is a document, actually a set of documents, which details the chain of owners of a particular parcel clear back to the original grant from the government to a private owner. Each time the property was sold and a deed recorded, some record should have been made. Ideally, there should be a record of each and every change in the title from one owner to another. Likewise all encumbrances and, similarly, their subsequent removal, should also have been recorded. All these records, in chronological order, serve as the abstract of title. The abstract itself is a copy of each document in the chain. A schematic representation of the abstract appears in Table 12.2.

A look at Table 12.2 would show a prospective owner many things. Assume it is 1983 and you wish to buy the property described in our table. You can see by looking at the abstract that F. Murphy appears to be the owner. Mr. Murphy appears to have good title because there is an unbroken chain from the original grant. We can see there is a mortgage against the property. Normally, the buyer would have a lawyer or title company search the records at the courthouse and bring the abstract up to date—that is, make sure all other recordings concerning the prop-

TABLE 12.2   ABSTRACT OF TITLE

Date	Transaction
11/13/1879	Government deeds to Mr. A. Brown . . .
6/30/1912	Mr. A. Brown dies. Property goes to daughter, Mrs. P. Jones . . .
3/18/1947	Mrs. Jones dies. Property passes to son, Mr. B. Jones . . .
8/23/1967	B. Jones deeds to F. Murphy . . .
8/23/1967	First Mortgage lien by First State Savings and Loan Co. . . .
10/2/1972	Mechanics lien filed against F. Murphy by Central Plumbing . . .
7/11/1973	Mechanics lien discharged by F. Murphy . . .

erty have been included since 1967. Through this mechanism, buyers can help establish their interest and the degree of their interest.

Title Insurance   Sometimes having the deed, an updated abstract, and even properly recording the deed is not enough. There are a number of things which can still cause difficulty for a recent buyer. If you wish to buy Mr. Murphy's property, you have the title search conducted on January 8, 1983, for instance. You are going to close the transaction on January 11, 1983. Suppose that on January 10, 1983, a legitimate, timely, mechanics lien is filed against the property. You may not get a clear title when you close. Also you did not know that Mr. Murphy has a wife, but is separated. She lives in Bayonne and does not know he has property. He does not know about the dower right and you do not know about the wife. Subsequent to your purchase, he dies, still married, and his wife finds out about the property. She steps forward to claim her dower right.

For these and other reasons, we have **title insurance.** Title insurance is helpful for two reasons. First, you will not get it until the insurance company does its own search. They may very well find that wife in Bayonne and let you know in time to do something about it. Second, once you do get the insurance, you are protected from loss by hidden interests. The title insurance company will take care of the claims.

There are several kinds of title insurance. Mortgagees (lenders) generally demand that you take out insurance in their benefit, so that the property will serve as sufficient collateral for the debt you will be incurring. Then the owner may take out the insurance for his or her fee interest. Just a warning here: be certain when you buy property that you specify that you wish title insurance for yourself as well as for the lender. Otherwise, you may think you are insured when in fact only the lender is. At the time of the closing of a sale transaction, title insurance is reasonably priced. It is much more expensive if you try to buy it later, for instance, after a year's time.

Other Evidence   Thus far we have seen that evidence of title may be established by having a deed, recording the deed, obtaining an abstract which is up-to-date, and buying title insurance. Another piece of evidence is possession of the property. Mr. A sells to Ms. B, who does not record the deed. Later Mr. A notices the deed has not been recorded by B, so A sells to Mr. C. C records the deed. Who is the owner? Probably, even though B did not record, if she has a deed, perhaps a cancelled check, and is in possession of the property, B will be the rightful owner. C will then have a cause of action against A, but that is all.

Another form of evidence may be obtained in some places. A few counties in the United States use the *Torrens system*. For example, when a buyer contemplates a purchase, he goes to a special court where he petitions the judge for a **Torrens Certificate.** When this certificate is obtained, it is absolute evidence of clear title. Before granting the certificate, the judge will, in essence, do a search of the title, advertise that the property is being transferred, and ask all concerned parties to present claims, and so forth. Once all claims are satisfied, the new owner can get clear title. On the surface, the Torrens system seems like a very good idea. The buyer will be well protected. However, the system is not in general use for a couple of reasons. First, it is very expensive to administer. Second, because the court cannot possibly advertise in every paper in the United States, legitimate claimants may not know the property is being transferred and they may lose their legal rights in the property, which is not fair.

Conveyance of Title

We have seen how buyers can show evidence of their interest in land and what degrees of interest they may have. Now we will see how these interests may be conveyed. There are a number of ways this can be done. These include the public and private grants, by gift, descent, adverse possession, and some miscellaneous other ways.

Public Grant   At some point in the history of the United States some governments owned all the land in the country by claim. Several governments were involved: Spain, France, England, Mexico, and the United States. A private citizen obtains land from the government by a **deed patent.** This is the first step in the title chain we saw earlier. Sometimes land was granted outright, without cost, and sometimes it was sold. The effect is the same either way.

Private Grant   The private grant of real property is accomplished in the owner's lifetime by exchanging a deed for some valuable consideration. One of two types of deed is most generally used, either the **warranty deed** or the **quitclaim deed.** The highest form of conveyance is accomplished with the warranty deed. With this deed the seller warrants that he or she has good and merchantable title to the property being conveyed. Contained in the warranty deed will be a phrase of some sort which conveys the title to the parcel described in the deed. There are also a series of covenants which serve to strengthen the title. In Iowa, for instance, the standard warranty deed says:

1. The grantors do here by covenant . . . that said grantors hold said real estate in fee simple;

2. That they have good and lawful authority to sell and convey (the property);

3. That said premises are free and clear of all liens and encumbrances whatsoever, except as specifically stated (in the deed);

4. That the grantors covenant to warrant and defend the premises against the lawful claims of others except those shown in the deed. Also,

5. All those signing also release all dower, homestead, and similar rights.

These covenants (1 through 4) above and the release of dower rights are common to most warranty deeds. The Iowa deed is written in somewhat more common language than the deeds used in other states. The covenants used have formal names which may be substituted in other jurisdictions. Covenants 1 and 2 above constitute the *Covenant of Seizin.* Covenant 3 is the *Covenant against encumbrances.* Covenant 4 is a combination of the *covenant of quiet enjoyment* and the *warranty of title.* All of these warranties inform buyers that they are getting good titles which should be free of any surprise claims and are theirs forever. If any of these covenants were broken by the seller, that seller is liable, even to a subsequent buyer.

A lesser form of conveyance is provided by the **quitclaim deed.** With this deed, the grantors merely state that they convey to the grantees all the interests held by said grantors. However, they do not have to have any interests to do this. No warranties are made that the sellers have any title to sell. Neither are there any assurances of protection from encumbrances for the grantees. These deeds are used when some possible "cloud" exists against the title held by the grantor.

In between the warranty deed and the quitclaim deed, in some states, is the **bargain and sale deed.** This deed does warrant that the seller has some interest in the property to convey. A bargain and sale may also contain an assurance that the grantor, at least, has not encumbered the property.

There are numerous other special deeds in various states. The important point to remember here is that as a buyer you get a deed which transfers to you the interest you wish to have and that you obtain as much protection from claims against your title as you can. As a seller you must make certain you do not promise something you cannot deliver to prevent claims against you later in the form of a lawsuit.

Conveyance by Gift   Property may be conveyed, without consideration, by gift during one's lifetime. A deed such as those previously described will still be used, but no mention will be made of consideration. Property may also be deeded at one's death through a will. This is known as **devise.** Again, the appropriate deed must be used, but no consideration is necessary.

Descent   When a person dies without a will, **intestate,** that person's property will be conveyed to his or her heirs in a way which conforms to the statutes controlling such matters. The state will decide how the interests are to be divided. Generally, some party will be given the authority to deed the appropriate interests to the rightful heirs in such a case.

Adverse Possession   It is possible in most states for someone to obtain property by simply taking it over. This is called **adverse possession.** The rules which control this are strict and designed to protect the rightful owner as much as possible. Generally, someone who wishes to obtain title in this way must sue for it. It must be proven that the person has occupied or possessed the ground as specified by statute. Generally, the occupancy must be

1. Open—for all to see;
2. Notorious or hostile—even when the owner has tried to prohibit it;
3. Continuous—You can't get kicked off, even for a day; and
4. For a sufficient, statutory time period.

Other requirements may apply in various jurisdictions. Probably, this is not as easy a way to obtain property today as it once was. However, it still happens and some property owners with a natural possibility of loss may put up fences or close a gate, say, to prevent the accidental satisfaction of these requirements.

An example of the use of restraints to prevent adverse possession may be valuable here. At Ohio State University there is a city street,

Neal Avenue, which traverses one end of the campus. To prevent the city from claiming this state property by adverse possession, the university closes a gate at each end of the street at the campus boundaries for one afternoon each year. This interrupts the continuity of use and prevents the transfer of title to the land on which the street is located.

Miscellaneous Situations   In addition to the preceding acquisition methods, property may also be acquired by condemnation, foreclosure, bankruptcy, accretion, or abandonment, to name a few. We will discuss condemnation later, and foreclosure will be covered in our discussion of financing. **Accretion** is the process of acquiring land through the action of nature. Water or wind may deposit land on or adjacent to a property, causing the land to increase. This process can also operate in reverse, in which case land may be lost by natural action. Bankruptcy and abandonment are fairly straightforward and often involve specific statutory requirements.

CHAPTER TWELVE SUMMARY

In this chapter we have examined some of the major legal determinants of value in real estate. First, we examined the basic definition of property rights in order to outline exactly what is meant by real estate. Then we proceeded to define the various estates, or degrees of ownership interest, an owner can hold in real property. Probably the most important form here is fee simple. This serves as the primary basis for home ownership and major investments. The other forms serve mostly for specific situations. Once we defined the degrees of interest, we described the various ways in which title to these interests might be conveyed as well as the various ways one can show evidence of title.

In terms of our model, we can see that the major effects of the legal area discussed so far lie in the following areas.

1. Value is a direct function of the degree of interest held. The more rights you have, the more valuable is your interest.

2. The evidence you have to support your claim to title may also be an important influence on value. An abstract showing "clouds" on the title will definitely reduce the value of an estate.

3. The method of conveyance is also important. A warranty deed is a much safer way for the buyer to acquire title.

KEY TERMS

Accretion	Fixtures	Realty
Adverse Possession	Freehold Estate	Remainderman
Bargain and Sale	Homestead Right	Tenancy in

Deed	Joint Tenancy	Common
Conventional Life	Intestate	Tenancy in Entirety
Estate	Legal Life Estates	Tenancy in
Curtesy Right	Less-Than-	Severalty
Deed Patent	Freehold Estate	Title Abstract
Determinable Fee	Qualified Fees	Title Insurance
Devise	Quitclaim Deed	Torrens Certificate
Dower Right		Warranty Deed
Fee Tail		

QUESTIONS FOR STUDY AND DISCUSSION

1. Distinguish between *real* and *personal* property. What are some legal tests for determining whether property is real or personal?

2. What is the highest form of interest one may own in real property? What distinguishes it from the lesser forms?

3. What is the difference between a *life estate* and an *estate of inheritance*?

4. Describe the operation of qualified fees.

5. Differentiate between *joint tenancy* and *tenancy in common*.

6. What constitutes evidence of title to real property?

7. What are some of the more important ways in which the title to real property may be conveyed?

8. What are the two most important types of deeds? Differentiate them by the warranties they make.

13
LEGAL FACTORS AFFECTING VALUE II– LESS-THAN-FREEHOLD INTERESTS

IN TABLE 12.1, we saw that there are a number of ways in which interest in real property may be held without regular ownership (freehold) rights. In this chapter, we will describe a number of these forms, including the important category of lease interests.

Lease Interests

General Characteristics

A **leasehold estate** allows the owner of the leasehold, or *leased fee,* as it may be called, to possess and use a piece of property without actually owning the right to transfer the property itself. Either through an expressed or implied contract, a fee owner may give another party the right to possess or use his or her property for some specified period. The *lessee* (owner of the leasehold and tenant) may build on the property, rent it to others, obtain financing, or whatever else is permitted by the agreement with the fee owner (*lessor*). What the lessee may not do, however, is transfer the right to own the leased property. Lessees may transfer the right to use or possess the property if this is agreed to, but they cannot sell the ownership of the fee itself. There are several types of leasehold interest.

1. *Tenancy* (estate) *for Years.*   The form of estate called **tenancy for years** specifies the right to possession and use for a specific period of time. The period can be measured in days, months, years, or whatever. However, the period is specified. Often, this type of tenancy cannot be cancelled by either party without the other's permission. This type of agreement may be for a substantial period of time—ninety-nine years is not rare. This type lease is often used for leasing land to a developer who may subsequently build a skyscraper, shopping center, or even a housing development on it.

2. *Periodic Tenancy.*   **Periodic tenancy** is agreed to for a specified base period, say, a month or a year, and the lease continues to renew itself automatically unless one of the parties cancels the agreement by proper notice. Many apartments and commercial leases are of this type.

3. *Tenancy at Will.*   The type of lease called **tenancy at will** has no specified term. It may be cancelled by either party with minimal notice. Often apartments may be leased "without a lease" under this form of tenancy. The landlord may present the tenant with some rules, demand rent in advance, and that will be the extent of the lease.

4. *Tenancy at Sufferance.*   **Tenancy at sufferance** is an illegal tenancy wherein the tenant occupies the property without the landlord's permission.

As we will see later, the leasehold interest is the basis for a number of important development and financing arrangements. Many of our large skyscrapers, shopping centers, and private housing projects are based on complex layers of leasehold interests.

Lease Types

The lease itself is a contract between the current owner of the rights to possession and use (the lessor) and the party to whom these will be transferred (lessee). The contract will specify what rights are to be transferred and for how long. In addition, the contract will specify what services, if any, the lessor will provide for the lessee. If the lessor is responsible for taxes and insurance or maintenance and repairs, this will be set forth in the lease contract. If all these services are provided, the lease is called a **service lease.**

Leases are divided into two general time frames. Leases lasting for twenty-one years or longer are called long-term leases. Others are called short-term leases. Another main feature of the lease contract is the amount of rent to be paid to the lessor. Rent can be fixed for the life of the lease or it may vary according to some schedule. There may be a cost of living adjustment, for example, to adjust for inflation. Many leases for retail stores call for the rent to be based on a percent of sales, perhaps with a minimum and/or maximum rental specified. There are probably about as many different types of lease arrangements as there are situations. We will now detail some of the more important forms and the situations for which they might be used.

Net Leases   A lease contract is basically a form of financing an interest in property. The fact that the lessor may provide services is really beyond the scope of financing per se. Long-term leases for commercial and industrial property are generally not service leases. They are *net leases* of some form. A **net lease** is one which fails to provide one or more of the standard services or one in which the lessee pays expenses such as taxes or insurance. Some leases call for the lessee to pay all the costs of using the property. All the owner supplies in such a case is 100% financing. This type of arrangement is called a net-net-net lease. **Absolute net leases,** as they are often called, are popular for certain kinds of structures. Supermarket chains, discount houses such as K-Mart, and some fast food stores use absolute net leases to finance properties. Absolute net leases, such as these with good tenants, make prime investments for wealthy individuals and financial institutions.

Long-Term Leases   The developers of a large project may find that mortgage financing for their project will not be enough. Many institutions lending on large projects are restricted to the amount of money they can lend. Loan-to-value ratios of over 75% are uncommon. If the project is very large, the amount of equity required can be a heavy burden. For this reason, it may be desirable to reduce the amount of equity needed by leasing the land under the project. With this as a basis, developers can obtain a larger total amount of financing.

In addition to land, buildings can also be leased. Straight lease agreements in land and buildings are often for long periods. This is especially true in the case of ground leases upon which complex improvements are to be put. If improvements on the land are to be financed, the lease must generally be for a period at least one year longer than the period of the loan. For this reason, the owners of the prospective leasehold are forced to seek a long-term lease in order to set up the financing required for the improvements.

Sandwich Lease   In complex development situations, the parties involved may make a complex lease arrangement called a sandwich lease. The **sandwich lease** may best be described by an example. A owns a piece of ground on which B wishes to build an office complex. A leases this ground to B, who becomes the ground lessee. B helps finance his development by subleasing to C, a professional building manager. C, in turn, subleases to a number of tenant–occupants—D's. Thus we have A, the owner, who leases to B, who subleases to C, who subleases to several D's. B is called a sandwich lessor and C is a sandwich lessee. These two are sandwiched between A and D, the owner and the occupants, respectively. We will examine a specific example of this in chapter 17.

Sale-and-Leaseback   Often property owners find that they would like to get back the cash tied up in their property without losing the use of the property. To solve this sort of problem, owners may execute a **sale-and-leaseback** arrangement. In this transaction, the current owner, A, transfers his interest to B and simultaneously executes an appropriate lease to permit him, A, the continued occupancy of the property. The sale-and-leaseback is useful in complex development situations. Any kind of lease contract can be used in the sale-and-leaseback transaction.

Leases as Collateral   Both the lessor and the lessee may use their interest in leased premises as security for other financing. The owner of the property (lessor) has a contract which guarantees a stream of benefits in the form of rent. Even though the lessor does not possess the property, he or she has a valuable interest. This interest may serve as valuable security for a loan.

Similarly, the rights of the lessee are also valuable. With a suitable ground lease, a lessee may make improvements which can be financed. The right to use the property has value and helps serve as security for the financing of leasehold improvements made by the lessee. These multiple financing arrangements will be explored later in the chapters on financing.

Conclusion

As you can see from the foregoing discussion, lease interests can be extremely flexible. Because a lease interest arises through a contract, any legal arrangement, agreed to by all the parties, can be devised. Leasing is also of interest because it is a method of financing property, as well as a form of interest in property. We shall examine the mechanics of leasing as a financing form in examples in chapter 17.

As we saw in the discussion of the sandwich lease, a land lessee need not possess the property that is being leased. The interest can be sub-leased to another party and the original lessee is simply the owner of a cash flow. In many ways, lease interests resemble securities investments. In large developments, sandwich lessors may have only a contractual monetary interest in the real property. In effect, their claim becomes much the same as that of a bondholder or other fixed income investor.

Because of the complexity of many leasing arrangements, the legal fees may be extremely high. For a well-written sale-and-leaseback contract on a relatively modest industrial investment property, it is not uncommon for the legal fees to run into several thousands of dollars. These arrangements should not be entered into without the services of competent legal counsel experienced in these types of contracts.

Other Miscellaneous Interests

The last major group of interests to be described involve a number of various types of arrangements which offer either a potential interest in real estate or the right to use property without possession.

Reversions

In our discussion of qualified fees and life estates, we noted that it is possible for one to have a *potential* interest in real property. This interest may or may not ever be realized. If the designated remainderman in a life estate does not outlive the original grantor, the interest will never be realized. Similarly, if the heirs of the original grantor of a qualified fee are not aware of a violation of the qualification or if a violation never occurs, there will be no real interest. These potential interests have no real value unless the proper conditions exist for them to be vested.

Easements

An **easement** gives one property owner or an independent party the right to use a specific part of the property of another for the purpose of gaining access to another parcel. Figure 13.1 shows several parcels in juxtaposition in a typical situation. Parcel B is located in such a way as to be "land-locked." There is no direct access from parcel B to a road without crossing the property of one of the surrounding neighbors. Under these circumstances, the owner of parcel B, called the **dominant tenement,** will be given an easement across the property of parcel A, called the **servient tenement.** This easement will be given to provide ingress and egress to parcel B. It will generally be granted in a way which does the least injury to the servient tenement. Only the dominant tenement can release the servient tenement from such an easement. This type of easement is called an **appurtenant easement.**

Other easements may be granted to provide access to utility poles, to allow people to have access to a beach, or some other similar purpose. Normally, the servient landowner will receive fair compensation in return for granting the easement. This type of easement is called an **easement in gross.**

Easements may be used to alter the value of a property. Consider the following example. A property owner in an eastern city owned a 45,000 square-foot parcel with good street frontage on two sides as shown in Figure 13.2. In this particular town, parcels had to be 30,000 square feet to be zoned commercial. An oil company wished to buy the parcel to

FIGURE 13.1   AN EASEMENT

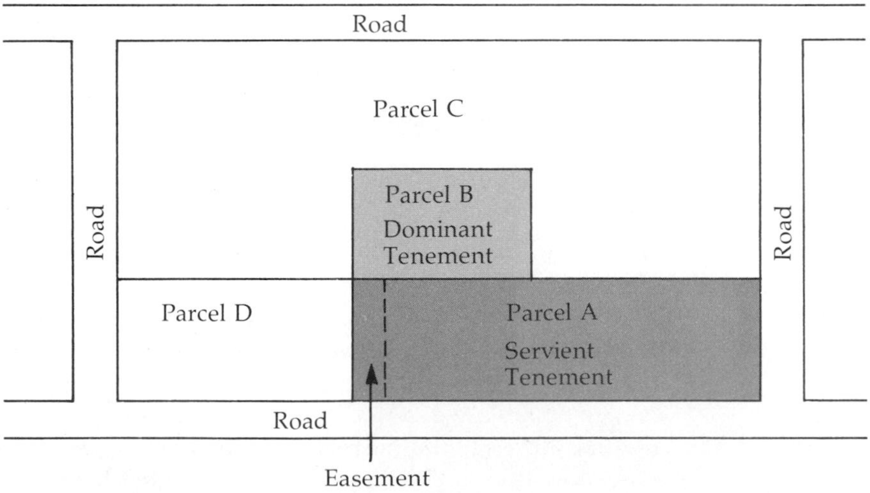

FIGURE 13.2   THE USE OF AN EASEMENT TO INCREASE VALUE

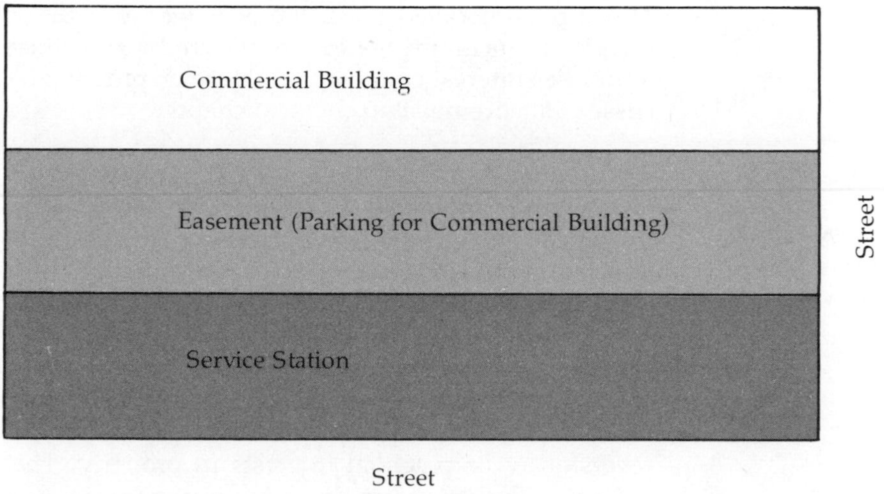

use for a service station. This company needed 30,000 square feet to obtain the necessary zoning but it needed only 15,000 square feet for the service station. If the oil company bought only what was needed for the station, it would not get the required zoning. If the company bought two-thirds of the property, it would have unused space and the owner would have a useless 15,000 square-foot parcel because that small parcel could not be zoned commercial. An interesting solution was used to solve this problem.

The oil company purchased the front 30,000 square feet (shaded in Figure 13.2) and gave the owner an easement on the back half of the property. The owner then used his remaining 15,000 square feet plus the 15,000 square-foot easement to package a 30,000 square-foot commercial parcel, using the easement for a parking lot with access through the side street. In this way, one 45,000 square-foot parcel was used to create two 30,000 square-foot parcels. Both parcels were zoned commercial and the owner increased the value of his property significantly by the thoughtful use of an easement.

License and Profit Rights

These rights allow the owner to use a property for a particular purpose. **License rights** refer to the right of use, such as fishing or hunting rights. **Profit rights** refer to the right granted by a landowner to another to remove minerals from a property. This right covers coal and oil leases, for instance.

Liens

One final important interest in land is the interest of a secured creditor. This interest is called a *lien*. If a borrower who has granted such an interest defaults on the obligation, the creditor may move to discharge his or her lien interest by the applicable legal proceeding. Liens will be discussed in more detail in the next chapter.

CHAPTER THIRTEEN SUMMARY

In this chapter, we have completed the description of the various types of interest one may hold in real property. The majority of the chapter was devoted to the lease forms which dominate much of the complex development in modern real estate. Leasing is not only a form of interest, but also a method to finance the purchase of certain rights in real property. Because it is a contractual arrangement, it is very flexible.

Other interest discussed included the easement, license, profit, and reversionary or potential interests in property. The latter types arise from the life estate form discussed in the previous chapter.

KEY TERMS

Absolute Net Lease
Appurtenant
   Easement
Dominant
   Tenement
Easement
Easement in Gross
Leasehold Estate

License and Profit
   Rights
Net Lease
Periodic Tenancy
Sale-and-Leaseback
Sandwich Lease

Service Lease
Servient Tenement
Tenancy at
   Sufferance
Tenancy at Will
Tenancy for Years

QUESTIONS FOR STUDY AND DISCUSSION

1. Describe the nature of the lease interest. Differentiate this interest from the ownership forms described in chapter 12.

2. Differentiate between a *tenancy for years* and a *periodic tenancy*. Under what circumstances would each be appropriate?

3. Why would a lender accept a lease as collateral for a loan?

4. Review the various reversionary interests described in chapter 12. How does each arise?

5. What is an *easement*? Why is an easement granted? Can an easement add to value? Can it detract from value? Why?

14
LEGAL FACTORS AFFECTING VALUE III– PUBLIC AND PRIVATE LIMITATIONS ON USE

A PROPERTY owned in fee simple gives its owner a number of rights. As we have seen, the owner theoretically owns the property from the center of the earth all the way out into the sky. Fee simple owners can do almost anything they want with their property. They can sell some of the rights separately. They can improve the property, farm it, or whatever they choose. However, this freedom is constrained by a number of factors. The major constraints include:

1. Deed restrictions;
2. Zoning and planning policies;
3. Building codes;
4. Police power;
5. Right of eminent domain;
6. Taxation; and
7. Encumbrances.

We will discuss each of these areas and how each affects value.

Private Limitations on Use

There are two major types of limitations that arise from the private sector which may constrain the landowner. Deed restrictions are set by the owner of a property and bind subsequent owners. Liens and other **encumbrances** may be initiated by the property owner or one of the owner's creditors. Liens may or may not have an effect on subsequent owners.

Deed Restrictions

We have already introduced this constraint in chapter 12. There are two types of deed restrictions. First, property owners in fee simple may voluntarily restrict the use of their property and continue these restrictions when they sell the property. Many new housing subdivisions have deed restrictions which restrict such things as fences and the use of signs and require such things as minimum house size and styles of architecture. These **voluntary deed restrictions** often appear in the deeds to condominiums also. The fact that they are voluntary makes them no less binding. (In the early 1970s, a homeowner in Virginia was forced to tear down a very expensive home he had just built because the neighbors felt the architecture ruined the appearance of the neighborhood.)

Voluntary deed restrictions run with the land. Each subsequent owner is forced to abide by these restrictions. In some cases, it is possible to get a variance through a petition of the neighbors, if that is allowed by the restrictions. Also, it is sometimes possible to have voluntary deed restrictions set aside in court if they become outmoded or are grossly unfair. Generally, the kind of restrictions we are discussing are meant to enhance or at least protect the value of a property. They generally have a positive impact on value. Finally, though there are similarities, voluntary deed restrictions should not be confused with zoning. Deed restrictions actually appear in the deed itself.

The second type of restriction which may constrain a fee simple owner arises from the qualified fee. The foregoing voluntary restrictions are basically qualified fees, but somewhat more complex. Sometimes the deed may only specify that a certain use may or may not be put to the property. While the voluntary restrictions may not specify reversion, a qualified fee may demand that if the restriction is violated, the owner may actually lose title to the original grantor or to the grantor's heirs.

Encumbrances

The second class of private limitations is the lien. A **lien** permits the lienor to obtain a potential benefit from the property if the owner does not repay his or her obligation. The lien will prohibit the owner from passing clear title to the property without discharging the obligation. Thus, when owners obligate themselves and cause a lien to go against their property, they greatly restrict their title and their interest.

An owner with a lien can sell his property subject to the lien with the permission of the lienholder. However, the title will not pass unencumbered. The new owner can only get clear title after discharging the lien. Mortgage liens probably have the least effect on value. Almost every residential property has a mortgage against it, so there seems to be little problem with this type of encumbrance. However, when a tax lien is involved and the disposition of the obligation is uncertain, the property may devalue significantly. Most tax sale properties are quitclaimed so the buyers have no warranty for the quality of their title. Under these uncertain circumstances, most buyers are uneasy about committing their funds, thus driving down the price of the tax-encumbered properties.

Mortgage Liens   The most common form of lien encumbrance is the **mortgage lien.** The mechanical operation of this lien will be described more fully in the discussion of financing forms. Basically, this lien involves the granting of a secondary interest in property by the owner to the creditor. If the owner conforms to all the contractual obligations of the debt to which the mortgage is tied, then when the debt is completely discharged the mortgage interest of the lender will be defeated and a clear title will once again revert to the owner.

Mechanics Lien   A second important lien form is the **mechanics lien.** This encumbrance arises when a property owner has services performed on the property by a contractor who is not paid. Many times an owner may have work performed by an electrician, a plumber, or other contractor over which a dispute may arise. The owner may feel the work done was inadequate or the price was too high. In either case, the owner chooses not to pay the contractor's fee. To protect himself the contractor (or *mechanic,* as he is called), who cannot repossess his work for nonpayment, is permitted by law the option of placing a lien against the property.

The process of obtaining a lien varies from state to state. The general idea is that after a suitable period of time and reasonable attempts to collect the debt, the contractor may file a lien against the property in the county recorder's office where the property is located. Not all states require that the owner be notified of this filing, though it appears to be in the contractor's interest to do so.

The mechanics lien arises in numerous situations. One of the most complex of these situations involves the building process. When a general contractor hires subcontractors to provide some of the work on a new structure, the question may arise for who is responsible for paying the subcontractors. In some states, the owner may be held responsible for the debts of the general contractor to the subcontractors even when the work has ostensibly been paid for. In such a case, a mechanics lien may be used to help ensure the subcontractor's interest.

Mechanics liens are common clouds in the title of property being transferred. When such liens exist, they must be discharged or a new owner cannot receive clear title. Because in many cases these liens can be filed at any time, the buyer must be careful not to acquire an encumbered title through a lien filed just before transfer, especially when the property is being quitclaimed.

Tax Lien   Another important lien is the **tax lien.** When property owners do not pay their taxes, the governmental authority involved may place a lien against the property, ultimately causing the property to be sold to settle the unpaid taxes. Often a property may be sold to settle a very small tax debt. It can be purchased at auction for much less than its appraised value. However, one should be warned that in most areas a property sold for taxes may be reclaimed by its delinquent owner, even after the sale. The conditions and time period involved vary greatly from state to state, but the effect is the same. An owner picking up a good piece of property at such an auction may lose a great deal later on when the property is reclaimed. Further, the title conveyed in such a sale rarely grants a very high degree of vested interest in the property, at least at the time of transfer. There have been, nonetheless, a great number of people over the years who have profited heavily from purchases made at tax auctions.

Public Limitations on Use

There are a number of ways in which governments or the public at large may limit the free use of real property. Some of these arise at the local level, a few arise at the state level, and some, such as air space regulations, pollution rules, and others, arise from federal statutes. We will now look at some of the more important public restrictions.

Zoning and Planning

One way in which property owners may find their freedom constrained is through zoning. Most communities recognize the *neighborhood effect* which alters property values. A tannery built next to a development of $100,000 homes will leave a neighborhood of $25,000 homes in its wake. Zoning is meant to prevent this condition. Various land uses are restricted to various segments of the city or county jurisdiction. Each piece of property under the control of the local zoning authority is assigned a particular zoning category which permits only certain land uses. These assignments should be made on the basis of the local master plan for area development. Typical zoning categories might include residential, industrial, commercial, and agricultural. Within these groups, there may be numerous subcategories.

There are a number of logical reasons for the use of zoning controls. The basic advantage lies in the ability to protect property values from damage or nuisances. Also, it tends to be based on planning, which is a good way to help develop the community and its resources. Proper zoning also helps control traffic patterns to enhance the linkages between major groups of land users.

Though zoning has a great deal of potential to enhance the value of property in any community, it is not always fair. The major problem with zoning actually arises out of its power to enhance value. A parcel of land with unfavorable zoning may lie fallow and undervalued for years. With advantageous zoning, the same parcel can multiply in value many times. Therein lies the problem. Local control of zoning offers a great temptation to the unscrupulous among us who would profit by their power to decide the fate of a parcel of land. Allowing a variance to a powerful local citizen to enhance his wealth in return for favors, of whatever type, defeats the purpose of the concept. In this way, zoning may be mistreated. The fact that zoning is sometimes based on politics, rather than economics, can lead to situations in which the whims of a few can raise the cost of community development out of proportion to the benefits and actually cause a loss to the area. Finally, the fact that zoning and planning may go hand in hand is of little value if the planning process is ill-conceived. Good zoning requires good planning.

Building Codes

Property owners may also be restricted in their freedom to use their property as they see fit because of building codes. Again, the idea behind building codes is basically sound. If a property is improved through quality construction, it should be more valuable and safer for its occupants. However, building codes, like zoning, are not without difficulty. First, building codes tend to be heavily influenced by special interest groups. Both labor and materials manufacturers have a vested interest in codes which force the inclusion of extra materials and labor. Codes tend to be built around a quantity basis rather than a performance basis. Second, building codes tend to be extremely conservative. Finally, building codes are a local phenomenon. They may vary widely from one area to another. Because they are local, the codes tend to be developed without the expertise which could be applied to a national code development program.

Police Power

For perfectly understandable reasons, property owners must give up a certain amount of their freedom to allow local authorities the right to enter their property in the interest of public safety. The community provides property owners with protection for their property. In exchange, it demands two things: taxes and the right to enter the property for the good of the community. Without this protection of police and fire departments, property values would undoubtedly be lower. In addition, insurance would be much more expensive, as it is in rural areas. There are some constraints on the exercise of police power, however. Several cases have been brought into the courts in recent years challenging the right to inspect buildings for fire hazards without search warrants.

Right of Eminent Domain

One of the more important constraints on the title of a property owner is the **right of eminent domain.** This right gives the government the ability to purchase property it needs for the good of the community. The right is also extended by statute to include not only the government itself, but also public service types of private industrial companies. Utilities and railroads, for example, have used this right to obtain needed property or rights of way.

The exercise of the right of eminent domain is called **condemnation;** it takes place in one of two ways. If the relevant authority wishes to obtain property, it generally offers a voluntary settlement first. This avoids costly court proceedings and perhaps the ill-feeling that sometimes accompanies condemnation. If the owner is unwilling to sell the property, the government may then condemn the property and obtain it through the courts. The settlement in such circumstances may or may not be as good as that which was offered voluntarily. Property owners generally force condemnation when they feel that they can make more money through the courts where the judge will award the "fair market value" of the property.

Condemnation is expensive, time-consuming, and may cause bitter feelings between the government and the citizenry. Occasionally we read stories of poor people holding out against the powerful machinery of progress to save their homesteads. This type of circumstance gives condemnation a very bad name. The effect of the impending condemnation of a property may have an unpredictable impact on its value. Sometimes, the knowledge of a road's going through property or the potential of condemnation for a civic center, for instance, will cause property values to rise in anticipation. It is alternatively possible that impending condemnation will cause property values to fall. This is partially a function of the use itself, the market for property, and how badly the local authority wants the property. The presence of alternative sites or routes, as in the case of a road, might have an effect.

The results of condemnation may be mixed, too. For example, assume a strip of properties has been condemned for a highway. Depending upon the circumstances, the condemned properties and even some adjacent parcels may fall in value because of the nature of the impending use. However, the value of other adjacent properties may rise dramatically in anticipation of being improved as restaurants, service stations, and so forth.

Taxing Power

Besides building codes and zoning, the most pervasive constraint on real property interests is the power of governments to levy taxes against the property. Generally, real estate taxes are used by local governments to raise funds for schools and government operation.

Local property taxes are called ad valorum taxes (against the value of the property). The general basis for these taxes is a function of two variables: how much money needs to be raised and the value of the property against which the taxes will be levied. The process should work roughly as follows. First, the taxing authority estimates the budgeted amount it wishes to spend to provide services to its constituents. Then the *assessed* (not appraised) *value* of the local property is determined. As we said in chapter 7, the assessment process varies widely across the country. Let us say for our example below that property is assessed at about 90% of its actual fair market value. Now the taxing authority compares its budget to the assessed value in order to obtain a *millage rate*.

For example, a modest community with a population of 30,000 has a budget of $8 million for all city services and schools. The assessed value of the property in the area is $320 million. Thus the basic millage rate would be determined as:

$$\frac{\$8,000,000}{\$320,000,000} = 0.025$$

This translates into a rate of $2.50 for each $100 of assessed value. Using this rate, the tax bill for a $40,000 home would be $1000:

$$\$40,000 \times \$2.50/\$100 \text{ or } \$400 \times \$2.50 = \$1000$$

This basic procedure can be applied with many variations. For instance, the incidence of the tax can be altered by adjusting the basis for assessment for various segments of property owners—residential or commercial or industrial. Several times in the 1970s, for example, the state of Iowa has required the various local taxing authorities to alter their valuations by a certain percentage. This caused the residential segment of the population to support an increasing amount of the tax burden. In 1978, the burden of property tax was substantially altered by the citizens of California, who voted themselves massive property tax relief through a referendum.

The amount of taxes levied against a property can have a great deal of impact on value. Generally, the higher the tax is, then the lower the value. Sometimes taxes which are higher than the additional services provided may be applied to a property. This results in **tax capitalization,** a situation in which more value is lost from the property because of taxes than is added in the form of services.

CHAPTER FOURTEEN SUMMARY

This chapter has presented a number of limitations which affect the ability of property owners to use their property with total freedom. There are others in addition to the seven types mentioned, but our list is representative.

The three chapters just completed may have seemed somewhat complex. It should be noted that these chapters have presented only a brief introduction to the legal aspects of real estate. Nearly every real estate transaction has some legal, financing, and tax issues to be settled. It is essential, especially in investment transactions, to use the services of legal counsel. It is also good to remember that when any doubt exists in a transaction the details, intents, and desires of all parties should be in writing.

We will discuss one other legal area, the contracts involved in transactions, in the chapter on brokerage in part 3.

KEY TERMS

Condemnation	Mechanics Lien	Tax Capitalization
Encumbrances	Mortgage Lien	Tax Lien
Lien	Right of Eminent Domain	Voluntary Deed Restriction

QUESTIONS FOR STUDY AND DISCUSSION

1. Explain the basic idea behind a *mechanics lien*.

2. Explain the nature of zoning restrictions.

3. For what purpose are building codes used? What are some of the problems with these rules? Would a national code system be better? Why or why not?

4. Explain the *right of eminent domain*. Who exercises this right? Why?

5. Describe the calculation of property taxes. By what methods might a municipal government be able to distribute the tax burden unfairly?

6. Describe the concept of the *voluntary deed restriction*. How does this differ from a qualified fee?

15

REAL ESTATE FINANCE I– INSTRUMENTS

BECAUSE OF its high value, relative to other commodities, most real estate transactions are financed. In this and the next two chapters, we will examine the instruments of real estate finance, the sources of these funds, and the effect of financing on value.

Types of Funds

There are two major sources of funds for financing any investment. Investors can contribute their own capital or they may use the capital of others. As we saw in chapter 8, the combination of owner and creditor capital tends, under the proper conditions, to increase the owner's overall return on an investment compared to all equity financing. In spite of the fact that owners may earn more with leverage, there are risks. If income should fall, the presence of excessive debt may cause the owners to lose their property. Debts and lease payments are contractual obligations. They must be paid from the property's cash flow before the owners get their money. If the income is too small to meet the obligations, the owners will be in default and may lose their property either through a foreclosure or bankruptcy suit.

Equity Funds

With the exception of lease financing, all types of leverage require some equity to lower the risk to the lender. Under normal circumstances, when owners wish to finance a property, they will have the title. This leaves the lenders with the need for some protection of their interest. The equity supplied by the owner provides a cushion of value for the lender so that if the property needs to be sold to settle the debt, any loss in value will be absorbed first by the owner.

There are several sources of equity funds for prospective owners. They may use their own savings, a major source of such funds. Investors may also liquidate some of their noncash assets such as securities or personal property to obtain equity funds. Equity may also be raised by borrowing. Often an investor may be able to borrow from relatives and friends without security or the kinds of restrictions that an institutional lender might demand. Even though this is not true equity, it is a viable substitute.

Another substitute for equity is leasing. If investors lease a property they need from the owner, they generally do not have to supply any equity at all. We will discuss this in more detail later.

Finally, an investor who does not have sufficient equity may sell shares to other investors, which may be done in numerous ways. The name for such an arrangement is **syndication.** Syndicates may be limited partnerships, corporations, trusts, or other miscellaneous joint ventures.

Creditor Capital

The leverage that an investor can obtain for financing real estate comes from borrowing and leasing. Borrowed funds can be obtained from institutions or individuals. Many borrowed funds obtained from individuals are secured from the seller of the property in the form of purchase money mortgages, land contract arrangements, or leases. Most institutional borrowing is in the form of mortgage loans or leases. In the next sections, we will take a detailed look at the major sources of funds available to finance real property.

Mortgage Loans

A **mortgage loan** is a loan secured by land or improved property. With this arrangement, the lender can cause the sale of the property to settle the debt if the borrower defaults on the loan.

Basic Structure

When a property owner borrows money using a real estate mortgage loan, the owner is committed in two ways. First, the borrower (mortgagor) signs a note with the lender (mortgagee) which is the evidence of the debt incurred. This note specifies the amount of money which is owed, the rate of interest to be charged, and the other terms of the debt. The borrower also makes a mortgage with the lender which offers specific real property as security for the debt. Often after receiving the mortgage the lender will record it in much the same way as a deed is recorded. Some states require this recording but most do not. The purpose of this act is to notify anyone who might be contemplating acquiring an interest in the property that there is a lien against the property.

A mortgage and its accompanying note may be separate or combined in a single document. The exact form of the mortgage varies from one region to another, but most mortgages have the same general contents.

Approaches to Mortgage Lending   There are two basic approaches to the type of interest a mortgage may have. In many states east of the Mississippi, mortgagees actually gain title to the property when the mortgage is executed. They receive a **mortgage deed.** When the mortgage note is satisfied, the title reverts back to the owner. In most states west of the Mississippi, the lien theory is used. In these instances, the lender only obtains a lien against the property. The actual effect of these two approaches may be similar in case of default.

In some states, especially in the South, the **deed of trust** is used in lieu of a mortgage. In this case, the borrower executes a deed of trust, passing the title to be held in trust by a third party who protects the interest of both the borrower and the lender.

Basic Data   The mortgage, at a minimum, must contain the legal description of the property and the names of the parties to the agreement. There must also be covenants which specify that the mortgagor does own the property in fee simple, warrants that the property is salable, and that the owner will defend the property against other claims. Finally, the mortgagor must provide for the release of any dower rights against the fee.

Defeasance Clause   The **defeasance clause** gives mortgagors the right to redeem their property, free and clear, after they have satisfactorily discharged their obligation to the lender. This clause is a two-edged sword because it also specifies that a borrower who does not pay loses all rights in the property.

Acceleration Clause   Because mortgage loans are generally amortized, that is, paid back in installments, they usually contain an **acceleration clause.** This clause specifies that if the borrower defaults on the loan, say, by missing a payment, the lender can declare the entire amount of the loan due and payable immediately. This permits the lender to sue for payment of the entire debt rather than one payment at a time.

Another version of the acceleration clause which is being used in some areas is the **due-on-sale clause.** This structure states that if the title to the property is assigned to anyone, the entire loan becomes due. This forces the buyer to renegotiate with the lender when the property is sold. Both of these versions of the acceleration idea are exercised at the option of the lender.

Rate-Change Clauses   Sometimes mortgage loan notes will contain a clause which permits the lender to raise the interest rate after a given interval of time or the prescribed notice. This is called an **escalator clause.** Another form of this arrangement is the **variable rate mortgage.** This type of loan permits the lender to raise or lower the interest rate according to some prescribed formula. This protects the lender when rates rise after the original loan is made and the borrower when rates fall. It makes long-term lending a bit more desirable when rates fluctuate a good deal.

Insurance Clause   Generally, a mortgagee will demand that the borrower insure his or her property against fire and other perils. This **insurance clause** requires that insurance be sufficient to cover the loss of the property so that the mortgagee's interest will not be endangered. This insurance should be set up so that the policy does not become void if the mortgagor is foreclosed for defaulting on the loan.

Prepayment Clause   The **prepayment clause** specifies the conditions under which a loan might be prepaid. Mortgages may vary a great deal in the way they treat prepayment. Some mortgages may actually prohibit prepayment of the principal. Others provide for the guaranteed prepayment of any part of the principal at any time. Finally, many mortgages provide for penalties or restrictions to be assessed at the option of the lender. These may specify the amount of the loan that can be repaid at any time or they may assess a monetary penalty if the loan is prepaid. Prospective borrowers who are interested in prepayment should try to negotiate the most favorable terms possible in this regard. We will discuss the economics of systematic prepayment in chapter 20.

Subordination   **Subordination** refers to the act of placing the priority of a loan below the priority of other financing. In a bankruptcy or foreclosure, various creditors are assigned particular priorities for receiving settlement of their debts. A first mortgage, called **senior mortgage**, has the highest priority for receiving the proceeds of a foreclosure sale. Junior, or subordinated, mortgages have lower priorities and must wait to receive payment until the senior debt is paid. In some cases, subordination will be necessary to structure the complex financing required for large-scale development. We shall discuss these circumstances later.

Mortgage Varieties

The most common form of the mortgage loan is the first mortgage or senior mortgage. There are many other types of mortgage loans which may be used in special situations.

Blanket Mortgage   An investor in the process of developing and selling a large tract of homes may find it economical to obtain a *blanket mortgage* on the entire group of homes (or even lots as the case may be). As each unit or lot is sold, the borrower (developer) will settle with the lender to release the unit from the blanket mortgage. Generally, the lender will require that more money be paid in than the proportion of the mortgage represented by that unit. For instance, assume a developer has fifty lots covered by a $500,000 mortgage. The lots are mortgaged for $10,000 each and will sell for $20,000 each. As each lot is sold, $15,000 of the mortgage will be retired. This ensures the lender that his security cushion will get bigger as the lots are sold. The reason for this precaution is that the choicest lots are likely to be sold first, reducing the secure position of the lender. This can be overcome by forcing the borrower to put in some extra money early.

Blanket mortgages are also used for corporate mortgages. A company like AT&T may sell first mortgage bonds, for example, to cover a number of properties in a given area. This situation makes use of another variety of debt, the bond. A *mortgage bond* is similar to a note except the debt has been divided into pieces so it can be sold to a number of individuals and institutions rather than just one large lender.

Open-End Mortgage   Often a firm finds it desirable to borrow, say, 50% of the value of a property and give a first mortgage, while reserving the right to borrow more against the same property. The important point here is not the ability to use the remaining 50% equity as security, per se, but that it can be used for additional first mortgage borrowing. First mortgages are generally less expensive than junior liens, so it is important to be able to expand first mortgage borrowing if the investor so desires.

Package Mortgage   A mortgage in its pure form is an instrument secured by real property. When a developer is building and selling homes, for instance, it may be desirable to include personal property under the mortgage. Stoves, dishwashers, or even furniture may be sold in the home and covered by a package mortgage loan. This may be convenient for the buyer, but it may be very expensive. Paying for a stove for thirty years at 9% through mortgage payments may mean that a home buyer can pay over $1000 for a $350 stove. Nevertheless, package mortgages are a popular device to help sell tract housing.

Junior Mortgage   A **junior mortgage** is one which has a lower priority than a first mortgage in case of a default. Generally, second and third mortgages are more expensive than first mortgage loans because of the lower priority and thus the higher risk involved. In the late 1970s the second mortgage has become a realistic tool for the small investor seeking to raise equity funds for investment purposes. Many homeowners have found themselves with a home which has a great deal of equity in it as a result of constant inflation throughout the decade. It is highly possible that a homeowner could find that a modest house purchased for, say, $25,000 in 1970 with a $20,000 mortgage is worth $60,000 in 1980 with a total equity of $40,000. It is relatively easy for the investor to obtain $25,000 from a second mortgage in such a circumstance.

Junior liens are often used to make up for a lack of equity. Suppose an investor wishes to purchase an apartment building for $300,000. She finds she can only borrow 75% or $225,000. The investor has only $25,000 to invest, so she negotiates a purchase money mortgage with the seller for $50,000 and subordinates it to her institutional loan. In this way, the buyer is able to substitute a $50,000 junior lien for her equity deficit. Numerous other examples of this type may be described.

Purchase Money Mortgage   Another form of mortgage financing is the **purchase money mortgage.** This is like a conventional mortgage arrangement except that the seller rather than a financial institution becomes the mortgagee. This is very similar in effect to the land contract. The main difference is in who holds the title after the transaction. With a land contract the seller retains the title. A purchase money mortgagor, in a lien theory state, gets the title and gives up a lien. Default under these circumstances requires strict foreclosure, which we will describe shortly.

Wrap-Around Loans The wrap-around loan is a fairly new form of loan which may be used to resolve a potentially difficult situation. We will examine this type of financing by example. A developer builds an office complex which cost $500,000 to create and he has a twenty-year first mortgage loan of $400,000 at 8% against it. After five years the developer gets an offer of $800,000 for his property. The buyer wishes to use a $600,000 mortgage to finance his purchase. However, the original first mortgage cannot be prepaid and still has a balance of about $350,000 outstanding. The buyer could take a second mortgage of $250,000 and solve his problem. However, such a second mortgage for fifteen years would carry a rate of 12% and payments of $36,700 per year. Table 15.1 shows the total payments that would be made if our buyer assumed the outstanding first mortgage and used a second mortgage for the rest of his needed funds.

The wrap-around mortgage was created for just such a situation. Our prospective buyer can obtain a $600,000 wrap-around mortgage for fifteen years with payments of $72,500 per year. The lender will take this payment and use it to pay the original lender his $40,750 annual payments and keep the rest. The new lender is, in effect, lending only $250,000 and is keeping $31,750 as his payment on that loan. This is an

TABLE 15.1 WRAP-AROUND MORTGAGE EXAMPLE

Original Mortgage: $400,000 at 8% for 20 years
    Annual Payment: $40,750
    Unpaid balance after 5 years: approximately $350,000

New Second Mortgage: $250,000 at 12% for 15 years
    Annual Payment: $36,700

Total Payments: $40,750 + $36,700 = $77,450 per year
Effective cost to borrower: 9.68%

Wrap-Around Loan: $600,000 at 8.56% for 15 years
    Annual Payment: $72,500
    Lender receives $72,500, pays $40,750 to the existing first mortgagee, and keeps $31,750
    Effective yield: $31,750 for $250,000 loan = 9.4%

effective rate of 9.4% with first mortgage protection. The borrower is able to reduce his effective cost to 8.56%.

There are numerous other forms and varieties of mortgage financing, though most are variations of the forms we have discussed. The important thing to see from the foregoing analysis is that an investor, builder, or developer has many options to help solve financing problems.

Remedies for Default

When borrowers default on their loans by missing, for instance, a couple of payments, the lender must decide what remedy to use. Generally, the lender will first assess the financial condition of the borrower at that point to determine why the default occurred. If the condition is temporary, the mortgagee will try to work with the borrower until the situation is corrected. If the borrower is in deep trouble and it is obvious that the lender cannot expect to receive further payment, then the lender will probably seek remedy in the courts.

Foreclosure is defined as the suit to end the **equity of redemption** of the mortgagor. When a default occurs the borrower has a right, in equity, to reclaim his or her property by paying all the accrued arrearage. The foreclosure suit is filed to end this right. There are two ways for the lender to treat this situation.

Strict foreclosure, which is infrequently used, is a suit to vest the title to the property in the mortgagee. If granted, the court gives the borrower one last chance to pay the debt. When the foreclosure is final, the borrower loses all rights in the property. Further, if the eventual sale of the property is insufficient to meet the outstanding obligation, the borrower is still liable for the deficiency.

In most cases, strict foreclosure is not used. Instead, the lender sues in a court of equity as in a strict foreclosure, but the suit ends in a decree of foreclosure and sale. The property is then sold to pay the debt. If the sale brings more money than is needed, the debtor gets the excess. Similarly, if the sale does not bring enough, the borrower is still liable for the deficiency.

When a foreclosure sale takes place, the lender may try to protect his interest by bidding on the property. This enables the lender to sell the property in the open market with a potentially higher price. The execution of the foreclosure sale varies widely from state to state. In some states, the lender is heavily protected in such situations, but in others, there is no such protection.

Another alternative approach to default involves the right to sue on the note rather than on the mortgage. The lender sues as a creditor and obtains a judgment against the borrower's property. This may be desirable if the mortgaged property is only a small part of the borrower's assets and there are not many other debts outstanding. If the debtor has numerous debts and his or her mortgaged real property is the best among them, then a foreclosure is the best remedy.

It should be noted that in some states when a foreclosure sale is closed, borrowers still have the right to redeem their interest. This is called the **statutory right of redemption.** In such cases, the buyer cannot get a clear title until this period is over.

Transactions Involving Mortgaged Property

When a property is sold with a mortgage lien against it, there are at least three ways of handling the situation. The buyer, if possible, may allow the seller to discharge the loan by refinancing the property with a new mortgage. The proceeds of the new loan will be used to pay off the old one. The old lien will thus be removed and a new one put on.

A second solution is for the buyer to assume the seller's existing loan. In this case, the buyer will make the payments on the loan as if it were his or hers. This process often allows that buyer to lower the cost of the transactions by avoiding the cost of refinancing. However, the seller remains *secondarily* liable for the loan if the buyer fails to pay the payments properly.

A property with an existing loan may also be sold *subject to* that loan. Here, again, the buyer makes the payments, but the original borrower remains *primarily* liable in case of default. This is not necessarily an advantageous way to sell a property. However, it is sometimes necessary. No matter what the position of the seller in the case of either an assumption or a "subject to" situation, the process of settling a default is bound to be messy, legally speaking.

Other Financing Forms

The mortgage loan is an important form of long-term financing. There are two other important long-term forms and several short-term sources of funds which are also used in real estate financing.

Land Contracts

The second major long-term source of funds is the **land contract,** or **contract for deed.** This form of financing is given by the seller to the buyer. The buyer executes a contract with the seller in which the buyer promises to pay for the property at a certain rate, often similar to the schedule of payments of an amortized mortgage. However, the seller retains title to the property until the contract terms are fulfilled. The buyer gets possession and the responsibility for the property, but not the deed.

A land contract is similar in form to any other type of contract. It will contain a property description and the basic terms under which the deed will be transferred. There are a number of specific covenants that buyers should demand, however. The type of deed to be transferred should be specified. If there are potential dower rights involved, the buyers should specify that these rights be waived in the contract. If they are not so waived, they need not be waived at the time of the deed transfer. Also, it is wise for the buyers to determine exactly what will happen if they should default. This may be an important point. A contract buyer must be sure to understand his or her responsibilities under the contract. The failure to live up to any of these responsibilities may cause a breach and the eventual loss of the interest in the property. Normally, the property must be kept insured and in good repair, for example.

Land contracts have been popular in transfers of farms and raw pre-development land. The use of a contract permits sellers to prorate any capital gain they have over the life of the contract. The buyers, alternatively, do not have the same sort of commitment with a land contract that they would have with a mortgage. If contract buyers find themselves unable to fulfill their contract, especially early in its life, they can walk away and the seller retakes possession. This last possibility is a two-edged sword. If buyers breach their contract late in its life, they may be in serious danger of losing a substantial interest in the property. In many cases, buyers will be protected by the courts and given the right to recover some of what they have put into the property. However, in the case of a breach, the buyers often find they will surely lose something.

Land contracts can be used to purchase improved properties as well as raw land, although land contracts are not terribly practical when sellers need their equity to purchase another property, such as with a personal residence. If a seller finds he can sell only on contract, yet he needs his equity, he may retain the right to put a lien against his fee. The seller can use this right to obtain a mortgage against the new property.

Land contracts are also used for two other important purposes. In many states, it has become a prevalent practice for lenders to demand that any mortgage balance outstanding become due if the title is transferred. This due-on-sale clause makes the transfer of property difficult without financial penalty. However, because a title does not pass until the end of the life of a land contract, this form of transaction may be used to thwart the due-on-sale clause. The buyer pays for the property in the usual manner of a land contract and the seller uses the payments to pay off the mortgage.

The last important function of the land contract is the postponement of capital gains taxes. Under the IRS code, property sold by installment sale does not have to be taxed for capital gains all at once. Basically, the total gain to be realized is prorated over the life of the contract. This is an important method for postponing what might otherwise be an onerous tax burden.

Leases

The third major form of long-term financing is the lease. Leases were described in some detail in chapter 13, and we will not repeat that discussion here. Most forms of lease arrangements are for reasonably long periods, or at least more than a year or so. The service-type lease and the month-to-month arrangements used by apartment renters are examples of short-term forms. Generally, most ground-rent (rental for land) agreements are long-term. Building leases are also often for extended periods, although many such leases have escape clauses. The escape clause is common for lessees such as fast food restaurants.

The use of lease forms in financing can have a dramatic impact on investment value. In chapter 17, we will explore the mechanics of some of the more exotic lease forms and show how they affect value.

Short-Term Financing

Often, real estate purchasers need money only for a short time. Usually, these sources are only interim forms required to bridge the gap between purchase and the final long-term financing. We will look at some of these next.

Construction Loans   When an investor is in the process of building a new improvement to a property, funds may be needed for the construction period. This type of financing must be handled differently from a regular mortgage because the improvement will not be completed through most of the life of the loan. Practices vary locally, but most lenders use some schedule to dispense funds for new construction when they are needed and the work has been completed. Often a speculative builder will be unable to receive the last 20% of the loan until the improvement is sold and a new loan closed. Construction funds may be given to the builder on a percent completion basis or they may be paid directly to subcontractors presenting bills for work completed. This choice will depend on the credit-worthiness of the builder.

Gap Financing   Often when an individual is moving from one house to another, the closings of the two transactions do not coincide. If an individual must use the equity from the home being sold as a downpayment for the house being purchased, there may be a gap to fill in between transactions. Banks and other lenders can be utilized here for short-term loans to cover the needed equity for closing the purchase transaction. Then, when the sale on the first home is closed, the gap loan can be discharged.

There are obviously other circumstances for which such financing might be used besides individual residence transactions. A form of gap financing may even be used by a large industrial borrower. If long-term interest rates are high, but expected to fall in a year or so, a large industrial borrower might arrange short-term financing to cover this period. This allows the borrower to wait until rates decline before being locked into a long-term financing arrangement such as a mortgage bond issue. In this kind of circumstance, it is often better for a borrower to pay a high rate of interest for one year than for thirty years.

Term Loans   Often, coupled with the development of a commercial property, there will be a requirement to purchase equipment or provide working capital. Even though these needs are not strictly required for the purchase of the real property, they may be necessary to enable the owner to use the property in its intended purpose. As part of the total financing package, the borrower may arrange a term loan at a bank for a period of three to five years, for instance, to help defray business start-up costs. As the venture becomes profitable, the loan can be converted to equity by paying for it with the profits retained in the business. This type of loan is not a real estate loan per se, but it does help free some of the borrower's capital to facilitate the real estate portion of the transaction.

CHAPTER FIFTEEN SUMMARY   This chapter has been concerned with the major instruments of real estate finance, primarily the mortgage loan, an important source of borrowing for the purchase of real estate. We described the basic features of mortgage loans and remedies for default of those loans, should the borrower fail to pay.

We also examined a number of other sources of funds, as well as various varieties of mortgage loans. These include construction loans, land contracts, leases, and miscellaneous forms of short-term financing. Leases may well be as important as mortgage loans in the overall scheme of things, but it is difficult to tell because as yet no reliable data have been published on the quantity of this form of financing.

KEY TERMS

Acceleration Clause	Foreclosure	Purchase Money
Contract for Deed	Insurance Clause	Mortgage
Deed of Trust	Junior Mortgage	Senior Mortgage
Defeasance Clause	Land Contract	Statutory Right of

Due-on-Sale Clause   Mortgage Deed   Redemption
Equity of   Mortgage Loan   Strict Foreclosure
    Redemption   Prepayment Clause   Subordination
Escalator Clause   Syndication
                                                   Variable Rate
                                                       Mortgage

**QUESTIONS
FOR STUDY
AND
DISCUSSION**

1. Explain the structure of the *mortgage loan.* What are the major clauses in a mortgage?

2. If a borrower defaults on the mortgage, what remedies does the lender have?

3. What is the difference between buying a property subject to a mortgage and assuming a mortgage?

4. What are the major types of seller-supplied financing available to a buyer?

5. Explain some of the major differences between straight mortgage debt and land contracts as financing tools.

6. How does a *land contract* differ from a *purchase money mortgage?*

16

REAL ESTATE FINANCE II– SOURCES OF FUNDS

NOW THAT we have examined a number of the important types of financing media for real estate, we will examine the market for funds and the institutional sources from which money may be obtained. We will also examine the government's role in the funds market. Because the housing and construction industry plays an important role in the total economy, the federal government has developed numerous ways to enter the market to facilitate its policy aims.

The Flow of Funds

The Role of Personal Savings

The primary source of funds for all new investment in the economy is personal saving. Ultimately, if individuals did not save, financial institutions would have no funds to lend and investment would slow to almost nothing. Thus, to understand the market for loanable funds, especially for mortgage money, first we must understand why individuals save, and second, what they do with these savings.

Why Individuals Save   When an individual receives income, there are two choices (excluding personal taxes)[1] for its disposal: consumption and savings. Each individual spending unit in the economy has certain needs for consumption in a given year. If these needs exceed disposable income, the individual may be considered a **deficit spending unit.** To make up the deficit, the individual may draw upon past savings or may borrow from some other source. If an individual has more disposable income than is needed, then this surplus will be saved for a future period (or used to pay back past borrowing). Such a spending unit is called a **surplus spending unit.** Surplus spending units are the ultimate source of loanable funds for deficit spending units.

Where Savings Go   Individual savers have many outlets for their savings dollars. Savings can simply be held as cash or demand deposits, which earn no return for savers. Alternatively, the funds can be invested to earn a return for savers while they are not needed. If investment is chosen, the savers have a number of possible media choices. First, direct investments can be made. The funds can be used to purchase securities, commodities, or direct interests in business and real estate ventures. In these cases, the individual saver is making the placement decision and assessing the risks and returns.

Often, however, people do not have the time, the inclination, or the

---

[1]Income after taxes is called *disposable income.*

expertise to make investment decisions. Further, the amount of savings may be too small to invest directly in a rational, economical way. In such circumstances, savers may deposit the funds with a **financial intermediary** who will make the investment decisions for them. The intermediary pays a return, usually from 5% to 8%, depending on the time for which the funds are deposited. The financial intermediary pools the savings of many small savers and then places the savings with the appropriate deficit spending units so that the intermediary may earn a return. The intermediary is effectively shifting the burden of the decision-making and the risk from the individual to the institution.

The role of financial intermediaries in our economy is an extremely important one. Without their services great numbers of deficit spending units, both individuals and businesses, would be in a much more difficult position to raise needed capital. The most important financial intermediaries include

1. Commercial banks—savings and trust departments;
2. Savings and loan associations;
3. Mutual savings banks;
4. Insurance companies, especially life insurance companies; and
5. Pension funds.

Not surprisingly, these institutions are the major sources of mortgage money for real estate.

There is one other source of funds which deserves some attention at this point. Commercial banks, as a system, may add to the total supply of loans outstanding by, in effect, creating money. The method by which they do this is a function of the structure of the system and the pattern with which deposits are acquired. Individual banks do not lend more money than they have on deposit, but as a whole system the banks can create money. This process is carefully controlled by the Federal Reserve System and greatly aids the process of capital formation. In general terms, the banking system may create about four to five dollars of new loans for every new dollar of deposits. However, in the same way if money (savings) is withdrawn from the system, bank-lending capacity must shrink as rapidly as it expanded. Thus, savings is even more important than merely the dollars saved, at least for commercial banks.

We may summarize the funds flow by saying that funds for lending come from three sources: individual savings, corporate profits, and, indirectly, from money creation. These funds flow into direct investments in business capital and deposits in financial intermediaries. The intermediaries then complete the process of investment by using the savings to make loans and finance the equity in new ventures.

The Market for Real Estate Finance

The market for real estate financing is divided into two parts: the primary and the secondary. The **primary market** is the one in which new loans originate. When an individual or financial institution makes a new mortgage loan, this is a primary market transaction. Similarly, new lease contracts or land contracts are made in the primary market. Such transactions are similar to the issue of new securities by a corporation. All these primary transactions create two common elements—an asset for the lender and a debt for the borrower.

Sometimes after a primary transaction has been consummated, the lender wishes to exchange the asset for cash or another asset which pays a higher return. If an investor buys one hundred shares of GM stock, it is not necessarily with the intention of holding it for a lifetime. The investment probably will be sold at a later date to use the cash for consumption or to reinvest at an improved return. If a savings and loan association makes a thirty-year mortgage at 8% interest and then interest rates rise to 9% in a few years, the savings and loan has a potential opportunity loss for the remaining life of the original contract. If the institution so desired, and could do so economically, it could sell the 8% mortgage to an investor at a discount and recover the money for reinvestment. This transaction would be in the **secondary market.** The efficacy of such a transaction will depend on the selling price. As we shall see, there are ways in which the federal government helps lenders dispose of mortgages in the secondary market, so that more new loans can be made, thus stimulating the construction industry.

Distribution of Mortgage Debt   Mortgage debt is held by three basic categories of lenders: individuals, institutions, and the government. In Table 16.1 we can see how the total debt is distributed among the major holders. Note the changes in this distribution over the five-year period. Table 16.2 shows the amount and distribution of mortgage lending for the principal financial institutions over the period from 1950 to 1976. Notice the large increase in loans outstanding over the period. Total institutional lending grew at 10% per year, compounded. Also notice the tremendous increase in the role of savings and loan associations during the period. Of the private institutions making mortgage loans, savings and loans account for half of the mortgage debt outstanding.

Interest Rates   As a result of heavy demands for mortgage funds, we saw mortgage interest rates at high levels in the 1970s. The rising costs of housing over that period forced borrowers to seek larger loans and the high inflation rates caused lenders to seek higher interest rates. Table 16.3 shows the rate for primary market mortgages from 1971 through 1977.

TABLE 16.1   DISTRIBUTION OF MORTGAGE DEBT BY
PRINCIPAL HOLDER

Holder	1977—1st Qtr. Billions $	%	1970 Billions $	%
Commercial Banks	154.0	17	99.3	16
Mutual Savings Banks	82.3	9	67.6	11
Savings and Loans	333.7	37	206.2	35
Life Insurance Companies	91.9	10	76.9	13
Federal Agencies	66.2	7	40.2	7
Mortgage Pools—Trusts	54.8	6	14.4	2
Individuals and Others	127.7	14	98.9	16
Totals	910.6	100%	603.5	100%

Loan Growth approximately 8.5% per year, compounded.

Source: *Federal Reserve Bulletin,* Feb. 1978, Table 1.54.

This completes our basic examination of the market structure for mortgage funds. We will now turn our attention to an examination of the various market participants in both the primary and secondary markets.

Private Primary Market Institutions

Savings and Loan Associations

The largest source of mortgage money for single-family residences is the nation's **savings and loan associations.** Savers open various types of time deposit accounts at these institutions, and the savings and loans use the money almost exclusively for mortgage loans. Savings and loans, as well as other financial institutions, are closely regulated as to the uses of their funds to protect the individual savers. Generally, they only make real estate loans and some investments in government securities. The loans made by savings and loans break down as follows:

A. One- to four-family residences

   1. Conventional first mortgage loans, up to 80% of the value of the property

   2. Insured mortgage loans, up to 95% of the value of the property

   3. Term loans

B. Commercial properties—mortgage loans up to 75% of value for

TABLE 16.2   DISTRIBUTION OF MORTGAGE DEBT AMONG MAJOR FINANCIAL INSTITUTIONS

| | 1976 | | 1950 | |
	Billions $	%	Billions $	%
Commercial Banks	146.6	23	13.7	26
Mutual Savings Banks	81.6	13	8.3	16
Savings and Loans	323.1	50	13.7	26
Life Insurance Companies	91.6	14	16.1	32
Totals	642.9	100%	51.8	100%

Loan Growth approximately 10% per year, compounded.

Source: *Statistical Abstract of the U.S., 1978*, Table 852.

TABLE 16.3   PRIMARY MARKET RATES OF INTEREST

Year	Rate
1971	7.75%
1972	7.60%
1973	7.95%
1974	8.90%
1975	9.00%
1976	9.05%
1977	9.00%

Source: *Dow Jones Business Almanac, 1978* (Homewood, Ill.: Dow Jones Irwin, 1978), p. 275.

up to twenty-five years. This is not a large part of the total savings and loan lending

C.   Land—loans up to 75% of value for up to five years. This is also not a large segment.

The most important group of loans made by these associations is the one- to four-family residence group. Savings and loans, besides lending the most money to this group compared to any other intermediary, also make the largest loans on a percentage of value basis. With an insured loan a buyer may borrow up to 95% of the value of the property. An insured loan is one which is insured by the government or a private firm such as MGIC. If the borrower defaults, the insurer will take care of at least part of any loss ultimately suffered by the institution. Savings and loans also make some miscellaneous loans such as for mobile homes. Finally, they also participate with other lenders in larger loans.

Along with the savings and loans, there is another institution which is very similar, the *mutual savings bank*. This is also a so-called thrift institution. Mutual banks are regionally important in the Northeast. Though there have been some structural changes in these institutions lately, they are still very similar to savings and loans in terms of their lending practices.

Commercial Banks

Commercial banks are not nearly as important a force in the real estate funds market as savings and loan associations. Generally speaking, banks are not as liberal in their lending policies as are savings and loans. Banks may make term loans up to five years in duration. They may make residential mortgage loans up to thirty years and 75% of value conventionally, 90% of value if insured. In addition, banks provide construction loans up to three years, mobile home loans, and leasehold loans. The lease must be at least one year longer than the life of the loan.

One important feature about bank lending for real estate is that banks have more liberal rules for the type of loans they can make. A bank can finance leaseholds and commercial development that cannot be handled by most savings and loans. For the prospective investor, however, it is a good idea to shop both types of institutions before committing to a particular source of funds. Terms and practices vary widely.

Insurance Companies

The kingpins of the big loan and creative financing markets in real estate are the **life insurance companies,** often in conjunction with mortgage companies. Life insurance companies, especially the larger ones, have a great deal of cash to invest annually, and real estate has proven to be a good outlet for these funds. A life insurance company makes a long-term contract with an insured person to give the individual a guaranteed return of some magnitude. Because of the long-term nature of a life insurance contract, the insurance company prefers long-lived, stable investments such as bonds, real estate mortgages, and leases to more volatile investments. However, because much money is often involved, life insurers prefer not to make individual single-family residential loans, since administration of these loans would become troublesome and costly.

For all these reasons, life insurers tend to stay with some particular groups of investments and fill an important role in the overall market:

1. *Large developments, residential or commercial.* Life insurers often participate in loans or ground leases to large-scale housing developers and commercial developers.

2. *Lease financing.* Life insurance companies buy leases for commercial property and participate in sale-and-leaseback arrangements.

3. *Package loans.* Life insurers often make arrangements with other intermediaries such as mortgage companies to buy large groups of residential and other small loans. These loans are often serviced and administered by other institutions for a fee.

4. *Participations and joint ventures.* Life insurance companies will provide equity funds in exchange for an interest in a large project as part of a joint venture with other companies or with individuals.

Life insurance companies have made a large commitment to financing housing and urban development in this country and play an important role in the large-scale development area. Because they are often willing to take a fairly low return on a long-term commitment of funds, they leave room for developers and others to make the economic gains required to stimulate private sector participation in the redevelopment of our cities.

Mortgage Companies

Although not large in terms of their total investment in real estate, compared to life insurance companies and savings and loans, **mortgage companies** play an important part in the overall fund-raising process. Mortgage companies serve as organizers in the market. These companies may go to a large insurance company, for instance, and obtain a commitment to buy perhaps $5 million of first mortgage loans at some rate of interest. The mortgage company will then make these loans and finally will sell them to the insurance company. After the sale the company will continue to service these loans for a fee.

Mortgage companies also make direct loans, participate in developments, acquire other loans, and warehouse loan funds. These companies also serve as brokers and manage real estate trusts. Though the names of these firms are generally not household words, they are important institutions facilitating real estate development in this country.

Pension Funds

One of the fastest growing sources of funds for real estate is the **pension fund.** A brief look at a sample of the pension fund liabilities of some of the larger companies will show that the pension funds are in for a long period of continued growth. Pension funds are a unique institution because one common type is exempt from income taxes. This, coupled with the high return and long-term yield on real estate, makes the pension fund a large-scale investor in this medium.

Pension funds generally do not invest as deeply in real estate as insurance companies—yet. However, they tend to be involved in a similar fashion. Pension funds buy packages of loans, make direct investments in large projects, and provide lease funds.

Real Estate Investment Trusts (REITs)

Perhaps no other financial institution connected with real estate has gotten as much publicity in the 1970s as the **real estate investment trust.** In the early 1970s, they achieved good success and everyone, including some of the nation's largest banks, got on the bandwagon. However, the economic downturn of the mid-1970s caused the over-leveraged REITs to turn sour. This put a great number of investors and institutions in financial distress.

A real estate investment trust is an institution which is organized much like a mutual fund or security investment trust. Shares are sold and money is borrowed to invest in real estate. REITs may lend money or invest directly in real estate and distribute the proceeds to the investors. If organized properly, an REIT can avoid most of the taxes which would otherwise be levied on its income. Because of their structure REITs may make many types of exotic financing commitments that other institutions cannot. However, many of these exotic commitments also have high risks. This fact is now well known by the managers of most of the nation's REITs.

To qualify for the tax breaks previously described the REIT must meet a number of organization conditions set by the IRS:

1. Ownership must be an unincorporated trust form with at least one trustee;
2. There must be at least one hundred owners;
3. The trust cannot be a personal holding company;
4. The trust may not act as a dealer;
5. Ninety percent of income must be from rentals, dividends, interest, or gains from real estate or securities;
6. Seventy-five percent of income must come directly from real property;
7. No more than thirty percent of income may come from short-term securities gains or from real property held less than four years; and

8. At least ninety percent of ordinary income must be distributed each year.

If these conditions are met, the REIT may avoid double-taxation on the distributed income.

Government Participation in the Primary Market

The federal government participates in the primary mortgage market two ways. First, it participates directly in the farm loan market by making direct loans to farmers for farm purchases. These loans are limited to 65% of the value of the farm and account for around $15 billion in outstanding loans.

The government also participates in the market by insuring loans made by financial intermediaries. These insurance programs are operated primarily through the FHA (**Federal Housing Administration**) and the VA (Veterans Administration).

FHA

The FHA has several basic aims. First, it is charged with insuring loans made by regular lenders to help stimulate their interest in mortgage lending. Second, the FHA sets building standards which must be met on homes bought under this program, thus helping to improve housing conditions. Finally, many specialized insurance and subsidy programs help stimulate specific market sectors which are important to certain population groups, such as the low-income, handicapped, or elderly. The programs of the FHA fall under the two titles of the Federal Housing laws. Title I allows the FHA to insure loans for repairs or additions to existing structures. Title II allows FHA to insure new construction and rental properties.

A complete listing of the **Title II programs** would take several pages of great detail. We will summarize the major programs to portray the flavor of the impact of these programs. Basically, when the FHA insures a loan, it sets up the conditions under which the lender may make the loan and then insures that the lender will be indemnified against a loss of the principal of the loan, should the borrower default. Both the housing and the lender must meet with FHA standards for the insurance to be approved.

Most of the insurance written under Title II falls under Section 203 of the Housing Act. This section provides insurance for one- to four-family dwellings. Other major programs provide insurance for rehabilitation of slum area dwellings and construction of low-income housing.

Section 221(d)(3) instituted rent subsidy programs for low-income and elderly or handicapped families. Housing in this program must be owned by nonprofit organizations or groups financed by several approved state and locally financed housing programs.

Two other programs were established under Sections 235 and 236 of the Housing Act of 1968. These programs provide subsidies to low-income families. Section 235 covers detached dwellings and Section 236 covers rental housing. The basic idea of both of these programs is that the government makes up the difference between the free market cost of the rent or mortgage payment and a fixed percentage of the dweller's income. There are limits on this subsidy and on the rate of return which may be earned by the landlords in these programs. However, these programs have made some significant contributions to the housing situation, in spite of early abuses in the programs.

VA

Like the FHA, the Veterans Administration also insures home loans. The VA loan programs are similar to the basic single-family program in FHA. Loans are generally made up to 75% of the value of the dwelling, though on occasion rates have been higher, up to 100%. Loans under this program may be either insured or guaranteed, the difference arising from the amount of the protection, the cost, and the way in which the lender receives compensation at default. The purpose of this program was originally to provide veterans with protection against inflation by allowing them to buy housing and helping to insure them a place to live.

Secondary Market Activities

In addition to primary market participation by the government, there are also a number of ways in which various agencies participate in the secondary mortgage markets. The two major sources of aid in the secondary market are the Federal National Mortgage Association (**Fannie Mae**) and the Government National Mortgage Association (**Ginnie Mae**).

FNMA

Fannie Mae is a quasi-public company which sells stock and bonds to the public, but is under the partial control of the federal government. Fannie Mae uses the funds raised from the public sector to buy mortgages from financial institutions. The returns on these mortgages are passed on to the firm's shareholders. The loans sold to Fannie Mae continue to be serviced by the seller. The selling of loans enables the lender to provide additional funds in the local area to facilitate home building and other real estate transactions. Generally, Fannie Mae buys insured mortgages, though it is empowered to buy conventional loans as well. Finally, in addition to distributing bonds, stock, and capital notes to raise funds, Fannie Mae may also sell certificates backed by "earmarked" pools of mortgages. These certificates are guaranteed by Ginnie Mae.

GNMA

Ginnie Mae was established in 1968. When Fannie Mae "went public" in that year, a void was created in the government's subsidy program to lenders. A problem often occurs in the market when insured mortgages are at rates of interest below the market rate. If a lender wishes to sell a below-market loan to an investor, a significant discount will often be required by the investor. This discount is necessary to convert the yield on the loan to a rate competitive with similar alternative investments. For example, a loan of $40,000 for thirty years at 8% carries a payment of $293.50 per month. For these payments to yield 9% over the same period the loan is only worth $36,475. This is a discount of 9% of the original loan amount.

To remove the problem of discounts plaguing lenders, Ginnie Mae is empowered to use government funds to buy such loans at par (here $40,000) and subsidize the discount in value. This process smooths the flow of funds in the secondary market. Ginnie Mae also buys insured loans with funds raised by the sale of **pass-through certificates.** These investments are becoming popular with large investors. The certificates basically "pass through" the receipts of the mortgage payments of the insured loans to the investors. Many issues of these certificates in the late 1970s offered rates of return in excess of 9%. This investment provides the individual investor with a way to participate in the high rates of return generated by the mortgage market without having to be a direct lender. Periodically, Ginnie Mae is used to facilitate other "one-shot" programs of the federal government to stimulate particular sectors of the housing market.

CHAPTER SIXTEEN SUMMARY

In this chapter we have looked at the market for funds used to finance real property purchases. The market itself was described in general terms first. We saw who the major participants are and how their roles have changed over time. Next we examined the nature of the major institutional sources in the primary market. These include banks, savings and loan associations, life insurance companies, and others. We then looked at the government participation in the market, both at the primary and secondary levels. We looked briefly at the role of the FHA, VA, FNMA, and the GNMA in both markets. We are now ready to look at the way financing may influence the value of property, with some interesting examples.

KEY TERMS

Commercial Banks
Deficit Spending
  Unit
Fannie Mae
Federal Housing
  Administration
Financial
  Intermediary
Ginnie Mae

Life Insurance
  Companies
Mortgage
  Companies
Pass-Through
  Certificates
Pension Fund
Primary Market

REIT
Savings and Loan
  Associations
Secondary Market
Surplus Spending
  Unit
Title II Programs

QUESTIONS FOR STUDY AND DISCUSSION

1. Explain the role of savings in the market for mortgage funds.

2. What role is played by financial intermediaries?

3. Differentiate between the *primary* and *secondary market* for funds. Who are the major participants in each?

4. Differentiate between the role played by savings and loan associations and commercial banks in the mortgage market. How do each of them compare to life insurance companies?

5. Describe the role played by the federal government in the primary funds market and the secondary market.

PROBLEMS FOR REVIEW

1. Using your present value tables, find the discount required to convert a thirty-year 8% loan of $50,000 into one yielding 9% (use annual payments).

17

REAL ESTATE FINANCE III— EFFECT OF FINANCING ON VALUE

IN THIS chapter we will examine the use of various combinations of the financing forms to show how they may be used to increase investment value. This chapter will tie together chapters 8, 15, and 16 by describing some of the more exotic ways developers can not only increase their wealth, but also operate with little or no capital investment.

The chapter is divided into two parts. First, we will look at how lease forms may be used to create increased project returns, while reducing the investment base. Second, we will view an example we have seen before, Super Supper Restaurant. The basic premise of that example will be expanded to show how returns on even a relatively minor project may be increased dramatically with creative financing. It is interesting to note that this latter example is a real one and all these financing options were actually available for the project.

Effective Use of Lease Financing Forms

The use of leases as financing vehicles may take one of several forms. In this part of the chapter we will look at four basic arrangements:

1. Straight ground rent;
2. Leasehold financing;
3. Sandwich leases; and
4. Sale-and-leaseback transactions.

Toward the end of the discussion you will see elements of several of these forms in the same example.

Straight Ground Rent

Often a landowner will execute a long-term straight lease with a developer to finance the cost of the land for a major project. This type of lease enables the ground lessor (developer) to avoid the need for equity to begin the project and permits the landowner to receive a fair return and avoid any capital gain which might have accrued to the land value, thus postponing the tax on that gain.

The use of the **straight ground lease** may permit a developer to avoid a great deal of equity financing on a project to be financed by debt. Assume a developer has an option on a piece of land on which he would like to build a shopping center. The developer finds an insurance company that wishes to finance the project with first mortgage financing. The land will cost $800,000 and the building will cost $2,700,000. When completed, the project will be worth $4 million. The developer would like to borrow the whole $3.5 million cost of the project, but the lender is limited to 75% of the project's value, or $3 million. To solve the problem, the builder foregoes his option and the insurance company buys the land and leases it to the developer. The builder borrows $2.7 million for the improvements, which is less than the 75% limit of $3 million. The ground lease is subordinated in priority to the mortgage. This approach has permitted the developer to build his project with no equity and the insurance company to increase its return because it holds the mortgage and the ground lease.

Often, ground lessors will wish to finance the cost of the ground they have bought. The interest of the ground lessor is called the **leased fee.** Financing a leased fee must be done with care. The general rule is that if a lessee will be making improvements which will be financed, then lessors will have to have any liens against their fee subordinated to the lease. This is necessary to protect the lessees in case the lessors default on their fee mortgage. If the mortgage had a superior claim and the owners defaulted, the lessees might lose their claim on the property under the lease. A developer who had just built a $20-million office building on leased ground would not like to have his claim disturbed. This situation is depicted graphically in Figure 17.1.

Leasehold Financing

In large-scale developments such as major office buildings, the developers often build on leased ground. Such improvements on leased ground are called **leaseholds.** In order to consummate these developments, the ground lessees must almost always use some form of financing. The primary source of funds for such a development is still the mortgage loan. However, this may really get complicated. The ground lessees already have an obligation to make lease payments, so the lender must feel comfortable that the leasehold will provide sufficient income to make all the contractual payments. If the lessees should default on their loan, the lender will have to pick up the lease payments to keep from losing the leasehold interest, which is the lender's security.

We can illustrate this by continuing the example started in Figure 17.1. Our ground lessee B wishes to build an office building on his leasehold. The building will cost $2 million and be financed with a $1.5 million, twenty-year, 9% mortgage. The mortgage will require total debt service of $164,000 per year. That means that the overall project will require net rent of $204,000, the mortgage payment plus the lease payment, just to cover financing costs. That is a heavy burden. The only security the mortgage lender has in these circumstances is the equity of $500,000 in the leasehold (a $2 million building cost less $1.5 million financing), and the rent which may be collected. We can see the overall position of the various parties in Figure 17.2.

As you can see by the figure, just a basic arrangement with a ground

FIGURE 17.1   FINANCING OF LEASED FEE

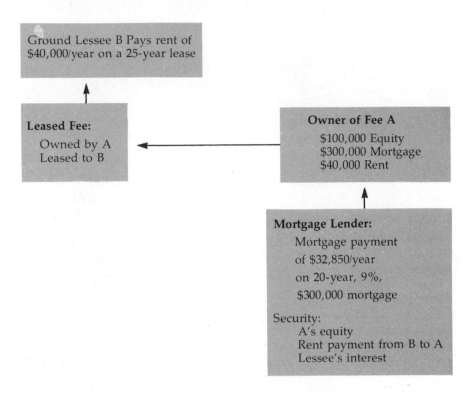

lessor and lessee who makes a leasehold improvement becomes complex. The questions of which interest will be subordinated to which other interest also becomes complex. Normally the lender to the leased fee will subordinate to the lease, so if A defaults B will remain undisturbed. If A has not borrowed, he will often subordinate his fee. This may cause him to lose his land if B defaults, but A would get a higher rent to compensate for this risk. One major advantage to these ground lease situations is that the owner of the leasehold can deduct the rent as an expense. This, in effect, provides a similar tax benefit to depreciation. Land cannot be depreciated, if owned.

Sandwich Lease

The sandwich lease is a useful arrangement of leases which makes it possible to distribute the services of a leasehold to the various tenants who ultimately wish to use the property. In real estate there are, by necessity, specialists. Certain types of firms and individuals find it ad-

FIGURE 17.2   LEASED FEE WITH LEASEHOLD FINANCING

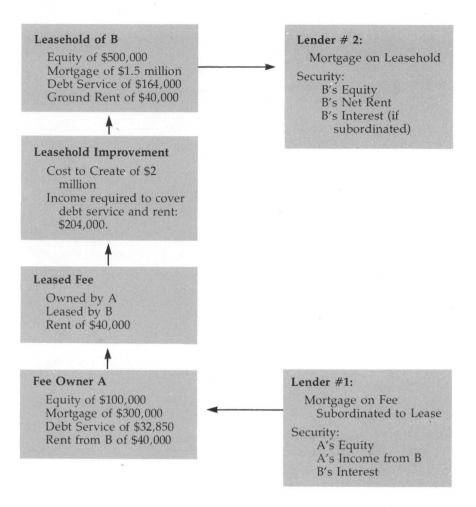

vantageous to gain their returns in certain ways. Life insurance companies, for instance, prefer long-term stable returns. For that reason, these institutions often become ground lessors.

Still other firms and individuals prefer to be developers. These individuals perform the tasks necessary to pull all the elements of a transaction together much like a movie producer does. Developers must line up the ground, the architects, the contractors, and eventually the tenants for the project. While this is going on, they are often at some risk. However, many developers do not like to take a permanent equity interest in their project, but find ways to sell it to others at the project's completion.

Finally, we have another group of specialists who may find it desirable to be responsible for subdividing the overall services of a large project. Such a firm or individual may lease an entire office building and then sublease it to the final tenants. These specialists are distributors, in effect. They make their profit on the spread between their rental income and their expenses, including their own rent.

The positions of all these specialists often create the sandwich leasing structure. For an example of this we can use the following sequence.

1. Smith buys (owns) ground.

2. Smith leases to Brown who develops the leasehold. Brown is a lessee to Smith.

3. Brown now subleases to Jones and gains a fixed rental income. This rent covers Brown's debt service and ground rent and yields a fairly fixed return. Brown will become the sandwich lessor to Jones.

4. Jones subleases property to various tenants to obtain his return. He, too, has a fixed rental cost. However, his rental income may vary depending on the job he does managing the property on a day-to-day basis. Jones is the sandwich lessee to Brown.

In this arrangement, Jones has no real investment. This is not always the case, as we shall see shortly. Brown may also not have much of an investment. The reason Brown includes Jones rather than going straight to the tenants is that he is a developer and makes his money by repeating the process, not by leasing office space.

Sale-and-Leaseback

When investors own property, they can only deduct depreciation on the improvement and interest on their debt financing from their income for tax purposes. Leasehold owners with a ground lease must still have some equity to support their property. By selling the rights that they own and leasing them back, the leasehold or fee owners may go beyond ground rent, eliminate their ownership, and increase their tax deductions.

Distilled to its ultimate, an owned investment property may yield just two types of benefits: periodic income and residual income. In our investment analysis discussion we said the decision to invest is based on a comparison of the present value of these two flows with the cash outflow required to acquire these flows. If property owners can generate a positive periodic cash flow without any equity commitment, then their return becomes infinite! The only thing given up by tenants who lease their entire interest is the residual value accruing to the owner. In fact, property owners who sell their fees and lease them back may find that they can sell the benefit stream to someone else for a capital gain in the future.

The point to emphasize here is that value comes from benefits, not from the physical nature of the property. The right to collect rent has value. It can be bought and sold just as the physical property can. It should also be noted that owners who sell property and lease it back may actually lower their cash flow because the depreciation they deducted as owners (on the improvements) did not represent a *cash* outflow. However, their investment is also reduced, perhaps to nothing. Overall, return on investment may rise. We will now illustrate some of these points with examples.

Example 17.1   Apex Company owns an office building which houses its corporate offices. The property was purchased in fee simple twenty years ago for $450,000. Of that amount, $50,000 was land. Annual depreciation on the property has been $10,000 per year. The basis of the property is now $250,000. Apex finds that it can sell the property for $500,000 and lease it back for twenty years for $58,750 per year. Apex earns 12% after taxes on its investments. Its tax rate is 50%. Table 17.1 shows the results of the sale transaction Apex is contemplating.

Presently Apex has $300,000 per year in cash operating income. The effect of the transaction on income is shown in Table 17.2. As you can see, the cash freed up by the sale-and-leaseback transaction can be put to work to increase income. However, we must remember a residual was given up here. We know that we would be indifferent if the present value of the residual given up by selling the fee is equal to the present value of the increased benefits. This calculation is shown below:

$$PV \text{ of residual} = \$16,925 \text{ increased annual cash}$$
$$\text{flow} \times PVAF_{20,12\%} = \$126,425$$

Since the present value of the residual is $126,425, we can work backwards to determine at what price the company would have to sell the building twenty years from now. This sale price would have to be more than $1,219,525 for Apex to be better off than they would be with the sale-and-leaseback. This appears somewhat doubtful. The building is

---

TABLE 17.1   SALE-AND-LEASEBACK—APEX COMPANY

Sale Price	$500,000
Less: Basis ($450,000 − $10,000 × 20)	250,000
Gain on Sale	$250,000

Tax: 25% of first $50,000 = $12,500
          30% of $200,000   =   60,000
          Total Tax Liability

Net Cash from Sale = $500,000 − $72,500 = $427,500

TABLE 17.2   EFFECT ON INCOME FROM
SALE-AND-LEASEBACK—APEX COMPANY

Current Income (Cash from Operations)	$300,000
Less: Depreciation (Noncash)	10,000
Income Before Tax	$290,000
Tax at 50%	145,000
After-Tax Income	$145,000

After-Tax Cash (After-tax income + Depreciation) = $155,000

Income After Sale-and-Leaseback	$300,000
Less: Rent	58,750
Income Before Tax	$241,250
Tax at 50%	120,625
After-Tax Income (Cash)	$120,625

After-Tax Income on funds generated by sale of building:
   12% Return on investment × $427,500 (Table 17.1)
   = $51,300

Total Cash Flow After Sale-and-Leaseback:		$120,625
	plus	51,300
		$171,925

Increase in Annual Cash Flow = $171,925 − $155,000 = $16,925

only worth $500,000 on the market today. We need to assume a steady inflation of 4½% per year from that value while the building deteriorates as it ages for the next twenty years.

In this example, we have looked at a typical situation where an owner sells a fee and leases it back so the money may be put to work elsewhere at a higher rate. Our presumption is that the office building provides no intrinsic earnings for the firm, but if its value were utilized elsewhere earnings would increase.

Example 17.2[1]   A more complex example may be used to illustrate how a developer may use sale-and-leaseback to finance a property. An investor–builder constructs a building on a piece of ground on which he holds a long-term lease. The building costs $11 million. The building is fully leased to tenants by the investor and rental income yields a cash flow of $1 million after ground rent has been paid. The project was originally financed with an interim loan from a group of large banks. The owner of the leasehold has to find a way to raise $11 million to pay back this loan.

---

[1]This example was suggested by a situation posed by William Atteberry, *Modern Real Estate Finance* (Columbus, Ohio: Grid, 1972), p. 114.

To accomplish this the developer, Mr. D, sells his leasehold to B, a large insurance company for $8 million. He assigns his ground lease to the same company. B becomes the ground lessee to A, the landowner. B owns the leasehold, which he subleases back to D for $600,000 per year. This yields a return of 7.5% for B and leaves D with a remaining cash flow of $400,000 ($1 million − $600,000).

Mr. D at this point is still $3 million short on the bank loan and he has a $400,000 cash flow as his chief asset. He sells the rights to this cash flow to C, another investor, for $3 million and leases these rights back for $300,000 per year. Mr. C has a $3 million investment and earns a 10% return cash on cash. Mr. D is now left with no debt, no investment, and a $100,000 return for his efforts. A diagram of this series of transactions appears as Table 17.3 below.

TABLE 17.3   SALE-AND-LEASEBACK

First Position

Ground Lessor—A	Builder-Lessee—D
Owns land; collects basic rent	Owns leasehold with $1 million cash flow; Return = $1 million/$11 million = 9%

Second Position

Ground Lessor—A	Institution—B
Owns land; collects basic rent	Pays $8 million for leasehold; Lease yields $600,000 per year; Return = 7.5%

Builder—D
Sublease from B for $600,000;
Net equity remains of $3 million;
Net income of $400,000;
Return = 13%

Third Position

Ground Lessor—A	Institution—B
Owns land; collects basic rent	Return on leasehold of 7.5%
Investor—C Pays $3 million for sublease; Leases it back for $300,000; Return = 10%	Builder—D Sub-sublease earning $100,000 on no investment

The type of sale-and-leaseback we have seen in Example 17.2 creates a sandwich lease with the investors who financed the transaction. This example shows how developers can finance a project by selling it, leaving a residual cash flow to reward them. The developers have no investment and are now free to repeat the process. As you can see from the example, just the rights to pieces of the cash flow have enough value to pay for the project.

There are some important factors to remember in sale-and-leaseback transactions as well as in straight leases. Normally, when a whole property is leased, the lessee may anticipate that the lease payments will be sufficiently high to yield the owners a return on their investment as well as the return of their capital. This would not necessarily be true in a short-term lease, but it probably will be for a long-term lease. Second, lessees must be careful to avoid options-to-purchase at predetermined prices. An option to purchase should be negotiated at arm's length at the end of the life of the lease. Otherwise the lease may be treated as a conditional sale by the IRS and the lessee will lose some of the tax benefits. This is also important for lessors. If the lease is wrongfully constructed, it may be construed by the courts to be a mortgage and it would have to be foreclosed in case of a default. With a lease, a tenant who defaults can be evicted, which is easier than foreclosure.

In addition to the straight sale-and-leaseback, there are also other varieties and combination forms. Again, these are only limited by the developer's creativity and that of his lawyer. Almost anything legal that the parties to a real estate project want to do can be worked out if the economics are right.

Effects of Financing on Value: A Case Study

Now that we have looked at various creative financing methods, we will look at how they can be used to change the value of a particular project. For this discussion, we will look at a fast food restaurant which is under development by an independent investor. A site has been located in a Midwestern state capital and the investor is trying to determine how best to finance the venture. This site has an abandoned restaurant building on it. The basic data on income are presented in Table 17.4. The four alternative financing arrangements will then be described. Finally, the resulting impact on value will be analyzed for each.

Alternative One

The investor finds that he can buy the building from the owner of the leasehold for $70,000. The owner of the land is also willing to sell for

TABLE 17.4   SUPER SUPPER RESTAURANT PROJECT

1. Conservative estimate of sales = $250,000 per year
2. Income before other expenses (cash) = $55,200 per year
3. Loan rate prevailing = 9%
4. Tax bracket of investor = 30%
5. Required rate of return on investment after taxes = 15%
6. Estimated property taxes = $3600;
   Estimated insurance = $3200
7. Holding period for investment purposes will be ten years; no reserve will be used because of the short life
8. Available property's price if sold on open market = $145,000; consists of land worth $75,000 and abandoned building worth $70,000
9. Land and building separately owned; ground rent currently $600 per month; land lease has eleven years to run; necessary improvements to building will cost $30,000 plus $10,000 needed for working capital
10. Residual value of property after improved expected to be $150,000 in ten years

$75,000. If the investor packages the property in this way he has determined that it will have a twenty-year life remaining and can be sold in ten years for $150,000 after he adds a few initial improvements. The project will be financed with a loan of $115,000 for ten years. His other funds will be equity. The value analysis is shown in Table 17.5. We have taken a shortcut approach to the value using the *average* interest expense, rather than the actual expense in each period, to make the comparison easier to see.

The net present value of this alternative for financing the project is $65,000. This represents an internal rate of return of 30%. Having this basic alternative in mind, the investor will now proceed to some more exotic approaches. The first of these will exploit the ground lease which already exists on the property. In the second creative alternative, we will look at a sale-and-leaseback of the property itself. Finally, we will look at an alternative in which everything but the working capital is leased.

Alternative Two

The present owner of the land at the subject site is willing to have the new investor pick up the lease and continue to pay the current ground rent. With this approach, our investor will abandon his building at the end of year 10, giving up its residual. The building purchase and initial improvements will be financed with a $75,000, ten-year, 9% loan. The new cash flow is found in Table 17.6. This is pure leasehold financing.

TABLE 17.5   ALTERNATIVE ONE

Operating Income (Gross)	$55,200
Less Taxes and Insurance	6,800
NOI	$48,400
Less: Building Depreciation (20 years)	3,500
Less: Improvements Depreciation (20 years)	1,500
Less: Average Interest[a]	6,400
Taxable Income	$37,000

Tax @ 30% = $11,100

NOI	$48,400
Less: Tax	11,100
Less: Debt Service	17,900
Net Cash Flow	$19,400

Present Value of Cash Flow for 10 years @ 15% = $97,350

Sale Price	$150,000
Less: Basis Land	75,000
Less: Basis Building	35,000
Less: Basis Improvements	15,000
Gain	$ 25,000

Tax on Gain = $6,250

Net Cash from Sale = $150,000 − $6,250 + $10,000 Working Capital Returned
= $153,750

Present Value of Residual = $38,000

Net Present Value = $97,350 + $38,000 − $70,000[b] = $65,350

[a] Loan payment @ $17,900/year for 10 years = $179,000 total payments and total interest of $64,000 ($179,000 − $115,000).

[b] Cash outlay of $10,000 working capital, $30,000 for improvements and $30,000 of equity for property.

As you can see this form of financing, in spite of the loss of the residual, raises the net present value to $75,000 from the $65,000 net present value in alternative one. This new approach represents an internal rate of return of 50%.

Alternative Three

Our intrepid restaurateur likes the potential 50% return promised by alternative two, but he would like to try for more. By diligent search, he has found an investor who will buy the whole property as it now sits for $145,000 and lease it back to the developer for $24,000 per year and pay the taxes besides. The developer will have to manage the im-

TABLE 17.6   ALTERNATIVE TWO

Cash From Operations	$55,200
Less: Taxes and Insurance	6,800
Less: Ground Rent	7,200
NOI	$41,200
Less: Depreciation (Building and Improvements)	10,000
Less: Interest (average)[a]	4,200
Taxable Income	$27,000

Tax @ 30% = $8,100

NOI	$41,200
Less: Tax	8,100
Less: Debt Service	11,700
Net Cash Flow	$21,400

Present Value @ 15% for 10 years = $107,400

Present Value of Working Capital Returned in 10th = $2,500

Total Present Value Benefits = $109,900

Cash Outlay = $10,000 Working Capital + $25,000 Equity

Net Present Value = $109,900 − $35,000 = $74,900

---

[a] Loan payments of $11,700 for ten years = $117,000; $117,000 − $75,000 = $42,000 total interest.

Note: Depreciation is based on a ten-year life in this alternative.

provements and working capital on his own. Otherwise, the project will be treated similarly to alternative two. The results appear in Table 17.7.

As you can see from the table, the net present value this way is the same as for alternative one. However, the internal rate of return is over 50%, much higher than that for alternative one.

Alternative Four

In this last situation, the developer has found an investor who will buy the whole package including equipment and improvements and lease it back for $26,000 per year. This produces the lowest cash flow over a ten-year period, but the highest net present value and an even higher rate of return. The results of this alternative are shown in Table 17.8. The net present value is a phenomenal $84,000 and the rate of return is more than 180% per year, compounded. If this return seems impressive, it is. Not only that, but the investor eventually abandoned this site as a possibility and put the restaurant on a site where the total rent, land and building was $500 per month guaranteed for ten years. With

TABLE 17.7   ALTERNATIVE THREE

Cash from Operations	$55,200
Less: Insurance	3,200
Less: Rent	24,000
NOI	$28,000
Less: Depreciation on Improvements (10 yrs)	3,000
Taxable Income	$25,000

Tax @ 30% = $7,500

NOI	$28,000
Less: Tax	7,500
Net Cash Flow	$20,500

Present Value of Cash Flow @ 15% for 10 years = $102,900

Present Value of Return of Working Capital = $2,500

Outflows of $10,000 for Working Capital + $30,000 Equity for Improvements.

Net Present Value = $102,900 + $2,500 − $40,000 = $65,400

TABLE 17.8   ALTERNATIVE FOUR

Cash from Operations	$55,200
Less: Insurance	3,200
Less: Rent	26,000
NOI = Taxable Income	$26,000

Tax @ 30% = $7,800

NOI	$26,000
Less: Tax	7,800
Net Cash Flow	$18,200

Present Value of Cash Flow = $91,400

Present Value of Working Capital Returned = $2,500

Outflows: Working Capital of $10,000

Net Present Value = $83,900

$100,000 in improvements, this new site will yield a return of 90% per year for ten years. This is less than alternative four, but it includes the fact that the new property is much more elaborate and twice as big.

From the four foregoing alternatives, we can see vividly how the nature of financing for a property can alter its value. By changing the financing here, we raised the return on the project from a solid 30% to over 180% per year. Real estate, almost more than any other investment, allows this type of possibility.

CHAPTER SEVENTEEN SUMMARY

This completes our discussion of real estate finance. In this chapter we have looked at the more exotic aspects of creative real estate finance. We looked at various types of mortgages and leases which can be used separately or in combinations to provide some startling results. There may be some who would question the need for this coverage, especially in detail. However, for potential investors, this is a key input to their value. Real estate finance is exciting and even small investors can use these techniques, as our restaurant example illustrated. The money is out there waiting for the more creative investors to utilize it effectively.

KEY TERMS

Leased Fee   **Straight Ground Lease**
Leasehold

QUESTIONS FOR STUDY AND DISCUSSION

1. Explain the operation of a sale-and-leaseback arrangement. What is it used for?

2. How does a sandwich lease work? What is it used for?

3. What factors must be taken into account when financing a leasehold?

PART 3

CHAPTER EIGHTEEN—LAND INVESTMENT AND DEVELOPMENT

Community growth is greatly influenced by real estate development. In this chapter we examine potential needs for development and how to select specific sites for it. Important features of the chapter include a discussion of the various stages of land development and some of the types of analysis that should be applied. One of the critical parts of this analysis is economic base analysis, which is discussed in detail.

CHAPTER NINETEEN—REAL ESTATE MARKETING

In this chapter we discuss real estate marketing. We view the brokerage functions as they might

SPECIAL TOPICS

affect values. We also discuss, in some depth, the various important contracts and documents associated with the transfer of real property.

CHAPTER TWENTY— HOME OWNERSHIP

The final chapter in this text is concerned with the nature of homeownership. We examine the various factors affecting the decision to own a home, as well as some important analytical processes associated with the decision to purchase a home. We look at the rent versus buy decision, the choice among various financing terms, and the overall value derived from home ownership. This chapter serves as a review and capstone to the book.

18 LAND INVESTMENT AND DEVELOPMENT

THIS CHAPTER has two main functions. First, it discusses land investment and development. Second, it shows how economic analysis mentioned in the previous chapters may be used to help determine the appropriate development investments for a given investor.

The discussion of investment analysis in chapter 8 set forth a general model that could be used for any type of real estate project. Here that model will be applied to real estate development. Because development involves changing the character of a parcel of real property, economic analysis will hold a key place in the process. This discussion is not intended to show the macro economic, or societal, implications of development. Rather, it centers on the micro process of investing in land and ultimately creating new real property values.

Land Investment

Land as an Investment

In his book on land investment, Maury Seldin points out that there are three important ways to accumulate wealth in society. These are "cornering" a resource market, obtaining a monopoly position in a market, and selling future expectations.[1] All three of these can be used to accumulate wealth by acquiring land.

Land has a number of important value characteristics. As a resource, land is fixed in quantity. Land can be improved in various ways to increase its productivity, but its resource amount is fixed. Land is not a homogeneous resource. Some land is of excellent quality. In Iowa, for instance, the farmland in many counties is among the best in the world and sells for over $4000 an acre as farmland. In other areas of the country where water is scarce and the soil is devoid of nutrients, land may sell for nearly giveaway prices. Because only a portion of the land is of a particular quality, it is possible for an individual to accumulate wealth by controlling a large portion of the high quality land in an area. Similarly, it is possible to become wealthy by creatively developing lower quality land.

It is an economic fact that land will be owned by the individuals most willing to pay for it. All resources allocated by the market will be bid for by those demanding it until the market is cleared. Generally, the bidding for land will stop when the land is gone or the investment value is reached and a higher price would mean the land is a bad investment. Contrary to the expectations of many, a Federal Reserve staff economist points out that an increasing percentage of farmland sold in the 1970s

---

[1]Maury Seldin, *Land Investment* (Homewood, Ill.: Dow Jones-Irwin, 1975), p. 3.

is being purchased by individuals who already own and operate farms.[2] This land was *not* being bought for investment or development purposes.

Land has one final characteristic which is important in any consideration of value. Land value is a function of politics. People have very strong feelings about those who profit from owning land. In our society, people demand the right to profit from their investments. However, even though society generally supports this right, with land there are limits. Because it is possible to obtain monopoly profits from land which can be misused, society also demands the right to control land use and ownership. Zoning laws in most communities dictate the types of ways to use land. Ownership restrictions such as anticorporate farming laws preventing large-scale ownership by corporations are in force in some states. In the late 1970s, a similar rule may break up farms in California under federal aegis.

Types of Land Investment

Land can be purchased in any one of several states of development for investment purposes: raw land, interim land, and development land.

Raw Acreage   **Raw land** is the least developed form of land. Generally such land is under some low density use and is not located in an area which will permit its use in some higher level of development. Raw land may be used for farming, extraction such as coal mining, recreation, or nothing at all. It is possible that land which is adjacent to a developed area is still in the raw stage because it is zoned for use only in agriculture, for example. Zoning is a function of the political process. In some areas, citizens in a community may decide that they do not want their city to grow, so they force their zoning group to prohibit further development of raw land on the city fringes.

Development Land   Land which is ready for development generally is characterized by three states. First, **development land** is located favorably so that its service linkages have reasonable economic costs associated with them. Second, development land has been zoned to permit higher intensity, higher valued improvements to be constructed. Unless the zoning for any parcel permits it to be developed under the appropriate use, the land will not realize its best value. Finally, development land is generally connected to necessary utilities or at least close to these utilities. Development land is available for such land uses as residential housing, commercial and industrial building, and complex multiple use developments. It may also be subdivided and sold in pieces for development by others.

---

[2]Marvin Duncan, "Farm Real Estate: Who Buys and How," *Monthly Review*, Federal Reserve Bank of Kansas City, June 1977, pp. 3–9.

Interim Land   Between raw acreage and development land is a category of land uses which help carry the land from its raw state to the place where it can be developed. As we will see shortly, raw land is an investment whose return comes chiefly from resale. This is a difficult state for many investors to maintain. To overcome the costs of carrying raw land it may be placed in an interim use. The definition of interim here is difficult to pin down. There are really a couple of classes of interim land situations:

1. Raw land which has never been developed, perhaps located on the edge of town, can be placed in an interim use such as a mobile home park, a miniature golf course, an outdoor movie theater, or a small amusement park. These uses provide the investor with sufficient income to help offset debt service, taxes, and other ownership costs while the land is becoming ripe for development.

2. Sometimes land has been developed in a use which is now no longer its best use. Changes in city economic patterns and other factors may render a particular land use relatively valueless. For example, in many large cities, service stations are relatively worthless as business enterprises. An appraisal of such property may show the building at say $5000 and the land at $95,000. A business investor can buy such property to serve as an interim land use. When new development patterns emerge the owner can then obtain zoning and sell the property or develop it. Under these circumstances what was formerly a prime use later becomes an interim use for a whole new round of development.

In general, a great variety of fairly permanent land uses can serve as **interim land** uses. Even garden apartments can be used. The important point is that an interim use is put on a site when it is obvious that the land cannot be used to its full potential, but still has a high potential value and will be expensive to maintain.

Benefits of Land Investment

As in any type of investment, the benefits of land investment come from two types of returns: periodic cash flows and terminal values. Land is an investment which often provides its returns only from terminal value. This may make some forms of land investment difficult for investors who need a certain amount of periodic income. Land can provide a wide variety of return combinations depending on the type of use under which it is held. This variety also offers a good deal of flexibility as we shall see in the following examples.

Land Investment Examples   In the next examples we will examine a parcel of development land as it might be owned in various ways. We shall look at the returns under each situation as well as the circumstances under which the land will yield the same return in all three situations.

Situation One:

An investor has an opportunity to buy a twenty-five-acre parcel of farmland on the edge of a community. The price of the farm is $3000 per acre, or $75,000 total. The land is close enough to the city that the investor feels certain he can merely hold the land for five years and sell it for a fair profit. The investor expects to sell the land for residential development purposes for $9500 per acre. The investor is in the 50% tax bracket. His after-tax return for this situation is 20% as illustrated in Table 18.1.

Table 18.1 shows what happens if the investor buys the land outright and holds it for five years. Notice that in addition to the initial equity the investor must also spend $1375 per year for property taxes. This is called a **carrying cost.** Cash flow on this project is negative until the last year's sale of the property. Carrying cost may be avoided by committing the property to an interim land use as may be seen in Table 18.2.

TABLE 18.1   LAND INVESTMENT—SITUATION ONE

Purchase Price: $75,000
  Present Value @ 20% ....($75,000)

Property Taxes per year: $2750
Less Tax Savings @ 50%:   1375
Net Property Tax: $1375
  Present Value @ 20% for five years ....($ 4,100)
Total Cost = Equity + Carrying Cost ....($79,100)

Proceeds from sale in five years:
  Sale Price $237,500
  Less Purchase Price   75,000
  Gain on Sale $162,500
  Tax @ 25% = $40,625

  Sale Price $237,500
  Less Taxes   40,625
  Net Proceeds $196,875
  Present Value at 20% $79,100
Net Present Value @ 20% ....$ 0

Overall rate of return if the parcel is sold for $9500 per acre is 20% per year.

TABLE 18.2   LAND INVESTMENT—SITUATION TWO

Purchase Price $75,000
Improvements   15,000
Total Investment $90,000
    Present Value @ 23.5% ....($90,000)

Cash Flow:
    Operating Income $15,000 per year
    Less Property Taxes   2,750
    Cash Income $12,250 per year
    Less Depreciation   3,000
    Taxable Income $ 9,250 per year
    Tax @ 50% = $4,625 per year

    Cash Income $12,250
    Less Taxes   4,625
    Cash Flow $ 7,625
    Present Value at 23.5% for 5 years $21,150

Sale Proceeds (see Situation One)
    Present Value at 23.5% $68,525
Net Present Value at 23.5% ....$ 325

Overall rate of return, assuming $9,500 per acre sale price, is 23.5%
    approximately.

Using a 20% return, the following situation may be constructed.
Here the sale price can be seen to be $7,900 per acre.

Sale Proceeds:
    Sale of Property $197,950
    Less Purchase Price   75,000
    Gain on Sale $122,950
    Tax @ 25% = $30,750

    Sale Price $197,950
    Less Taxes   30,750
    Net Proceeds $167,200

    Present Value at 20% $67,200

    Present Value of Investment at 20% ....($90,000)

    Present Value of Annual Cash Flow at 20% $22,800

Net Present Value at 20% .... $ 0

Situation Two:
    In this approach the investor buys the acreage for $75,000 and then
    spends an additional $15,000 to create a miniature golf course on

part of the property. This will help defray carrying costs and accomplish two things. First, the overall rate of return on the property may be increased. Second, the investor may achieve the same 20% return as in Situation One, but he may sell the property for less than $9500 per acre, making it available for a wider variety of final development uses. This is illustrated in Table 18.2.

Thus, we can see under an interim land use the return can be raised to 23.5%, or the land can be sold for $7900 instead of $9500 and still yield the investor 20%. This lowers the risk to the investor and improves his flexibility.

Situation Three:

Having seen the possibilities, our intrepid investor now decides to see what will happen if he buys this property on contract. The downpayment is 25% and the balance is financed at 9% with five equal installments. It is assumed that the property can be sold for $9500. Table 18.3 shows the results of the analysis.

As we can see, the investor can expect to earn a 34% return if he finances the property as shown, and sells the property for $9500 per acre. This is a significant increase in return compared to the other two situations. The reader may confirm that our investor could sell the property for $5560 per acre and still earn 20% on his investment.

Summary   In these examples we have seen how an investor may use an interim land use, combined with appropriate leverage, to increase the return on a parcel of predevelopment land. We also have seen how the risk and flexibility might be altered under the various situations. This is only a brief glance at the variety of ways developers may hold acreage for development. The possibilities are unlimited, even with this brief example. You can also see how a variety of investment needs can be served by the investor's approach to holding the property.

Risks in Land Investment

The general risks which apply to land investment are the same as for other types of investments. However, in some situations there are certain differences. A pure land investment such as Situation One has a very low business risk and no financial risk. Situation One depends entirely on the market, so there is a good deal of market risk. Land investments in general have little or no purchasing power risk. How-

TABLE 18.3   LAND INVESTMENT—SITUATION THREE

Loan Situation (approximation method)

Downpayment (25%)	$ 18,750	
Add Improvements	15,000	
	$33,750	

Present Value of Initial Outlay at 34% ....($33,750)

Loan Payment at 9%	=	$14,460
Total Payments	=	$72,300
Total Interest	=	$16,050
Average Interest	=	$3,210

Carrying Cost

Operating Income	$15,000
Less Property Tax	2,750
Cash Income	$12,250
Less Average Interest	3,210
Less Depreciation	3,000
Taxable Income	$ 6,040

Tax @ 50% = $3,020

Cash Income	$12,250
Less Taxes	3,020
Less Debt Service	14,460
Carrying Cost	($ 5,230)

Present Value at 34% for 5 years ....($11,820)

Sale Proceeds (see Situation One)
Present Value at 34% $45,570

Net Present Value at 34% .... $ 0

ever, when land is financed as by the land contract in Situation Three, there is a significant financial risk.

Besides market risks, financial risks, and a certain amount of business risk when interim land is held, there is one other significant risk in land investment. Because land value depends on its use and land use generally depends on zoning, there is a good deal of political risk. A change in city administration and planning policy could completely alter the investment value of a parcel of land. This risk is subtle, but no less devastating than any other. Investors may become trapped in a parcel with unfavorable zoning and either find themselves with an opportunity loss or a real loss, depending upon whether the parcel is sold.

Forces Affecting Land Values

The value of a parcel of land is affected by a complex combination of factors. Figure 10.5 showed how all the various physical, financial, and economic influences worked in a general way to influence values. Here we can point to some forces behind some of the features in the earlier model. A number of social and economic factors lie behind the changes in land values manifested in the last twenty to thirty years.

Urbanization   The first major movement which greatly altered land values in the United States was the movement of population from rural to urban areas, called **urbanization.** This move was not possible until agricultural productivity rose sufficiently to permit the movement of people from the farm. The coincident rise of industrial capability gave these displaced people jobs and moved them toward the urban areas. The demand for housing and industrial and commercial sites in the urban areas caused land values to escalate. Simultaneously, farmland also rose as increased productivity made it more profitable. This urban movement had its greatest surge in the first half of the twentieth century.

Suburbanization   As urban areas swelled in population and the quality of life deteriorated, people began to move out of the cities and into the suburbs. Linkages became too long and expensive at the edges of the city. People living outside and working and shopping in the downtown area became disenchanted, so the development of the suburbs began in earnest in the mid–twentieth century. By the late 1960s most large cities were circled by outerbelt freeways and major arteries on which were located large shopping centers and office buildings. Thus, people living on the edge of town could shop and work without going into the city.

The move to the suburbs, or **suburbanization,** has had some heavy repercussions on land values. Obviously, land on the edges of cities near major traffic arteries has risen dramatically in value in the last twenty years. Meanwhile, in the 1960s and 1970s land values in downtown areas have become soft in many areas. Transportation costs, as they rise, detract from a property's value. Many downtown parcels in large cities such as New York and Philadelphia have lost their values. However, they have not lost enough to become ripe for development under highest and best use.

It should be noted here that even though the general trends described in these last two sections are strong and pervasive, they are not universal. Some large cities, such as Houston and Minneapolis, have fairly vital downtowns. Even some of the older Eastern cities such as Philadelphia are moving ever so slightly in the direction of spot development downtown. An example would be the Society Hill section of Philadelphia. In general, however, the greatest rising trends in value are still at the edges of our larger urban areas.

Interurbanization   Another trend which has affected land values is the general process of proximate cities flowing toward each other, filling in the space between them. This process, called **interurbanization,** takes place first along major interurban highways and spreads back away gradually. The Dallas–Fort Worth and Arlington, Texas area is one example. The whole coastal area in Southern California is another notable example. This movement has created some significant values, but also some problems. Commuting and other frictional costs required for this type of development place a social cost on development, because of the use of scarce fossil fuels.

How the trend in interurbanization will continue in the years to come is a big question. It may be that the growing expense attached to commuting will first hurt this movement and then begin to force the redevelopment of the downtown urban areas. An investor with the appropriate vision may find land in the right urban areas an excellent investment in the decades to come.

Population Trends   In chapter 10 we mentioned that the general characteristics of the population in a local area will influence property value. Shortly we will see how to look at these characteristics from a decision-making point of view. It is important to point out here that the future of land values depends not so much on historical trends as on future shifts in population demographics. What will the population be in five years is a more appropriate question than what has happened for the last five years. For urban value analysis, especially in large cities, finding the turning points for changes in the situation will be the important thing. When will the trend away from the city stop?

Local Economics   Again, in chapter 10, we pointed to the importance of local economics. The nature of a city's economic base is an important factor affecting future demand. Cities which depend on one or two major industries or employers may find themselves in a great deal of trouble if something happens to one of those major employers. Some years ago when Studebaker and two other major employers left South Bend, Indiana, the city suddenly found itself in dire economic straits. Development is very uncertain in such situations. Land may also be cheap, however, and if the city comes back, as South Bend did, many speculators may make heavy profits.

In general, the ideal situation is probably a broad strong economic base of export (primary) employment. The exact nature of the base will determine the characteristics of land use to a certain extent, however. For instance, Columbus, Ohio, is a capital city with heavy employment in government and satellite service agencies. There is also a large state university in the city. These two features, coupled with the types of professionals they attract, causes a heavy segment of the population to be white collar middle class with a fair amount of affluence. This gives the city a different character than a city which has a broad base of heavy industry such as Gary, Indiana. Large cities develop an economic character which influences their population and, in turn, land values.

Local Politics   The role of politics was alluded to earlier in the discussion of risk. Because land is a local phenomenon, the demand for it and its control are also local. What a city intends to do with itself has a direct bearing on land values. The economic influences just discussed indirectly affect the character of a city. The direct manifestation of this character shows itself through city planning, goal statements, and other outputs. The value of land in a city with a stated goal of no growth or controlled growth is obviously going to be affected by these particular goals.

City planners, directed by their constituents to a certain extent, may dictate land use and thus its value. It is therefore important for the developer to understand what uses will be acceptable and where demand lies before investing. Because planners and developers, as well as the citizens, may not always agree on what land uses are best, conflicts arise. The way in which these conflicts are settled is important. If a city is too restrictive, it need not be a problem because the courts may react to encourage freer development. On the other hand, it is always better if conflicts may be settled reasonably by the parties involved. Such a climate is much more conducive to creative development.

The Process of Land Investment and Development

Now that we have seen the nature of land as an investment and what influences its value, we can look at the analytical process that may be used to select a particular alternative. This section will really conclude a great deal of the material discussed in the book up to this point. We have looked at cash flow analysis before, but we have not really tried to go behind the numbers from a process standpoint.

The basic process of investing in land for profit or development may be summarized by Figure 18.1.

FIGURE 18.1   LAND INVESTMENT PROCESS

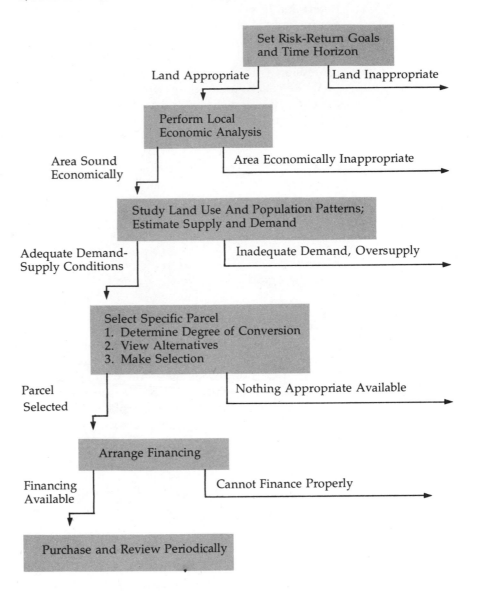

Preliminary Determinations

Before making any investments, the investor must determine what level of risk and return is desired. If the investor has a propensity for some high risk–high return investments, land for development may be an appropriate alternative. The next step is then the determination of a desired time horizon. A land investment may require a fairly long time to mature to the appropriate value. This means the investor must be ready to be patient.

Local Economic Analysis

The purpose of local economic analysis is to determine the economic structure which underlies the local real estate market. The best approach here is to analyze the current situation and one or two selected past years to help spot any trends which may be developing. As you may recall, the process of local economic analysis is aimed at finding the relationship between service and export (primary) employment in the community. This relationship will help to identify changes in the demand for certain land uses.

For this discussion, **service employment** will refer to workers whose output is primarily consumed within the community. Primary or **export employment** refers to output consumed primarily outside the community. The most important basis for primary employment is manufacturing.

There are three approaches which may be used to establish the necessary relationships. The first uses a set of employment ratios to help establish the "ideal" ratios for given categories of employment, which may then be used to sort out service and export categories. The second method is the location quotient. The third method involves the use of input–output analysis.

Ratio Method   In the United States as a whole, essentially *all* the employment in certain broad categories such as retail and wholesale trade, government, and finance is service employment. It may be assumed that in *any* city the proportion of the population engaged in a given category should be the same as the national proportion. If the proportion of the workforce in a given category is higher locally than the national pro portion, any excess may be said to be exported. If the proportion is not high enough, then the community must import some of these services. Some formulas may be derived as

---

Trade and Service Categories

1. The national proportion, P_i, may be found for any trade or service category, E_i:

$$\frac{\text{Total employment in U.S. in } E_i}{\text{Total U.S. population}} = P_i$$

2. The amount of local service employment in the E_i category is

$P_i \times$ local population

3. The amount of export employment in the E_i category for the community is

Total local employment in E_i
Less the service employment found in (2) above.

An example of these calculations is summarized for Black Hawk County, Iowa, in tables 18.4 and 18.5. Table 18.4 shows the basic data for mid-1976 and Table 18.5 shows the division of employment. The trade employment calculation is illustrated as

1. $\dfrac{\text{Total U.S. employment in trade}}{\text{Total U.S. population}} = \dfrac{16,521,000}{210,000,000} = 7.87\%$
2. $7.87\% \times \text{Local population} = 7.87\% \times 132,400 = 10,416$
3. Total local trade employment $- 10,416 = 12,300 - 10,416 = 1,884$ (export trade employment)

For various manufacturing employment groups the service employment is estimated by population proportion. The population of the local area consumes its fair share of total output and sends the rest to others. We can estimate the service and export division as

---

Manufacturing Categories

1. $\dfrac{\text{Population locally}}{\text{Population in U.S.}} = P_j$

2. $P_j \times$ total employment in category E_j = service portion of category E_j

3. Total employment locally in E_j minus the service portion in E_j from (2) above = export portion in E_j

---

This procedure was used to divide the manufacturing category in Table 18.5.

Having produced the total breakdown of service and export employment, these two categories can be related by the **ratio method**. Traditionally, the ratio is struck between service and export employment totals. For our example this ratio is about 1.6 service workers for each export worker. If any major employers are known to have ratios of service to export employment which differ from the expectations above, then that employer's workforce can be withheld, divided properly, and then added into the numbers derived from the formulas.

TABLE 18.4   BASIC EMPLOYMENT DATA FOR BLACK HAWK CO.,
IOWA, 1976

Place of Work	Local [a]	U.S. [b] (thousands)
Manufacturing	19,500	19,923
Construction	2,600	3,675
Trade	12,300	16,521
Finance	1,800	4,127
Services	11,600	17,931
Government	10,000	14,055
Total Civilian Nonfarm Workforce	57,800	76,891,000
Population	132,400	210,000,000

[a] Source: Iowa Office of Employment Services.
[b] Source: *Statistical Abstract.*

TABLE 18.5   ECONOMIC BASE ANALYSIS FOR
BLACK HAWK CO., IOWA, 1976

Category	Service	Export	Total
Manufacturing	12	19,488	19,500
Construction	2,317	283	2,600
Trade	10,416	1,884	12,300
Finance	2,602	(802)	1,800
Service	11,305	295	11,600
Government	8,861	1,139	10,000
Totals	35,513	22,287	57,800

$$\text{Ratio of service to export} = \frac{35,513}{22,287} = 1.6 \text{ times}$$

It is interesting to note that in the finance category shown in Table 18.5 there is a deficit of 800 export workers. There is a large insurance company just over the county line which employs between 750 and 800 workers.

Given the overall ratio, many kinds of information can be generated. If the population is expected to change by a certain amount, the amount of employment in each category can be predicted. Also, if it is known that an employer will be creating a certain number of jobs in the area, this can be used to predict changes in population. For example, John Deere and Company has announced that it will add 2000 jobs in our sample county region between 1977 and 1980. If all ratios hold, the estimated change in employment may be extrapolated as:

1. Unemployment is low, so all the jobs will require new workers.

2. 2000 export jobs × 1.6 = 3200 extra service jobs. Total new jobs = 5200.

3. Proportion of population employed $= \dfrac{57,800}{132,400} = 44\%$.

4. Expected change in population = 5200/44% = 11,800

5. Assuming at least half of these people already live in the county (teenagers for example), then over 5000 people will need housing, or around 2000 dwellings will be needed. Many new service establishments will also be demanded.

This analysis shows the tremendous impact a few new jobs can have on the demand for real estate development. We might note here that there are no ideal service to export ratios. Further, the ratios may not be stable over time. As new export jobs are added, there will be a lag before service employment catches up. Thus, samples of these ratios should be taken periodically to track the cycles.

Location Quotient   The **location quotient** method enables the analyst to estimate the service–export ratio by job category. The procedure works as

$$\frac{\dfrac{\text{Employment in category } E_i \text{ in community}}{\text{Population in community}}}{\dfrac{\text{Employment in category } E_i \text{ in U.S.}}{\text{Population in U.S.}}}$$

If this ratio is greater than one, the implication is that the category is export-oriented. If the ratio is less than one, the category is service-oriented. Table 18.6 shows these calculations. An alternative calculation may be made by substituting total workforce for population in the preceding ratio. This is helpful if the proportion of the population in the workforce is significantly different in a local area than it is nationally. Sample figures for this formulation also appear in Table 18.6. Notice these alternative calculations correspond more closely to the first approach we took in Table 18.5. This is a function of labor force participation. In the United States as a whole 37% of the population is employed. In Black Hawk County, Iowa, it is 44%.

Input–Output Analysis   **Input–output analysis** is a complex technique used by some economists to trace the movement of national product between industries in the economy. A given industry obtains its resources from many sectors of the economy and sends its output to many other sectors. By tracing these movements, a great deal of information

TABLE 18.6   LOCATION QUOTIENTS, BLACK HAWK CO., IOWA, 1976

Category	Quotient Using Population	Quotient Using Workforce
Manufacturing	1.55	1.30
Construction	1.14	0.94
Trade	1.18	0.99
Finance	0.69	0.58
Service	1.03	0.86
Government	1.13	0.95

can be obtained about economic structure. New techniques are now being devised to extend these techniques to local economic situations. The tables are difficult to construct and the local application is still in its infancy. However, as this is developed more fully, it should provide a more detailed picture of the local economic scene and land use development.

All of these techniques are designed to help the analyst understand economic structure and help foresee trends which may affect land use analysis. They are not meant to be exact, but merely representative of overall gross structures.

Estimate Demand and Supply

If the investor–developer finds a satisfactory economic basis for investment, the next step is to translate basic data into supply and demand estimates. In order to make a determination of the value of a parcel of land suitable for development, the investor must identify potential uses. To do this requires an estimate of the demand for various land uses. Local data may be obtained to show the proportion of the total area in the community put to these uses. These and other data can be used to estimate the potential demand for additional development in certain uses.

A basic part of the demand analysis is an estimate of population change. This can be done by looking at census and economic base data. Both of these sources can be correlated to estimate the overall number of persons and the composition of the population in future periods. Gross population numbers can be converted to households to estimate housing demand and the demand for certain services. The important thing to remember in this analysis is that total demand and changes in trends need to be predicted. Also, the time horizons must match. If a parcel is not located for immediate development, then demand predictions are not as important, but they are also more difficult to make.

Once the analyst has determined the demand for various land uses, the figures must be compared to supply estimates for these uses. This process should highlight uses where demand is expected to exceed supply. These potential uses can then be examined with standard techniques such as those discussed in chapter 8.

Tempering the foregoing supply–demand analysis are the inputs of city officials and their attitudes toward growth and development. Can the uses in demand be zoned on available parcels? This kind of question must be answered.

Select a Specific Parcel

Having determined what land uses will be in demand, the investor must look to the selection of a specific parcel. The type of parcel will depend on what stage of the development process the investor desires. When the investor has decided on the degree of conversion desired, the process can then turn to the selection of alternative sites suitable for the estimated uses. Standard investment analysis based on cash flow forecasts can be used to select among the alternatives.

The watchword here is patience. The investor must be willing to be patient during the purchasing process. The land investor–developer cannot be in a hurry to buy or to sell.

Complete Transaction

If a parcel is found which will satisfy the needs of the investor, it may be purchased. Financing might be needed. If so, it must be arranged and the transaction closed. After a purchase is consummated comes one of the most important parts of the process—project review. It is important to continually update the input data used in the decision so the investor can be assured that the decision is still going as planned. If something happens to change the situation, then the investor must decide whether to retain the parcel.

Analysis of Specific Types of Land

Different levels of conversion require different considerations in analysis. If an investor simply wishes to speculate in raw land, consideration must be given to the long-run use, the potential for favorable zoning, and so forth. However, these elements are not terribly critical in terms of detail. As long as the land is sold before development is imminent, only general knowledge is needed. The raw land investor must decide how to finance the property and whether or not an interim use should be placed on the land. This analysis may look something like the examples we discussed at the beginning of this chapter.

Land which is ripe for development can be purchased by one of two types of investors. If two or three years are required, a land investor can buy and resell to a developer in say three years. If development is imminent then the investor must have detailed input regarding use, zoning, and other important factors. This type of purchase may be much less risky than a raw land deal, but offers less opportunity for a substantial holding gain.

CHAPTER EIGHTEEN SUMMARY

In this chapter we have dealt with land investment and development. We have seen how historical population trends and the structural characteristics of cities affect land values. The moves to suburbanization and interurbanization have both changed the pace of land investment. We then looked at the process of decision-making for land investor–developers. The process was shown in model form in Figure 18.1. One of the most important features of the analytical process involves analysis of the economic base in the community. As we have seen before, the strength of the basic export employment in a local area has a great impact on the demand for development. We examined three ways to look at the economic base. Base analysis is the key input to the demand estimate which helps determine the alternative uses for a parcel. The decision-making process is completed by the analysis and selection of the potential parcels available for the uses which will be in demand at the appropriate time.

KEY TERMS

Carrying Cost
Development Land
Export
  Employment
  Input–Output
  Analysis

Interim Land
Interurbanization
Location Quotient
Ratio Method

Raw Land
Service
  Employment
Suburbanization
Urbanization

QUESTIONS FOR STUDY AND DISCUSSION

1. How does land as an investment vehicle differ from securities investments? Explain how raw land differs from fully developed property as an investment.

2. Differentiate between *raw, interim,* and *development* land. How does each differ in its investment and physical characteristics?

3. A number of important social forces were mentioned as having influenced the value and direction of land investment. Describe these major forces. How has each affected value?

4. Historically the forces affecting land values can be isolated. More important, however, is what factors will be affecting values in the future. What major factors and trends in United States society will be affecting land values in the next twenty years? Why?

5. Describe the basic process one would use to isolate a parcel of land for development.

6. Using the *Statistical Abstract* and data from the community employment service where you are currently living, follow the guidelines in Tables 18.4 and 18.5 to determine the service to export ratio overall for the local area. Are there any special distinguishing characteristics in your city's economic base which will probably affect future development?

7. Pick a large city or SMSA in the United States or use the data from (6) above. Using statistical data concerning population trends and economic characteristics, project the underlying demand for land development in the next ten years. Possible sources of data are the *Statistical Abstract*, U.S. Census, and local chamber of commerce or economic development agency in the city chosen.

19 REAL ESTATE MARKETING

MARKETING REAL estate is sometimes complex. Because the specifics of such a discussion are to a great degree a function of state law, our discussion will be a general one.

The chief operative in marketing real estate is the broker. This chapter will examine the role of brokers—their duties, as well as their obligations. We will also examine the functions performed by brokers in addition to facilitating market transactions. Finally, we will examine some of the important principles behind successful real estate marketing and how a transaction might take place.

Brokerage

The main intermediary in a real estate transaction is usually a broker or the broker's authorized agent. In general, a **broker** is someone who serves the marketing process by bringing two parties together so that a transaction may be consummated.

In the marketing process for any good, commodity, or service, it is often necessary for there to be agents or institutions of some kind to facilitate transactions. For goods which are manufactured by a few large firms and sold to many people, the channel of distribution generally contains several levels of firms such as wholesalers or distributors and retailers. Sometimes the number of suppliers is large and the number of customers equally large or larger. This is a situation in which a go-between can serve a useful function. Figure 19.1 shows a situation archetype in which a broker may serve to facilitate marketing.

To bring the multiple buyers and sellers together in this type of situation requires one of two arrangements. One alternative is for the buyers and sellers all to come together in one place so that they may exchange information about the nature of the goods and the price. This is done in secondary securities markets like the New York Stock Exchange and in commodities markets like the Chicago Board of Trade. The other alternative is for brokers to position themselves between buyers and sellers and serve both parties to facilitate transactions.

A grocer who wants to buy a certain commodity has numerous producers to choose from. The grocer may make the choice at a commodity market area in a large city, say New York, or use a food broker who finds sellers and puts them in contact with the buyer for a fee. A broker may also act for a seller who needs to contact a number of buyers. The seller could either have a sales force or use an agent or broker to provide this service for a fee.

The broker in these examples serves as an information magnet or central point to which buyers and sellers may come to find potential parties with whom they can consummate a transaction. Brokers are used in many forms of business besides real estate. Food products, stocks,

FIGURE 19.1   HOW A BROKER FACILITATES MARKETING

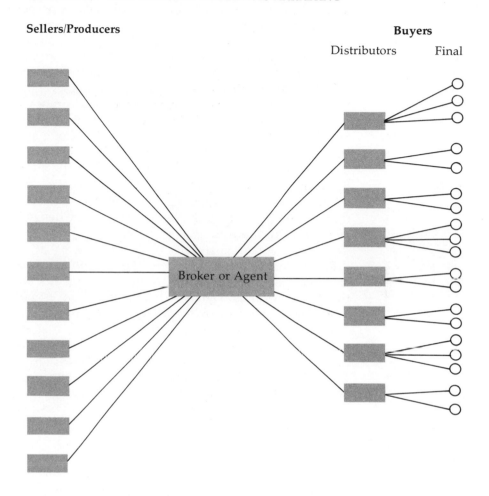

commodities, petroleum products, and certain industrial goods are all sold through brokers in some situations. However, a broker is not required. If a seller can find a buyer without the broker, so be it. Nevertheless, brokers do provide a useful function. Many buyers and sellers cannot economically provide sufficient sales personnel or purchasing agents internally to perform the necessary functions for them. The broker may be anybody's part-time salesperson or purchasing agent.

Functions of a Real Estate Broker

Facilitating Sales   The real estate broker's chief function is to bring buyers and sellers together to consummate a transaction. Brokers advertise their services, list properties available for purchase, and keep in contact with buyers to inform them of available properties.

In addition to their traditional role in facilitating sales of properties, brokers also may help arrange property exchanges. These complex transactions often require the services of many professionals. Brokers will often maintain contacts with several different outside professionals such as lawyers, financial consultants, and officers of financial institutions who can help to consummate a complex transaction.

In many complex deals involving larger properties for investment, industrial, or commercial uses, a qualified broker may aid the parties in the process of negotiating the terms of the agreement. Some sellers do not wish to use this service, as it may indirectly alter the net value of the property. Someone must pay for the services. Even so, there are many occasions when the ability to reach a final agreement, not only on the price but also on the terms of sale, may depend on the ability of an experienced broker.

Property Management   Brokers perform other services in addition to the preceding traditional ones. Many investors buy property purely for the cash flows and do not wish to manage the investment directly. Often management services are provided by a broker for a fee. Property management services may include simple tasks such as rent collection and leasing of the property, or they may include a full range of activities. Some property managers will come into a new project with the full responsibility for filling the property with tenants, hiring maintenance personnel, servicing the tenants, and even keeping the books for the owner. Obviously, the more services that are provided, the higher the fee. Generally, the fee is based on some percentage of the *effective* gross income.

A full service management job involves many activities. First, the property manager must lease the available space. This involves finding the tenants and negotiating the lease agreements. Any time a portion of the property becomes vacant a new tenant must be found quickly. This is one reason why fees are based on effective gross. The manager cannot earn a fee to manage a vacant unit. The full service manager is also responsible for setting up the budgets for running the property and sticking to them. Services must be provided and paid for. Because the manager will lose the fee if rent due is not collected, the credit standing of tenants will be an important concern during the renting process. The manager must also keep good records so that all monies received and disbursed can be accounted for. As a full service manager, the broker may be held responsible for the funds and property being managed.

The property manager generally performs the task under contract with the owner. The contract should specify the exact nature of the tasks to be performed and the compensation. Often such contracts will contain a "hold harmless" clause protecting the manager from liability should a tenant have a cause of action against the owner.

Miscellaneous Functions   Brokers may serve many miscellaneous functions which relate to the basic tasks just described. A broker, if properly qualified, may sell insurance, act as an auctioneer for property, be a notary public, serve as a trustee for an estate, or serve as an escrow agent. All these functions and more are possible. However, many of these involve licensing or at least a legal responsibility which requires the broker to operate with some care. There are some limitations on the activities of brokers which will be discussed later.

Duties of a Broker

Agency   Generally, when acting on behalf of others, a real estate broker is acting as an *agent*. **Agency** is a legal arrangement in which one or more persons enter into a contractual agreement to act on behalf of another party or parties, called **principals**. Agency can be established for any legal purpose by any parties who are able to make a valid contract. In addition to any contractual agreements, agency is subject to a number of standard legal responsibilities and restrictions.

A real estate broker becomes an agent for a specific party through some kind of contract or agreement. A seller may employ a broker through the use of a listing agreement such as that to be described later in this chapter. A broker may be authorized to sell a property through an open listing, an exclusive listing, or with the exclusive right to sell. As we will see, these various levels of exclusiveness carry different degrees of protection for brokers in terms of their compensation.

As with any contract, an agency may be terminated by mutual assent. A principal may also terminate his or her agency without the permission of the agent, provided it does not violate the contract or provided the agent does not have a legal interest in the object of the agency. If a broker owned part of a parcel of land and was hired as an agent to sell it, the agency could not be involuntarily terminated by the principal. When a listing contract is terminated by a seller, the broker ordinarily is protected against the loss of the commission at least until the original contract term has expired.

A buyer, too, may employ a broker as an agent. Generally, buyers merely use the services of a broker for information and the broker is the agent for the seller. However, this is not always true.

Obligations as an Agent   Because the broker may be given a good deal of authority as an agent for one of the principals in a transaction, the broker must act responsibly. There are a number of important restrictions and duties involved.

Brokers may not use their position for personal profit at the expense of a client. If brokers were to use their position improperly, they might find a buyer unknown to the seller, buy the property themselves, and resell it for a profit. This is obviously not allowed. That does not prohibit brokers from buying properties offered to them in an open fashion, however. The dividing line between transactions of this type, which are allowed, and those which are "shady" may be a fuzzy one indeed.

Because brokers often handle the funds of the parties to a transaction, there must be a proper accounting of all such funds. When brokers act as a fiduciary to the parties in a transaction, there are, again, a whole set of precise legal responsibilities assigned to this role. Money or property involved in a transaction must not be commingled with that of the brokers' firm.

Brokers often hire salespeople or other subagents to help them with their duties. The broker is responsible for acts committed by these people even when such acts are unknown to the broker. Agency agreements are made in confidence and with trust. Brokers who use subagents do so at their own risk.

Because brokers are in a position of trust, they must obviously be careful not to do anything that will jeopardize the interest of the principal. Brokers must do what is stipulated. They must be careful not to misrepresent the object of the agency, and they certainly should not make any purposefully false statements. To prevent a buyer's being hurt, the Statute of Frauds requires all agreements concerning transactions in land or real estate to be in writing. However, if a broker has made statements which later cause a transaction to be aborted, that broker may be liable to the principal for any loss suffered. An honest mistake made by an agent cannot be held against the agent, unless it was the result of gross negligence.

One final question we may deal with in this discussion involves for whom the broker is an agent. The broker is the agent for the seller, in general. The seller, by convention, pays the commission in a real estate transaction. When the broker has been duly authorized to act as an agent for both parties to a transaction, all parties must be notified and specifically authorize the arrangement. Because of the obvious potential for conflicts of interest in such circumstances, this type of situation cannot continue without the knowledge and consent of all parties.

Limitations   Brokerage is a profession which must be regulated. The responsibilities are much like those of a doctor or a lawyer and might be easily abused by the unscrupulous. Because of the quantity of money involved in a typical real estate transaction, the loss that could potentially be suffered through a wrongful act is large. Brokers must be licensed and must take a fairly rigorous examination in order to get their license. However, the standards for these examinations do vary widely from state to state.

Because brokers deal in transactions which very often involve legal work, they must be careful not to perform any functions that are the province of the legal profession. Lawyers, too, must be qualified and certified by examination. If a broker is not also a lawyer (which some are), he or she cannot perform legal work, but must instead use or recommend the services of a qualified legal professional.

Brokerage Fees

The major functions performed by real estate brokers are generally performed for a fee called a **commission.** In order to be in a position to collect a commission for services performed, the broker must first show an authorization to perform the service. A broker must be employed to collect the commission. The broker must also be licensed. Finally, the broker has to produce a buyer who is ready, willing, and able to consummate a transaction. Generally, brokers are entitled to their commission when a valid contract for sale has been executed between a seller and a bona fide purchaser. There may be one or two problems on this last point, however.

Generally, a purchaser, if possible, will execute a purchase contract subject to being able to obtain reasonable financing. If the financing is not obtained, the transaction is cancelled. The principal does not really want to pay the commission in such a case and should not be forced to. For that reason, it is a good idea for a seller to obtain in writing a statement that the commission will not be paid until the title actually passes.

There are other reasons besides failure to obtain financing for a transaction not to occur. Sometimes a buyer may decide to back out of a transaction before closing. This is not done without penalty, but the fact remains that the property has not been sold. Under these circumstances the seller does not really wish to pay the broker a commission even though it is not the broker's fault. Generally, the broker will waive the fee voluntarily in exchange for a portion of the penalty paid by the defaulting buyer. Again, an agreement in writing here is preferable to a verbal understanding.

If the seller defaults on a transaction which has been contracted for at the seller's approved price, the seller will probably have to pay the commission anyway.

Another important factor in determining the ability of a given broker to collect a fee for a transaction is whether or not the particular agent was instrumental in bringing buyer and seller together. The broker must show actual participation in the transaction.

Real Estate Contracts

The process of transferring real estate often involves the use of many legal documents. The nature and structure of these documents, mostly in the form of contracts, may have an important influence on the value of the owner's interest. A poorly written contract may result in legal problems which can be resolved only in the courts. It is important for prospective buyers or sellers to determine what they want from their transactions and make certain that the documents used in the transactions appropriately reflect these desires. Before beginning our discussion in detail, we will look at the legal elements of a contract. We will then discuss some of the major contracts used in transactions for real property.

Elements of a Contract

A contract is an agreement between parties, each promising to do something in exchange for some consideration. A contract must be a voluntary agreement in order to be binding. If one of the parties is under duress, the agreement is not binding. There are several other elements which must be present for a contract to be made.

A contract starts with an offer by one party and an acceptance by another. This may be an offer to perform a service, to buy a car, or to buy a parcel of real estate. In real estate there may be two or more parties to the contract. Generally, however, there will be two sides: purchaser(s) and seller(s). When real estate is the object of a contract, generally the original offer is an offer to buy. If the seller turns this down and, in turn, offers to sell for some alternative to the original offer, this becomes a *counteroffer* by the seller. The buyer may make another counteroffer and so forth. This will continue until the two parties agree or until they decide to terminate the process.

The parties to a contract must be competent for the agreement to be binding. Competence means that the parties are able to legally accept the responsibility of the contract. Persons who are insane, intoxicated, or underage may not make binding contracts. There are some exceptions for minors. Minors may make contracts which are binding on both sides, but they may also make certain kinds of contracts which are binding only on the other side. A minor may *disaffirm* (or back out of) a contract to buy or sell real property in some states. A prospective buyer or seller who contracts with a minor should find out how such contracts are treated in his or her state.

Every contract must be for a legal object. A contract cannot be binding if it violates the law or involves an object which itself is illegal. A contract to burn down a house, for instance, cannot be enforced in court.

Finally, a contract requires each party to give consideration. For many contracts, the fact that each party makes some promise he or she intends to keep is sufficient consideration. Money, services rendered, and the promise not to do something may also be deemed sufficient consideration. When one party to a contract offers to provide a service and the other side accepts, but does not specify what will be done in return, there may not be a binding contract.

If a contract is violated by one of the parties, the other party has the right to seek a remedy in the courts. The injured party may either sue for damages suffered or may, in some cases, sue for *specific performance*. When specific performance is given as the remedy by the court, the party in violation will be forced by the court to do what was originally promised, rather than pay damages. Such a remedy is not always possible, however.

Most contracts can be made either orally or in writing. However, contracts for the transfer of real property must be in writing. A contract to list property with a realtor does not involve transfer of the ownership and can be oral. Sale contracts and land contracts, however, must be in writing to be enforced. Further, when the contract must be in writing, as in this case, oral agreements or understandings not written into the document cannot be enforced. This is an important concern when consummating a sale contract in real estate. Oral agreements concerning fixtures, for instance, will not be enforced in court.

A contract is most important when people do not fulfill their responsibilities. If all parties do what they are supposed to, there should be no problems. For this reason, both parties should have sufficient protection built into the contract to provide them with the remedies they need in the event of a breach. Additionally, both parties should make certain that it is clear what will constitute a breach of contract. Finally, a contract can always be altered if all parties agree. Similarly, any contract may be cancelled if all parties agree.

Listing Agreements

When a broker is involved in the process of selling real estate, a seller generally signs a listing agreement with the selling agent. This agreement is a type of employment contract and must conform to the rules we have set forth previously. Generally, the listing contract includes the following elements.

1. Names of the parties to the agreement.

2. A legal description of the property to be sold. A good agreement should also include a list of all items to be sold with the property about which there might be some question. This precaution may avoid a good deal of friction when it comes time to execute a sale contract.

3. Price and terms of sale. This will be an initial asking price. Also, the seller can specify whether he or she wishes to sell with a mortgage assumption, for cash on contract, or whether other terms are desired.

4. Duration of the listing. This clause will specify how long the seller will employ the agent in an official capacity.

5. Commission rate and terms. This specifies the consideration to be given by the seller to the broker.

6. Duties and rights of agent. This specifies what the agent will do and on what terms. There are several types of listings based on the degree of exclusivity given to the agent. We will discuss these shortly.

A broker may take a listing for a piece of real estate under one of three basic agreements. These are the open listing, the exclusive agency, and the exclusive right to sell.

Open Listing   An **open listing** is given to a broker when the seller wishes to permit many brokers to work on the property. With an open listing, any broker who has an agreement with the seller can sell the property and obtain the agreed-upon commission. Even the seller may sell the property, thus avoiding the commission entirely. A broker who wishes to earn a commission must be the first to execute a binding sale document with a buyer who is ready, willing, and able to buy.

This type of listing is thought to be advantageous by some sellers because they can employ more people to work on their property. There is a problem, however. Few brokers want to work very hard under this type of arrangement since they have too much to lose. It is doubtful that this is a realistic form of broker–seller arrangement except when there are many more brokers than properties to list.

Exclusive Listing   A broker who is an exclusive agent is assured that he or she is competing with no other brokers to sell the property. Only one **exclusive agency** will be working at a time. However, the owner can sell the property and avoid the commission.

Exclusive Right to Sell   The **exclusive right to sell** is the highest security agreement for a broker. With this arrangement the broker will receive the commission regardless of who sells the property. In many such agreements, the broker may even be entitled to the commission if the property is sold after the agreement is terminated. Many such agreements hold that if the property seller obtains a purchase contract from a bona fide buyer up to, for instance, three months after the agreement terminates and if the broker first showed the property to that particular buyer during the term of the contract, then the broker will receive the commission.

This type of agreement is restrictive for the seller, but allows the broker to concentrate on the job of selling the property without the risk of losing the commission. This method of listing is preferred by most brokers. There is a problem here, nevertheless. Because the seller is committed to one broker, the number of contacts the seller can have is limited. This situation can be overcome with multiple listing.

Multiple Listing   In a number of cities many brokers will belong to a **multiple listing** service. With this arrangement the broker may be given the exclusive right to sell for say thirty days. If the broker does not sell during that time, then the listing will be transmitted to the other members of the service. If one of them sells the property, that broker will get a percentage of the agreed commission and the listing broker will get the remainder of the commission. If the listing broker eventually does sell the property, he or she will get the lion's share. This type of arrangement provides the best of both worlds—the effort of the exclusive right to sell and the wide contacts available with an open listing.

Effect on Value   The effects on value of a listing agreement are subtle, but nonetheless significant. If the agreement is worked out properly, sellers will have a much better chance to obtain the full value of their homes in the market. A dissatisfied listing broker may only make a half-hearted attempt to sell the property, and the seller is the loser.

Contract for Sale

The main contract involved in a real estate transfer is the **contract for sale.** This is the agreement signed by both the buyer and the seller agreeing to transfer the property. Normally, there are a number of common elements in most of these agreements which will be listed next. In general, these elements closely parallel the elements of a contract discussed earlier in this chapter.

Normally, the sale contract will begin with a date. This helps pinpoint the time of execution and sets limits for compliance. The next element is the name of each party to the contract. If the seller has a wife who might have a dower right, it is important that she sign the agreement, even if she is not an owner. Otherwise, she cannot be forced to sign away her rights on the deed. The property must be described legally so that there is no question of the object of the contract. This description should include any personal property which will be sold with the real property. Only the writing in the contract is binding. An important element of the contract is the price of the property and the terms of payment. This should be spelled out in detail. How much is to be paid and when should be included. Earnest money will have to be paid to bind the parties in the contract.

The contract should also list any encumbrances on the property. A list specifying the various encumbrances, including such things as zoning, should be given. Generally, there is some open-ended wording which includes all encumbrances of record at the time of closing. This prevents subsequent voiding of the contract resulting from events occurring after the contract is signed.

There are a number of important miscellaneous clauses specific to real estate contracts which may be present in some form. The contract may specify any peculiar rights to adjoining roads or water which pass with the land. The contract will also specify that a deed will be delivered and the type deed to be delivered. Along with the deed itself, the contract may specify that the title should either be marketable or insurable. This gives the most flexibility from the seller's point of view. A title may be marketable and not insurable, and vice versa. It may also be desirable for either the buyer or the seller to insist, in writing, that the closing where both deed and money are exchanged be definitely on or before the time limit stipulated by the agreement. In many simple transactions, this is of no consequence. However, when the buyer or seller has another transaction hanging on the consummation of the one in question, it may be very important.

Many times it is wise to have a clause in the contract stating who will be liable for any violations of the law in effect at the time of sale. Without this clause the buyer may be liable. Another important set of clauses will be concerned with the apportionment of items which reflect accrued liabilities or prepaid expenses, in the case of income real estate. The portion of the taxes paid in advance will have to be returned to the seller. Similar arrangements may have to be made for prepaid utilities and insurance, to name a few.

Finally, the contract should have a statement concerning the remedy for breach by either party. This may help to avoid a costly, time-consuming court battle if one or the other of the parties fails to fulfill his end of the contract. Another clause which may be important is an escape clause. If possible, the buyer will generally try to condition the purchase upon the ability to obtain financing. In transactions where the market for the subject property is tight, the buyer may not be able to obtain such a stipulation. This is especially true with the purchase of prime income property.

Although this is not an exhaustive list of the clauses of real estate sales contracts, it does include most of the important ones. It is important to note, once again, that the services of a good attorney may be helpful before you sign anything. Once the damage is done it is too late. It is what is in writing that counts.

Miscellaneous Agreements

The two contracts we have just discussed are common to almost every real estate transaction. There are a number of other contracts and agreements which are used less frequently.

Escrow Agreement   When a real estate sales agreement is reached, it is common to designate someone, either a third party or the broker, to serve as the escrow agent. All consideration, whether money or deeds, is given to the escrow agent to hold. At the closing all consideration will be transferred simultaneously to the appropriate parties. This practice assures all parties that they will receive what they have coming to them in the transaction and that they will be protected from losing what they have contributed. The **escrow agreement** can be either a separate document executed at the time of the sale agreement or included in the sale contract itself. The escrow agreement should include the names of the parties and the escrow agent to be designated. The terms and conditions of the escrow—what is to be delivered, when and where it should be delivered—should be set forth. What will be done if one of the parties fails to deliver should be made clear.

Offer to Purchase—Binders   Before the execution of the formal sale contract, or in lieu of it, the parties to the impending sale may execute an *offer to purchase* or a *binder*. The **offer to purchase** is a form of the sale contract which is not a complete contract. It may include as little information as the names of the parties, the description of the property, and the price. Many versions of this may exist.

A binder is a mini-contract which binds the parties to execute a formal purchase agreement at a later date. It will contain the elements of a contract, but it will not be as involved as the formal agreement. The purpose of this is that it can be executed quickly, giving all parties time to develop a good sale contract. Generally, a certain amount of earnest money will be given to bind the contract, because it removes the property from the market. If the parties cannot reach agreement on a formal contract within the allotted time called for in the binder, generally, the seller will keep the earnest money or part of it and return the property to the market. This contract, rather than asking for the delivery of the deed, calls for delivery of another contract.

Options   Another important agreement used in the transfer of property is the option. An **option** is used for keeping a property off the market. This is done in exchange for consideration. A builder or developer, for instance, may not know how much money he or she will have or when. If such a person finds some land and wishes to buy it but does not have the money, an option can be executed to prevent the land from being sold out from under the developer. When an option agreement is reached, the seller will ordinarily insist that it be executed only on large pieces of the property, in order to prevent the buyer's selecting only the prime parts of the parcel. It is also general practice to attach to the option the contract which will eventually be used to buy the property.

Sale Transactions

Some of the major brokerage functions can best be illustrated through a description of a real estate sale transaction.

Listing the Property

The first step in a sale transaction is the listing process. The seller executes a **listing agreement** with the broker specifying the property to be sold, the price, the nature and duration of the agency, the rate of the commission, the names of the parties, and any other pertinent information affecting the listing conditions. Once the property is listed, the broker should actively seek buyers for the property. Many techniques are used to attract buyers: advertising, word of mouth, personal contact, and the open house. In many places the open house is not considered an especially productive approach. However, in other areas where the open house is well accepted by the public it may prove an efficient way to establish personal contact and show the property.

Offer to Purchase

Real estate professionals say that for every property there is one right buyer and the service they provide is to find that buyer. When a buyer is found for the listed property, the buyer must make an offer. This is often done through an *offer to purchase*. We previously described this document. The offer to purchase is generally accompanied by earnest money, a cash deposit which commits the buyer to purchase. For a personal residence an earnest money deposit of $500 or $1000 is common. For commercial and industrial properties 10% of the price is not unusual. If the seller refuses the offer, the money is returned.

As you may recall, the offer to purchase is not necessarily a contract. It may include as little as the names of the parties, the property description, the amount of the offer, and a promise to sign a contract within some reasonable time period. When this offer is transmitted in writing, the seller may then accept or make a counteroffer. The process of negotiation continues until an agreement is reached or one of the parties backs away.

If the straight offer to purchase is used to begin the purchase, a contract is usually executed shortly thereafter to bind the parties to a transfer. If a contract is used instead of an offer to purchase, the parties are bound at the time of acceptance.

Contract for Sale

Generally, the parties to a sale transaction will eventually sign a sale contract prior to the property's actual transfer. The contract for sale must have all the elements of a contract. As we said earlier, the parties to this agreement should make certain that the contract spells out any important considerations they want accounted for. Oral agreements made in conjunction with the transaction cannot be enforced in court. Some of the important features are listed here.

1. Parties to the agreement. The wife must sign if she is to be required to sign the deed.
2. Property description, including personal property to be sold.
3. Time the contract is to run.
4. Price and monies owed by the buyer.
5. Distribution of costs. Who will pay taxes and other closing costs?
6. Type of deed to be delivered by the seller.
7. What will be done in case of a default by one of the parties.
8. Other miscellaneous information.

Closing Process

After the sale contract has been executed, the sellers, buyers, and the broker usually have many activities to perform. Generally, the buyers must arrange financing for the purchase. Often the contract will specify that if suitable financing cannot be arranged, the buyers will not be bound by the contract. The sellers generally are responsible for bringing the abstract of title up to date. This is usually done shortly before the actual transfer of the title. The sellers must take care of any outstanding liens against the property so that a clear title can be transferred. The sellers may also have to perform repairs in some cases, depending on the condition of the property.

Often the broker in a transaction may be instrumental in arranging many of the tasks above-described. The broker will also arrange for the actual closing of the transaction. During the time between the signing of the contract and the transfer of the property, any monies or other consideration will be held in escrow by the broker or an outside escrow agent. The escrow agreement specifying how this is to be handled can be executed separately or as part of the sale contract.

When the closing day finally arrives, if all preliminaries have been completed satisfactorily, the closing may take place. At the closing "ceremony" all consideration is exchanged and the sale is consummated. The money deposited and owed by the buyer is paid to the seller. The deed is transferred to the buyer and the broker. When appropriate, the buyer will execute the final financing arrangement and be provided an abstract or opinion of good title. The final step in the transfer involves the recording of the deed and perhaps the mortgage.

As we stated earlier, one of the duties of brokers is to account for all monies in their charge. At the time of the closing, a document known as a **closing statement** is executed. This shows how all the money is to be distributed. The normal features involved in this statement are itemized here.

A. *Seller's Statement*

   1. Received: Purchase price = deposit + balance owed.

   2. Disbursed: Commission to broker, legal fees for closing costs such as abstract costs, termite inspection, and other costs.

   3. Adjustments for accrued taxes. The seller is responsible for taxes and insurance owed up to the day of transfer. If an escrow account for these items has been maintained up to this point, the account is adjusted and the seller gets a refund for any funds paid in for future taxes. This receipt will be added to the purchase price.

B. *Buyer's Statement*

   1. Received: deed.

   2. Disbursed: purchase price, closing costs to lender such as loan fees, points, and other costs. Also, any legal costs incurred by the buyer on his or her own behalf will be disbursed. Finally, the buyer will pay for the accrued escrow account for taxes and insurance if this applies.

The broker will generally take his own check and disburse the buyer's and seller's funds for legal fees and closing costs. Because of the way in which taxes are normally paid, this adjustment is usually a bit tricky. Both parties to the transaction should be assured that this has been handled properly. It is also important to note that real estate contracts and closings may be extremely complex. It is not unwise for both the buyers and sellers to have all documents checked by a lawyer before signing. A sample closing statement appears as Table 19.1.

Effect of Brokerage on Value

We have seen how a broker plays an important role in the transaction process as well as in other functions concerned with real estate. One question which may be posed at this point is whether or not brokerage activity has any effect on real estate value and prices. There is no good way to ascertain this from research, so the following is somewhat speculative.

From what we know about the market and the way it operates, it is possible to argue that the presence of brokers in transactions has a positive effect on value. For a given property, the more potential buyers

TABLE 19.1   SAMPLE CLOSING STATEMENT

Dwelling Sold for		$33,000.00
Seller: Mr. and Mrs. John Jones		
Purchaser: Mr. and Mrs. Ralph Phillips		

Seller's Statement

Selling Price		$33,000.00
Mortgage Balance	$28,033.52	
Current Interest	186.87	
168 Days of Taxes Due	219.96	
Previous Year Tax Due	477.90	
Abstract Continuation Fee	41.00	
Termite Inspection	10.00	
Deed Preparation	15.00	
Balance Due to Seller	4,015.75	
	$33,000.00	$33,000.00

Purchaser's Statement

Purchase Price		$33,000.00
Assumption Fee		75.00
Recording Fee		2.50
Mortgage Balance	$28,033.52	
Current Interest	186.87	
168 Days Taxes Due	219.96	
Prior Year Tax Due	477.90	
Amount Required to Close	4,159.25	
	$33,077.50	$33,077.50

Disbursement of Amount Required to Close		
Abstract and Recording Fees	$	43.50
Assumption Fee		75.00
Termite Inspection		10.00
Deed Preparation		15.00
To Sellers		4,015.75
		$ 4,159.25

who are informed and are actively seeking the property, the more likely the price may be bid upward. A seller who tries to sell a property alone may not be able to attract sufficient bidders to receive the real value of the property in the market. It may also be argued that the property management and other functions performed by real estate professionals may help attract good tenants to a property, thus adding to its value.

However, the services above-performed are not free to the user. The next question we must ask, then, is whether or not the possible value added by these professionals is enough to offset their costs. It would be difficult to prove, but it is possible that a good deal of the inflation in property values, especially in residential transactions, is a function of the need for the seller to recoup the commission, which he or she must pay for the sale. The important value figure to consider here is the net proceeds to be received by the seller as a result of the sale. Value is not necessarily measured by the gross price of a property.

We may never resolve the issue, but from a decision standpoint, a potential user of real estate services should try to assess whether the services will provide enough benefits to justify their cost.

CHAPTER NINETEEN SUMMARY

In this chapter we have briefly examined the role of real estate professionals, especially brokers, and the way in which these people contribute to the process of transferring property. In the first part of the chapter we examined the functions performed by real estate brokers and their agents. Brokers facilitate the sale of property, take fiduciary responsibilities, manage property, and provide many other services. We next turned our attention to the duties and obligations of the broker as an agent. Agency is a complex legal area, and the broker must perform his or her duties with care. We next examined many of the key legal agreements involved in property transactions. Finally, we examined a typical property transaction, looking at the various steps in the process and examining the role of the broker. We finished the chapter with a brief discussion of the effect of the brokerage function on the value of property.

KEY TERMS

Agency
Broker
Closing Statement
Commission
Contract for Sale

Escrow Agreement
Exclusive Agency
Exclusive Right to Sell
Listing Agreement
Multiple Listing

Offer to Purchase
Open Listing
Option
Principals

QUESTIONS FOR STUDY AND DISCUSSION

1. Real estate has traditionally been transferred with the assistance of brokers or agents. Why? What characteristics of the real estate market make this type of marketing operative the most practical?

2. Enumerate the major functions performed by real estate brokers. Describe each of these functions.

3. What are the principal duties of the real estate broker to the client? What legal position does the broker assume in the relationship with a client? Where do sales personnel fit in?

4. What must brokers do to assure that a fee will be received for services rendered? Must a listing contract be in writing?

5. Briefly enumerate the steps in the process of completing a sale transaction with a broker. What is the function of escrow in this process?

6. What purpose is served by the *closing statement?* What are its usual contents?

7. Can the fact that real estate is generally transacted through brokers have any effect on its value?

20 HOMEOWNERSHIP

THE MOST common opportunity most people have to invest in real estate is through homeownership. Homeownership, through the medium of the single-family dwelling, has long been an important part of the American dream. The green grass and freedom associated with a home are treated on much the same level as motherhood and apple pie by many Americans. As we shall see in this chapter, homeownership is not always a financially rewarding alternative. Further, homeownership carries a great deal of responsibility with it which should be carefully considered before a purchase is made. In this chapter we will consider the pros and cons of homeownership, some of the more commonly encountered technical considerations, the appropriate financial analysis one might perform before purchasing a home, and some social issues involved in home buying.

Pros and Cons of Homeownership

The variables which favor homeownership are generally subjective. As was stated above, the issue of homeownership is largely an emotional one which has its roots in the pioneers and homesteaders of our early history. As we shall see shortly, there are some potential financial benefits to homeownership, but they do not apply in every case. It may be possible that a person who is subject to frequent moves as a result of employment may be better off renting. We will also point out the hidden costs of homeownership.

A homeowner has two important potential benefits. One of these relates to freedom and privacy. A family which owns its own home, within the limits of the law, zoning, and deed restrictions, may do what it wishes with the property. However, in today's society the potential restrictions may be sizable. Many suburban neighborhoods have substantial deed restrictions, as do many condominium developments. These restrictions may specify the minimum square footage of the dwelling, the amount of brick to be used in construction, the architectural style of the home, the type of fences permitted, and other similar features. All of this can be extremely restrictive. Some of these restrictions have been struck down in the courts, but many still exist.

The other benefit that may come from homeownership is the financial benefit. In the 1970s inflation exceeded 6% per year on the average for each year in the decade. Home prices increased at least as fast as the general price level in many places. Because the average home is heavily financed, the leverage helps give the buyer a great financial gain on the investment in a home. Example One shows how this might look on a typical property.

Example One:

The Peters family bought a home on January 1, 1970, and sold it on December 31, 1979. During the ten years, the price of the home rose an average of 5% per year. The original price of the home was $30,000, financed by a mortgage of $22,500 at a 7% interest rate for thirty years. Disregarding the tax benefits and expenses associated with ownership, how much did the Peters family earn on their original investment?

First, we must compute the final selling price. With an inflation factor of 5%, the price may be figured as follows:

$$\text{Selling price} = \text{Purchase price} \times FVF_{10,5\%}$$
$$= \$30,000 \times 1.629 = \$48,870$$

The next step is to see what the Peters earned over the ten-year period. When they sold the home they received $48,870 less the mortgage balance owed. Using the table in Appendix 1 to the text, we see that after ten years the Peters family still owed 86% of the original mortgage, or $19,300 ($22,500 × 0.86). Thus, the net proceeds of the sale, before taxes, are:

$$\text{Net proceeds} = \$48,870 - \$19,300 = \$29,570$$

Now we may check to see what pre-tax rate of return is implied by this investment. Using the present value table we find

$$PV = FV \times PVF_{10,i}$$

Since their downpayment was $7,500 ($30,000 − $22,500),

$$\$7500 = \$29,570 \times PVF_{10,i}$$
$$PVF_{10,i} = 0.254$$

The present value factor for ten years at 15% is 0.247; for 14% for ten years the factor is 0.270. This implies the return is roughly 15% before taxes. The stock market in the 1970s returned much less than 10% before taxes.

From this example we can see that the great leverage in a home can potentially lead to substantial returns even when a relatively low inflation rate is involved. This example did not account for a number of analytical factors which would have altered the results. We will cover all of these in more detail in the following examples.

Apart from the benefits of homeownership, the homeowner may face a good deal of responsibility. Renters generally do not have to worry about maintenance and tax expenses, as these costs are built into the rental payment. Further, someone else does the work. Homeowners face all the maintenance expenses required to keep their homes in good shape. For maximum value to be maintained, the home must be kept up. This means regular painting, repairs, gardening chores, replacement of worn-out items such as the roof, carpeting, or furnace. All these things are the responsibility of the landlord in a typical rental situation. Further, homeowners face a good deal of liability for things which happen on their property. If someone slips on the sidewalk in the winter, the homeowner may face a huge lawsuit. If a neighbor's child falls off the swing in the homeowner's backyard, again there may be a lawsuit. A lawsuit without proper insurance can make owning a home a gigantic headache.

There are obviously pros and cons to homeownership. One way to evaluate some of them is to try to quantify the costs and evaluate them financially. We will approach this analysis on a step-by-step basis in the next section. It must be stated that not all the factors can be quantified. For example, the willingness to assume responsibility may carry more or less weight with some potential home purchasers. These nonquantifiable variables are omitted from the analysis, but they nevertheless influence the final decision.

Financial Analysis of Homeownership

To sort out the costs and benefits of homeownership, we will use a comparative approach. The analysis will view a typical home and a typical apartment in a Midwestern city in the 1970s. Through comparative analysis of the incremental costs and benefits, we will try to see which alternative is superior, financially.

Costs Associated with Renting

The basic cost associated with renting is the rental payment. Typically, a rent payment for an apartment includes maintenance, periodic remodeling, and taxes. Renters often pay the utility bill, though utilities may also be included as part of the rent. If the apartment owner pays the utilities, the only other important expense to renters besides the rent itself is insurance on personal belongings and liability coverage for the actual apartment dwelling unit. The public parts of the building are covered by the landlord. No tax deductions are currently allowed for any of these expenses.

Benefits Associated with Renting

The main cash benefit associated with renting is the opportunity to earn a return on the funds which would have been available for use as a downpayment if a home had been purchased. The return on these funds will be subject to tax, as would be any other investment earnings. One question arises in the analysis of this benefit. What is a fair rate of return to allow for these benefits? We will look at this question two ways. First, we will assume only bank rate interest can be earned. Then we will see what happens if it is assumed the investor earns a somewhat higher return.

Costs Associated with Homeownership

Homeownership involves many costs. First, the major cost is the mortgage payment. The interest at today's rates may make this a sizable burden. Looking at Table Set 2 in Appendix 1, the monthly payment on a $40,000 mortgage at 9% or thirty years is

$$\text{Annual payment} = \$40,000 \times AF_{30,9\%}$$
$$= \$40,000 \times 0.0973 = \$3,892$$
$$\text{Monthly payment (approximately)} = \$3,892/12 = \$325 \text{ per month}$$

Over ten years the total payments made will be almost $39,000. For the whole life of the mortgage the owner will pay in almost $120,000, or three times the price of the house (assuming no downpayment). This means the owner is paying $80,000 in interest over thirty years to buy the home.

The owner also has to pay taxes, insurance, maintenance costs, and utilities for living in the home. Taxes on a home of this size in 1977 might have ranged from $0 in states like Louisiana to well over $1000 in many other states. Maintenance expenses are somewhat difficult to generalize. For new homes 1½% to 2% per year of the value of the property is a fair approximation. For an older home 3% might not be unusual. Insurance costs for a typical home in the late 1970s, including appropriate liability insurance, is probably at least $180 per year. This cost is much higher in rural areas or situations in which construction methods and neighborhood variables call for increased rates. Utility expenses are obviously of great concern, but are difficult to estimate as a general rule. These costs will vary greatly from one location to another, from one type of dwelling to another, and by family size. Energy costs are rising, however, so utility bills will probably be increasingly more expensive in the 1980s and beyond. In comparing renting and buying, utilities may be considered to be similar and are not relevant in the differentiation of the two alternatives. However, if differences in utility expenses are known to exist between the two dwellings or if utilities are included in the rental payment itself, then it is necessary to include these incremental costs in the analysis.

Benefits Associated with Homeownership

There is no return in cash associated with occupying a home. In fact, there may be an opportunity cost because the family's cash is invested in a home rather than some other source. A complete tax deduction is allowed for the interest part of the mortgage payment and the local tax expense associated with homeownership, however. Also, if a home is sold for a profit and the proceeds are retained, the gain is given preferential tax treatment. Further, if a new home is purchased soon enough after the sale, the gain may be postponed under certain circumstances.

Basic Data—Sample Analysis

We are now ready to consider an example of the analytical process which might be used to explain the benefits and costs of homeownership. The situation will be presented first, followed by the analysis. We must make some assumptions here, but they will be as realistic as possible and they can be adjusted, depending on how critical they are.

In 1975 the Peters family was considering the purchase of a home. At that time they occupied a 1400-square-foot, three-bedroom apartment. The apartment was brand new, had all the basic amenities of a similar-sized house, and rented for $300 per month, including a garage and the use of common facilities such as a swimming pool. Insurance and utility costs for the apartment were $5 and $100 per month on the average, respectively.

In 1975 in the area where the Peters lived a 1400-square-foot ranch-style house with a garage and amenities similar to the apartment would have cost about $40,000. A conventional loan of $32,000 at 9% for thirty years could have been obtained to finance the home. Closing costs and moving expenses would have been about $1500 for the transaction. Maintenance and upkeep was estimated at $50 per month. Insurance would have been $15 per month, and utilities would have been similar to those in the apartment. Property taxes would have been at least $70 per month. The monthly mortgage payment for the loan would have run about $257 per month or $3090 per year. The Peters were in the 30% tax bracket and could have safely invested at 8% before taxes. They wished to know if they should stay where they were or make the move to the house. They felt they would stay in the house ten years, unless they were transferred out of the area about three years later.

To make this analysis a bit more realistic, we will attach a 5% inflation rate to the expenses and the value of the house. This may be treated by adjusting the present value factors for each expense.

To properly compare the costs of these two alternatives, we will compare the present values of the two cost-benefit streams. Because of the uncertainties attaching to the impact of inflation and other factors, the Peters have determined that the appropriate *before-tax* rate of return which should be used to evaluate these costs is 10%. Given their tax bracket this rate of return translates into 7% *after taxes*.

Before-tax return × (1 − tax rate) = After tax
10% × (1 − 0.3) = 7%

This 7% rate will be applied to all the cost and benefit flows which will be examined. It represents an opportunity rate of return which is appropriate for the risk level.

Analysis—Renting

Costs   The costs associated with the rental alternative are summarized as

Rent $300 per month
Insurance $ 5 per month
Utilities $100 per month
  Total $405 per month
Annual cost = $405 × 12 months = $4860

Assuming these expenses all grow at 5% compounded, we may find the present value after taxes as follows:[1]

1. Real rate of return = after-tax rate less inflation

   Real rate = 7% − 5% = 2%

2. Present value of annual costs = cost × $PVAF_{10,2\%}$

   $PV = \$4860 \times 8.98 = \$43,650$

Thus the basic cost of renting for ten years may be seen to have an equivalent value today of $43,650.

---

[1]The *real rate of return* refers to a rate adjusted for inflation. The same *PV* can be obtained by compounding expenses at 5% and using 7% *PV* factors for each of the ten years.

SPECIAL TOPICS

Benefits   One of the most important financial benefits of homeownership is the terminal cash flow obtained when the property is sold. If a family rents rather than buys its residence, a comparable cash flow may be obtained by investing the money which was *not* used as a downpayment in some medium such as a savings account. Other higher yielding investments might be considered, but in our example the Peters chose to earn the rate paid on long-term savings certificates. The cash received at the end of the appropriate time horizon is the terminal value of renting.

In this case, we said the Peters family could save at 8% before taxes or 5.6% after taxes. Thus, if they chose to rent and save the amount that would otherwise have been used for a downpayment, the ending benefit can be found as[2]

$$\text{Future value} = \text{Amount invested} \times FVF_{10,5.6\%}$$
$$FV = \$9500 \times 1.724 = \$16,375$$

We may find the present value of this terminal flow by applying the present value factor at the Peters' opportunity rate of return of 7% after taxes.

$$PV = \$16,375 \times PVF_{10,7\%}$$
$$= \$16,375 \times 0.508 = \$8,320$$

This is the equivalent value today of the residual obtained under the rental alternative. Because $9500 was paid for this residual, it has a negative net present value of

$$\$8320 - \$9500 = (\$1180)$$

Net Cost of Renting   The net cost of renting is the cost of all the rental expenses, plus the negative value associated with the residual. The net cost of renting for the Peters for ten years is

$$\$43,650 + \$1,180 = \$44,830.$$

We may now turn our attention to the cost of the ownership alternative.

---

[2]The *amount invested* includes the downpayment and the closing costs of $1500, neither of which had to be expended under the rental alternative.

Analysis—Owning

Costs   The costs associated with ownership are summarized as

Operating Costs:	
Maintenance	$ 50 per month
Insurance	$ 15 per month
Utilities	$100 per month
Total	$165 per month
Property Tax	70 per month
Mortgage	257 per month

Annualized, the preceding costs are

Operating costs	$1980 per year
Property Tax	$ 840 per year
Mortgage	$3090 per year

The burden of these costs will be reduced by the benefits associated with the deductibility of the interest and property tax expenses. Table 20.1 shows the tax shelter associated with the costs of owning. The interest in the table is not averaged, but is based on an annual amortization for simplicity. The present value of the net costs after taxes is shown in Table 20.2.

As you can see, because of the tax benefits it is cheaper to buy the house than rent the apartment, even if the residual to be received from the sale of the house is not considered.

Residual Benefits   The house in question could be purchased at $40,000. If it grew in value by 5% a year, in ten years it would sell for

$$\text{Future value} = \$40,000 \times FVF_{10,5\%}$$
$$= \$40,000 \times 1.63 = \$65,200$$

The net proceeds of the sale may be determined in the following manner:

1. Gross price − Commission of 7% = Net price

   $65,200 − $4565 = $60,635

2. Gain on sale = Net price − Cost (includes closing)
   $$= \$60,635 - \$41,500 = \$19,135$$

3. Tax on sale (15%) = $19,135 × 0.15 = $2,870

TABLE 20.1   COSTS ASSOCIATED WITH OWNERSHIP

Year	(1) Mortgage Payment	(2) Operating Costs[a]	(3) Interest	(4) Property Taxes[a]	(5) Total Tax Shield (3 + 4)	(6) Tax Savings (5 × 0.3)	(7) Cash Flow (1 + 2 + 4 − 6)
1	$3090[b]	$1980	$2880	$ 840	$3720	$1115	$4795
2	3090	2080	2860	880	3740	1120	4930
3	3090	2180	2840	925	3765	1130	5065
4	3090	2290	2820	970	3790	1135	5205
5	3090	2405	2795	1020	3815	1145	5370
6	3090	2525	2770	1070	3840	1150	5535
7	3090	2650	2740	1125	3865	1160	5705
8	3090	2785	2705	1180	3885	1165	5890
9	3090	2925	2670	1240	3910	1175	6080
10	3090	3070	2635	1300	3935	1180	6280

[a] A 5% inflation rate has been applied to the first year's costs.
[b] Figures have been rounded to the nearest $5.

4. Proceeds, net of tax = $60,635 − $2,870
$$= \$57,765$$

5. Proceeds, net of mortgage balance[3]

$57,765 − $28,810 = $28,955

The present value of these benefits after taxes is

$$PV = \$28,955 \times PVF_{10,7\%}$$
$$= \$28,955 \times 0.508 = \$14,710$$

Subtracting the original cash outlay of $9500 yields a *net benefit* of $6210 for the residual.

Net Cost of Owning   The net cost of ownership, thus, becomes

$37,900 − $6200 = $31,700

---

[3] The *mortgage balance* may be found from Table 20.1 by subtracting column 3 from column 1, summing the principal repayment amounts, and subtracting this total from the original mortgage amount.

TABLE 20.2   PRESENT VALUE—COSTS OF OWNING

Year	After-Tax Cash Flow	$PVF_{n,7\%}$	Present Value
1	$4795	0.935	$4485
2	4930	0.873	4305
3	5065	0.816	4130
4	5205	0.763	3990
5	5370	0.713	3830
6	5535	0.666	3685
7	5705	0.623	3555
8	5890	0.582	3430
9	6080	0.544	3305
10	6280	0.508	3190
			$37,885

Total Cost: approximately $37,900

Summary of Analysis

The basic cost outflows of renting at present value were $43,650. The comparable costs for the ownership example were $37,900. This represents a savings to ownership of $5750 in today's terms. In both cases, the Peters have $9500 to invest. In one case, it is invested at 5.6% after taxes, resulting in total earnings residual of $16,375. In the other, it is invested in the house which inflates at 5% per year and is leveraged. The residual for ownership was seen to be $28,955. At present value, the rental residual is worth $8320 compared to $14,710 for the home. This is a net extra benefit of $6390 for the homeownership alternative. The final cost comparison is approximately $13,100 ($44,830 − $31,700) in favor of ownership.

To make these comparisons more useful, we can convert the present value costs to an annualized basis. Using a 7% after-tax rate of return, an **equivalent annual cost** (*EAC*) for each flow can be created as follows:

$EAC = PV$ cost $/ PVAF_{10,7\%}$
EAC of renting $= \$44,830/7.024 = \$6,380$ per year
EAC of owning $= \$31,700/7.024 = \$4,513$ per year

We can say that owning the house costs the equivalent of $4500 per year, net. Renting on the same basis costs $6380 per year. This is a savings of $1880 per year on an equivalent basis.

Three-Year Analysis

We will now see how these two alternatives relate on the basis of a three-year holding period. The comparison of the basic costs is shown in Table 20.3. The numbers are from previous calculations.

The table shows that for three years renting is $435 more expensive on a present value basis. The question, however, is what the effect is on the residual. The renter may invest $9500 at 5.6% after taxes and end up with a future value of

$$\$9500 \times FVF_{3,5.6\%} = \$9500 \times 1.18 = \$11,190$$

Under the ownership alternative the residual is more complex. In three years a $40,000 house might sell for

$$\$40,000 \times 1.16 = \$46,300$$

assuming a 5% inflation rate. This price yields a capital gain and net proceeds as follows:

1. Net price (after commission) = $43,060
2. Gain = $43,060 − $41,500 = $1560
3. Tax on gain = $1560 × 0.15 = $235
4. Net proceeds = $43,060 − $235 = $42,825
5. Net of mortgage balance = $42,825 − $31,310
$$= \$11,515$$

Looking at this analysis we see that the residual value of the house is $11,515, compared to $11,190 for renting. The rent residual has been invested in the bank and can be brought back to the present at 7%, after tax opportunity rate. This yields a present value of $9130. The house residual is also brought back at 7% and has a present value of $9400.

TABLE 20.3   THREE-YEAR COST COMPARISON

Year	Cost of Renting	Cost of Owning	Net Cost of Renting	$PVF_{n,7\%}$	Present Value
1	$4860	$4795	$ 65	0.935	$ 60
2	5100	4930	170	0.873	150
3	5355	5065	290	0.816	235
					$435

Advantage of Owning: $435

Thus, the renting alternative is only $270 worse from the viewpoint of the residual. The net difference between the two alternatives is $700. For periods of less than three years, it is quite probable the rental would be the less-expensive alternative.

Conclusion

This analysis has been detailed and complex. However, we can draw some general conclusions. First, it appears that in our economy, when comparable properties are compared from an owning versus renting point of view, the owning alternative will be less expensive in the long run for two reasons. Owning a house gives one the ability to earn an inflation return on the *whole* property. This provides a great deal of leverage which is unavailable to the renter–investor. Also, the tax benefits available to owners enable them to lower the cost of ownership dramatically.

A second conclusion which may be drawn is that for short periods homeownership may be costly. If a person is involved in a job which calls for frequent transfers to new locations, ownership may be a problem from a financial standpoint.

Technical Considerations

The decision to acquire a home is a complex one, as we have seen. Aside from the foregoing comparisons between owning and renting, there are a number of other considerations that should be taken into account. One question which must be answered is what size house a buyer can afford. There are several ways to settle this issue, as we shall see. Another question involves the mortgage prepayment. Finally, one last issue involves the question of how large a mortgage an owner should take on. We shall look at each of these questions in turn.

Size of House

There are several approaches to the decision of what size house to purchase. Mortgage lenders use rules of thumb when making decisions about the size of a mortgage that a family can afford. There are two important considerations from a financial standpoint. Many lenders use the rule that no more than 25% of a person's income should be used for a mortgage payment or no more than 35% should be used for total debt payments, including car payments and so forth. Another rule is that a mortgage should not exceed 2.5 times a family's annual income. Some lenders have reduced this to 2 times in recent years because of increased mortgage rates. Using these rules of thumb can show a family how the lender will view the potential mortgage commitment.

Another approach is based on the family budget. A prospective homeowner should begin with take-home income and then deduct all fixed expenses such as debt payments, insurance, and others. From this amount the family should subtract living expenses such as food, utilities, and so forth. Finally, total annual costs for clothing, entertainment, medical bills, and the like should be averaged to a monthly basis and deducted. What is left would be available to pay housing costs: the mortgage payment, maintenance, taxes, and insurance. This approach is safer and tends to force the family to put its expenses into a perspective.

Prepayment Question

With many mortgage loans it is possible to prepay the principal gradually over the life of the loan. Prospective homeowners should know the potential benefits of **prepayment.** The basic idea works as follows. Every mortgage has a particular number of payments assigned at the beginning. A thirty-year mortgage has 360 payments. Each month borrowers must pay the regular payment. However, borrowers might decide, for instance, that each month they will pay the regular payment and the *principal only* from the next payment. Through the life of the mortgage, this will reduce the total number of payments to one half. This procedure will not save any principal, but it will save a great deal of interest over the life of the loan.

If this procedure were followed over the life of a thirty-year, 9% loan of $32,000, the total savings before taxes would be roughly $30,000. The total payments for a $32,000 loan would be $92,700 if nothing were prepaid. Dividing the total payout of $62,700 (when prepayment occurs as we stated) by 180 payments yields an average monthly payment of $348. This is $90 more on the average than the monthly payment without prepayment, during the first fifteen years of the regular loan. The present value of this extra amount at 8% on an annual basis is:

$$PV = \$90 \times 12 \text{ months} \times PVF_{15,8\%}$$
$$= \$1080 \times 8.56 = \$9245$$

This is the extra cost of our approach to prepayment in present value terms. It assumes the homeowner would invest the $90 each month at a before-tax rate of return of 8%. However, in the last fifteen years, $257 per month is saved. This could also be invested, instead of being used to pay off the mortgage. This is worth in present value terms

$$PV = \$257 \times 12 \text{ months} \times (PVAF_{30,8\%} - PVAF_{15,8\%})$$
$$= \$3090 \times (11.26 - 8.56)$$
$$= \$3090 \times 2.70 = \$8343$$

Thus, even though a great deal of interest is saved, the benefits of this procedure do not exceed the costs, at least at 8% on a before-tax basis. Similar analyses can be used to evaluate prepayment for other rates of return which the investor might receive, for other prepayment schedules, and on an after-tax basis.

Size of Loan

In today's world of rising home prices, a person who buys a house and then begins moving every five years or so is faced with the decision of whether to put all the resulting equity back into a new house. Again, we will illustrate an approach to this situation by example.

A homeowner buys a house for $40,000 with a $32,000 9% mortgage for thirty years. Five years later the home is sold for $51,000 less a commission of 7%, or $3570. The mortgage balance is $30,675 at that point. Thus, the owner removes equity of $51,000 less $3570 less $30,675, or $16,755. The owner is now going to buy a new home costing $52,000. This postpones the gains tax. The question is whether to use the whole $16,755 as equity on the second house, or again take an 80% mortgage.

If the homeowner decides to use all equity from the first house, the loan would be for $35,245 ($52,000 − $16,755). The mortgage payment would be $283.60 per month at 9% for thirty years, or approximately $3400 per year.

If he decides to assume an 80% loan, he would be borrowing $41,600 (80% × $52,000). The equity required would be $10,400, which leaves $6355 of his total equity from the first house unused. This mortgage payment would be $334.70 per month or about $4000 per year.

The smaller equity alternative (taking an 80% loan) frees $6350 for investment. At 8% interest, $500 would be earned by this sum each year. After taxes of 30%, this would leave about $350 in net earnings.

At the end of another five years his second house is sold for $66,000, less a commission of $4600. This leaves proceeds of $61,400 before the mortgage balance. The remaining balance on the small loan would be $33,900. The large loan would have a balance of $40,100. Table 20.4 shows the cash flows associated with these two alternative loan sizes. They are somewhat conservative flows.

If the homeowner uses the interest he receives from investing the $6,350 at 8% to defray the larger mortgage payments associated with this alternative, we can see from Table 20.4 that the smaller mortgage plan has a slight advantage.

PV of $90 savings for 5 years @ 8% = $350
PV of lost residual of $150 @ 8% = (100)
Net benefit to smaller loan   = $250

the process has been pervasive, it has not been enjoyed as fully by some minority groups. Nathan Glazer points out that the proportion of blacks in the suburbs is roughly one-half the proportion in society as a whole (5.3% versus 11%).[4] This lack of proportion has existed because of past discrimination and economic considerations. The facts that suburban housing is generally more expensive and that black income levels are generally lower have combined to cause the decreased proportion.

The problem here from a social standpoint is that, unlike employment, private housing is in no way assigned by a central authority. Antidiscrimination laws can guarantee an *equal opportunity* to buy a house, but not equal economic qualifications. Deed and zoning restrictions specifying minimum housing sizes or single-family homes only, for example, increase costs and values and reduce the ability of minorities to purchase available housing. Any attempts to force this situation to change will have a potentially profound effect on the value of suburban housing. Striking down zoning laws in an indiscriminate fashion may well do irreparable damage to land use planning. For the potential homeowner the future effects of social considerations may be an important variable.

The discussion of this issue is an emotional one. Our society is committed to reducing social injustice. However, in the housing area, the policy issues are difficult and the mechanics nearly impossible without potentially altering the whole fabric of development and homeownership.

CHAPTER TWENTY SUMMARY	In this chapter we have examined the factors which need to be analyzed in the consideration of home ownership. Our analysis has been concentrated on various financial inputs to the decision. We have viewed the major costs and benefits from a financial viewpoint. We also saw the power of the tax deductions and leverage of ownership, as well as the effect of possession time, on the decision. We then turned our attention to several technical decisions that might arise during the homeownership decision. These include the questions of how large a house to buy, whether to prepay the loan, and what percentage mortgage to hold, given the size of the house purchased. Finally, we concluded with a brief discussion of some social issues involved in homeownership.

KEY TERMS   **Equivalent Annual Cost**   **Prepayment**

---

[4]Nathan Glazer, *Affirmative Discrimination: Ethnic Inequality and Public Policy* (New York: Basic Books, 1975), pp. 130–167.

QUESTIONS FOR STUDY AND DISCUSSION

1. Identify some of the major costs and benefits associated with home-ownership. Can all the costs be quantified?

2. Why is homeownership often cheaper in a long-run situation? When may renting be cheaper than owning a home?

PROBLEMS FOR REVIEW

1. Consider the costs associated with the following home. A home may be purchased for $50,000 today and sold in ten years for $70,000, less a commission of 7%. The home will be financed with a $40,000 mortgage at 9% for thirty years. Other expenses that will be incurred are as follows:

Utilities—$120 per month
Insurance—$20 per month
Property tax—$80 per month
Maintenance—$60 per month

The owner is in the 30% tax bracket and can invest at 10% before taxes. Ignore inflation in your calculation. Find the net present value of the costs associated with this home. What is the equivalent annual cost?

APPENDICES

TABLE OF CONTENTS

1
THE NATURE
OF REAL ESTATE
AND ITS VALUE

REAL ESTATE is an interesting, exciting subject. During the course of our discussions, we will look at many facets of this complex subject. We will look at the nature of real property, what gives it value, and learn how to estimate its value. We will also look at the real estate business and will talk about how real estate is marketed and developed. Finally, we will discuss how to analyze investments in real property, both in income real estate and single-family dwellings for personal residences.

When you have finished with your initial exposure to our subject at the end of this book, you will have much of the basic preparation required to enter your apprenticeship in this profession, if you choose. Similarly, if you choose to use your knowledge to make valuable investments in real property, you should have a good, basic background for this purpose. Finally, if an academic pursuit of real estate is your desire, this book should provide a sound foundation of terms and concepts upon which you can build.

Why Study Real Estate?

Real estate is possibly the most basic of all the assets a person may own. Our dwellings, farms, factories, monuments, and public buildings are all real estate. To understand the nature of real estate is to understand much of what is significant in the history of civilization. Land has been at the heart of many wars and conflicts. Owning land is a basic human instinct.

In addition to its historical significance, there are other reasons for studying real estate. For average people in a free society such as ours, the major investment of their lifetimes will be their homes. Understanding the nature of real property and what gives it value can help the prospective homeowner make this decision in a wise and rational way. Income property is likewise an important investment vehicle. In an economy subject to inflationary pressures, land and improved property can be an extremely sound way to combat the ravages of inflation. By understanding the nature of real estate value and how to estimate it, investors can make investment decisions more wisely.

There are also some social reasons for studying real estate. In our society, there are a number of resources that we can no longer take for granted. Clean air, clean water, and sufficient, decent, economic housing for all are no longer givens in our society. By studying real estate and the factors affecting its development, we can learn more about how to conserve these scarce resources. The development of our cities will be an important determinant of the future economic health of our country. But, as we will see later, it is not always easy to facilitate natural urban development in the free enterprise system. There are major social, political, and economic considerations which must be resolved to solve our development problems.

The Nature of Real Estate

Property Rights

In order to understand the nature of real estate, we must first define the concept of property. Ownership of an asset, or *wealth* as it may be called, is often considered to be mere possession or use of an object. The concept of *property* is more expansive. The ownership of property refers to a **bundle of rights** in the property. These rights may include:

1. The right to use the property for some purpose for gain or satisfaction;
2. The right to dispose of the property as the owner sees fit;
3. The right of possession of the property even though the property may not be used by the owner; and
4. The right to extract minerals from beneath the property.

The distinction between wealth and property may seem too subtle for consideration, but it is extremely important in the field of real estate. All property rights have value. These rights may be purchased or sold in any number of combinations. Once we consider property in terms of rights, rather than as a unified physical object, the possibilities for creative investment become endless. For instance, many buildings in large cities are built on *air rights*. In such a case, the only right the building owner has in the land under the building is the right to use a certain portion of the air above the land. This ability to make such flexible use of an asset may help maximize its value.

Legal Nature of Real Estate

Legally, real estate includes the land and everything directly and permanently attached to it. This concept is a fairly simple one, but, in certain circumstances, it may be difficult to determine exactly what is attached to the land. In the highest form of ownership, called **fee simple,** the landowner owns from the center of the earth out into the sky, in addition to the surface and improvements. Fee simple is what gives the landowner control over air rights and mineral rights. Although we have implied that the owner of a fee simple has tremendous freedom, he is still subject to the control of laws, taxes, zoning, and so forth.

As we shall see later, there are a number of important legal considerations which will affect the value and use of real property. We will examine these briefly in this chapter and in detail later on.

Physical Nature of Real Estate

Although it may not be obvious, real estate is largely an urban, manufactured product. Although only 8% of the total land area in the United

States is in private nonfarm uses, 55% of the value is in these land uses (see Table 1.1). Additionally, as with any other resource, raw land must have value added to it to make it productive. Even raw land which is used for mineral extraction must be developed to provide value to the user.

Another important characteristic of real property is its unique property. Each parcel of real estate is different. Even if two identical sets of improvements are added to neighboring parcels, the resulting properties will be at least somewhat different. Their locations are different, as may be their physical characteristics. Generally, however, it is the fixity of location of each and every parcel that certainly differentiates it from every other parcel.

Besides being fixed in location and quantity, land is also indestructible.[1] Finally, real estate parcels are generally fairly large and have such a high value that financing is required. These characteristics, and others we will discuss later, all affect the value of real estate.

Real Estate as an Investment

Let us consider the investment qualities of real estate. Real property is important as an investment medium in our society, enjoying many inherent advantages over other investments such as securities. It should be noted that we are talking here about productive real estate *investment*, as opposed to *speculation*. The difference between investment and speculation is a subtle one. Investment is basically a state of mind, an attitude. The desire to commit funds for a long term, coupled with the desire to achieve a reasonable rate of return, is **investment.** Investment

TABLE 1.1   DISTRIBUTION OF MAJOR LAND USES AND VALUES, 1975

Land Use	Square Miles	Percent	Value (Billions)	Percent
Private Farm	1,700,000	47%	$336	26%
Private Nonfarm (Major Urban Areas)	300,000	8%	$705	55%
Public Land	1,200,000	45%	$243	19%
Other	400,000			
Totals	3,600,000	100%	$1284	100%

Sources: Compiled from *Statistical Abstract*, U.S. Census Department, 1978, and *Land Use Planning Abstracts*, Volume 2, 1976.

---

[1]Obviously, there are occasions when natural disasters may alter the physical characteristics of a parcel, but, in general, it is basically indestructible.

returns generally include both periodic returns and appreciation. **Speculation** is characterized by a desire to "make a killing," generally in the short run, and often yields only capital gains, not periodic returns.

As a general rule, real estate investments compare very favorably to investments in securities. The returns are comparable to those earned on common stock investments. However, as we shall see in chapter 8, real estate investments are different from securities investments in many ways. Probably the most important current characteristics of real estate investments are their ability to hedge against inflation, the flexibility with which they may be financed, and their potential manageability.

Real Estate as a Business

In addition to considering real estate as an investment, we will also discuss the nature of real estate as a business. There are several aspects to this consideration. First, income property is itself a business enterprise. There are revenues, expenses, profits, and cash flows just as there are in manufacturing or retailing.

Another view of real estate as a business concerns the construction industry. In 1976 5% of the U.S. national income of $1400 billion was derived from the contract construction industry.[2] Construction includes residential dwellings, commercial buildings, industrial property, and public works. The construction industry is important in our society because a number of other industries depend heavily on new construction. When the number of new housing starts falls, the demand for heavy appliances and, indirectly, the demand for such materials as sheet steel also falls. The construction and building materials industries are fairly labor-intensive and unemployment is greatly affected by their success. Conversely, however, the construction industry is extremely sensitive to the level of employment in the economy. If people are not working, they cannot afford new homes. The construction industry is also very sensitive to the level of interest rates, because construction must be heavily financed.

Finally, the marketing of real property is also an important business. In 1976 the real estate business accounted for national income of $115 billion or 8% of total national income.[3] In addition, the real estate industry has the largest investment per employee of any industry in the economy, almost $400,000 per person in 1958 dollars. This is over three times greater than for any other industry.[4]

In addition to marketing, the real estate profession also provides many other important services. The appraisal of real property is an important function which facilitates the operation of real estate market

---

[2]*Statistical Abstract,* U.S. Census Department, 1978.
[3]*Statistical Abstract,* U.S. Census Department, 1978.
[4]Ibid.

activity. Income property is managed by property management companies for landlord investors. This management function greatly facilitates the investment in real property by large institutional investors such as insurance companies. Finally, the real estate profession provides a number of advisory and development services to the investor and homeowner. Real estate decisions are often difficult and complex, necessitating the use of professional advice to facilitate these decisions.

Real Estate Value Concepts

The overall approach to the subject of real estate in this book will be to look at value. We will see what value is, how to estimate it, and what factors affect it. In the rest of this chapter, we will view the general structure of value and provide a look at things to come.

The concept of value is complex indeed. There are many types of value—market value, accounting value, investment value, and others. In this section, we will define and compare some of the important value concepts as they relate to real estate. Figure 1.1 is a graphic representation of the key relationships.

Market Value

One measure of the value of any investment, including real estate, is the *market value*. Historically, market transactions provide an objective record of the periodic changes in the value of an asset. One definition

FIGURE 1.1   REAL ESTATE VALUE

Factors Affecting Value   Types of Value

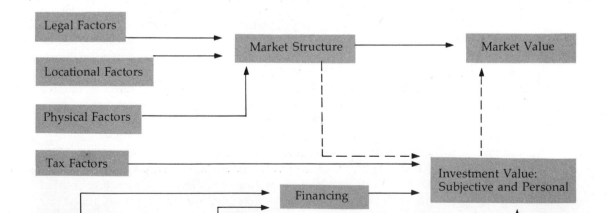

of market value is that it is the price a willing, informed buyer will pay and a willing, informed seller will accept in the open market. One assumption we must make here is that each party to the transaction has sufficient information to judge whether the price is fair. We must assume neither party is under duress. If the seller must sell to obtain money to buy another property or if the buyer must buy property regardless of price, the price cannot be considered a fair market price. Some people also feel that the market price cannot be considered a truly representative value if there are insufficient buyers and sellers in the market. If only one buyer looks at a property and makes an offer, the transaction may not be considered a fair market value. Likewise, when insufficient numbers of similar properties are available in the market to give the buyer a free choice, transactions may not be at real fair market prices.

A classic definition of **fair market value** is that it measures the ability of an asset to command goods in exchange. It is not just a dollar measure, but a relative measure of real value. Market value may also be defined as the present value of future amenities. This condition will be described in more detail when we discuss the appraisal of income real estate in later chapters. Under this latter definition, we recognize the idea that the value of an asset is derived from its productivity. With residential real estate, this concept is a difficult one to operationalize. We are mainly accepting this definition as an explanatory concept in the residential case. Finally, we may view the market value as a consensus notion. Again, the value is the result of competitive forces in the market, the so-called "free market" activity. This concept of consensus also intimates that, in the market, similar properties will sell for similar prices. It is this last idea that will serve as the basis for the market comparison approach to appraisal.

Investment Value

The process of setting market prices is built on negotiation. Offers, counteroffers, and, eventually, acceptances from both parties are necessary elements. However, one of the other necessary elements is every market participant's idea of what the value should be. This subjective view is the **investment value**.

For buyers, the investment value for a property is the *most* they are willing to pay, given personal constraints such as other investment opportunities, personal income tax rate, and preferences for risk. The buyer is viewing all the amenities of the property such as potential benefits and risks and is making a subjective evaluation applicable only to him or her. The investment value serves as an upper bound for actual market negotiations.

For sellers, the investment value is the *least* they will accept given personal investment constraints. For sellers, the investment value is a lower bound in the market price negotiations. In order for a transaction to finally take place, the eventual buyer and seller must have investment values sufficiently separated to allow negotiation to take place. No transactions will occur without mutual benefits to the parties.

Our assessment of investment values will contain many of the elements of market value estimation. The difference will be the addition of personal considerations.

Cost

A glance at Figure 1.1 will show that the third important value concept is that of cost—an objective concept. The **cost to create** for a property is the total cost required to put the property in a condition which will permit it to be utilized in the purpose for which it was intended. These costs may include materials, labor, architect's fees, closing costs, etc. A property will not necessarily sell for its costs, even when new. Often cost will equal value for new properties, but there are a number of reasons why this equality may not exist.

In a small city, two adjacent lots are available for development. Each is priced to sell for $75,000. A developer purchases one lot and spends $375,000 to build a large building on that property. He then sells the developed property for $500,000, which is $50,000 over his total cost. How is this possible? A prospective buyer could buy the other lot, spend the same $375,000, and create an identical building for only $450,000.

There may be a number of explanations for this phenomenon. First, there is the time element. By buying the completed building, the user can begin to use the property immediately, giving him an opportunity savings. Second, it could be that parking is needed for the building and it would not be available if both lots were occupied. It is possible that costs might have risen so that another identical building could not be built for $375,000. Finally, perhaps there would not be sufficient business for two buildings of that size in that area. Thus, it can be seen that value is based on a complex combination of variables. Only when a transaction occurs will we know the relationship between value and cost.

Factors Affecting Value

We will now turn our attention to a number of factors affecting the various values we have defined. Another look at Figure 1.1 will show what will be covered in this section.

Physical Characteristics

There are a number of physical characteristics of a property which will affect its present and future value. For example, we must consider the characteristics of the site itself, such as its size and shape. A small, irregularly shaped plot will probably be of less use in an urban setting than a good-sized rectangular one. Improvements also affect the value of the property.

Locational Factors

This area of value analysis considers the relationship of one parcel of real estate to other parcels providing various services. One of the key concepts in location theory is the *neighborhood* concept. A neighborhood is an area of land uses, such as single-family residences, which has a coincident relation to an outside influence, such as a factory. All parcels whose values are affected by the factory are in the same neighborhood.

Locational analysis is also concerned with the spatial relationships between parcels of property. Each parcel is *linked* to every other parcel to which it is connected for services. **Linkages** are measured by the costs of movement between parcels, called **frictional costs.** Generally, a particular site is chosen for a certain use in such a way to minimize total costs. We will be discussing both physical and locational factors in chapter 11.

Legal Factors

One of the most complex areas of real estate is concerned with its legal characteristics. We will be looking at a number of these in several of the chapters in parts 2 and 3 of the text. We will be discussing seven major areas:

1. The nature of property rights
2. Property description
3. The degrees of ownership interest in property
4. The nature of lease interests in property
5. How property rights are conveyed from one party to another
6. Public and private limitations on the use of property, and
7. The various contracts used to complete property transactions

As we shall see, all of these factors may affect property values.

Tax Factors

Investment value requires the analysis of two important factors: taxes and financing. Real estate is an important tax shelter. We will be looking at this more closely in chapter 7.

There are a number of areas where taxes have an impact. First, real estate is a business when it is owned for investment purposes. As a business, certain expenses, especially depreciation, are tax-deductible.

This consideration protects some of the cash flow of the investment from taxes, enhancing its value. Further, when property is owned in partnership or proprietorship, any losses sustained can protect income from other sources from taxes, adding to personal cash flow.

One must also consider the type of depreciation allowed for tax purposes. Different types of properties allow different methods of depreciation which will affect value. A further tax effect must be considered at the time of the sale of the property. If the property has increased in value, the profit is taxed at a more favorable rate.

Financing

The other major factor affecting investment value is the type financing available to the investor. The tax-deductibility of interest, coupled with the fact that interest is a fixed charge, provides the investor with *leverage*. As we shall see in chapter 8, leverage may increase the value of a real estate investment. At the same time, leverage may also increase the risks involved.

Financing, its cost and availability, is a function of a number of factors. Financing is generally obtained from one of two major sources: institutions in the market and the seller of the property. The market includes a number of institutions, such as savings and loans, banks, insurance companies, and mortgage companies. The cost and availability, and the terms surrounding financing from these institutions, are heavily influenced by economic conditions.

The primary form of financing for real property is the *mortgage loan*. The mortgage loan may have various structures, but most are similar. In addition to the mortgage, there are other types of financing arrangements which may be utilized to increase the value of the property. These include the land contract, the straight lease, the sale-and-leaseback, and construction financing. We shall examine all the various financing sources, instruments, and their effect on value in chapters 15 to 17.

Economic Factors

The value of real property is affected both directly and indirectly by the economic environment. The structure of economic markets, both for property itself and for the inputs to the construction industry, has an obvious impact on value. The structure of the financial markets and the influence of the government in these markets affects how investors and homeowners will obtain needed financing. The economy is greatly affected by governmental influence, both direct and indirect, which, in turn, affects real estate values. We shall examine these and other influences in the model of real estate markets in chapter 10.

CHAPTER ONE SUMMARY

In this chapter we have set the stage for the discussions of real estate and its value which will follow. We defined various value concepts such as market value, investment value, and cost. We also looked at the concept of property and what it means. A model was presented to show how all the value concepts are affected by the characteristics and environment of real estate. In part 1 to follow we will examine in detail the analysis and estimation of real estate values.

Part 2 will present in detail the important characteristics affecting real estate value. Part 3 will be a discussion of real estate marketing and development. We will look at the function of brokers. We will also briefly examine the brokerage business and discuss some specific activities surrounding the market transaction, such as closings and listings. The last part of the text will discuss real estate development, raw land investment, and homeownership.

The upcoming discussions on value may challenge you a great deal. If you can master these concepts, however, you will have the foundation you need for some successful endeavors in real estate. As you study the subject, you may find that things will fit together better if you keep in mind the interrelationships shown in Figure 1.1.

KEY TERMS

Bundle of Rights	**Fee Simple**	**Investment Value**
Cost to Create	**Frictional Costs**	**Linkages**
Fair Market Value	**Investment**	**Speculation**

QUESTIONS FOR STUDY AND DISCUSSION

1. Differentiate between the concepts of *wealth* and *property*.

2. What is the difference between *investment value* and *market value* in real estate?

3. What attributes does real estate have that make it attractive as an investment alternative?

4. What types of factors directly affect the market value of a piece of real estate?

5. If a man purchases a single-family residence from his father, the price paid may not necessarily represent the "fair market value" of that real estate parcel. What conditions must be met if the father wishes to receive the "fair market value" for his residence?

PART 1

CHAPTER TWO—BASIC VALUE CONCEPTS I

In this chapter we will examine the concept of present value, which serves as the foundation for economic decision-making. We will look at a number of important techniques and the computational analysis required for their use.

CHAPTER THREE—BASIC VALUE CONCEPTS II

The process of valuation in real estate often depends on a version of present value analysis called capitalization. In this chapter we will discuss capitalization, the determination of capitalization rates, and the decision rules which are used in modern investment analysis.

CHAPTER FOUR—INTRODUCTION TO APPRAISAL

This chapter describes the general process by which the market value of real estate may be estimated. The discussion begins with a general discussion of real estate markets. Following this, we will look at the process of appraisal in general terms.

CHAPTER FIVE—MARKET AND COST BASIS APPRAISING

This chapter will discuss two of the three classic appraisal techniques. The market approach is based on the premise that similar properties will sell for similar prices. The cost approach is based on the idea that no property should sell for more than it costs to reproduce it exactly.

CHAPTER SIX—INCOME APPRAISING

Income properties are often appraised based on the value of their income

VALUE CONCEPTS AND ANALYSIS

benefits. This kind of appraising draws heavily on the material presented in chapter 3. We will see how to estimate income, what benefit streams are relevant, and how value is estimated in various situations.

CHAPTER SEVEN—TAX CONSIDERATIONS

One of the primary factors affecting the investment value of real property is the tax structure. In this chapter we will discuss the various taxes affecting real estate with special emphasis on the federal tax structures. Because the tax laws change so frequently, we will keep the discussion fairly general, making reference to the tax laws whenever this is necessary.

CHAPTER EIGHT—INVESTMENT ANALYSIS

This chapter is concerned with investment analysis. Investment analysis is similar to income appraisal but is more personalized. The first part of the discussion will be concerned with the investment process in general. The second part will be concerned with the calculations required for investment analysis of real estate.

CHAPTER NINE—CAPITAL ASSET PRICING AND RISK ANALYSIS

There are a number of areas in appraisal and investment analysis which interface with finance and economic theory. This chapter will present the modern theory of capital asset pricing and the risk–return analysis as it relates to traditional real estate analysis. We will discuss the nature of risk, the relationships between risk and return, and the management of risk through portfolio diversification.

2

BASIC VALUE
CONCEPTS I–
PRESENT VALUE

AS WE will define it, an investment is a proposition in which the investor trades a current sum for the expectation of receiving some future benefit(s). The purpose of this chapter will be to examine this concept in general. We will develop the basic tools of valuation applicable to all investments and especially to real estate. The concepts we will develop will be based on the productivity of an asset arising from its future benefits. The theory from this section will be inherent in all our methods of evaluating real estate.

Factors Affecting the Value of Cash Streams

The benefits of any investment are the cash flows which will accrue to the owner over the life of the project. We use *cash* benefits because everything must eventually be paid for in cash. The investor must beware of substituting traditional accounting profits for these benefits because, as we shall see later, the tax laws can make these figures misleading.

The most obvious factor affecting the value of a stream of cash benefits is its *amount*. All other things being equal, the average investor prefers a larger benefit stream. More simply stated, more money is preferred to less. Suppose someone approaches you on a street corner and offers you a choice of propositions. First, if you give him $100, he will give you back $150 one year from now. Alternatively, if you give him $100 now, he will give you back $125 one year from now. Your preference would be for the first alternative.

There are other considerations, however. To illustrate, we return to our street corner and consider two new propositions. In the first, we are told that if we put up $100 today, we will receive $200 in two years. In the second proposition, we are told we can put up $100 today and receive $200 in five years. Which would you you prefer? Why? The average investor would prefer the first proposition, even though the amounts are the same in both cases, because it returns your money faster. Money can be used for two basic functions: current consumption and investment (or savings). The sooner we can do either, presumably the more satisfaction we may obtain. Thus, our second factor is the *timing* of money flows. Current dollars are preferred to future dollars, especially because of the prospect for reinvestment.

Finally, there is a third factor we must consider. Assume two more proposals. First, the man on the corner makes a proposal whereby you may leave $100 with him and return five years later and receive $200. Alternatively, the U.S. government makes you the same proposition. Which is more likely to fulfill its obligation? The third factor then is *risk*. All other things being equal, the average investor prefers certainty to uncertainty and would more likely accept the second of the two proposals.

We have three factors to evaluate when considering the value of any money flow. These factors are the amount (quantity), the timing, and the risk (quality) of the flow. Any system of analysis which does not account for all three of these factors may cause an investor to make erroneous decisions. This condition is not to imply that simply accounting for these elements in just any way will ensure success. It simply means that failure to account for all three factors may be disastrous.

With these basic ideas in mind, we are now ready to develop a set of techniques which will let us find a useful, unified value for a money flow. The techniques developed in this chapter will account for all three of the factors affecting the value: quantity, quality, and timing. You frequently will be referred to the tables in Appendix One at the end of this text. Before beginning the following sections, you may find it useful to glance at the tables briefly to familiarize yourself with them. It might also be noted here that the symbols used for the various present value tables are nontraditional and designed to help you remember the various concepts. For this reason, a glossary of these symbols (Appendix to chapter 2) is included at the end of the chapter.

Values of a Single Sum

Future Value of a Single Sum

Perhaps the simplest form of investment proposal to evaluate is one in which the investor risks a certain sum today in exchange for a single benefit at some future date. The total value of this benefit is the **future value**. To analyze this situation, we will define some symbols.

Let: P = the beginning amount invested;
    i = the rate of return earned on the investment;
    I = the dollar return on the investment; and
    F = the future value of the investment.

To simplify matters, we will assume all investment periods equal one year for the present time. Later we will vary this assumption.

Now assume for a moment you were to put $1000 into a savings account which paid 6% interest per year. What would you earn in one year? Answer:

I = $1000 × 6% × 1 year
  = $1000 × 0.06
  = $60

You would earn $60. We can also see that, in general, the earnings in one year equal the amount invested multiplied by the rate of interest expressed as a decimal, $I = P \times i$.

The total value of our investment at the end of one year is given as F and is the sum of the amount we started with plus our earnings. Thus,

$$F = P + I$$
$$= \$1000 + \$60$$
$$= \$1060$$

We may restructure what we have seen so far using some algebra as follows:

$$F = P + I$$
$$F = P + Pi$$
$$F = P (1 + i) \qquad [2.1]$$

To demonstrate that this last equation [2.1] works in our problem, substitute the proper numbers as:

$$F = \$1000 (1 + 0.06)$$
$$= \$1000 (1.06)$$
$$= \$1060$$

Thus, we can see either form of the equation will work, but [2.1] is simpler to use.

Example 2.1

Find the value of $4300 invested at 8.5% for one year using equation [2.1].

$$F = \$4300(1.085) = \$4665.50$$

At this point we must differentiate between the two kinds of interest one can earn on an investment: simple interest and compound interest. **Simple interest** refers to the situation in which interest is received on an investment and paid to the investor. The investor will then leave only the principal amount to earn more interest in the next period. Thus, the return in each period is the same since the *same amount* is invested each time. The *dollar return* in each period is represented by I.

The investor, alternatively, may deposit the interest he has received in each period, which means that in each period the investment will grow by the amount of interest earned in the previous period. When this process occurs automatically, it is called compounding or **compound interest.** Note the effect of compounding on our investment in the sequence in Table 2.1. We will use equation [2.1] for these calculations.

In Table 2.1, we can see the advantage of compound interest. Here the total value was $3.60 more with compounding than with simple interest. The assumption we will make throughout this book is that the investor will *always reinvest earnings at the assigned earnings rate.* Therefore, compounding will occur. We can see how this multiple period process works here.

For the first period: $F_1 = P (1 + i)$
For the second period: $F_2 = F_1 (1 + i)$

Note how the amount from the first period, F_1, becomes the P for the second period. We can change this last relationship into the terms of the original investment, P, as:

$$\begin{aligned} F_2 &= F_1 (1 + i) \\ &= P (1 + i) (1 + i) \\ &= P (1 + i)^2 \end{aligned}$$

For any number of periods F_n will be found similarly:

$$F_n = P (1 + i)^n \tag{2.2}$$

TABLE 2.1   SIMPLE VS COMPOUND INTEREST

Simple Interest		Compound Interest
$1000 × 0.06 = $60 Withdraw interest	Period 1	$1000 × 0.06 = $60 Leave interest and principal
$1000 × 0.06 = $60 Withdraw interest and principal	Period 2	$1060 × 1.06 = $1123.60 Withdraw total amount
$1000 investment + 120 earnings ———— $1120 total value	Status at end of Period 2	$1123.60 total value

where n represents the number of periods. The quantity $(1 + i)^n$ may be a complicated number to find if the number of periods is large, so tables have been constructed for various rates of interest, i, and various numbers of periods, n. These tables are called future value tables or compound sum tables. You have one in the appendix at the end of the book. A sample is included as Table 2.2.

To account for the tables, we will reformulate equation [2.2] to fit the idea of a table value. The term $FVF_{n,i}$ is the Future Value Factor for n periods at i rate of interest and will be substituted for the quantity $(1 + i)^n$. Thus:

$$F_n = P \times FVF_{n,i} \qquad\qquad [2.3]$$

Returning to our original example of a $1000 investment for two years at 6% interest, using the table the solution may be found as:

$$\begin{aligned} F_2 &= \$1000 \times FVF_{2,6\%} \\ &= \$1000 \times 1.124 = \$1124 \end{aligned}$$

The difference between $1124 and $1123.60 from Table 2.1 is because of the rounding of the last digit in the future value table.

To practice these concepts, we will look at the next two examples.

TABLE 2.2   FUTURE VALUE FACTORS

Period	6%	7%	8%	9%	10%
1	1.060	1.070	1.080	1.090	1.100
2	1.124	1.145	1.166	1.188	1.210
3	1.191	1.225	1.260	1.295	1.331
4	1.263	1.311	1.360	1.412	1.464
5	1.338	1.402	1.469	1.539	1.610
6	1.418	1.501	1.587	1.677	1.772
7	1.504	1.606	1.714	1.828	1.949
8	1.594	1.718	1.851	1.992	2.144
.	.	.	.	.	.
.	.	.	.	.	.
.	.	.	.	.	.

(column header spanning 7% and 8%: $i =$)

Example 2.2

Using the Future Value Factors in Table 2.2, find the future values requested.

1. $2500 invested for six years at 9%.

$$F_6 = \$2500 \times 1.677 = \$4192.50$$

2. $5200 invested at 6% for 8 years.

$$F_8 = \$5200 \times 1.594 = \$8288.80$$

One final note here is necessary, which will allow us to relax the assumption about yearly periods of investment. In some certificate accounts the earnings are at, say, 8% per year compounded quarterly. For such cases, the table may still be used. To find the appropriate value, first divide the interest rate by the number of compounding periods in one year. Next, multiply the number of years by the number of compounding periods in one year. Finally, use these two new figures for i and n in the table. Thus, 8% per year compounded quarterly becomes 2% per period. If the number of years to be considered is two years, then eight periods (4 × 2) are involved. Hence, $n = 8$ and $i = 2\%$.

$$\begin{aligned} F_8 &= \$1000 \times FVF_{8,2\%} \\ &= \$1000 \times 1.172 = \$1172 \end{aligned}$$

Here F_8 represents eight *periods* or two years. Compare this to an investment of $1000 at 8% for two years with annual compounding instead of quarterly compounding.

$$\begin{aligned} F_2 &= \$1000 \times FVF_{2,8\%} \\ &= \$1000 \times 1.166 = \$1166 \end{aligned}$$

Clearly, compounding for periods less than one year will increase earnings somewhat for the same stated interest rate and same period of investment.

Example 2.3

Find the future value of a $6300 investment for five years at 12% compounded quarterly.

$$\begin{aligned} F_{20} &= \$6300 \times FVF_{20,3\%} \\ &= \$6300 \times 1.806 = \$11,377.80 \end{aligned}$$

Present Value of a Single Sum

The method of finding future values that we have just seen is a useful step toward our goal of evaluating income streams. However, there are some problems with the future value idea.

1. If investments are made for differing lengths of time, they are difficult to compare in a fair manner.

2. Generally, what we "know" about an investment is its *expected benefit*. We want to evaluate this benefit to see if it is sufficient to justify its cost.

3. We have already seen that the most valuable dollars are the ones we have in the present. These are the dollars we may choose to give up to make investments. Comparing only future values fails to account for this.

Because of these problems we must devise a scheme that helps us to compare each alternative investment we have in common terms—what the investment is worth to us today in current, investible dollars—termed the present worth or **present value** of the investment. It may also be viewed as the *maximum*, or exact, amount of money one would be willing to give up today in order to get the benefits expected.

To solve for this value, three things must be known: the expected benefit, the length of time until the benefit is received, and the rate of interest expected to be earned. We already have a formula for this value, equation [2.2],

$$F_n = P \ (1 + i)^n$$

In this instance we know F, i, and n. Thus, we must solve for P, the present worth or maximum initial investment.

$$P \ = \ \frac{F_n}{(1 + i)^n}$$

To make this equation more convenient to use we may rewrite it as:

$$P \ = \ F_n \ [\ \frac{1}{(1 + i)^n} \ ] \qquad\qquad [2.4]$$

The quantity $[1/(1 + i)^n]$ has been put into a table, just as the future value factors were. In fact, it is just the reciprocal of the future value factor. This leaves us with a simplified equation:

$$PV = F_n \times PVF_{n,i} \qquad\qquad [2.5]$$

where $PVF_{n,i}$ is the *Present Value Factor* for n years at i rate of interest. The table for these values is also in the appendix and a partial table appears in Table 2.3. Notice that now we will be using PV to stand for the present value, rather than P for the beginning investment. Mathematically, there is no difference between P and PV. For investment analysis purposes, however, it is more meaningful conceptually to speak of present values rather than beginning investments.

We will now look at an example of present value calculation. Assume you can make an investment at 6% for two years. Assume the expected benefit from this investment is $1124. What is its present value? Using equation [2.5], we find:

$$PV = F_2 \times PVF_{2,6\%}$$
$$= \$1124 \times 0.890 = \$1000$$

Thus, the present worth of this investment is $1000, which means that $1000 is the *most* you should pay out today to earn 6% on your investment. It also means that if you paid less than $1000, you would actually be earning more than 6% and the investment would be a bargain. We will discuss this idea in greater detail later. If you had to pay more than $1000, on the other hand, it would not be worthwhile to make this investment, as you could presumably invest $1000 elsewhere at 6% and get exactly $1124 in two years. Two examples of present value calculations appear here.

TABLE 2.3   PRESENT VALUE FACTORS

Period	6%	$i =$ 8%	10%
1	0.943	0.926	0.909
2	0.890	0.857	0.826
3	0.840	0.794	0.751
4	0.792	0.735	0.683
5	0.747	0.681	0.621
6	0.705	0.630	0.565
.	.	.	.
.	.	.	.
.	.	.	.

Example 2.4

1. What is the present worth of $5000 received five years from now if you wish to earn 8%?

$$PV = F_5 \times PVF_{5,8\%}$$
$$= \$5000 \times 0.681 = \$3405$$

2. What is the present value of $8000 received six years from now assuming a 10% return?

$$PV = F_6 \times PVF_{6,10\%}$$
$$= \$8000 \times 0.564 = \$4512$$

Streams of Benefits

Present Value of Benefit Streams

We have just seen that the concept of present value is very useful for analyzing investments which involve the receipt of only one benefit. In fact, we will use this approach to evaluate the residual or terminal values of investments. However, many types of investment proposals involve receipts of multiple benefits over a period of years. Such an investment benefit stream is called an **annuity**.

Irregular Annuity   One type of investment proposal, an **irregular annuity**, is shown schematically in Figure 2.1. In this example, each pay-

FIGURE 2.1   IRREGULAR ANNUITY

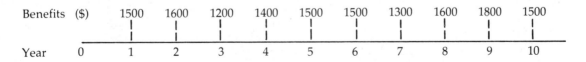

Benefits ($)   1500   1600   1200   1400   1500   1500   1300   1600   1800   1500

Year   0   1   2   3   4   5   6   7   8   9   10

ment is different for the most part. When this is the case, the method used to evaluate the stream of benefits is to find the present value of *each* benefit separately as if it were a single investment situation. These present values are then summed to find the total present value for the annuity. To summarize, the present value of an annuity of n payments, or PVA_n, is:

$$PVA_n = PV_1 + PV_2 + PV_3 + \ldots + PV_n$$
$$= [F_1 \times PVF_{1,i}] + [F_2 \times PVF_{2,i}] +$$
$$[F_3 \times PVF_{3,i}] + \ldots + [F_n \times PVF_{n,i}] \qquad [2.6]$$

Using this format, we may find the present value of the stream in Figure 2.1 at 8%. Refer to Table 2.4.

TABLE 2.4   PRESENT VALUE OF AN IRREGULAR ANNUITY

Year	Benefit ($)	Present Value Factor @ 8%	Present Value ($)
1	1500	0.926	1389
2	1600	0.857	1371
3	1200	0.794	952
4	1400	0.735	1029
5	1500	0.681	1021
6	1500	0.630	945
7	1300	0.583	757
8	1600	0.540	864
9	1800	0.500	900
10	1500	0.463	694
Total	14,900	6.709	9922

$$PVA_{10,8\%} = \$9922$$

Example 2.5

Find the present value of the following stream of benefits at 10%: year 1—$2700; year 2—$3000; year 3—$4200; year 4—$3800; and year 5—$3600.

Year	Benefit	*PVF* @ 10%	Present Value
1	$2700	0.909	$2454
2	$3000	0.826	$2478
3	$4200	0.751	$3154
4	$3800	0.683	$2595
5	$3600	0.621	$2236
Total			$12,917

$$PVA_{5,10\%} = \$12,917$$

Level Annuity   The approach just described will work on any investment no matter what kind of flows of benefits it has. However, observe what happens when each payment in the annuity is the *same*. This is called a **level annuity.** We will use equation [2.6], except that we will assume F is the same in each period. In this case, we will use B to stand for the *equal annual benefits*, which allows us to factor B out of the series, leaving:

$$PVA_n = B \; (PVF_{1,i} + PVF_{2,i} + PVF_{3,i} + \ldots + PVF_{n,i})$$

This expression may also be written as:

$$PVA_n \; = \; B \; \sum_{y=1}^{n} PVF_{y,i} \qquad\qquad [2.7]$$

The sign sigma, Σ, means that the expression just following should be calculated for each value in the series and then added up. There is a value for each year, denoted as integer values of y. The phrase

$$\sum_{y=1}^{n} PVF_{y,i}$$

means you should find the PVF for the interest rate i and each year from 1 to n and add them all up.

To save time, we can devise a table for these amounts. This sum for any given number of years is called the *Present Value Annuity Factor, PVAF*. This yields the computational formula:

$$PVA_n = B \times PVAF_{n,i} \qquad\qquad [2.8]$$

These $PVAF$ factors also appear in the appendix and in Table 2.5.

To illustrate the present value calculation for a level annuity, assume you can purchase a stream of ten payments of $1500 each to be received at the end of each of ten years. Your investments all currently earn 8%.

$$
\begin{aligned}
PVA_{10} &= B \times PVAF_{10,8\%} \\
&= \$1500 \times 6.710 = \$10,065
\end{aligned}
$$

Note that the present value factor 6.710 from the $PVAF$ table is the same as the total of the ten individual factors used in the example in Table 2.4. The slight difference is due to a rounding error in the table values.

TABLE 2.5   PRESENT VALUE OF LEVEL ANNUITY FACTORS

Period	7%	8%	$i =$ 9%	10%
.	.	.	.	.
.	.	.	.	.
.	.	.	.	.
6	4.766	4.623	4.486	4.355
7	5.389	5.206	5.033	4.868
8	5.971	5.747	5.535	5.335
9	6.515	6.247	5.995	5.759
10	7.024	6.710	6.418	6.145
.	.	.	.	.
.	.	.	.	.
.	.	.	.	.

Example 2.6

Using the present value annuity factor table, find the present value of a level annuity of $6000 a year for eight years at 7%.

$$PVA_8 = B \times PVAF_{8,7\%}$$
$$= \$6000 \times 5.971 = \$35,826$$

Perpetuity   There is one other type of annuity, which is evaluated differently from the other two. This is the perpetual annuity or perpetuity. A **perpetuity** is a level annuity which has benefits lasting indefinitely. To avoid an abundance of strenuous math, we will approach this type of benefit stream intuitively. Imagine you wish to make the *minimum* investment you could to yield $1000 per year forever and permit you to earn 10%. In order to obtain a benefit of $1000 per year forever, you must obtain the *entire return from interest*. In fact, your return should be *all* the interest earned. If you earn more than $1000 the first year and only withdraw $1000, your investment would grow. On the other hand, if the interest is less than $1000, your investment will eventually shrink to nothing. Table 2.6 demonstrates what happens to a $3790 investment made to yield $1000 per year. It can be seen that by the end of the fifth year there is no more principal remaining and the annuity will end.

The value of the perpetuity may be found by solving for the investment, assuming each year's return is exactly the interest earned. Thus:

$$B = PV \times i \text{ , or}$$
$$PV = B/i \tag{2.9}$$

28   VALUE CONCEPTS AND ANALYSIS

TABLE 2.6   NON-PERPETUAL ANNUITY

Initial Investment $3790		
Interest First Year @ 10% $379		
From Principal ....__621__	− __621__	
First Payment $1000	$3169	Principal Balance: End of First Year
Interest Second Year @ 10%...... $317		
From Principal ....__683__	− __683__	
Second Payment..............$1000	$2486	Principal Balance: End of Second Year
Interest Third Year @ 10% $249		
From Principal ....__751__	− __751__	
Third Payment $1000	$1735	Principal Balance: End of Third Year
Interest Fourth Year @ 10% $173		
From Principal ....__827__	− __827__	
Fourth Payment $1000	$ 908	Principal Balance: End of Fourth Year
Interest Fifth Year @ 10% .... $ 91		
From Principal ....__908__	− __908__	
Fifth Payment $1000	$ 0	Principal Balance: End of Fifth Year

The value, then, is the benefit payment divided by the interest rate. In our hypothetical situation, we find:

$$PV = \$1000/10\% = \$10,000$$

Example 2.7

Find the present value of a perpetuity of $7200 per year at 8%.

$$PV = \$7200/0.08 = \$90,000$$

The process shown in this section is called **discounting** or **capitalization** and will be discussed in more detail in the next chapter.

A Tip on Technique   Sometimes you will have an annuity which is mostly level, but not completely. In this situation, you may combine methods of calculation. An example is provided here.

Example 2.8

You wish to know the present value of the following annuity at 8%: year 1—$1500; year 2—$1500; year 3—$2000; year 4—$1500; year 5—$1500; and year 6—$1500.

This may be thought of as a level annuity of $1500 per year, plus a single payment of $500 in the third year. The value is given by:

$$PV = (\$1500 \times PVAF_{6,8\%}) + (\$500 \times PVF_{3,8\%})$$
$$= (\$1500 \times 4.623) + (\$500 \times 0.794)$$
$$= \$6934.50 + \$397$$
$$= \$7331.50$$

This method saves time since the entire six-year stream need not be evaluated as an irregular annuity.

Summary   We may now summarize our three annuity calculations and then proceed to some miscellaneous concepts.

1. Irregular Annuity—equation [2.6]

$$PVA_n = (F_1 \times PVF_{1,i}) + (F_2 \times PVF_{2,i}) + (F_3 \times PVF_{3,i}) + \ldots + (F_n \times PVF_{n,i})$$

2. Level Annuity—equation [2.8]

$$PVA_n = B \times PVAF_{n,i}$$

3. Perpetuity—equation [2.9]

$$PV = B/i$$

Future Value of an Annuity

When cash is invested for a period of time, the future value at the end of the period is given by equation [2.3]. However, we have not discussed what happens when money is *accumulated* over a period of time. Say, for instance, parents are saving for their child's education. If they put $1000 per year away at the *end* of each year for ten years, how much will they accumulate after the ten-year period? The answer is fairly simple. The first payment at the end of year one accumulates interest for nine years; the second payment accumulates interest for eight years; the third payment accumulates interest for seven years, etc. The last year's payment earns no interest. Thus, the value of the accumulation may be shown by the equation:

$$FA_n = (S \times FVF_{n-1,i}) + (S \times FVF_{n-2,i}) + \ldots + (S \times FVF_{1,i}) + S$$

This may also be written as:

$$FA_n = S(1 + \sum_{y=1}^{n-1} FVF_{y,i}) \qquad\qquad [2.10]$$

Here FA_n is the *Future Annuity* at the end of n periods and S is the level payment to be saved. The last factor,

$$(1 + \sum_{y=1}^{n-1} FVF_{y,i})$$

is found in a table in the appendix. This quantity will be called the *Accumulation Factor*, AF. Thus the value of an accumulation of n periods at i rate of interest is given by:

$$FA_n = S + AF_{n,i} \qquad\qquad [2.11]$$

We will now turn to an example. Assume that $1000 is accumulated each year for five years at 7%. What is the future value?

$$
\begin{aligned}
FA_5 &= (S \times FVF_{4,7\%}) + (S \times FVF_{3,7\%}) + \\
&\quad (S \times FVF_{2,7\%}) + (S \times FVF_{1,7\%}) + S \\
&= (\$1000 \times 1.311) + (\$1000 \times 1.225) + \\
&\quad (\$1000 \times 1.145) + (\$1000 \times 1.107) + \$1000 \\
&= \$1311 + \$1225 + \$1145 + \$1070 + \$1000 \\
&= \$5751
\end{aligned}
$$

Alternatively this may be calculated using the AF table:

$$
\begin{aligned}
FA_5 &= S \times AF_{5,7\%} \\
&= \$1000 \times 5.751 \\
&= \$5751
\end{aligned}
$$

Example 2.9

Find the future value of an accumulation of $3500 per year for nine years at 6%.

$$
\begin{aligned}
FA_9 &= S \times AF_{9,6\%} \\
&= \$3500 \times 11.491 = \$40,218
\end{aligned}
$$

This concept is useful in some circumstances, but often we know the total amount we want to save and we wish to solve for S, the amount we must save periodically. For this amount, we will move to the idea of a sinking fund.

Sinking Fund

A savings fund accumulated to a desired future amount is a **sinking fund.** Suppose we know that our child's education will cost $10,000. The question is: what must we save each year for ten years at 6% to accumulate this amount? The basic equation may be found by algebraic manipulation of equation [2.11]:

$$FA_n = S \times AF_{n,i} \text{ or}$$
$$S = FA_n \, (1/AF_{n,i}) \qquad\qquad [2.12]$$

We can see that we can find the amount to be accumulated each year by multiplying the desired end result, FA_n, by the reciprocal of the accumulation factor. There is also a table for this reciprocal. It is a table of Sinking Fund Factors SFF, and appears in the appendix. Thus:

$$S = FA_n \times SFF_{n,i} \qquad\qquad [2.13]$$

We can now find the solution to the problem using this equation and the SFF table:

$$S = FA_{10} \times SFF_{10,6\%}$$
$$= \$10,000 \times 0.076$$
$$= \$760 \text{ per year}$$

This answer may be checked by reversing the process. If $760 is accumulated each year for ten years at 6%, how much will be saved?

$$FA_{10} = \$760 \times AF_{10,6\%}$$
$$= \$760 \times 13.181$$
$$= \$10,017$$

The concept of the sinking fund will be especially useful later when we talk about replacement reserves.

Example 2.10

An investor wishes to accumulate $10,000 in eight years. If he can invest at 7%, how much will he have to save at the end of each year?

$$S = FA_8 \times SFF_{8,7\%}$$
$$= \$10,000 \times 0.097$$
$$= \$970 \text{ per year}$$

Amortization of Loans

Another concept we will consider is that of **loan amortization.** Loan amortization refers to the division of a loan obligation into a schedule of payments. The present value of an annuity showed us how to evaluate a stream of benefits for a particular period of time. Now imagine you are a lender who has just lent someone $20,000 to be paid back in ten years in equal installments to yield you, the lender, 8%. You should recognize the amount lent as the present value of a ten-year annuity. To refresh your memory, equation [2.8] gives the value of a level annuity:

$$PVA_n = B \times PVAF_{n,i}$$

With a little algebra we can solve for B, the amount of each of the level payments to be received:

$$B = PVA_n \, (1/PVAF_{n,i})$$

We can see that we can find the payment, B, by dividing the amount of the loan, PVA_n, by the present value annuity factor. Restated:

$$B = \frac{\text{Loan Amount}}{PVAF_{n,i}} \qquad\qquad [2.14]$$

The quantity ($1/PVAF_{n,i}$) has been converted into a table of *AM*ortization Factors, $AMF_{n,i}$, and is located in the appendix. Equation [2.14] may be restated as:

$$\text{Loan Payment} = \text{Loan Amount} \times AMF_{n,i} \qquad\qquad [2.15]$$

The problem may be solved using the table of amortization factors as:

$$\begin{aligned}
\text{Loan Payment} &= \$20,000 \times AMF_{10,8\%} \\
&= \$20,000 \times 0.149 \\
&= \$2980 \text{ per year}
\end{aligned}$$

The problem could also be solved using the annuity table:

$$\begin{aligned}
B &= \$20,000/PVAF_{10,8\%} \\
&= \$20,000/6.710 \\
&= \$2980 \text{ per year}
\end{aligned}$$

Example 2.11

A loan of $40,000 at 6% is to be amortized over fifteen years. What should the level payment be?

Loan Payment = $40,000 $\times$ $AMF_{15,6\%}$
     = $40,000 $\times$ 0.103
     = $4120 per year

To be completely realistic, several points of clarification are in order here. First, loans are really made involving an annual payment such as the one described in our preceding discussion. To find the monthly payment involves using a table which consumes a great deal of space. This table has not been included but is generally available in any library or at a local financial institution. We can approximate the monthly payment very closely by dividing the annual payment by 12. In example 2.11, we would approximate the payment as follows:

Monthly payment = $4120/12
        = $343 per month

The actual monthly payment from this loan would be $338. As you can see, our approximation technique results in only a small error. Further, the error will always be conservative.

A second point that should be made is that not all loans on real estate are *fully amortized* as are the ones we previously discussed. Fully amortized means that during the life of the loan the entire principal and the appropriate interest will be paid. Generally, fully amortized loans have a level payment, consisting of a different proportion of principal and interest each period. Sometimes, however, the lender may use other arrangements for the repayment of the loan:

1. *Level Amortization of Principal.*   With this format, the principal of the loan will be divided into equal parts and the appropriate interest on the unpaid balance will be added to each payment, making the first payment the biggest and the last payment the smallest.

2. *Interest-Only Payments.*   Under certain circumstances, lenders make loans in which the borrower only pays the interest for the first few years, followed then by a period of amortization. Many times, in such a loan, the entire principal will not be paid at the end of the term. Here a final large payment, called a *balloon,* must be made to discharge the obligation.

3. *Variable Payments.*   With the high interest rates prevailing in the mid-to-late 1970s, various institutions in some states began experi-

menting with loan payment schedules which start with low payments and gradually get higher during the life of the loan. These payments follow the growing income of a young family, making it easier for them to own a home.

One final point may now be made. We have not discussed any calculations for these odd variations here to avoid confusing you with too much detail. With the numerous business calculators and programmable calculators, not to mention home computers which are now prevalent, most of these calculations can be easily made. See the references at the end of the book for some sources relating to this material. In fact, all of the calculations requiring tables from this chapter can be done far more easily on a good business calculator.

CHAPTER TWO SUMMARY

This completes our discussion of the basic tools of cash flow evaluation, often called *discounting* or *capitalization*. We looked at several concepts, seven of which will be especially useful in our study of real estate analysis. To refresh your memory, we will list the seven computational equations and the appropriate table references in the appendix at the end of this chapter.

In this chapter we have spent most of our time dealing with the techniques and concepts relating to the process of evaluating cash flows. In following chapters we will discuss the decision situations which will require these tools and will frequently refer to the equations summarized at the end of this chapter.

KEY TERMS

Capitalization	Future Value	Perpetuity
Compound Interest	Irregular Annuity	Present Value
Deferred Annuity (see the appendix to this chapter)	Level Annuity	Simple Interest
	Loan Amortization	Sinking Fund
Discounting		

QUESTIONS FOR STUDY AND DISCUSSION

1. Why do we consider only cash when discussing investment value?

2. What three primary considerations must be accounted for when a cash stream is evaluated?

3. Why is present value used to evaluate alternative investments rather than another concept, such as future value?

4. What is meant by *capitalizing* a stream of benefits?

5. This chapter mentioned annual and quarterly compounding. Can you think of other types of compounding which are frequently used? What do you suppose *continuous compounding* means? What type of compounding would yield you the greatest return on your investment?

PROBLEMS FOR REVIEW

1. You invest $5000 at 8% for five years. What is your end value?

2. Find the future value of $6000 at 10% for seven years.

3. You invest $8000 at 8% for five years. Your earnings are compounded quarterly. What is your future value?

4. At 8% interest, how long will it take your investment to double in value?

5. You invest $5000 for five years. At the end of this period, you receive $7700. What rate of interest did you earn?

6. You have invested $6000 at 6% interest and received $9565. For how many years did you invest?

7. Which is worth more to you: $10,000 received eight years from now or $5000 today? Your investment rate is 8%.

8. Would your answer to question 7 be different if you would earn 9%? 10%?

9. You have invested $5000 and received $7520 in seven years. At what rate have you invested? Can you solve this problem using more than one table in the appendix?

10. What is the present value of a level annuity of $3000 per year for ten years at 10%?

11. Find the present value of a level annuity of $4200 per year for seven years if you are earning 6%.

12. You can make an investment which yields the following benefits at the end of each year for five years: year 1—$2500; year 2—$2000; year 3—$3000; year 4—$2800; and year 5—$3500. What is the present value of this investment at 9%?

13. You have been given the choice between two alternative investments. One provides you with a stream of five benefits as follows: year 1—$2000; year 2—$2500; year 3—$4000; year 4—$3000; and year 5—$3500. The other investment is a single sum of $17,350 to be received at the end of five years. You are investing to earn 8%. Which would you prefer to invest in?

14. You can purchase an investment which will yield benefits of $5000 per year indefinitely. What should you pay for this investment if you wish to earn 10%?

15. You have a prospective investment which will yield $1000 semiannually for five years. What is the present value of this proposal if you earn 10% on an annual basis?

16. An investment is available to you which will allow you to earn $2000 per year for eight years and a bonus of $10,000 at the end of the eighth year. What is its present value at 7%?

17. You find an investment proposal which will yield $5000 per year for eight years, the first payment to be received at the end of the tenth year. What is the present value at 8%?

18. You wish to save $20,000 in fifteen years. How much should you deposit each year to accomplish this if you are saving at 8%?

19. You are planning to save $2500 per year for eight years at 7%. How much will you accumulate?

20. You have just borrowed $30,000 at 6%. How much will you have to pay each year to pay this loan back in twenty years?

APPENDIX
TO CHAPTER 2

Glossary of Symbols
Factors from Tables
Computational Formulas with Table References
Deferred Present Value

Glossary of Symbols

F = Future value of a single sum

P = Present value or initial investment

PV = Present value or initial investment (or P)

i = Rate of return, also called discount rate or capitalization rate

I = Interest earnings from an investment ($)

n = Number of periods over which an investment is to be considered

PVA = Present value of an annuity

B = Uniform benefit of a level annuity or perpetuity

Σ = Summation sign which means to add up a number of calculations to derive a sum

FA = Future value of an annuity; arises when an amount is saved periodically for a certain number of periods

S = Sinking fund payment; refers to amount being saved periodically

Factors from Tables

FVF = Future Value Factor

$(1 + i)^n$

PVF = Present Value Factor

$1/(1 + i)^n$

$PVAF$ = Present Value of an Annuity Factor

$\sum\limits_{y=1}^{n} PVF_{y,i}$

AF = Accumulation Factor

$1 + \sum\limits_{y=1}^{n-1} FVF_{y,i}$

SFF = Sinking Fund Factor

$1/AF_{n,i}$

AMF = Amortization Factor

$1/PVAF_{n,i}$

Computational Formulas with Table References

1. Future Value of a Single Sum
   FVF Table

   $$F_n = P \times FVF_{n,i} \qquad [2.3]$$

2. Future Value of a Level Accumulation
   AF Table

   $$FA_n = S \times AF_{n,i} \qquad [2.11]$$

3. Present Value of a Single Sum
   PVF Table

   $$PV = F_n \times PVF_{n,i} \qquad [2.5]$$

4. Present Value of a Level Annuity
   PVAF Table

   $$PVA_n = B \times PVAF_{n,i} \qquad [2.8]$$

5. Present Value of a Perpetual Annuity
   no table

   $$PV = B/i \qquad [2.9]$$

6. Sinking Fund Payment
   SFF Table

   $$S = FA_n \times SFF_{n,i} \qquad [2.13]$$

7. Amortization of a Loan
   AMF Table

   $$\text{Loan Payment} = \text{Loan Amount} \times AMF_{n,i} \qquad [2.15]$$

Deferred Present Value

Sometimes it becomes necessary to consider the present value of an annuity that does not begin until sometime in the future, a **deferred annuity**. For example, assume you are going to receive an annuity of $10,000 a year for twenty years, beginning eleven years from now. What should you be willing to pay for this today if you wish to have your investment earn 8%?

First, we must treat the annuity. An annuity of twenty years at 8% has a present value of $98,180 calculated as follows:

$$PV = B \times PVAF_{20,8\%}$$
$$= \$10,000 \times 9.818$$
$$= \$98,180$$

However, this calculation tells you the present value as it will be ten years from now (at the beginning of the eleventh year). Thus,

we must bring this present value back to today as follows:

$$PV = F \times PVF_{10,8\%}$$
$$= \$98,180 \times 0.463$$
$$= \$45,457$$

This means that an investment of $45,457 today will earn enough interest at 8% to begin paying a $10,000-a-year annuity in eleven years, which will last twenty years beyond that.

A similar answer may be obtained by realizing that this problem merely represents an annuity of thirty years with the first ten years missing. Therefore, the answer may also be found by deducting one factor from another as follows:

$$PVAF_{10\,-\,30,8\%} = PVAF_{30,8\%} - PVAF_{10,8\%}$$
$$= 11.258 - 6.710$$
$$= 4.548$$

Our solution becomes:

$$PV = \$10,000 \times 4.548$$
$$= \$45,480$$

FIGURE 2.2 DEFERRED ANNUITY

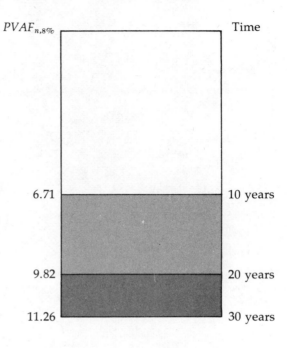

$PVAF_{n,8\%}$ ... Time

6.71 — 10 years

9.82 — 20 years

11.26 — 30 years

This technique may also be used for deferred single sum present value problems. This latter approach may be viewed in Figure 2.2.

The benefits equal $10,000 per year at the end of each of the years 10 through 30 (the beginning of the eleventh year). The present value factors on the left of Figure 2.2 show the relative investment required to generate each ten-year block of the annuity. Each ten-year block provides ten payments. Since we do not want the first ten years, we can subtract the present value of the missing block from that for the whole column.

3

BASIC VALUE
CONCEPTS II –
CAPITALIZATION

BEFORE WE begin our presentation of real estate appraisal and investment analysis, we will describe some basic concepts that we will be using throughout our discussions. First, we will look at a number of different types of income streams that may be assumed to apply to real estate investments. We will examine the general process of evaluating these various streams. Then we will examine the concept of capitalization rates and how they may be calculated.

Real Estate Income Streams

There are two major components of the returns (benefits) from an investment. First, the investment earns a periodic return, *interest*, for instance, on its outstanding value. Second, when the investment has a finite life, a portion of its value is *recaptured* and returned to the investor each year. The first component of return is called the **return on investment** (ROI). The second component is called the **recapture of capital** (ROC). We will be illustrating these concepts for various types of income streams, starting with the level annuity.

Level Annuity

In Table 2.6 we portrayed an investment which, if purchased for $3790, would return 10% to the investor in a stream of five $1000 annual payments. The data from this investment are summarized in Table 3.1 and shows the two components of return clearly. Note that the outstanding balance is determined by subtracting the year's principal recapture from the previous year's outstanding balance.

TABLE 3.1   LEVEL ANNUITY

Year	Income	Interest @ 10%	Capital Recapture	Year End Outstanding Balance
1	$1000	$379	$621	$3169
2	$1000	$317	$683	$2486
3	$1000	$249	$751	$1735
4	$1000	$173	$827	$ 908
5	$1000	$ 91	$909	$ 0
total	$5000	$1209	$3791	

As we can see from the table, a portion of the original investment is returned each year, so the net investment decreases each period. This principal recapture is the recapture of capital. Also notice how in each year's income of $1000 a portion consists of a 10% return on the outstanding value. This amount is the return on investment component. The *level annuity,* then, *when purchased at its present value automatically provides both components of return.* This type of income stream is shown schematically in Figure 3.1.

We have seen how convenient it is to find the present value of a level annuity. Further, we have noted that the normal value calculation automatically allows for ROI and ROC. However, we can *only* use this type of valuation method if we expect that the income we will receive from a property will actually be a *constant, finite stream.* Indeed, we will be able to make this assumption in some cases, but there are other assumptions that may also be made.

Straight-Line-Declining Income

Another common assumption is that the income declines over time. The cash flow resulting from a real estate investment, especially one held for the entire productive life of the asset, declines because of two factors. **Net operating income** (NOI) is defined as gross income less operating expenses. Often, gross income declines and, at the same time, operating costs rise as the asset moves through its life. In fact, the definition of **economic life** is the length of time it takes for net operating income (excluding depreciation) to decline to zero. This decline in NOI is shown

FIGURE 3.1   PRESENT VALUE OF LEVEL ANNUITY

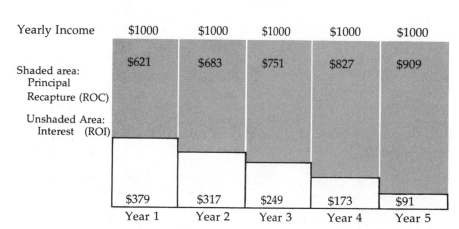

Yearly Income	$1000	$1000	$1000	$1000	$1000
Shaded area: Principal Recapture (ROC)	$621	$683	$751	$827	$909
Unshaded Area: Interest (ROI)	$379	$317	$249	$173	$91
	Year 1	Year 2	Year 3	Year 4	Year 5

in Figure 3.2. It must be noted that whenever we refer to "income" we will mean either NOI or cash flow, not gross income.

The question is: How can these declining streams be evaluated? We cannot use the level annuity method. There is a convenient way to do the evaluation, however. We may assume that the stream declines in such a way so that it provides a *constant recapture of principal*. This is a **straight-line-declining income stream.** We merely divide the first year's income by a **capitalization rate** composed of a return on investment (ROI) component and a recapture of capital (ROC) component.

To find the capitalization rate, we first determine what rate of return we wish to have on our investment (ROI). Then we determine what we estimate that the economic life of the asset will be. The rate of recapture (ROC) is found by dividing 1 by the life of the asset. For instance, if an asset is expected to have a five-year life, then the rate of recapture is 20% per year:

$$1/5 = 20\%$$

The overall rate of return, capitalization rate, in this circumstance is then calculated by adding the return on investment to the recapture rate. Let us say we required a 10% return on the investment. The overall capitalization rate would then be 30%:

$$10\% + 20\% = 30\%$$

FIGURE 3.2   DECLINING INCOME STREAM

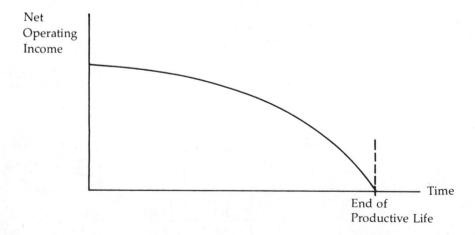

Example 3.1

Calculate the appropriate recapture rates for these useful lives.

1. Useful life of ten years.

   Recapture rate = 1/10 = 10% per year

2. Useful life of fifteen years.

   Recapture rate = 1/15 = 6.67% per year

We can now proceed to an evaluation of a prospective investment. Let us say we have a five-year investment which is expected to produce a straight-line-declining income stream with a first-year cash flow of $3000. What is the value of this investment if we require a 10% return on investment? The capitalization rate is 30%, as shown previously, so the value would be $10,000:

$$PV = \$3000 \text{ first-year income} / 30\% = \$10,000.$$

The data from this investment are shown in Table 3.2. Note how the stream declines over the life of the investment, while providing both components of return.

The declining income stream may also be shown schematically as in Figure 3.3.

This method of dividing the first-year income by the capitalization rate conveniently provides the present value of this specifically shaped income stream. This income stream may also be recognized as an irregular annuity and could also be evaluated by taking the present value of each year's income using the appropriate values from the present value table, *PVF*, though the process would be far more laborious. This step may be verified by the student as an exercise.

TABLE 3.2 DECLINING INCOME STREAM

Year	Income	Interest @ 10%	Recapture of Capital	Year End Outstanding Balance
1	$3000	$1000	$2000	$8000
2	$2800	$ 800	$2000	$6000
3	$2600	$ 600	$2000	$4000
4	$2400	$ 400	$2000	$2000
5	$2200	$ 200	$2000	$ 0
Total	$13,000	$3000	$10,000	

FIGURE 3.3   STRAIGHT-LINE-DECLINING INCOME STREAM

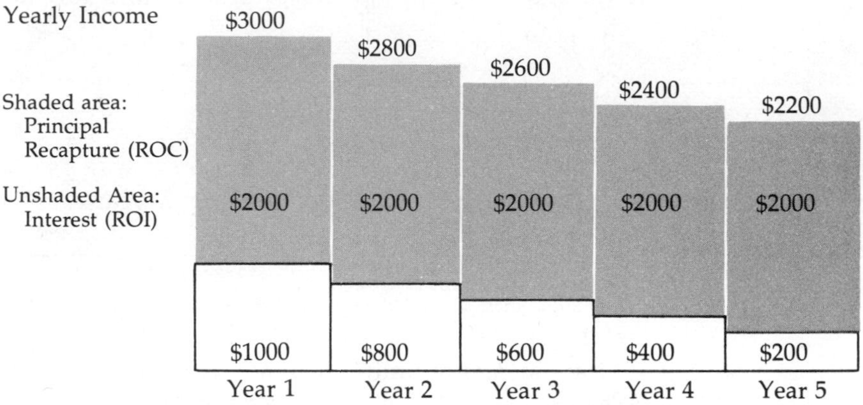

Example 3.2

Assume an investment will have a straight-line-declining income stream with a first-year income of $5000. Find the value of this stream if you require a 12% return on investment and the rate of recapture is 8%.

Capitalization rate = 12% + 8% = 20%
PV = $5000/20% = $25,000

Other Income Streams

The previous two types of income patterns are probably two of the most practical and widely used in basic analysis. Level annuities are generally used when the asset is held less than its productive life, as is often the case. In these cases, the investment may not be held long enough for income to begin to decline. The level annuity is also assumed in some types of classic appraisal situations, often with older properties. The straight-line-declining income stream is most often used in classic income appraisal analysis for property improvements and for investments held for the entire life of the asset.

While some assets have finite lives—buildings, for example—land has an infinite life. For this kind of investment, we usually apply the perpetuity as the model of the income stream. The value of this type of income stream is simply found by dividing the expected annual income by the rate of return required (refer to equation [2.9]). Such an income stream is shown schematically in Figure 3.4.

Example 3.3

Assume the benefits depicted in Figure 3.4 are for a parcel of land and are expected to be $10,000 per year indefinitely. If the required ROI is 10%, what will the value of this land be?

$PV = \$10,000/0.10 = \$100,000$

There are situations in which none of these model income streams is appropriate. It may be that income rises and then declines as illustrated in Figure 3.5.

Versions of this latter type of income stream are used, particularly by sophisticated analysts. There are special tables which help analysts find the proper present value. However, the basic approach we used to determine the value of an irregular annuity may also be used if we partition the income as shown by the vertical lines in Figure 3.5.

This completes our discussion of various types of income streams. Some problems utilizing the models presented thus far will follow at the end of the chapter.

FIGURE 3.4   PERPETUAL ANNUITY

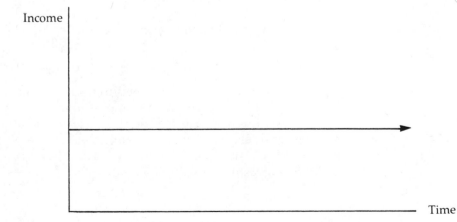

FIGURE 3.5   INCOME STREAM UNADAPTABLE TO BASIC MODELS

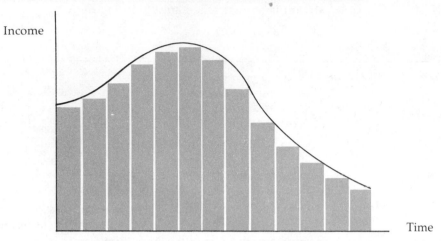

Capitalization Rates

So far we have just skirted the question of capitalization rate on investment returns. We have generally assumed the rate of return for our example problems. In this section we will discuss the question more carefully.

The rate of return on an investment is obviously compensation. The question is: compensation for what? First, it is compensation for time. When people make an investment, they give up the ability to consume. For the time the consumption must be postponed, investors need compensation. Second, the return on an investment is compensation for risk. We have said that investors are risk-averse. For that reason, they must be compensated for the risks they take. Finally, the rate of return represents an opportunity rate. The **opportunity rate of return** is the *highest* return the investor is giving up on an alternative investment to the one under consideration at the *same risk level*.

Opportunity Rate of Return

The process of investing is assumed to take place in the context of alternatives. For every investment proposal which one can view at a given level of risk, it is assumed that there is at least one other proposal that may be considered at that risk level. Let us say that at a given level of risk, which we shall denote as risk level x, a hypothetical investor can make five investments with various known returns as shown in Table 3.3.[1]

---

[1] The concept of a risk class or risk level will be discussed in more detail in chapter 9.

APPENDIX ONE
—COMPOUND INTEREST TABLES

Table Set 1
PVF, PVAF, FVF, AF

Table Set 2
Amortization Factors

Table Set 3
Sinking Fund Factors

Table Set 4
Loan Amortization Tables

APPENDIX TWO
—REFERENCES

APPENDIX THREE
—GLOSSARY OF TERMS AND SYMBOLS

APPENDIX ONE
COMPOUND INTEREST TABLES

Table Set One—Compound Interest

These tables contain the four basic present and future value factors as defined in chapter 2. These factors are all based on *annual compounding* of the nominal rate of interest.

PVF = Present Value Factor
$PVAF$ = Present Value Annuity Factor
FVF = Future Value Factor
AF = Accumulation Factor

Table Set Two—Amortization Factors

This table shows the amortization factor which is multiplied by the principal amount of a loan to find the *annual* payment on the loan. The payments so determined are level. The annual payments may be divided by twelve to derive an approximate monthly payment.

Table Set Three—Sinking Fund Factors

This table shows the factors required to determine the amount that must be saved annually to accumulate a dollar at the end of n years.

Table Set Four—Loan Amortization Tables

These tables present the percentage of an annual loan payment which is interest for each payment in the given loan and the percentage which the remaining balance is of the original loan amount at the end of each period. Payments are on an *annual basis* rather than a monthly one.

TABLE SET ONE
COMPOUND INTEREST:
PVF, PVAF, FVF, AF

ANNUAL COMPOUND INTEREST TABLES, INTEREST = 3%

Year	FVF	AF	PVF	PVAF
1	1.030	1.000	0.971	0.971
2	1.061	2.030	0.943	1.913
3	1.093	3.091	0.915	2.829
4	1.126	4.184	0.888	3.717
5	1.159	5.309	0.863	4.580
6	1.194	6.468	0.837	5.417
7	1.230	7.662	0.813	6.230
8	1.267	8.892	0.789	7.020
9	1.305	10.159	0.766	7.786
10	1.344	11.464	0.744	8.530
11	1.384	12.808	0.722	9.253
12	1.426	14.192	0.701	9.954
13	1.469	15.618	0.681	10.635
14	1.513	17.086	0.661	11.296
15	1.558	18.599	0.642	11.938
16	1.605	20.157	0.623	12.561
17	1.653	21.762	0.605	13.166
18	1.702	23.414	0.587	13.754
19	1.754	25.117	0.570	14.324
20	1.806	26.870	0.554	14.877
25	2.094	36.459	0.478	17.413
30	2.427	47.575	0.412	19.600
35	2.814	60.462	0.355	21.487
40	3.262	75.401	0.307	23.115
50	4.384	112.797	0.228	25.730

ANNUAL COMPOUND INTEREST TABLES, INTEREST = 5%

Year	FVF	AF	PVF	PVAF
1	1.050	1.000	0.952	0.952
2	1.102	2.050	0.907	1.859
3	1.158	3.152	0.864	2.723
4	1.216	4.310	0.823	3.546
5	1.276	5.526	0.784	4.329
6	1.340	6.802	0.746	5.076
7	1.407	8.142	0.711	5.786
8	1.477	9.549	0.677	6.463
9	1.551	11.027	0.645	7.108
10	1.629	12.578	0.614	7.722
11	1.710	14.207	0.585	8.306
12	1.796	15.917	0.557	8.863
13	1.886	17.713	0.530	9.394
14	1.980	19.599	0.505	9.899
15	2.079	21.579	0.481	10.380
16	2.183	23.657	0.458	10.838
17	2.292	25.840	0.436	11.274
18	2.407	28.132	0.416	11.690
19	2.527	30.539	0.396	12.085
20	2.653	33.066	0.377	12.462
25	3.386	47.727	0.295	14.094
30	4.322	66.439	0.231	15.372
35	5.516	90.320	0.181	16.374
40	7.040	120.800	0.142	17.159
50	11.467	209.348	0.087	18.256

ANNUAL COMPOUND INTEREST TABLES, INTEREST = 6%

Year	*FVF*	*AF*	*PVF*	*PVAF*
1	1.060	1.000	0.943	0.943
2	1.124	2.060	0.890	1.833
3	1.191	3.184	0.840	2.673
4	1.262	4.375	0.792	3.465
5	1.338	5.637	0.747	4.212
6	1.419	6.975	0.705	4.917
7	1.504	8.394	0.665	5.562
8	1.594	9.897	0.627	6.210
9	1.689	11.491	0.592	6.802
10	1.791	13.181	0.558	7.360
11	1.898	14.972	0.527	7.887
12	2.012	16.870	0.497	8.384
13	2.133	18.882	0.469	8.853
14	2.261	21.015	0.442	9.295
15	2.397	23.276	0.417	9.712
16	2.540	25.673	0.394	10.106
17	2.693	28.213	0.371	10.477
18	2.854	30.906	0.350	10.828
19	3.026	33.760	0.331	11.158
20	3.207	36.786	0.312	11.470
25	4.292	54.865	0.233	12.783
30	5.743	79.058	0.174	13.765
35	7.686	111.435	0.130	14.498
40	10.286	154.762	0.097	15.046
50	18.420	290.336	0.054	15.762

ANNUAL COMPOUND INTEREST TABLES, INTEREST = 7%

Year	FVF	AF	PVF	PVAF
1	1.070	1.000	0.935	0.935
2	1.145	2.070	0.873	1.808
3	1.225	3.215	0.816	2.624
4	1.311	4.440	0.763	3.387
5	1.403	5.751	0.713	4.100
6	1.501	7.153	0.666	4.767
7	1.606	8.654	0.623	5.389
8	1.718	10.260	0.582	5.971
9	1.838	11.978	0.544	6.515
10	1.967	13.816	0.508	7.024
11	2.105	15.784	0.475	7.499
12	2.252	17.888	0.444	7.943
13	2.410	20.141	0.415	8.358
14	2.579	22.550	0.388	8.745
15	2.759	25.129	0.362	9.108
16	2.952	27.888	0.339	9.447
17	3.159	30.840	0.317	9.763
18	3.380	33.999	0.296	10.059
19	3.617	37.379	0.277	10.336
20	3.870	40.995	0.258	10.594
25	5.427	63.249	0.184	11.654
30	7.612	94.461	0.131	12.409
35	10.677	138.237	0.094	12.948
40	14.974	199.635	0.067	13.332
50	29.457	406.529	0.034	13.801

ANNUAL COMPOUND INTEREST TABLES, INTEREST = 8%

Year	FVF	AF	PVF	PVAF
1	1.080	1.000	0.926	0.926
2	1.166	2.080	0.857	1.783
3	1.260	3.246	0.794	2.577
4	1.360	4.506	0.735	3.312
5	1.469	5.867	0.681	3.993
6	1.587	7.336	0.630	4.623
7	1.714	8.923	0.583	5.206
8	1.851	10.637	0.540	5.747
9	1.999	12.488	0.500	6.247
10	2.159	14.487	0.463	6.710
11	2.332	16.645	0.429	7.139
12	2.518	18.977	0.397	7.536
13	2.720	21.495	0.368	7.904
14	2.937	24.215	0.340	8.244
15	3.172	27.152	0.315	8.559
16	3.426	30.324	0.292	8.851
17	3.700	33.750	0.270	9.122
18	3.996	37.450	0.250	9.372
19	4.316	41.446	0.232	9.604
20	4.661	45.762	0.215	9.818
25	6.848	73.106	0.146	10.675
30	10.063	113.283	0.099	11.258
35	14.785	172.317	0.068	11.655
40	21.725	259.057	0.046	11.925
50	46.902	573.770	0.021	12.233

ANNUAL COMPOUND INTEREST TABLES, INTEREST = 9%

Year	FVF	AF	PVF	PVAF
1	1.090	1.000	0.917	0.917
2	1.188	2.090	0.842	1.759
3	1.295	3.278	0.772	2.531
4	1.412	4.573	0.708	3.240
5	1.539	5.985	0.650	3.890
6	1.677	7.523	0.596	4.486
7	1.828	9.200	0.547	5.033
8	1.993	11.028	0.502	5.535
9	2.172	13.021	0.460	5.995
10	2.367	15.193	0.422	6.418
11	2.580	17.560	0.388	6.805
12	2.813	20.141	0.356	7.161
13	3.066	22.953	0.326	7.487
14	3.342	26.019	0.299	7.786
15	3.642	29.361	0.275	8.061
16	3.970	33.003	0.252	8.313
17	4.328	36.974	0.231	8.544
18	4.717	41.301	0.212	8.756
19	5.142	46.018	0.194	8.950
20	5.604	51.160	0.178	9.129
25	8.623	84.701	0.116	9.823
30	13.268	136.308	0.075	10.274
35	20.414	215.711	0.049	10.567
40	31.409	337.882	0.032	10.757
50	74.358	815.084	0.013	10.962

ANNUAL COMPOUND INTEREST TABLES, INTEREST = 10%

Year	FVF	AF	PVF	PVAF
1	1.100	1.000	0.909	0.909
2	1.210	2.100	0.826	1.736
3	1.331	3.310	0.751	2.487
4	1.464	4.641	0.683	3.170
5	1.611	6.105	0.621	3.791
6	1.772	7.716	0.564	4.355
7	1.949	9.487	0.513	4.868
8	2.144	11.436	0.467	5.335
9	2.358	13.579	0.424	5.759
10	2.594	15.937	0.386	6.145
11	2.853	18.531	0.350	6.495
12	3.138	21.384	0.319	6.814
13	3.452	24.523	0.290	7.103
14	3.797	27.975	0.263	7.367
15	4.177	31.772	0.239	7.606
16	4.595	35.950	0.218	7.824
17	5.054	40.545	0.198	8.022
18	5.560	45.599	0.180	8.201
19	6.116	51.159	0.164	8.365
20	6.728	57.275	0.149	8.514
25	10.835	98.347	0.092	9.077
30	17.449	164.494	0.057	9.427
35	28.102	271.024	0.036	9.644
40	45.259	442.593	0.022	9.779
50	117.391	1163.909	0.009	9.915

ANNUAL COMPOUND INTEREST TABLES, INTEREST = 12%

Year	FVF	AF	PVF	PVAF
1	1.120	1.000	0.893	0.893
2	1.254	2.120	0.797	1.690
3	1.405	3.374	0.712	2.402
4	1.574	4.779	0.636	3.037
5	1.762	6.353	0.567	3.605
6	1.974	8.115	0.507	4.111
7	2.211	10.089	0.452	4.564
8	2.476	12.300	0.404	4.968
9	2.773	14.776	0.361	5.328
10	3.106	17.549	0.322	5.650
11	3.479	20.655	0.287	5.938
12	3.896	24.133	0.257	6.194
13	4.363	28.029	0.229	6.424
14	4.887	32.393	0.205	6.628
15	5.474	37.280	0.183	6.811
16	6.130	42.753	0.163	6.974
17	6.866	48.884	0.146	7.120
18	7.690	55.750	0.130	7.250
19	8.613	63.440	0.116	7.366
20	9.646	72.052	0.104	7.469
25	17.000	133.334	0.059	7.843
30	29.960	241.333	0.033	8.055
35	52.800	431.663	0.019	8.176
40	93.051	767.091	0.011	8.244
50	289.002	2400.018	0.003	8.304

ANNUAL COMPOUND INTEREST TABLES, INTEREST = 15%

Year	FVF	AF	PVF	PVAF
1	1.150	1.000	0.870	0.870
2	1.322	2.150	0.756	1.626
3	1.521	3.472	0.658	2.283
4	1.749	4.993	0.572	2.855
5	2.011	6.742	0.497	3.352
6	2.313	8.754	0.432	3.784
7	2.660	11.067	0.376	4.160
8	3.059	13.727	0.327	4.487
9	3.518	16.786	0.284	4.772
10	4.046	20.304	0.247	5.019
11	4.652	24.349	0.215	5.234
12	5.350	29.002	0.187	5.421
13	6.153	34.352	0.163	5.583
14	7.076	40.505	0.141	5.724
15	8.137	47.580	0.123	5.847
16	9.358	55.717	0.107	5.954
17	10.761	65.075	0.093	6.047
18	12.375	75.836	0.081	6.128
19	14.232	88.212	0.070	6.198
20	16.367	102.444	0.061	6.259
25	32.919	212.793	0.030	6.464
30	66.212	434.745	0.015	6.566
35	133.176	881.170	0.008	6.617
40	267.864	1779.090	0.004	6.642
50	1083.657	7217.716	0.001	6.661

ANNUAL COMPOUND INTEREST TABLES, INTEREST = 20%

Year	FVF	AF	PVF	PVAF
1	1.200	1.000	0.833	0.833
2	1.440	2.200	0.694	1.528
3	1.728	3.640	0.579	2.106
4	2.074	5.368	0.482	2.589
5	2.488	7.442	0.402	2.991
6	2.986	9.930	0.335	3.326
7	3.583	12.916	0.279	3.605
8	4.300	16.499	0.233	3.837
9	5.160	20.799	0.194	4.031
10	6.192	25.959	0.162	4.192
11	7.430	32.150	0.135	4.327
12	8.916	39.581	0.112	4.439
13	10.699	48.497	0.093	4.533
14	12.839	59.196	0.078	4.611
15	15.407	72.035	0.065	4.675
16	18.488	87.442	0.054	4.730
17	22.186	105.931	0.045	4.775
18	26.623	128.117	0.038	4.812
19	31.948	154.740	0.031	4.843
20	38.338	186.688	0.026	4.870
25	95.396	471.981	0.010	4.948
30	237.376	1181.882	0.004	4.979
35	590.668	2948.341	0.002	4.992
40	1469.772	7343.858	0.001	4.997
50	9100.438	45497.191	0.000	4.999

ANNUAL COMPOUND INTEREST TABLES, INTEREST = 25%

Year	FVF	AF	PVF	PVAF
1	1.250	1.000	0.800	0.800
2	1.562	2.250	0.640	1.440
3	1.953	3.812	0.512	1.952
4	2.441	5.766	0.410	2.362
5	3.052	8.207	0.328	2.689
6	3.815	11.259	0.262	2.951
7	4.768	15.073	0.210	3.161
8	5.960	19.842	0.168	3.329
9	7.451	25.802	0.134	3.463
10	9.313	33.253	0.107	3.571
11	11.642	42.566	0.086	3.656
12	14.552	54.208	0.069	3.725
13	18.190	68.760	0.055	3.780
14	22.737	86.949	0.044	3.824
15	28.422	109.687	0.035	3.859
16	35.527	138.109	0.028	3.887
17	44.409	173.636	0.023	3.910
18	55.511	218.045	0.018	3.928
19	69.389	273.556	0.014	3.942
20	86.736	342.945	0.012	3.954
25	264.698	1054.791	0.004	3.985
30	807.794	3227.174	0.001	3.995
35	2465.190	9856.761	0.000	3.998
40	7523.164	30088.655	0.000	3.999
50	70064.923	280255.693	0.000	4.000

TABLE SET TWO
AMORTIZATION FACTORS

AMORTIZATION FACTORS

			Interest Rate		
Year	8%	8½%	9%	9½%	10%
5	0.250	0.254	0.257	0.260	0.264
10	0.149	0.152	0.156	0.159	0.163
15	0.117	0.120	0.124	0.128	0.131
20	0.102	0.106	0.110	0.113	0.117
25	0.094	0.098	0.102	0.106	0.110
30	0.089	0.093	0.097	0.102	0.106
35	0.086	0.090	0.095	0.099	0.104
40	0.084	0.088	0.093	0.098	0.102

TABLE SET THREE
SINKING FUND FACTORS

SINKING FUND FACTORS

			Interest Rate			
Year	5%	6%	7%	8%	9%	10%
1	1.000	1.000	1.000	1.000	1.000	1.000
2	0.488	0.485	0.483	0.481	0.478	0.476
3	0.317	0.314	0.311	0.308	0.305	0.302
4	0.232	0.229	0.225	0.222	0.219	0.215
5	0.181	0.177	0.174	0.170	0.167	0.164
6	0.147	0.143	0.140	0.136	0.133	0.130
7	0.123	0.119	0.116	0.112	0.109	0.105
8	0.105	0.101	0.097	0.094	0.091	0.087
9	0.091	0.087	0.083	0.080	0.077	0.074
10	0.080	0.076	0.072	0.069	0.066	0.063
11	0.070	0.067	0.063	0.060	0.057	0.054
12	0.063	0.059	0.056	0.053	0.050	0.047
13	0.056	0.053	0.050	0.047	0.044	0.041
14	0.051	0.048	0.044	0.041	0.038	0.036
15	0.046	0.043	0.040	0.037	0.034	0.031

continued

SINKING FUND FACTORS (CONTINUED)

Year	5%	6%	7%	8%	9%	10%
			Interest Rate			
16	0.042	0.039	0.036	0.033	0.030	0.028
17	0.039	0.035	0.032	0.030	0.027	0.025
18	0.036	0.032	0.029	0.027	0.024	0.022
19	0.033	0.030	0.027	0.024	0.022	0.020
20	0.030	0.027	0.024	0.022	0.020	0.017
25	0.021	0.018	0.016	0.014	0.012	0.010
30	0.015	0.013	0.011	0.009	0.007	0.006
35	0.011	0.009	0.007	0.006	0.005	0.004
40	0.008	0.006	0.005	0.004	0.003	0.002
50	0.005	0.003	0.002	0.002	0.001	0.001

TABLE SET FOUR
LOAN AMORTIZATION TABLES

TEN-YEAR LOAN

	8%		9%		10%	
Year	(1)	(2)	(1)	(2)	(1)	(2)
1	54%	93%	58%	93%	61%	94%
2	50	86	54	86	58	87
3	46	78	50	78	53	79
4	42	69	45	70	49	71
5	37	60	40	61	44	62
6	32	49	35	50	38	52
7	26	38	29	39	32	40
8	21	27	23	27	25	28
9	14	14	16	14	17	15
10	7	0	8	0	9	0

(1)—Interest as a percentage of total loan payment
(2)—Balance at year end as a percentage of total loan

FIFTEEN-YEAR LOAN

Year	Interest Rate					
	8%		9%		10%	
	(1)	(2)	(1)	(2)	(1)	(2)
1	68%	96%	73%	97%	76%	97%
2	66	92	70	93	74	93
3	63	88	67	89	71	90
4	60	83	64	84	68	85
5	57	78	61	80	65	81
6	54	73	58	74	61	76
7	50	67	54	69	58	70
8	46	61	50	62	53	64
9	42	54	45	56	49	57
10	37	47	40	48	44	50
11	32	39	35	40	38	42
12	26	30	29	31	32	33
13	21	21	23	22	25	23
14	14	11	16	11	17	12
15	7	0	8	0	9	0

(1)—Interest as a percentage of total loan payment
(2)—Balance at year end as a percentage of total loan

TWENTY-YEAR LOAN

| | 8% | | 9% | | 10% | |
Year	(1)	(2)	(1)	(2)	(1)	(2)
			Interest Rate			
1	79%	98%	82%	98%	85%	98%
2	77	95	81	96	84	96
3	75	93	79	94	82	94
4	73	90	77	91	80	92
5	71	87	75	88	78	89
6	68	84	73	85	76	87
7	66	81	70	82	74	83
8	63	77	67	78	71	80
9	60	73	64	75	68	76
10	57	68	61	70	65	72
11	54	64	58	66	61	68
12	50	59	54	61	58	63
13	46	53	50	55	53	57
14	42	47	45	49	49	51
15	37	41	40	43	44	45
16	32	34	35	35	38	37
17	26	26	29	28	32	29
18	21	18	23	19	25	20
19	14	9	16	10	17	11
20	7	0	8	0	9	0

(1)—Interest as a percentage of total loan payment
(2)—Balance at year end as a percentage of total loan

TWENTY-FIVE-YEAR LOAN

| | Interest Rate | | | | | |
| | 8% | | 9% | | 10% | |
Year	(1)	(2)	(1)	(2)	(1)	(2)
1	85%	99%	88%	99%	91%	99%
2	84	97	87	98	90	98
3	83	96	86	96	89	97
4	82	94	85	95	88	95
5	80	92	84	93	86	94
6	79	90	82	91	85	92
7	77	88	81	89	84	90
8	75	85	79	87	82	88
9	73	83	77	85	80	86
10	71	80	75	82	78	84
11	68	77	73	79	76	81
12	66	74	70	76	74	78
13	63	71	67	73	71	75
14	60	67	64	69	68	72
15	57	63	61	65	65	68
16	54	59	58	61	61	63
17	50	54	54	56	58	59
18	46	49	50	51	53	54
19	42	43	45	46	49	48
20	37	37	40	40	44	42
21	32	31	35	33	38	35
22	26	24	29	26	32	27
23	21	17	23	18	25	19
24	14	9	16	9	17	10
25	7	0	8	0	9	0

(1)—Interest as a percentage of total loan payment
(2)—Balance at year end as a percentage of total loan

THIRTY-YEAR LOAN

			Interest Rate			
	8%		9%		10%	
Year	(1)	(2)	(1)	(2)	(1)	(2)
1	90%	99%	92%	99%	94%	99%
2	89	98	92	98	94	99
3	88	97	91	98	93	98
4	87	96	90	97	92	97
5	86	95	89	96	92	96
6	85	94	88	94	91	95
7	84	92	87	93	90	94
8	83	91	86	92	89	93
9	82	89	85	90	88	92
10	80	87	84	89	86	90
11	79	85	82	87	85	89
12	77	83	81	85	84	87
13	75	81	79	83	82	85
14	73	79	77	81	80	83
15	71	76	75	78	78	81
16	68	73	73	76	76	78
17	66	70	70	73	74	75
18	63	67	67	70	71	72
19	60	63	64	66	68	69
20	57	60	61	62	65	65
21	54	55	58	58	61	61
22	50	51	54	54	58	57
23	46	46	50	49	53	52
24	42	41	45	44	49	46
25	37	35	40	38	44	40
26	32	29	35	32	38	34
27	26	23	29	25	32	26
28	21	16	23	17	25	18
29	14	8	16	9	17	10
30	7	0	8	0	9	0

(1)—Interest as a percentage of total loan payment
(2)—Balance at year end as a percentage of total loan

APPENDIX TWO
REFERENCES

This list of references may be used to supplement the information provided in this text. These sources are arranged by subject matter category. For further references, the reader may consult the bibliographies cited in these references.

General References A number of general sources are available in real estate literature. The following references represent a range of viewpoints.

Hines, Mary Alice. *Principles and Practices of Real Estate.* Homewood, Ill.: Richard D. Irwin, 1976.

Ratcliff, Richard U. *Real Estate Analysis.* New York: McGraw-Hill, 1961.

Schenkel, William M. *Modern Real Estate Principles.* Dallas, Tex.: Business Publications, Inc., 1977.

Semenow, Robert. *Questions and Answers on Real Estate.* 8th Ed. Englewood Cliffs, N.J.: Prentice-Hall, 1975. This work is a good source of detailed information for someone interested in pursuing a real estate license.

Smith, Halbert C., Tschappat, Carl J., and Racster, Ronald. *Real Estate and Urban Development.* 2nd Ed. Homewood, Ill.: Richard D. Irwin, 1977.

Unger, Maurice A. *Real Estate, Principles and Practices.* 5th Ed. Cincinnati, Ohio: Southwestern Publishing Co., 1974. This is a broad, practically oriented reference.

Weimer, Arthur M., Hoyt, Homer, and Bloom, George. *Principles of Urban Real Estate.* 6th Ed. New York: Ronald Press, 1972.

Real Estate Appraisal and Investment Analysis The following sources may be used to obtain more details concerning real estate appraisal and investment analysis. The Ring and the American Institute books contain excellent coverage of the traditional as well as the more sophisticated techniques of appraisal. The American Institute book also has a large bibliography which relates to real estate value analysis.

American Institute of Real Estate Appraisers. *The Appraisal of Real Estate.* 6th Ed. Chicago: American Institute of Real Estate Appraisers, 1973.

Beaton, William R., and Robertson, Terry. *Real Estate Investment.* 2nd Ed. Englewood Cliffs, N.J.: Prentice-Hall, 1977.

Ellwood, L. W. *Ellwood Tables for Real Estate Appraising and Financing.* 3rd Ed. Chicago: American Institute of Real Estate Appraisers, 1970.

Kahn, Sanders A., Case, Frederick E., and Schimmel, Alfred. *Real Estate Appraisal and Investment.* New York: Ronald Press, 1963.

Ring, Alfred A. *The Valuation of Real Estate.* 2nd Ed. Englewood Cliffs, N.J.: Prentice-Hall, 1970.

Roulac, Stephen E. *Modern Real Estate Investment: An Institutional Approach.* San Francisco: Property Press, 1977. This work is extremely comprehensive and up-to-date in all aspects of real estate investment.

Smith, Halbert C. *Real Estate Appraisal.* Columbus, Ohio: Grid, 1976.

Wendt, Paul F., and Cerf, Alan R. *Real Estate Investment Analysis and Taxation.* New York: McGraw-Hill, 1969.

Real Estate Finance   Two good sources of detailed information on real estate finance are listed.

Atteberry, William. *Modern Real Estate Finance.* Columbus, Ohio: Grid, 1972.

Hoagland, Henry E., Stone, Leo D., and Brueggeman, William B. *Real Estate Finance.* 6th Ed. Homewood, Ill.: Richard D. Irwin, 1977. An excellent detailed source, especially in the area of government programs.

Real Estate Law

Kratovil, Robert. *Real Estate Law.* 5th Ed. Englewood Cliffs, N.J.: Prentice-Hall, 1969.

Taxation

Federal Tax Course—1978. Englewood Cliffs, N.J.: Prentice-Hall, 1977. A good, basic reference to tax problems in general, including references to the IRS Code.

Urban and General Economics (Housing Markets)

Goulet, Peter G. "Discriminant Analysis of Low-Income Housing: A Study of Non-Price Factors Influencing Housing Choice Decisions." Unpublished Ph.D. dissertation, Ohio State University, 1970.

Muth, Richard F. *Cities and Housing.* Chicago: University of Chicago Press, 1969.

————. "The Demand for Non-Farm Housing." In *The Demand for Durable Goods*, edited by Arnold C. Harberger, Chicago: University of Chicago Press, 1960.

————. *Urban Economic Problems.* New York: Harper and Row, 1975. This book covers a broad range of urban economic issues.

Reid, Margaret. *Housing and Income.* Chicago: University of Chicago Press, 1968.

Samuelson, Paul. *Economics.* 9th Ed. New York: McGraw-Hill, 1973. This text presents an encyclopedic coverage of general economics.

Segal, David. *Urban Economics.* Homewood, Ill.: Richard D. Irwin, 1977. This text has a good, basic coverage of urban economic theory.

Land and Real Estate Development   The works below provide a cross-section of basic information concerning the analysis of land and development opportunities.

Graaskamp, James A. *A Guide to Feasibility Analysis.* Chicago: Society of Real Estate Appraisers, 1970.

Kinnard, William N., Jr. *Industrial Real Estate.* 2nd Ed. Washington, D.C.: Society of Industrial Realtors, 1971.

Seldin, Maury. *Land Investment.* Homewood, Ill.: Dow Jones–Irwin, 1975.

Miscellaneous References   The following references include a list of journals, data sources, and other miscellaneous references which may provide input to the study and practice of real estate.

Journals

Appraisal Journal. Published by the American Institute of Real Estate Appraisers. This is a good, general source of articles on current issues in appraisal and investment analysis.

Land Economics. Published by the University of Wisconsin. This is a top-level theory journal.

Data Sources

Dow Jones–Irwin Business Almanac. Edited by Sumner Levine. Homewood, Ill.: Dow Jones–Irwin, published annually. This book contains a range of data such as business ratios, price level data, financial and monetary aggregates, and national income data.

Institute of Řeal Estate Management. *Apartment Building Income and Expense Analysis.* Chicago: Published annually. This is an annual source for income and expense data for apartment building by type as well as location.

Marshall Valuation Service. Los Angeles: Marshall and Swift Publication Co. This is a major source of cost data for appraisal practitioners.

Savings and Loan Fact Book. Chicago: U.S. League of Savings Institutions. This is a source of detailed data on housing and savings and loan role in real estate finance, by region.

Statistical Abstract of the U.S. Washington, D.C.: Bureau of the Census, prepared annually. This reference contains detailed information on population, business, and other economic and social variables.

Urban Land Institute. *Dollars and Sense of Shopping Centers.* Washington D.C., 1972. This is a source for data on shopping centers.

Other Sources

Estes, Jack C. *Interest Amortization Tables.* New York: McGraw-Hill, 1976. This is a paperback version of the monthly amortization tables for loans.

Calculator Analysis for Business and Finance. Texas Instruments, Inc., 1977. This proprietary publication provides detailed insight into the use of a business calculator for the solution of many types of real estate and financial analytical problems. The methods are based on a particular Texas Instruments calculator, but may be applied to others as well with minor conversion. Other paperback books of this type are also available for RPN logic calculators.

APPENDIX THREE
GLOSSARY OF TERMS AND SYMBOLS

This appendix includes terms which appear in this text in a real estate context. Most of these terms have been listed as Key Terms in one or more of the chapters. Not all Key Terms have been listed here, as some are basically common knowledge.

Following the terms is the list of symbols which appeared at the end of chapter 2.

GLOSSARY OF TERMS

Absolute Net Lease—An agreement in which the tenant is responsible for all the expenses of operating and maintaining the leased property.

Abstract (of title)—A document which describes the chain of title for a parcel of real property.

Accelerated Depreciation—Any of the methods of accounting for depreciation which allow a property owner to write off larger amounts of the value in the early years of the property's life.

Acceleration Clause—A clause found in mortgage contracts which allows the creditor to consider the entire debt due if the borrower defaults.

Accretion—The natural process by which a parcel of land increases in size, as through the deposit of soil by wind or water.

Adjusted Basis—The book value of a capital investment for tax purposes as reckoned at the time of sale. The adjusted basis includes original cost, plus improvements, less depreciation and transfer costs.

Adjusted Gross Income—An important subtotal in the calculation of taxable income, consisting of gross income, minus adjustments.

Ad Valorem Tax—A tax based on the value of an asset. Property tax is a prime example.

Adverse Possession—A process by which a party may earn the title to a piece of real property by using it against the wishes of the owner.

Agency—A legal relationship in which one person acts on behalf of another.

Amortization—The progressive repayment of a portion of a loan with periodic regularity.

Annuity—An investment arrangement which returns a finite stream of benefits to its beneficiary.

Appraisal—The process of estimating the fair market value of an asset.

Assessed Value—The value of a piece of property for tax purposes, generally determined by an agent of the taxing authority involved.

Band-of-Investment (technique)—A method of determining the appropriate rate of return for value analysis. This is also called the weighted average cost of capital, found by considering the average rate needed to compensate each form of capital used to finance the asset being evaluated.

Bargain and Sale Deed—A deed used to transfer the rights in property. This type of deed does not warrant clear title, but does warrant that some rights are owned by the grantor.

Baseline—One of the two major constructs used to describe the location of property under the survey method. Baselines run east and west.

Basis—The cost of a capital asset for tax purposes.

Bid-Rent (theory)—An economic concept which describes the way in which parcels are allocated in the market on the basis of willingness to pay.

Book Value—*See* Adjusted Basis.

Broker—An important real estate functionary who handles the transfer of property between buyer and seller.

Budget (line)—The amount of money a consumer has to spend for goods and services in a given period.

Builders Detail Method—One of four methods for determining the cost of replacement for appraisal purposes.

Building Capitalization Rate—A rate of return used to value improvements for a given property in income appraisal.

Building Income—The income associated with the improvements on a property for appraisal purposes.

Building Residual Technique—An approach to income appraisal which assumes the value of the land is known.

Built-Up Rate of Return—*See* Summation Method.

Business Risk—The probability of loss that a business firm may incur through either internal or external factors.

Capital Asset Pricing Model—A theoretical approach to the valuation of capital assets based on the premise that the rate of return is a function of time and systematic risk for a particular asset.

Capital Gain—The profit generated by the sale of a capital asset. Long-term gains occur when the asset has been held for more than one year and short-term gains occur when the asset has been owned for less than one year.

Capitalization—The process of calculating the value of a stream of cash benefits.

Capitalization Rate—The rate of return used to find the value of a stream of cash benefits.

Capital Loss—The sale of a capital asset for less than its adjusted basis.

Carrying Cost—A negative periodic cash flow associated with real property investment.

Central Business District (CBD)—The core of an urban area.

Characteristic Line—The relationship of the return on a given capital asset to the return on the market.

Closing Statement—A document used to show how consideration is disbursed at the closing of a property sales transaction.

Coefficient of Determination (R^2)—The proportion of the variation in a dependent variable which is accounted for by a regression relationship.

Comparable Property—A property used to serve as a reference to determine the value of another property using the market approach to appraisal.

Comparative Market Method—The method used to derive the replacement cost of a structure in the cost approach to appraisal.

Component Depreciation—A method whereby a property improvement may be depreciated in parts at different rates for different lives.

Compound Interest—Interest earned on reinvested earnings from previous periods.

Condemnation—The process by which the right of eminent domain is exercised.

Contract—An agreement between parties in which all participants promise to exchange something of value.

Contract for Deed—*See* Land Contract.

Contract for Sale—A contract in which one party agrees to deliver the deed to a property and the other party agrees to give consideration in exchange.

Conventional Life Estate—An ownership interest which lasts for the life of the grantor or someone designated by the grantor.

Correlation Coefficient (R)—A measure of the degree of relationship between two variables.

Cost Approach—A means of appraisal, based on the concept that a property improvement should be worth the depreciated cost to replace it.

Cost-to-Create—The total cost required to build an improvement and to ready it for its intended service.

Covariance—A measure of association between two variables which accounts for their individual volatility and their correlation.

Curable Depreciation—A loss in economic value which can be removed by the application of some additional value. Depreciation is curable when the value added exceeds the cost to produce it.

Curtesy—The interest of a husband in the property of his wife.

Debt Service—The periodic payment required to meet a loan obligation, often including both principal and interest.

Declining Balance Depreciation—An accelerated depreciation method in which a particular rate is applied to the remaining undepreciated balance of the asset.

Deductible Expense—Any business expense which may be subtracted from gross income to determine taxable income.

Deed—A document which serves as evidence of title to real property.

Defeasance Clause—A clause in a mortgage which states that the borrower will have his title returned when the obligation is paid.

Deferred Annuity—A stream of benefits which will be received in the future.

Deficit Spending Unit—A spending unit which has a demand for more resources in a given period than it has in periodic income.

Dependent Variable—A variable whose value is contingent upon the value of another variable or variables.

Depreciation—The periodic loss in economic value of a capital asset.

Depreciation Recapture—The process by which some of the depreciation taken for an asset is "recaptured," treated as ordinary income at transfer.

Determinable Fee—An interest in land which is conditioned on the performance of some act.

Development Land—Land which is ready to be developed to some highest and best use.

Devise—The process of transferring property through a will.

Diminishing Marginal Utility—The consumption of additional units of goods or services with less satisfaction than previously acquired units of the same goods or services.

Discounting—Finding the present value of a benefit or stream of benefits.

Diversification—The combining of assets into groups so that the risk of the overall combination is lower than the risk of the individual assets.

Dominant Tenement—One who has an easement for ingress and egress to a landlocked property.

Dower—The rights of a wife in the property of her husband.

Due-on-Sale (clause)—A clause in a mortgage contract which allows the lender to demand payment if the title to the mortgaged property is transferred.

Easement—An interest in property which allows a party or parties to have access to the property of the party who grants it.

Economic Base (analysis)—The general structure of the economic relationships in a local community. The analysis of this base generally involves the calculation of the relationship between service and export employment in the community.

Economic Life—The period of time during which a property provides positive economic benefits.

Economic Obsolescence—The loss in value which results from a property's being located on a less-than-advantageous site.

Economic Rent—Excess return which accrues to a landowner over and above the required return for the property.

Effective Gross Income—The gross income of a property, less vacancy and collection losses.

Efficient Portfolio—A group of assets which maximizes returns for a given level of risk.

Eminent Domain—The right of municipalities and designated authorities to force the sale of private properties for public purposes.

Encumbrance—A restriction of the rights of an owner in property.

Equity of Redemption—The right of an owner–borrower to redeem property after a loan default, but before foreclosure is complete.

Escalator Clause—A mortgage clause which allows the lender to raise the rate of interest after the contract is in force.

Escrow—A legal device which allows parties to a transaction to deposit their consideration with a third party for simultaneous future transfer.

Exclusive Listing—One type of listing arrangement between a broker and client.

Exclusive Right to Sell—A listing arrangement which gives the broker the highest protection of his commission.

Expected Value—The expected outcome of an economic proposition with risk which is a function of the possible states of nature and the probabilities of their occurrence.

Export Employment (or basic employment)—The employment of workers who produce goods or services consumed outside the community.

Fair Market Value—The price a willing, informed buyer will pay and a seller will accept in a free and open market transaction.

Fannie Mae—Federal National Mortgage Association.

Fee Simple—The highest form of property ownership.

FHA—Federal Housing Administration.

Filtering—The long-run adjustment process which helps bring real estate markets into demand and supply equilibrium.

Financial Intermediary—An institution which uses the savings of individuals and businesses to make loans to deficit spending units.

Financial Risk—The possibility of losses that accrue to an investment because it is financed partially with debt.

Fixed Expenses—Expenses which are a function of time rather than volume of production, including property taxes and insurance.

Fixtures—Personal property which becomes real property because of its attachment to the real property.

Foreclosure—A suit brought by a mortgage lender to end the borrower's right of equitable redemption.

Freehold Estate—The general category of land ownership rights in contrast to less-than-freehold estates such as leaseholds.

Frictional Costs—The costs associated with travel from one parcel of real estate to another.

Functional Obsolescence—The economic loss in value of a property improvement which results from its inability to perform its intended use efficiently.

Future Value—The value of an investment sum left at compound interest for a period of time.

Ginnie Mae—Government National Mortgage Association.

Gross Income—The total of ordinary income for tax purposes *or* the total rent which may be collected on an income property if no vacancy occurs.

Ground Lease—A lease agreement, generally, long-term, which gives the lessee (tenant) the right to use and improve a parcel of land.

Highest and Best Use—That use of a parcel of land which allows the highest income to accrue to the land as a residual.

Homestead Right—The right of a family to have a portion of its interest in property protected from certain creditors.

Housing Cycle—The economic cycle which describes the level of construction of housing over time.

Housing Service—The sum of the benefits, both monetary and psychic, which accrue from a particular form of housing occupancy.

Income Approach—An appraisal technique which estimates value based on a capitalization of the expected future benefits accruing to a property.

Incorporeal Rights—The rights to possession or use without title, such as easements or profit rights.

Incurable Depreciation—Obsolescence which cannot economically be repaired.

Independent Variable—A variable which takes on values not contingent upon the values of other variables.

Indifference Curve—An economic construct which describes various combinations of goods or services which may be consumed to provide a given level of satisfaction.

Input-Output Analysis—A form of economic analysis which describes the sectors of the economy to which the output of a given sector flows.

Interim Land—Land which is not ready for full development at highest and best use, but requires some improvement to pay carrying costs.

Internal Rate of Return—The rate of discount which causes the net present value of an investment to be zero.

Interurbanization—The process by which development takes place between urban limits, gradually causing the areas to meld together.

Intestate—A person who dies without leaving a will.

Intrinsic Value—The value of a property based on its inherent qualities, apart from market value.

Investment—A situation in which a sum of money is exchanged for the right to receive future benefits.

Investment Value—The value of a property based on its future benefits as they relate to an individual investor; a personal estimate of value.

Joint Tenancy—The equal and shared ownership of two or more parties in a piece of property. In order for this to be valid, certain unities must exist.

Junior Mortgage (lien)—A security agreement in which rights are purposefully subordinated to those of another creditor.

Land Contract—A contract under which a buyer contracts to buy the title to a property after the payment, over time, of certain sums of money. Title remains with the seller until the payments are made.

Land Income—The income which accrues to the land portion of a property.

Land Residual Technique—A method of income appraisal which is based on a known value for the improvements on the land.

Lease—A contract between parties which gives one party (or parties), the lessee, the right to use property controlled by the other party, the lessor.

Leased Fee—A parcel of land or property which is leased.

Leasehold (estate)—An owned interest of a lessee which is situated on a leased fee.

Legal Life Estate—A category of interests in land which includes dower and curtesy rights, among others.

Leverage—The magnification of an investment owner's earnings which results from the presence of fixed cost expenses, such as interest, in the income stream. This term commonly refers to the use of debt financing.

Liability to Replace—A method for calculating the value of obsolescence in the cost approach to appraisal. The method is based on the percentage of present value lost through shortened life.

License (rights)—The right to use the property of another. An example of this right would be the permission granted by a farmer to allow hunters to use his land.

Lien—A security interest in a property which gives the lienor the right to extract a portion of the value of the property as satisfaction for an obligation in default.

Linkage—The hypothetical connection between two parcels of real estate used for the flow of services from one parcel to the other.

Liquidity—A characteristic of investments which describes the ability to sell the asset readily for cash at a high percentage of its intrinsic value.

Listing Agreement—An agreement or contract between a broker and the seller of a piece of property which specifies the rights and duties of each.

Location Quotient—A method of analyzing the economic base of a community.

Market—A place, hypothetical or real, where buyers and sellers come together to transfer goods or property.

Market Comparison Approach—An appraisal approach in which value estimates are based on prices of existing, recently transferred properties of like characteristics.

Market Risk—The chance that an investor will lose money because the value of the investment falls in the market.

Market Value—See Fair Market Value.

Mechanics Lien—A lien placed on property by someone who performs services on the property without receiving the proper compensation.

Metes and Bounds—A method of describing property location using landmarks and standard distance and direction measures.

Millage Rate—The rate of taxation applied to the unit of assessed value for property tax purposes.

Mortgage Deed—A deed used in some states which theoretically vests the title to the property with a mortgage lender for the life of the loan.

Mortgagee—The creditor in a mortgage loan arrangement.

Mortgage Lien—A security agreement executed in favor of a mortgage lender (*see* Lien).

Mortgage Loan—A method of borrowing money to purchase property in which the lender agrees to lend money and receives a promise to pay, as well as a security interest in the property.

Mortgagor—The borrower in a mortgage loan agreement.

Multiple Listing—An arrangement in which cooperating brokers automatically are given the same listing.

Neighborhood—A contiguous area of land uses, all of which are subject to the same outside influences.

Net Lease—A form of lease agreement in which the lessee agrees to take some responsibility for maintenance and upkeep of the property.

Net Operating Income (NOI)—The difference between effective gross income and total expenses, excluding interest and depreciation.

Net Present Value—The difference between the present value of the benefits of an investment (cash inflows) and the present value of the costs (outflows) at the investor's required rate of return.

Nonsystematic Risk—The group of investment risks which are not associated with the activity in the investment market. These are the risks which may be theoretically reduced through diversification.

Offer To Purchase—An agreement, not necessarily contractual, through which a buyer offers to purchase real property.

Open Listing—An agreement which allows the seller to employ someone other than the broker to sell the property with the potential loss of commission to the broker who is a party to the open listing.

Operating Expenses—Variable expenses such as utilities and maintenance associated with the operation of real property.

Opportunity Rate of Return—The highest yield that would be sacrificed when an investor chooses a particular investment.

Option—An agreement giving one party the right to keep a priority position for making an offer to purchase a particular parcel of real estate. Sometimes this is called the right of first refusal.

Ordinary Income—The periodic income and certain income from capital transactions which is subject to income taxation at regular (as opposed to preferred) rates.

Pass-Through (certificate)—A type of financial instrument backed by pools of guaranteed mortgages.

Periodic Tenancy—A lease agreement for a specific period of time which automatically renews itself if not cancelled appropriately by one of the parties.

Perpetuity—A level annuity of infinite duration.

Personal property—Property other than real property.

Physical Deterioration—The loss in value of an improvement owing to structural wear and tear.

Platting—A method of property description based on the information contained in a map called a plat plan filed with the appropriate governmental authority.

Plottage—The phenomenon which occurs when several small parcels of property are combined to make a larger parcel worth more than the sum of the parts.

Political Risk—The risk that investment value will be adversely affected by the action of a political authority.

Population Density Gradient—The relationship between population density and distance to the CBD.

Prepayment Clause—A mortgage agreement clause which specifies possible conditions under which the loan might be prepaid.

Present Value—The value today of a sum of money to be received in the future, given a specified interest rate.

Primary Mortgage Market—The market in which a mortgage loan is originated.

Principal Meridian—The north–south line used as a basis for property description in the survey method. *Also see* Baseline.

Principle of Contribution—The net present value decision rule. Nothing should be done to improve a property unless the present value of the improvement exceeds its cost. This principle also serves as the dividing line between curable and incurable obsolescence in the cost approach to appraisal.

Principle of Substitution—The basis for market appraising which states that properties providing similar service should sell for similar prices.

Profit (right)—The right to extract minerals from a property (mineral rights) is an example of profit.

Property Rights—The concept of ownership as a bundle of rights.

Purchase Money Mortgage—A lending agreement in which the seller, rather than an institution, takes a mortgage from the property owner.

Purchasing Power Risk—The risk that a loss of purchasing power will be suffered in an investment, usually attributed to fixed income investments.

Qualified Fee—A fee interest which has been conditioned to the performance or non-performance of some act or acts.

Quantity Survey Method—A means of determining the replacement value of an improvement for cost-based appraisals.

Quitclaim (deed)—A deed which transfers all the rights of the seller in a property without warranting that any rights are in fact owned by that seller.

R—*See* Correlation Coefficient.

R²—*See* Coefficient of Determination.

Range—A directional measure used to designate the location of a township in the survey method of property description.

Rate of Recapture—The rate at which an investor's capital must be returned in a wasting asset investment. This rate equals one divided by the economic life of the investment.

Rate of Return—*See* Return on Investment.

Ratio Method—One method for determining the ratio of service to export employment in economic base analysis (*see* Location Quotient).

Raw Land—Land which is undeveloped or unimproved; generally, farmland, recreation land, or fallow land.

Real Estate Investment Trust (REIT)—A particular type of investment company set up to buy equity interests in real property or to lend money on such property for the benefit of the shareholders of the trust.

Realty—Land and any improvements permanently and directly attached to the land; also called real property.

Recapture of Capital—The amount of an investment income stream which represents a return of the investor's capital.

Rectangular Survey—A method for describing the location of land in some states; also called the government survey.

Regression Line—A line, either straight or curved, which represents a "best fit" relationship between a dependent variable and one or more independent variables.

Remainderman—The designated beneficiary in a legal life estate.

Rent Gradient—The relationship between relative rent levels on property and their distance from the CBD.

Reserve for Replacements—A cash reserve established for the purpose of replacing wasting parts in a rental property improvement.

Residual Cash Benefits—The net cash proceeds from the sale of a real estate investment.

Return on Investment—The overall relationship between the return earned by an investment and the investment's value, excluding the return of capital.

Risk Premium—The rate of return which is earned for taking extra risk in the investment market.

Sale-and-Leaseback—An arrangement whereby a property owner sells a property and simultaneously leases it back from the buyer.

Sandwich Lease—A leasing arrangement with four levels of parties such that the two in the middle are in effect "sandwiched" by the ultimate lessor and ultimate lessee.

Secondary Mortgage Market—The investment market in which holders of existing mortgages may sell these mortgages for cash.

Section—An area of land containing 640 acres or one square mile.

Section 1231 Property—Certain capital assets which qualify for preferential treatment under the IRS Code.

Section 1245 Property—Section 1231 Property, including real property.

Section 1250 Property—Section 1231 Property, including personal property.

Security Market Line—The regression line which relates returns in the investment market to the level of risk in the market.

Senior Mortgage—A lien which has a prior claim on the assets pledged as security for a loan.

Sensitivity Analysis—A process used to discover the importance of the influence of a particular variable on the outcome of a decision.

Service Employment—The level of employment in a community attributed to workers producing goods for consumption within the community.

Service Lease—A lease agreement in which the lessor provides services to the lessee.

Servient Tenement—The owner of a property across which there is an easement for ingress or egress from a landlocked property.

Simple Interest—Interest which is earned and withdrawn from an investment, rather than being reinvested for compound earnings.

Sinking Fund—A savings fund which is accumulated to a desired future amount. (*See* Reserve for Replacements, for example.)

Speculation—The commitment of investible funds which is characterized by a desire for a short-run capital gain rather than a longer term, steady return.

Stabilized Income—The long-run, normal, expected income from a rental property; also called normalized income and used for appraisal and investment analysis.

Stagflation—A condition in the economy characterized by slow growth or stagnation accompanied by inflation.

Standard Deviation—A statistical measure of the variation inherent in the values which can be assumed by a given variable; a measure of risk; the square root of variance.

Statute of Frauds—A section of the law which specifies that certain agreements must be in writing to be valid.

Statutory Right of Redemption—A period, allowed in some states, during which a mortgagor can redeem property lost through foreclosure.

Straight-Line-Declining Income Stream—An income stream which declines each year by a constant amount.

Straight-Line Depreciation—The depreciation method which operates by allowing a constant write-off in each period during the life of the depreciable asset.

Strict Foreclosure—The technique of foreclosure which permits the lender to simply take over the property under foreclosure.

Subject Property—A property under appraisal.

Submarket—A section of a property market defined by the relative homogeneity of the properties and their occupants, often in a contiguous area.

Subordination—The process of placing a particular loan in a lower priority position than that of other loans.

Suburbanization—The social phenomenon associated with the shift in population to the outlying regions of urban population centers.

Summation Method—A method for determining the appropriate rate of return for an investment. A series of risk premiums is added to the basic return for the postponement of consumption.

Sum-of-Years'-Digits Depreciation—A depreciation method which employs a contrived formula based on the sum of the digits of the useful life of an asset in years.

Surplus Spending Unit—A spending unit which has more funds available for consumption than it needs in a given period.

Syndicate—A group of investors who combine in some formal organization to invest in an asset or assets.

Systematic Risk—That portion of total risk of an asset attributed solely to the behavior of the market for the asset.

Taxable Income—The income amount on which income tax liability is calculated.

Taxable Operating Income—In this text, the sum of net operating income and the reserve for replacements.

Tax Capitalization—The subtraction of more value from a property through increased taxes than is added in services.

Tax Lien—A security interest which is taken in a property whose owner fails to pay taxes rightfully due.

Tax Shelter—Any expense which is deductible as a shield against income tax. A property whose income is negative shelters some other income from taxes.

Tenancy in Common—Joint ownership which does not have the unities of joint tenancy. An owner can sell an interest without disrupting the tenancy.

Tenancy in Entireties—Joint tenancy involving a husband and wife.

Tenancy in Severalty—Individual ownership.

Tenancy at Sufferance—Inhabiting a property against the wishes of the owner.

Tenancy at Will—A tenancy without specific period which may be cancelled by either party with proper notice.

Tenancy for Years—A single term lease without a specific automatic renewal for a like period; often noncancellable.

Title Insurance—Insurance protection which indemnifies a property owner against the claims of other interests.

Topography—The "lay of the land"; physical characteristics of the surface of a site.

Torrens Certificate—A document issued in some jurisdictions in which a clear title is adjudicated in Torrens Court.

Township—A square land area six miles on a side; equal to thirty-six sections.

Trust Deed—A deed transferring the title of property to a trustee; often used in some states as a substitute for the traditional mortgage arrangement.

Unit-in-Place Method—A method of determining the replacement cost of a building improvement.

Urbanization—The social phenomena which describes the movement of population to cities.

Variable Rate Mortgage—A mortgage with an interest rate which varies with the market.

Variance—See Standard Deviation.

Voluntary Deed Restrictions—Any one of a number of possible restrictions placed on the use of property by a grantor. Not all are as restrictive as qualified fees.

Warranty Deed—A deed for transferring ownership which provides the new owner with legal guarantees as to the quality of the title.

Yield—See Internal Rate of Return.

Zoning—A process used by governmental authorities for restricting the use of particular sites.

GLOSSARY OF SYMBOLS

F = Future value of a single sum

P = Present value or initial investment

PV = Present value or initial investment (or P)

i = Rate of return, also called discount rate or capitalization rate

I = Interest earnings from an investment ($)

n = Number of periods over which an investment is to be considered

PVA = Present value of an annuity

B = Uniform benefit of a level annuity or perpetuity

Σ = Summation sign which means to add up a number of calculations to derive a sum

FA = Future value of an annuity; arises when an amount is saved periodically for a certain number of periods

S = Sinking fund payment; refers to amount being saved periodically

Factors from Tables

FVF = Future Value Factor

$$(1 + i)^n$$

PVF = Present Value Factor

$$1/(1 + i)^n$$

$PVAF$ = Present Value of an Annuity Factor

$$\sum_{y=1}^{n} PVF_{y,i}$$

AF = Accumulation Factor

$$1 + \sum_{y=1}^{n-1} FVF_{y,i}$$

SFF = Sinking Fund Factor

$$1/AF_{n,i}$$

AMF = Amortization Factor

$$1/PVAF_{n,i}$$

INDEX